Mr. Scott Wirtzm
1228 Denniston S
Pittsburgh, PA 15217

MW00356160

To
Polly
A trailblazer for women in the
legal profession — wonderful!
— Joe Fried

"GUIDANCE, NOT GOVERNANCE"

"GUIDANCE, NOT GOVERNANCE"

Rabbi Solomon B. Freehof and Reform Responsa

Joan S. Friedman

Hebrew Union College Press
Cincinnati

Library of Congress Cataloging-in-Publication Data

Friedman, Joan S., 1953–
  "Guidance, not governance": Rabbi Solomon B. Freehof and Reform responsa/ Joan
S. Friedman.
        pages cm
  Includes bibliographical references.
  ISBN 978-0-87820-467-0
1. Freehof, Solomon Bennett, 1892–1990. 2. Reform Judaism. 3. Responsa—1948- 4.
Responsa—1800–1948. I. Title.
  BM755.F693F75 2013
  296.1'854—dc23
                                                                    2013003153

The Hebrew Union College Press acknowledges with gratitude

The Allen H. and Selma W. Berkman Family Fund
Marcus Aaron
Patricia S. Lemer
Elaine, Edwin and the Honorable Gene Strassburger

whose generosity supported the publication of this book

To the memory of
my *bobie* Tillie Friedman ז״ל
who wanted an education
and for
my aunt Eleanor Friedman
with love and gratitude

CONTENTS

FOREWORD

It is a great pleasure for me to write this Foreword to *"Guidance, Not Governance": Rabbi Solomon B. Freehof and Reform Responsa* by my colleague and friend Joan Friedman. I have known Rabbi Friedman for more than thirty years. We both attended HUC-JIR in New York during the 1970s and we worked together as teachers at the Union for Reform Judaism's Camp Kutz during that time. I was also honored to serve as one of the readers of her Columbia University doctoral dissertation on Rabbi Freehof, and I am especially pleased that she has so skillfully built upon that work to produce this extremely important volume on Rabbi Freehof's responsa.

In the pages of this book, Dr. Friedman provides a highly comprehensive and insightful presentation and analysis of the legal opinions of the late Rabbi Freehof. She applies her own considerable knowledge of Jewish law and texts as well as her sophisticated academic training as a critical historian to her work on Freehof's legal writings. In so doing, Friedman fills a major lacuna in modern American Jewish history by highlighting the distinct and prominent place that Freehof and his writings possess in the ever evolving history of American Reform Judaism. She indicates in captivating historical prose how Rabbi Freehof came to write this literature and how he advanced to his position as the *posek elyon*, the foremost legal decisor, of the American Reform community. Friedman also provides great insight into the state of Reform and American Judaism throughout much of the century by offering a first-rate discussion of the most prominent issues with which Rabbi Freehof and the Reform community struggled throughout the 1900s. Even as she discusses the fine points of his writings and Jewish legal tradition in exquisite detail, Friedman never ignores the question of the greater significance Rabbi Freehof and his responsa hold for an understanding of the history and character of Reform Judaism. Indeed, it is this latter point that bears emphasis as one reflects on the importance of this book and its place within the larger context of Jewish and Reform Jewish history.

It is a truism to assert that the genre of rabbinic literature known as *she'elot u-teshuvot* (responsa) has been critical to the development of Judaism for more than a thousand years. In the responsa, leading rabbis throughout the centuries have applied the insights, meanings, norms, and precedents provided by the literary and legal texts (Bible, Talmud, Codes, and earlier responsa) of the Jewish past to the pressing and often novel issues of a present age. A single responsum is a crossroads where text and context meet in the ongoing tradition of Jewish legal interpretation. That modern-day Orthodox Jews would continue to understand this genre of rabbinic writings as central to their understanding of Jewish religious tradition is hardly surprising. After all, they view fidelity to law as the defining characteristic of Judaism.

Many Reform Jews have a different understanding. Their affirmation of autonomy and their sense of antinomianism cause them to question and even reject a connection between law and Judaism. Martin Buber captured the reason for this Reform sensibility when he contended that the champions of Jewish law in modern times had fossilized the Jewish legal tradition and in so doing "kept living religiosity at a distance." He indicted these Jewish jurists for transforming "the law into a heap of petty formulas" that allowed decisions regarding "right and wrong to degenerate into hairsplitting casuistry."

Nevertheless, the history of the Reform Movement indicates that not all Reform Jews have adopted this stance in regard to the relationship between Reform and Jewish law. When, in 1819, the first edition of the Hamburg Temple Prayerbook appeared, contemporaneous champions of Orthodoxy savagely attacked it in *Eleh Divre HaBrit*, a collection of responsa compiled and edited by the Hamburg Rabbinical Court. The opinions contained within this volume marshaled Talmudic and other halakhic sources against the innovations introduced by the Reformers into Jewish prayer.

M. I. Bresselau, an editor of the Hamburg Temple Prayerbook, responded to the Orthodox in a Hebrew-language volume, *Ḥerev Nokemet Nekam Brit*, and contended that the authors of *Eleh Divre HaBrit* had misinterpreted some and ignored other classical rabbinical sources in making their case against the Hamburg Reformers' liturgy. Drawing upon earlier halakhic works (*Or Nogah* and *Nogah Hatsedek*) in defense of Reform, Bresselau did not confine his response to a critique of what he claimed was an Orthodox misuse of rabbinic literature. He also cited much rabbinic material to defend the Hamburg Reformers. Nor was Bresselau alone among the Reformers in offering such a statement. David Caro, in his *Brit Emet* (1820), also condemned the Orthodox response as misinformed, and he too gathered together alternative halakhic sources to provide a traditional warrant for the deeds of the Reformers.

While historians and partisans continued to debate the merits of each side's arguments in the dispute, "what remains of abiding interest [in this affair]," as our teacher Jakob Petuchowski observed, "is the fact that the early Reformers should have felt the need to defend themselves in that particular arena, and with these particular weapons. Nothing demonstrates more clearly than this that the farthest thing from their mind was the formation of a new Jewish sect, let alone the founding of a new religion. The Judaism to which they wanted to bring reform was a Judaism based on Bible, Talmud and Codes; and it was by an appeal to these accepted bases of Jewish life that they sought to justify their place *within* Judaism."

Rabbi Gunther Plaut, commenting upon the same episode, analyzes it much as Petuchowski did and notes that the literature of the Reformers in this dispute "is couched in the same language which Orthodoxy had used." These initial proponents of Reform, Plaut asserts, "demanded that any change from the past be founded in genuine Jewish tradition." In so doing, these men, in Plaut's opinion, established a pattern for later generations of Reform leaders who "insisted that all of tradition was significant, that reform had to grow organically from it, and that a renewal of Judaism could only come from a continuity of spiritual development."

For Rabbi Plaut, who eventually succeeded Rabbi Freehof as a chairman of the CCAR Responsa Committee, and for Rabbi Petuchowski, as well as countless other twentieth-century Reform leaders like Rabbi Moshe Zemer of Israel and Rabbi Walter Jacob of Rodef Shalom in Pittsburgh, this continuity required that Reform Judaism affirm and draw upon its legal traditions in meeting the demands of the present. Otherwise, Reform would be inauthentic and unfaithful to the spirit that has marked Judaism throughout history.

Joan Friedman demonstrates that Rabbi Freehof believed this in the deepest recesses of his being. She thus begins her book by placing his writings within a chain of Jewish legal writings produced by his own teachers Kaufmann Kohler and Jacob Lauterbach and concludes her analysis by discussing the legacy Rabbi Freehof bequeathed American Reform Judaism through her examination of the CCAR Responsa Committee in recent years. In so doing, she demonstrates the ongoing relevance and importance of Rabbi Freehof to contemporary Reform Judaism and to those who yet desire that Reform reject the "revolutionary spirit" of those who would eschew the legal elements of Judaism altogether. Thus Rabbi Freehof emerges here as teacher and guide for those Reform Jews today who insist that Reform Judaism—to be authentic—must not ignore the legal patrimony that is the inheritance of all Jews. Dr. Friedman's manifold scholarly talents and her informed judgments that are so evident in this book give all of us concerned with Reform Judaism today much for which to be grateful and much from which we can learn.

David Ellenson
February 24, 2013
14 Adar, 5773 (Purim)

ACKNOWLEDGMENTS

Profound thanks are due to many people without whose help this book would not exist. First on the list is Prof. Michael A. Meyer of Hebrew Union College-Jewish Institute of Religion, who introduced me to the academic study of Reform Judaism in a course at the Hebrew University more years ago than I would like to admit and, more recently, guided me in turning my dissertation into a book and then waited patiently for it. Next is Dr. Walter Jacob, Rabbi Emeritus of Rodef Shalom Congregation in Pittsburgh, who was unfailingly kind, generous, and helpful when I first started my research on Freehof—even hosting me in his home for the duration of my first research trip to Pittsburgh, though it was also the first week of his retirement. He has been unfailingly kind, generous, and helpful ever since then.

I am grateful that Prof. Yosef Hayim Yerushalmi z"l accommodated my changed focus in the graduate program at Columbia University, and that I had the privilege of having Prof. Aryeh Goren as my dissertation director there. Conducting my original research at HUC-JIR in Cincinnati was a wonderful experience. Current Responsa Committee chair Prof. Mark Washofsky was always willing to discuss some "Freehofiana" with me, not only perceptively but with his customary wit. Chief Archivist Kevin Proffitt and the reading room staff of the American Jewish Archives, and Administrative Librarian Laurel Wolfson and Senior Associate Librarian Dan Rettberg of the Klau Library shared their expertise and cheerfully found me everything I needed. Extra thanks go to Laurel and Dan for more recently helping me long distance, sometimes on very short notice. Rodef Shalom Congregation's former rabbi, Mark Staitman, generously arranged for Freehof's papers to be sent to the Klau Library so I could have extended access to them. Since the congregation created its own archive and catalogued Freehof's papers within it, archivist Martha Berg has facilitated my access to his files on a number of occasions and has graciously helped me relocate material I had found previously. On my first visit to Pittsburgh Dr. Jacob arranged a visit with Mrs. Lillian

Freehof z"l, who kindly showed me the home she shared for many years with her late husband and pointed out several decorative items that were products of his carpentry hobby. Dr. Freehof's niece, Mrs. Theresa Schwartz, shared recollections of her uncle and sent me some invaluable family photographs. Several rabbinical colleagues read sections and offered encouraging comments along the way, most notably Rabbi Dow Marmur. My dear teacher Dr. A. Stanley Dreyfus z"l and his wife Marianne hosted me on two research trips to New York City and shared personal reminiscences of Dr. Freehof. It saddens me that I did not complete this project before Stanley's death.

This book has reached completion while I have been teaching at the College of Wooster, where Professors Anne Nurse, Chuck Kammer, Mark Graham, Madonna Hettinger, Greg Shaya, and Peter Pozefsky have guided and mentored me in making the transition from part-time visitor to full-time faculty member. Though being housed in two departments adds to the number of meetings I have to attend, I could not ask for more companionable, supportive, or encouraging colleagues than the members of Wooster's Departments of History and Religious Studies. Additionally, the Junior Faculty Research Boot Camps have been a great way to write while enjoying time with friends and, alas, indulging in too many munchies.

Financial support for the dissertation came in the form of several fellowships and grants: from the Jacob Rader Marcus Center of the American Jewish Archives, a Loewenstein-Weiner Fellowship in American Jewish Studies and the Bernard and Audrey Rapoport Fellowship; from the National Foundation for Jewish Culture, the Jewish Foundation for Education of Women Fellowship of the Maurice and Marilyn Cohen Fund for Doctoral Dissertation Fellowships in Jewish Studies; from Columbia University's Center for Israel and Jewish Studies, a Fellowship. My treasured friends Deborah Reichler and Shoshana Keller provided financial support through the Isaac Schnitzer Fund for Graduate Study. At Wooster the book was helped along by a Henry Luce III Fund for Distinguished Scholarship Award in Fall 2009, which freed up time for writing by relieving me of one course.

I owe enormous thanks to Sonja Rethy, the editor at the Hebrew Union College Press. I'm a pretty good writer, but she showed me—as I remind my students—that there is always room for improvement. She has also been extremely patient with all of my questions as I go through the publishing process for the first time.

Finally, I am blessed to share the joy of this book's publication with my family. Our daughters Judith and Esther have announced it on their Facebook pages and have had a good time trying to decide whom to cast as Solomon Freehof in the movie version, and our new son-in-law Matt accepted working on the book as a valid reason for not running the Cleveland Turkey Trot. On a more serious note, there are no words adequate to express the gratitude I owe my partner Nancy. In one way or another this project has been part of our life for all the time we have known each other. She never lost confidence in my ability to complete it, even when I was not so certain. In the last several years she took on more than her share of household responsibilities so I could work undisturbed, and ate a lot of meals alone while I ate at my desk. Her loving companionship is what makes everything worthwhile.

ברוך הטוב והמטיב

Wooster, Ohio
17 Adar 5773
27 February 2013

ABBREVIATIONS

B.	Babylonian Talmud
EH	Even HaEzer
Hil.	Hilkhot, "Laws of"
ḤM	Ḥoshen Mishpat
OH	Oraḥ Ḥayim
R.	Rabbi
ShA	Shulḥan Arukh
SM"G	Sefer Mitsvot Hagadol
Tur ShA	Tur and Shulḥan Arukh
Y.	Palestinian ("Jerusalem") Talmud
YD	Yoreh De'ah

INTRODUCTION

By virtue of his great learning, his wide-ranging activity on behalf of the Central Conference of American Rabbis (CCAR) and the Union of American Hebrew Congregations (UAHC), the personal respect and affection his colleagues had for him, and his sheer longevity, Solomon Bennett Freehof was one of the central figures of American Reform Judaism in the twentieth century. This book is the first critical study of his crowning achievement, his responsa.

Son of a *sofer* and *mohel* from Ukraine who claimed descent from the first Lubavitcher Rebbe, Freehof was born in London in 1892 and moved with his family to Baltimore in 1903. He entered the Hebrew Union College (HUC) in 1911 and was ordained in 1915, a year after receiving his B.A. from the University of Cincinnati. He immediately joined the College faculty as an instructor in liturgy and remained there until 1924, with time off in 1918–19 for chaplaincy service with the AEF in France. While teaching at HUC he earned a Doctor of Divinity degree with a dissertation on "Personal Prayers in the Talmud." In 1924 he became rabbi of Kehilath Anshe Mayriv Congregation in Chicago, and in 1934 moved to Pittsburgh to serve as senior rabbi of Rodef Shalom Congregation, retiring in 1966. He died in 1990.

Freehof was one of the most influential members of the CCAR in the twentieth century. He served on its Liturgy Committee for over twenty years and was its chairman during the 1930s when it carried out a major revision of the *Union Prayer Book*. He served as vice-president of the CCAR in 1941–43 and president in 1943–45, years when the intense controversy over Zionism that culminated in the founding of the American Council for Judaism threatened to split the Reform rabbinate and the movement. During World War II he also chaired the CCAR's Emergency Committee on Placement, recruiting rabbis for the military chaplaincy and overseeing their replacement in civilian pulpits. From the outbreak of the world war until after the end of the Korean War he also chaired the Responsa Committee of the National Jewish Welfare Board's Committee on Army and Navy Religious Activities (CANRA), a position which required him to work closely with Conservative and Orthodox rabbis to decide questions of Jewish ritual practice in a military context. Throughout his career he was an active member of the UAHC-CCAR Joint Commission on Jewish Education, authoring a number of books on liturgy and Bible for youth and adults. From 1959–1967 he served as President of the World Union for Progressive Judaism, traveling frequently to Europe, Israel, and South Africa.

As senior rabbi of the largest and most prestigious synagogue in Pittsburgh, Freehof was a prominent figure in the local community. He excelled at fulfilling that rabbinic role so near and dear to earlier generations of American Jews, representing Judaism to the Christian community. This he did primarily through his Sunday morning lecture-sermons and his Wednesday morning book reviews. A dynamic and gifted preacher and public speaker, he regularly drew an attendance of hundreds, by no means limited to the Jewish community. He was also a frequent speaker on radio and in various public forums.

Freehof is best known, however, as Reform Judaism's most distinguished authority on questions of Jewish law and practice. His interest in halakhah dated back to his student days, as he recalled years later: "[Professor of Talmud Jacob Z.] Lauterbach naturalized me into the halakhah."[1] His status as Lauterbach's outstanding protégé was the reason he became the CCAR's representative on the military Responsa Committee. That experience, in turn, provided him with the expertise to emerge in the late 1940s as the CCAR's chosen authority on questions of Jewish practice. He wrote his first responsum for a CCAR colleague in 1942 and joined the CCAR Responsa Committee in 1947. In 1955 he succeeded Israel Bettan as chairman of the committee, remaining in that position until 1976. He continued to answer questions until his death, though the bulk of his responsa were written between 1950 and 1970. In addition to the thirty-three responsa he submitted to the CCAR during his chairmanship, between 1960 and 1990 he published eight volumes including nearly 600 responsa, while sending out informal responses to at least that number of inquiries.

Freehof's responsa cannot be understood apart from the ongoing debate within Reform Judaism over ritual observance—what Reform Judaism demanded of its adherents, who had the authority to make that determination, and on what basis. Freehof, who supported the reappropriation of ritual that began in the interwar years but opposed any attempt to declare ritual observances obligatory, advocated turning to responsa for guidance because in a Reform context they were merely advisory, and because they would serve to reconnect Reform Jews with the riches of the halakhic literature, mistakenly jettisoned in Reform's earlier, more radical phase. In conjunction with his call for more use of responsa as the most appropriate way to guide Reform Jewish practice, he proposed an original theory identifying the evolutionary principle underlying the halakhah with the same evolutionary principle he saw at work in Reform Judaism, which he identified as minhag. This theoretical framework served as the basis for his 1944 book, *Reform Jewish Practice and its Rabbinic Background*, which in turn informed all his subsequent responsa work.

The years of Freehof's peak activity coincided with the disintegration of what Jonathan Sarna has termed the prewar Jewish "subculture," as Jews increasingly entered the larger arena of American life.[2] The popular "tri-faith" model of American religiosity placed Jews as a religious group on equal footing with Protestants and Catholics. The sharp decline in antisemitism in the wake of Hitler's genocide facilitated the entry of Jews into neighborhoods, colleges and universities, and professions where they had previously not been welcome. The Jewish community's center of gravity moved from the city to the suburbs, where Jews lived in greater or lesser concentrations sprinkled among a Christian majority, rather than in identifiably Jewish urban enclaves. This new social context offered unprecedented opportunities, but also raised unprecedented challenges, particularly for Reform Jews, whose religious ideology and orientation were born out of the desire to be part of the society around them, and for whom halakhic boundaries lacked *ipso facto* validity.

Not surprisingly, therefore, questions on mixed marriage, conversion, Jewish status, gentile participation in the synagogue, and in general what is or is not "Jewish"—what Freehof called questions about "living in an open society"[3]—constituted a plurality of his published responsa and an even larger plurality of his unpublished correspondence. Indeed, even after the CCAR had adopted his rules regarding marriage, mixed marriage, and conversion—and, by implication, Jewish status—individual rabbis and laypeople turned to him for guidance in situations where the boundaries between Jewish and not Jewish were ambiguous or blurred. As he proudly wrote in 1978, "All these are new questions, the product of modern life. Orthodoxy brushes them aside. Reform Halacha faces them and deals with them."[4]

The postwar decades also redefined the fault lines within American Jewry. The line between "German" Reform Jews and the rest of the Jewish community virtually disappeared. In 1921 young Rabbi Jake Marcus confided to his diary that since Sol Freehof wanted to marry "a girl who is cultured, educated, and good looking and will not wince when a Yiddish word is spoken . . . ," the two friends had concluded that they had better marry "Russian" girls, because "if a boy of Russian descent married a girl of German descent the chances are that she would look down upon him and his family and the marriage would not be successful."[5] But the distinction between the "Russians," whose numbers overwhelmed the "Germans," mattered less and less as immigration became a thing of the past. The tide of postwar prosperity moderated or eliminated the economic disparities between the two groups, while the growing number of college-educated east Europeans reduced the "culture" gap. The presence of so many east Europeans in the Reform rabbinate and the corresponding interwar shift away from classical Reform made it easier for more east Europeans to enter the movement in the postwar years. While east Europeans had been joining Reform temples between the world wars, those households tended to be exceptionally highly acculturated and very well off.[6] The postwar east European influx—many of whom had first been exposed to Reform by Reform military chaplains, whose services were often less identifiably Reform in order to be inclusive[7]—was less willing to divest itself of its *Yiddishkayt.* Instead of the carefully controlled, top-down reappropriation of ritual set in motion by Rabbi Jacob Schwarz and the Commission on Ceremonies, change was now unsystematic and might be initiated by the rabbi or by some fraction of the membership. Many congregations experiencing conflicts over the presence or absence of "traditional" practices turned to Freehof to resolve their problems.

Even as the fault lines separating Reform Judaism from the rest of the Jewish community disappeared, however, a new fault line was developing, between an increasingly militant Orthodoxy and the rest of the community. Freehof's attitude toward Orthodoxy was a complex amalgam of respect for learning, nostalgic yearning for the warm piety his parents and his childhood home exemplified for him, disdain for the rightward shift of contemporary authorities, and a deep intellectual conviction that adherence to Orthodoxy was flying in the face of history. Though he resisted Reform attempts to create a code in part because he did not wish to create controversy with the Orthodox, at the same time he was a fierce opponent of attempts to enforce Orthodox standards of observance upon Jewish communal institutions and events.

The fault line between religious and secular ethnic ideologies of Jewish life also faded in the postwar years. The establishment of the State of Israel in 1948 rendered moot the controversy over Jewish nationalism and brought virtually all American Jews together in support of the new state. Synagogue affiliation, like church affiliation, reached an all-time high, with the result that the synagogue, rather than the JCC or any other explicitly cultural or ethnic institution, emerged as the definitive American Jewish institution. Though ethnicity had lost the battle to be the defining principle of American Jewish life, nevertheless, in many, if not most, of the new suburban synagogues, religion was just a cloak for ethnic solidarity, with attendance generally higher for social and cultural events than for services. However, for Reform leaders like Freehof, who had a deep commitment to a Jewish religious path rooted in distinctive beliefs, the absence of emphasis on the religious element in synagogue life was a problem. Freehof therefore defended the legitimacy and authenticity of *Reform* as opposed to Orthodoxy or Conservatism, and also of *Judaism* as opposed to Jewishness (even while affirming Jewish peoplehood).

Freehof himself was no neo-traditionalist. In many ways his own notion of Reform Judaism could be labeled "a broad and pleasant middle-class establishmentarianism . . . [,] the Jewish segment of the new North American religion."[8] But he did succeed admirably in making Reform Jews aware of their connection to the rabbinic tradition, and in putting the question of the relationship between Reform and halakhah squarely back in the movement's consciousness for the first time since its earliest days.

Chapter 1 of this study describes the role of responsa in the early Reform movement and the establishment of the CCAR's Responsa Committee, and surveys the Responsa Committee's activity prior to Freehof's chairmanship.

Chapter 2 outlines the convergence of circumstances that led to Freehof's emergence as an arbiter of Reform practice even prior to his accession to the chairmanship of the Responsa Committee. Ironically, his opposition to a code of Reform practice played a significant role in this development, as did the expertise he acquired during World War II as chairman of the Responsa Committee for Jewish military chaplains, as well as his general prominence within the CCAR.

Chapter 3 analyzes Freehof's views on ritual observance and halakhah in Reform Judaism. It shows that Freehof charted a centrist course in the currents of Reform thought. Though he approved of the Columbus Platform's renewed appreciation for ritual, he opposed encouraging—or expecting—Reform Jews to return to ritual practices they had abandoned, arguing that popular minhag should be determinative unless it was at odds with Jewish values. The theory of the relationship between halakhah and minhag—law and custom—he expounded in the introduction to his 1944 *Reform Jewish Practice and its Rabbinic Background* was the basis on which all his subsequent responsa work rested.

Chapters 4–8 analyze his published responsa and unpublished correspondence on a select number of topics: marriage and divorce, especially mixed marriage (Chapter 4); conversion and Jewish status (Chapter 5); Shabbat and kashrut (Chapter 6); and the limits of appropriate Reform practice (Chapters 7 and 8). The large number of questions he received about these topics indicates that these were the issues that troubled Reform rabbis and laypeople in the postwar decades. In Chapter 9 I offer my conclusions about the significant aspects of Freehof's responsa.

Chapter 10 concludes this study by examining the work of the Responsa Committee since Freehof. In truth, this subject deserves its own book. In this limited context I have chosen to focus only on what I consider the most important aspects of the post-Freehof Responsa Committee: its increasingly participatory process; the central role of all three post-Freehof committee chairs in the project to create Reform halakhah; and the committee's heightened profile within the Reform movement as the result of its involvement in several highly public and controversial issues.

Readers expecting close analysis of Freehof's halakhic reasoning will be disappointed. In most cases I have not done so because, paradoxically, it is not crucial for understanding the positions he took. Given his purpose in consulting the legal literature as well as his negative evaluation of Orthodox decisors of the modern era, it is not surprising that he felt free to ignore the conventions of halakhic jurisprudence. I have focused, however, on several instances when he was egregiously tendentious in his use of the sources, because these reveal significant elements of his thought.

It is my hope that this study of Freehof's responsa will not only raise his prominence in scholarly considerations of Reform Judaism, but will also add to the understanding of American Judaism and religion in America broadly considered.

1

RESPONSA IN REFORM JUDAISM

Responsa and the CCAR Responsa Committee possess a relatively high profile within contemporary Reform Judaism. In an era when virtually every organization has a website as its public face, the CCAR website includes links to Reform responsa right along with links to the resolutions and platforms it has adopted over the years of its existence.[1] Within the last two decades, members of the CCAR turned to the Responsa Committee for answers on controversial topics such as the role of the non-Jew in the synagogue and rabbinic officiation at same-sex ceremonies even while the movement as a whole was weighing those issues. Not infrequently, senior rabbinic students write theses on Reform responsa and related topics.

Yet this high profile for responsa is relatively new within Reform Judaism, and dates only to Freehof's ascendancy as a decisor.[2] Although the CCAR's Responsa Committee dates back to 1906, before the Freehof era its products were, with few exceptions, of marginal concern to both rabbis and laypeople. For more than half a century prior to 1906, responsa had been virtually absent from Reform Judaism.

Responsa in Nineteenth-Century Reform Judaism

Prior to the encounter with modernity, Jews (excepting Karaites and isolated groups such as the Beta Israel of Ethiopia) constituted, in Moshe Halbertal's phrase, a classic text-centered community.[3] The text at the center of the Jewish community was the Torah, both written and oral, as exemplified in the Talmud. Jewish life was lived within the "four cubits of the halakhah," the law as expounded in the Talmud and the literary edifice of commentaries, codes, responsa, and so forth, erected upon it.

Of all forms of halakhic literature, responsa by definition deal most

1

immediately with the actualities of individual and communal life. Responsa are, as it were, the "shock troops" of the halakhah: In their pages we find the record of rabbinic Judaism's encounter with what is new and different. It is therefore no surprise that the earliest battles in the war over religious reform were waged through the medium of responsa literature.

The earliest phase of Reform responsa began in 1810, when Israel Jacobson's Westphalian Consistory issued a letter permitting the consumption of legumes on Passover. In response to criticisms from other rabbis, Consistory member Rabbi Menaḥem Mendel Steinhardt published *Divre Iggeret*, in which he included a responsum that presented all the relevant halakhic sources and the reasoning by which the members of the Consistory had arrived at their decision, as well as other responsa defending the liturgical changes effected in the synagogues under their jurisdiction. Then in 1818 Eliezer Liebermann published *Nogah HaTsedek*, a compilation of responsa justifying the innovations introduced into the service by the Berlin reformers. The following year, alarmed by the establishment of a similar reform-minded temple in their community, the rabbinic court of Hamburg called on other opponents of reform to issue responsa refuting the arguments advanced in Liebermann's collection. The result, *Eleh Divre HaBrit*, was a compilation of twenty-two opinions from forty rabbis, all condemning the reforms defended and justified in *Nogah HaTsedek*.[4]

As Halbertal explains, in a text-centered community

> agreement on a common text defines the boundaries of the community and makes it cohesive. The shared text may be a source of conflicting beliefs and practices, but the community recognizes that it alone must be used to justify them all. . . . It is a procedural agreement that all practices, beliefs, or institutions, whatever they may be, are to be justified in reference to the text, as an interpretation of the text. In a text-centered community . . . interpretation becomes the main and central form of justification. Legal practice is similarly bounded by such procedural agreement. Courts can produce radically opposing rulings; what binds them together is agreement about the text that is the ground for the rulings.[5]

Under this definition, it is not surprising that most scholars agree that both the pro- and anti-reform opinions in these volumes were traditional responsa because of their shared assumptions about text and procedure.[6] However, even at the time, some opponents of change accused the reformers of intellectual dishonesty in their use of the sources.[7]

By the time the next battle of the texts broke out in 1842, the ground rules had definitely begun to change. During the prolonged controversy in Breslau between traditionalist Solomon Tiktin and modernist Abraham Geiger, the latter's supporters solicited and published seventeen responsa; Tiktin published a counter-collection. Coincidentally, around the same time the members of the Hamburg temple also published a responsa collection defending their new prayerbook against traditionalist condemnation.[8]

These texts were not traditional responsa; rather, their appearance marked the beginning of the second phase of Reform responsa. First, all appeared in German, not Hebrew. As Freehof later observed, this abandonment of Hebrew was "evidence that the controversy was moving out of the main stream [*sic*] of responsa debate," since only Hebrew-language documents would be shared among Jewish scholars the world over.[9] Second, while the Geiger and Tiktin collections did appeal to rabbinic sources, the issue at hand was not one of practice but of principle—whether the critical study and interpretation of sacred texts was compatible with a religious understanding of them. Finally, the Hamburg temple collection included very few appeals to halakhah but very many to philosophical and theological concepts.[10]

From the 1840s on, responsa as a genre disappeared from the reformers' literary output, for several reasons. First, as "Reform" and "Orthodoxy" gradually coalesced into two opposing blocs there was no need for, or purpose to, debate between them; they were satisfied either to ignore or condemn each other. Certainly once Liberal Judaism attained its dominant position in central European communities it had no need to engage in this sort of textual polemic.[11] Second, although many reformers continued to turn to the rabbinic sources for guidance in determining the course of reform, they employed the non-traditional hermeneutic of the *Wissenschaft des Judentums* in the analysis and interpretation of those texts. The text was essential not for its normative guidance but for elucidation of Judaism's historical development, for determining which elements of Judaism were timeless and essential and which were merely the products of historical contingency and therefore subject to change.[12] As Halbertal observes, in a text-based community, even when all agree on the canon, disagreement about what constitutes legitimate interpretation will cause a split in the community.[13] Third, the more radical reformers viewed the rabbinic corpus and the entire edifice of "rabbinism" as an unfortunate by-product of the centuries of oppression and exile, and were eager to dispense with it altogether.[14]

Reformers essentially replaced the responsa process with a different type of decision-making mechanism—parliamentary procedure. In place of the individual eminent scholar to whom questions were to be addressed, the reformers organized conferences and synods where decisions about religious practice were arrived at through collective actions taken by majority vote. At the three European rabbinical conferences and two synods, it made no difference whether a participant arrived at his individual position through a traditional reading of the sources, an historical critical reading of the sources, or some other process altogether. In David Ellenson's words, "The absence of [responsa] literature by the 1890s reveals that Reform Judaism ultimately came to abjure law as a defining characteristic of the movement and marks its departure from the classical legal canon of rabbinic civilisation [*sic*]. . . . It was a Reform . . . that was no longer tied to 'the authority of precedent' to sanction its actions."[15]

Despite its theoretical willingness to act without concern for halakhic precedent, Reform Judaism remained in practice relatively conservative in Germany, where the tight communal structure of the *Kultusgemeinde* and, eventually, the threat of Orthodox secession predisposed communal leaders toward compromise. Radicals like Samuel Holdheim's secessionist Berlin congregation remained the exception. But there were no constraints at all on Jewish religious life in America (i.e., the US and Canada), to which a number of the more extreme reformers therefore gravitated. In the new world radical Reform ideology and practice blossomed in the second half of the nineteenth century. Although Reform did not emerge in America without controversy, in the absence of an entrenched traditional rabbinate there was no recognized authority to issue responsa condemning the practices of American congregations that chose to institute reforms. There were also no rabbis like Aaron Chorin, arguing for reform out of a traditional context. Those reformers who did ground their decisions in the rabbinic literature either employed the historical critical method of Wissenschaft scholarship in their textual analysis or read the tradition in a selective fashion.

As in Europe, three positions emerged among American rabbis and religious leaders with regard to the Talmud and its authority. The Orthodox held that the Oral Law was of divine origin and that the decisions of the Talmud and codes were therefore binding; the text was sacred and was not subject to critical evaluation, nor could new interpretive methods be applied to it. The radical Reformers rejected any sort of submission to Talmudic authority, however understood. Indeed, some of them went so far in rejecting "rabbinism" that they also rejected any notion of the rabbi as possessor of religious authority.[16]

Between those two extremes lay a wide and ill-defined center, occupied in Europe by both the Positive-Historical school and the majority of reformers, and in the US by the moderate reformers. The vast majority of rabbis and scholars who occupied this center applied the tools and lessons of Wissenschaft scholarship to the rabbinic corpus. These centrists eventually divided into Reform and Conservative camps over the issue of the binding authority of the halakhah. Those within the Reform camp differed widely among themselves over how much value they assigned to the historical forms represented by the Talmud. Nevertheless they shared Abraham Geiger's historical approach, which led them to agree that the Talmud, however distasteful its practices to modern spiritual sensibilities, was an essential part of the development of Judaism.[17] Therefore, nineteenth-century American reformers did not write responsa for the same reasons that their European counterparts did not: There was no group for whom the traditional responsa process was adequate or necessary to address the new issues at hand.

Isaac Mayer Wise, in his perpetual quest to unify American Jewry, had envisioned the Union of American Hebrew Congregations as precisely that, a body encompassing all American synagogues; he founded the Hebrew Union College in 1875 to train rabbis to serve these American congregations. By the time he established the Central Conference of American Rabbis, however, it was with the express intent of organizing a rabbinic body with a distinctly Reform orientation.[18] The CCAR as a body would shape the form and content of American Judaism (which, for Wise, would inevitably become synonymous with Reform Judaism), leaving behind the era in which "every man did that which was right in his own eyes" (Jud. 21:25). Wise envisioned the CCAR deciding collectively on what reforms should be made and how they should be carried out.

> The united Rabbis of America have undoubtedly the right – also according to Talmudical teachings – to declare and decide, anyhow for our country, with its peculiar circumstances, unforeseen anywhere, which of our religious forms, institutions, observances, usages, customs, ordinances, and prescriptions are still living factors in our religious, ethical and intellectual life, and which are so no longer . . . All reforms ought to go into practice on the authority of the Conference, not only to protect the individual rabbi, but to protect Judaism against presumptuous innovations and the precipitations of rash and inconsiderate men. The Conference is the lawful authority in all matters of form.[19]

When the rabbis assembled at the first meeting of the Central Conference of American Rabbis in 1890, to the extent that they were concerned with precedent it was the precedent of the European reformers. To establish an ideological orientation for their deliberations they voted to take the proceedings of all previous modern rabbinic conferences and synods "as a basis for the work of this Conference, in an endeavor to maintain, in unbroken historic succession, the formulated expression of Jewish thought and life of each era."[20] It went without saying that their deliberations, including decisions concerning matters of religious practice, would be conducted according to parliamentary procedure and majority rule. Thus, like the European rabbinical conferences and synods, the American rabbis were not bound by precedent. They made no commitment to any criteria or guidelines for arriving at the individual decisions according to which they cast their votes. American Reform rabbis, like their European counterparts, read the traditional texts more or less critically, or felt free to ignore them altogether. This is evident in the written record of the CCAR's first major controversy over a matter of ritual practice, the debate over *milat gerim* in 1891.[21]

This debate constitutes a sort of American parallel to the 1840s German *Gutachten*, although here the discussion was within the Reform camp, not between Reform and Orthodox. The responses to Henry Berkowitz's inquiry included in the 1891 *CCAR Yearbook* were all written in English; some had appeared in the Jewish press. They were not responsa in the traditional sense, although one respondent referred to Berkowitz's question as "certainly belonging to the class of modern שאלות ותשובות."[22] By definition, of course, they were non-traditional in that they all accepted the legitimacy of questioning a matter of halakhah regarded as settled by all the major codes.[23] But they also diverged widely in the interpretive process by which they made their arguments. Aaron Hahn, chosen to deliver the paper against requiring *milat gerim,* relied entirely on sources in the Talmud and responsa to derive a conclusion that differed from the codified halakhah. By contrast, Isaac Schwab, who argued at great length for it, employed a Wissenschaft approach to a wide variety of texts, Jewish and non-Jewish, to demonstrate the historical importance of circumcision to the Jewish people. None of the published responses remotely resembled a traditional responsum; most cited far fewer rabbinic sources than had Aaron Hahn. Most were in favor of eliminating the requirement and expressed their opinions without reference to any Jewish sources, but made their arguments on the basis of contemporary considerations. Isaac Mayer Wise stated that while he believed *milat gerim* unnecessary and not required by the Torah, nevertheless he would not act individually but only if it was "adopted by [a] legitimate body, conference, or synod," since he was "not willing, in so important and incisive a question, to be an innovator on [his] own authority."[24] When the CCAR plenum finally voted on the question the following year, they decided by a vote of twenty-five to five to drop the requirement of ritual circumcision for adult male converts.[25] (In the same year they voted to allow cremation, after hearing papers in favor of the change in both 1891 and 1892.[26])

The Creation of the CCAR Responsa Committee

Between 1890 and 1914 the CCAR concerned itself primarily with imposing some order and uniformity upon the chaotic and variegated practice of American Reform congregations. At least on a pragmatic level, unity of praxis reflected unity of purpose and a shared vision of Reform Judaism. Nevertheless there remained an implicit tension between a concept of Judaism in which ritual was not a proper subject of religious law, and the need to reach agreement on what constituted appropriate Reform praxis. There was also tension between moderates and radicals—between those who saw reform as evolutionary and those who saw it as revolutionary. These tensions fueled open controversy on several occasions when members of the Conference held strong but conflicting views on the nature of Reform praxis, and ultimately led to the establishment of the Responsa Committee. When members of the CCAR first began to discuss the possibility of writing "responsa," however, what they had in mind was something very different from what the term had historically connoted.

In 1904 the CCAR established a committee to compile a manual of life cycle rituals for use by all its members, in keeping with the desire for liturgical consistency within the young movement. At the 1906 convention the committee presented its draft and reported that they had also asked President Kaufmann Kohler and Professor Gotthard Deutsch of the Hebrew Union College to "formulate a number of Halakot or laws, which should serve as a guidance for Reform Rabbis."[27] Kohler explained that this was being done in response to requests for guidance from younger rabbis, in particular, who did not know what constituted proper Reform practice in life cycle rituals. The committee report stressed that these were to be guidelines only, not obligatory decisions. Nevertheless, the term "Halakot" elicited a storm of protest, and Kohler was forced to backtrack, insisting, "Neither Dr. Deutsch nor I want to dictate. We want simply to counsel and to assist those who request enlightenment."[28]

A lengthy and heated discussion ensued, with the proposal's opponents arguing that even in setting down guidelines for Jewish observance Reform was in danger of becoming a new Orthodoxy. In the words of Samuel Schulman: "I do not think that we should say whether a mourner should mourn for three or five days. . . . When they come to me with questions of this kind I let them settle it for themselves. I let their conscience dictate to them. They may mourn for a week or they may go to work the next day, if it is necessary."[29] In the end the assembled rabbis reached a compromise. It was resolved "that an extra appendix be added to the Year Book, such appendix to contain questions that might, from time to time be submitted concerning Jewish customs and traditions, together with appropriate answers."[30] Kaufmann Kohler was appointed to chair the committee that would provide the answers to these questions. Thus was born the CCAR's Responsa Committee.

Samuel Schulman, who had bitterly opposed Kohler's "Halakot" proposal, explained why he favored this solution: Establishing a Responsa Committee was merely a way to recommend that younger colleagues who didn't know what to do in "a matter of practice," do what had been done "from time immemorial in Israel: write to older men and men of learning and experience for an answer, and . . . be guided in their conduct with due deference and reverence for such authority and information . . . " Since "such answers may be valuable . . . they should receive some form of permanence in our Year Book."[31] David Philipson, equally opposed to introducing any "Halakot" into Reform Judaism, endorsed the proposal as well, noting that "If the Conference were to act on these responsa and make it an action of the Conference, it might look like the offering of a new Shulkan Aruk. If they are simply the responsa of an individual, or of a committee of three, they remain an individual matter."[32] Philipson's distinction added an element that would prove crucial in the future, i.e., the notion that a decision of the Responsa Committee would be merely one possible solution to any issue, representing no more than the best effort of one or several rabbis to offer a course of action based on their agreed-on reading of the tradition. As a "private" effort, it would not carry the authoritative weight of a decision reached by the Conference as a whole through a majority decision of the rabbis present and voting at a plenum. Thus the CCAR formalized a situation in which non-precedent-based decisions (majority vote) carried more weight than precedent-based decisions (responsa).

The Responsa Committee under Kaufmann Kohler

The original members of the Responsa Committee appear to have been selected either for their reliability in adhering to Kohler's views or for their influential status within the CCAR. Two prominent radicals were included, Bernhard Felsenthal of Chicago's Sinai Congregation and Jacob Voorsanger of Temple Emanu-El of San Francisco. Other members were Joseph Krauskopf of Philadelphia's Keneseth Israel Temple; Max Landsberg of Temple B'rith Kodesh of Rochester, NY; Sigmund Mannheimer, the elderly Hebrew Union College librarian; Julius Rappaport, Beth-El Congregation, Chicago; and Joseph Stolz from Isaiah Temple in Chicago. It is doubtful that the committee functioned at all in its first six years. Felsenthal and Voorsanger died in 1908 and Mannheimer in 1909; the *Yearbooks* from 1909 through 1912 list only Kohler and HUC Professors Gotthard Deutsch and/or David Neumark as members of the committee. The 1911 *Yearbook* notes that Kohler gave an oral committee report at the convention, but no record of its content was included in the volume. Not until 1913 did he issue the committee's first recorded decisions, most of which were not even responses to questions submitted but rather his exposition of issues that would have been included in the "Halakot" section of the proposed Ministers' Handbook: the impropriety of bar mitzvah in a Reform context, where the proper ceremony was now confirmation for both boys and girls; saying Kaddish for a deceased parent for twelve months rather than eleven; times when weddings may be solemnized; and the propriety of sounding the *shofar* in the synagogue when Rosh Hashanah falls on Shabbat.[33] All of these earliest "responsa" are examples of historical critical scholarship applied to the rabbinic texts and reflect the type of analysis Kohler had described in his 1907 paper, "The History and Functions of Ceremonies in Judaism."[34] There, basing himself on his father-in-law David Einhorn's view that ceremonies are needed "as symbolic expressions of the priest-mission assigned to the Jewish people," Kohler elaborated a process by which the historical development of Jewish rituals could be studied scientifically in order to determine whether in the present they were to be retained, rejected, modified, or replaced in order to inculcate piety and spirituality among contemporary Jews.

While most of the earliest responsa served as platforms for Kohler to articulate his views, these years are also noteworthy for setting *de facto* precedents in the creation of responsa and their use by the CCAR. Kohler delegated the writing of some responsa to members of the committee; David Neumark's stinging dissenting opinion on bar mitzvah established the precedent that the committee did not have to render a unanimous decision.[35] These earliest responsa established a boundary between questions that were appropriately handled by the Responsa Committee and questions requiring consideration by the CCAR as a whole. Kohler himself articulated the committee's limitations when he refrained from deciding questions of forbidden marriages:

> Now in matters involving great principles in which the immaculate purity of the offspring, the Pesul Mamzeruth, the unblemished family record, is at stake, no individual rabbi, however radical or however learned he may be, ought to act single-handedly and on his own authority, but submit the question to a larger body for a thorough discussion and careful deliberation to have it decided by a *Conference of Rabbis*, that after having weighed the various views against each other may claim competence and authority for its final solution.[36]

In other words, the Conference could allow latitude in "ceremonials," but not in fundamentals of Jewish life such as personal status.

Finally and most significantly, the Responsa Committee articulated a perspective that generally militated against radical reform. It did this in two ways. First, by explicitly attributing importance to the rabbinic tradition: The committee's mission was to arrive at decisions through studying traditional rabbinic sources, although they read those sources critically rather than as traditional norms. Members of the CCAR meeting in plenary session, by contrast, were free to decide issues based on whatever criteria they saw fit, without regard to precedent. Second, one of Kohler's 1913 responsa—the only one precipitated by an actual question submitted to him—demonstrates that a responsum could serve as an intentional bulwark against what he, at least, viewed as extreme radical Reform.

Kohler reported to the 1913 CCAR convention that, in response to an inquiry from Rabbi Martin Meyer of Temple Emanu-El in San Francisco, he had written a responsum on whether the Torah reading could be done completely in the vernacular. The responsum is a model of Wissenschaft scholarship harnessed to the service of moderate reform. Kohler began by explaining that the proper procedure, according to the tradition, was to read all the Hebrew and then translate it into the vernacular. In the past, however, there had been two "deplorable" departures from this practice: that of the Alexandrian Jews, who read only in the Greek and, as a consequence of losing touch with the Hebrew, were assimilated into the Greek-speaking Christian world, and that of the traditional synagogue, which discontinued the vernacular translation and thereby turned the Torah reading into a meaningless rote performance. Today, said Kohler, in order to "revive the ancient spirit of genuine devotion" by making the Torah reading meaningful again, the "recommended" course of action was to read at least a small portion in Hebrew, translate it, and follow it with a "Scriptural lesson" from Prophets or Writings in the vernacular. "By such reading . . . the impressiveness of the ancient custom is greatly enhanced *and at the same time the continuity of the Synagogue tradition maintained.*" [emphasis added] [37] Kohler, who had no difficulty breaking with synagogue tradition when it suited him, was clearly dismayed by the prospect of change that he considered too radical, so he structured his responsum to arrive at the desired conclusion.

What Kohler did not include in the record, but was probably known to most, if not all, of those present, was that Meyer was among the minority of rabbis who favored taking this step. He had introduced it at Temple Emanu-El, but enough members opposed it to overrule him, and voted to reinstitute the Hebrew reading.[38] The reaction of the assembled rabbis to this one decision illustrates what would happen repeatedly in the future whenever the Responsa Committee issued a decision on a "hot button" issue: Those in agreement with the decision sought to have it adopted as CCAR policy; those opposed to the decision rejected such a move. In this instance, the CCAR first voted to accept the committee report and include it in the *Yearbook*, in accordance with the process agreed on six years earlier. However, David Philipson then moved that the decision on Torah reading be adopted by the Conference as a resolution and sent to the questioner. Joseph Stolz and Samuel Schulman, understanding the implications of Philipson's motion, wanted no part of it. Said Schulman, who as president was chairing the plenum, "In the creation of the Committee on Responsa, it was intended to establish a moral authority in this country. . . . However, it should not be adopted as the sense of the Conference. We shall print this report, but the individuals may do as they like."[39]

Philipson then made a milder proposal that the Conference adopt

Kohler's suggestion and write a letter to the congregation stating that it was the CCAR's "opinion" that a section of the Torah be read in Hebrew and translated into the vernacular. Moses Gries, whose congregation had also dispensed with the Hebrew Torah reading, objected. Making this an official Conference position, he argued, would mean that all congregations that did not have a Hebrew Torah reading were incorrect in their practice. Unable to arrive at a statement of policy that would satisfy both Kohler's and Gries's views, the rabbis gave up and agreed that Kohler would send his individual responsum to the congregation.

Although the rabbis continued to wax enthusiastic about the educational value of the committee's work, they did not necessarily feel the need to take advantage of it. Kohler begged his colleagues on at least two occasions to submit their questions.[40] In the absence of actual questions, it appears that he continued to produce responsa on topics that he felt needed to be addressed, thus creating yet another avenue to extend his already considerable personal influence over Reform Judaism in North America. On one occasion, at least, he seems to have behaved too highhandedly for his colleagues to endure. The responsum he submitted as his 1915 report (which has not been preserved and whose subject is not known) was not only rejected when it was read at the convention in his absence, but even criticized there by one of his faculty members, Professor of Talmud Jacob Lauterbach, who deplored its lack of sources: "In a report of this character, the authority should be given for every decision so that the younger rabbis may see the development of the ideas involved. The answers should show on what basis the responsa were given." David Philipson complained that the other members of the Responsa Committee needed to see the report before it was submitted, and that the committee also needed to "formulate some principle [concerning procedures] which shall guide them in their work."[41]

Between 1913 and 1921, when Kohler passed the committee chairmanship to Lauterbach, thirty-one responsa appeared in the *CCAR Yearbook* (see Table I). Those submitted by questioners and those initiated by Kohler show a striking difference. Kohler initiated the writing of five responsa relating to synagogue or liturgical practice and six on questions of death and mourning, but received only one question in both of those areas, the controversial issue of eliminating the Hebrew Torah

Table I: CCAR Responsa Committee Questions, 1913–1921[42]

Year	Author/s	Title	Question Submitted	Category
1913	Kaufmann Kohler, David Neumark	Times When Marriages Should Not Take Place	NO	*Synagogue/liturgy*
1913	Kaufmann Kohler	Bar Mitzvah	NO	*Synagogue/liturgy*
1913	David Neumark	Bar Mitzvah	NO	*Synagogue/liturgy*
1913	Kaufmann Kohler, David Neumark	Reading the Torah Portion in the Vernacular	YES	*Synagogue/liturgy*
1913	Kaufmann Kohler, David Neumark	Blowing of the *Shofar* on Sabbath	NO	*Synagogue/liturgy*
1913	Kaufmann Kohler, David Neumark	Length of Time for Recital of Kaddish	NO	*Death and mourning*
1913	Kaufmann Kohler, David Neumark	Mourning Customs	NO	*Death and mourning*
1914	Kaufmann Kohler, David Neumark	The Educational Value of Yahrzeit	NO	*Death and mourning*
1914	Kaufmann Kohler	Kaddish and Distinctions Between the Dead	NO	*Death and mourning*
1914	Kaufmann Kohler	Standing During Recital of Kaddish	NO	*Death and mourning*
1914	Kaufmann Kohler	Marriage With a Mother's Sister or Half-Sister (Aunt or Half-Aunt)	YES	*Forbidden relations*
1914	Kaufmann Kohler	Burial of Non-Jewish Wives in Jewish Cemetery	NO	*Jews and gentiles*
1916	Kaufmann Kohler, Jacob Lauterbach	Burial of Non-Jewish Wives in Jewish Cemetery	YES	*Jews and gentiles*
1916	Kaufmann Kohler, Jacob Lauterbach	Forfeiture of Congregational Membership by Intermarriage	YES	*Jews and gentiles*
1917	Kaufmann Kohler, Jacob Lauterbach	Employment of Non-Jews in a Jewish Cemetery	YES	*Jews and gentiles*
1917	Kaufmann Kohler, Jacob Lauterbach	Burial of Jews in Section of Non-Jewish Cemetery	YES	*Jews and gentiles*
1917	Kaufmann Kohler, Jacob Lauterbach	Choice of Cemetery	YES	*Jews and gentiles*
1917	Kaufmann Kohler, Jacob Lauterbach	Marriage With a Step-Aunt	YES	*Forbidden relations*

Year	Author/s	Title	Question Submitted	Category
1918	Kaufmann Kohler, Julius Rappaport	Rabbi Officiating at Christian Scientist's Funeral	YES	*Jews and gentiles*
1918	Gotthard Deutsch	Kosher Kitchen in Military Camps	YES	*Jews and civil society*
1918	Kaufmann Kohler	*Nolad Mahul*	YES	*Miscellaneous*
1919	Gotthard Deutsch	Use of Pyrex Dishes for Meat and Milk	YES	*Miscellaneous*
1919	Gotthard Deutsch	Sale of a Synagogue	YES	*Miscellaneous*
1919	Gotthard Deutsch	Divorce of Insane Husband	YES	*Forbidden relations*
1919	Kaufmann Kohler	Rabbi Officiating at Mixed Marriage	YES	*Jews and gentiles*
1919	Kaufmann Kohler	Burial of Non-Jewish Wives in Jewish Cemetery	YES	*Jews and gentiles*
1919	Gotthard Deutsch	Burial of Non-Jewish Wives in Jewish Cemetery	YES	*Jews and gentiles*
1919	Kaufmann Kohler	Children of Mixed Marriages	YES	*Jews and gentiles*
1920	Julius Rappaport	Fermented Wine Not Required for Sacramental Purposes	YES	*Jews and civil society*
1920	S. Felix Mendelsohn	How Should a Loan in Foreign (Russian) Currency, Exchanged in Another Country (United States), Be Repaid?	YES	*Miscellaneous*
1921	Gotthard Deutsch	Burial on a Holy Day	NO	*Death and mourning*

reading. Clearly members of the CCAR felt capable of determining their own congregations' liturgical style and guiding their congregants' life cycle events. Among the questions submitted to the Responsa Committee in those years, two stemmed from the effect of current events, the world war and Prohibition; four others were miscellaneous inquiries. But by far the largest group dealt in some way with relations between Jews and Gentiles—more specifically, with the consequences of life in a society where Jews were free both to marry Gentiles and to maintain their affiliation with the Jewish community. What Reform rabbis needed above all in these years, apparently, was help in defining the boundary between Jews and non-Jews.

The Responsa Committee after Kohler

In 1921 Jacob Lauterbach succeeded Kaufmann Kohler as Chairman of the Responsa Committee. Lauterbach's responsa "tended to be long explorations of the history of Jewish rituals with citations from a wide range of materials, some rabbinic and some not."[43] However, Lauterbach valued the halakhic tradition far more than Kohler did, famously identifying halakhah as prophetic ethics applied to daily life,[44] and made far more extensive use of Talmudic citations than Kohler had. Lauterbach suffered from ill health and in 1934 passed the chairmanship to HUC Professor of History Jacob Mann, who died in 1940. Mann's responsa tended to be quite short with limited text citations. He had had no involvement with the committee prior to his appointment and evinced little interest in it during his six years as chairman. Under Mann "the committee hardly functioned," forwarding only one committee report to the CCAR. Walter Jacob suggests that he may have been appointed to limit the committee's activity, though aside from the question of women's ordination (see below), the committee had never taken a stance that created controversy in the CCAR and did not receive much attention from the membership.[45]

Neither man followed Kohler's practice of initiating responsa; most questions came from individuals, although the CCAR leadership requested the responsum on birth control and the HUC Board of Governors requested Lauterbach's responsum on the ordination of women. The questions they received were rather a different mix from those received by Kohler, as Table II shows.

With precedents already established from the Kohler years—for those who wanted to consult them—to cover many of the problematic aspects of relationships between Jews and gentiles, the Responsa Committee's agenda in the interwar years is not quite so easily categorized. There were relatively few questions about liturgical practice. The question of forbidden marriages continued to arise because the CCAR had yet to adopt a definitive position on it, while individual rabbis continued to be asked to officiate at such ceremonies. Burial of non-Jewish spouses in Jewish cemeteries was clearly a perennial question, as were mourning and burial practices in general.

The issue of women's ordination led to a significant difference of opinion between the Responsa Committee and the Conference as a whole. Professor Neumark's daughter Martha had successfully completed the program of rabbinic study at HUC and wanted to be ordained. The faculty had voted in favor of the ordination of women in theory (with Professors Lauterbach and Freehof voting against[46]), but were hesitant about actually doing it; they referred the matter to the Board of Governors, who turned to Professor Lauterbach as head of the Responsa Committee for his opinion. The matter was controversial enough that a discussion of his vehemently negative responsum was placed on the agenda of the CCAR's 1922 convention. After a spirited discussion the Conference rejected it and overwhelmingly endorsed a statement asserting that ". . . we declare that woman cannot justly be denied the privilege of ordination."[47] Nevertheless, since the Conference did not have the authority to tell the College what to do, their disagreement was moot.

Several of the interwar responsa do share one distinctive characteristic: They address questions reflecting the growing presence of east European Jews in the ranks of Reform Judaism. Two of Lauterbach's responsa, on head covering and naming, are among the best known of this genre. In these and in his article on the custom of breaking the glass at weddings[50] he deployed his vast halakhic erudition to demonstrate that wearing a *kippah*, naming a child after a deceased relative, and breaking a glass at weddings—three of the most visible and common east European practices, whose absence in Reform Judaism was cited as proof of Reform's lack of *Yiddishkayt*—were, in fact, mere folk customs with no basis whatsoever in halakhah, and that there was no rational basis for maintaining them.

When Jacob Mann died in 1940 the CCAR leadership named Freehof's friend Israel Bettan, Professor of Midrash and Homiletics at HUC, as his replacement. Bettan served until 1955, when he stepped down upon taking the presidency of the CCAR. His responsa tended to be extremely light on citations from rabbinic sources and heavy on appeals to Reform principles and ideology. When he took over the Responsa Com-

Table II: CCAR Responsa Committee Questions, 1922–36[48]

Year	Author/s	Question	Category
1922	Jacob Lauterbach	Removal of Dead Body to Another Grave	*Death and mourning*
1922	Jacob Lauterbach	Ordination of Women as Rabbis	*Miscellaneous*
1922	Jacob Lauterbach	Marriages Between New Year and Atonement	*Synagogue/ liturgy*
1923	Jacob Lauterbach	Direction of Graves in Cemetery	*Death and mourning*
1923	Jacob Lauterbach	Placing Small Sticks in the Hands of the Deceased When Placing in the Grave	*Death and mourning*
1923	Jacob Lauterbach	Marriage With a Mother's Sister or Half-Sister (Aunt or Half-Aunt)	*Forbidden relations*
1923	Jacob Lauterbach	Blowing of the *Shofar*	*Synagogue/ liturgy*
1923	Henry Berkowitz, Jacob Lauterbach	Burial from the Temple, Also With Reference to Burial of Suicides	*Death and mourning*
1923	Jacob Lauterbach	Emblem of the Tribe of Levi [on a tombstone]	*Death and mourning*
1924	Jacob Lauterbach	Who Shall Read From the Torah?	*Synagogue/ liturgy*
1924	Jacob Lauterbach	Ritual for Disposal of Damaged *Sefer Torah*	*Synagogue/ liturgy*
1925	Jacob Lauterbach	Autopsy	*Death and mourning*
1925	Samuel Cohon	Marriage With Brother's Widow	*Forbidden relations*
1927	Jacob Lauterbach	Birth Control	*Jews and civil society*[49]
1927	Jacob Lauterbach	Work on New Synagogue on Sabbath by Non-Jews	*Jews and Gentiles*
1927	Jacob Lauterbach	Positioning of Synagogue Entrance and Ark	*Synagogue/ liturgy*
1928	Jacob Lauterbach	Worshiping With Covered Heads	*Synagogue/ liturgy*
1932	Jacob Lauterbach	Orthodox Jew as Partner in Firm Keeping Open on Sabbath	*Sabbath*

Year	Author/s	Question	Category
1932	Jacob Lauterbach	Lapse of Time Before Setting a Tombstone	*Death and mourning*
1932	Jacob Lauterbach	Naming of Children	*Death and mourning*
1932	Jacob Lauterbach	Validity of Rabbinic Opinions	*Miscellaneous*
1932	Jacob Lauterbach	The Jewish Jubilee	*Miscellaneous*
1936	Jacob Mann	Repairing Damaged Sefer Torah	*Synagogue/ liturgy*
1936	Anonymous	Burial of Non-Jewish Wives in Jewish Cemetery	*Jews and gentiles*
1936	Jacob Mann	Less Than a Minyan of Ten at Services	*Synagogue/ liturgy*
1936	Jacob Mann	Games of Chance in Connection With Fund Raising	*Miscellaneous*
1936	Jacob Mann	Burial of Non-Jewish Wives in Jewish Cemetery	*Jews and gentiles*
1936	Julius Rappaport	Burial of Non-Jewish Wives in Jewish Cemetery	*Jews and gentiles*

mittee it was "moribund with an uncertain future."[51] In a span of eleven years (1940–1950) he submitted only six responsa to the CCAR; then in the next five years (1951–1955) he submitted twenty. As Chapter 3 will show, this was because of Freehof.

The questions Bettan received reflected the new circumstances of postwar American life. Over one-quarter of these responsa (seven of twenty-six) deal with questions of medical ethics or other matters related to the enormous changes in health care following World War II. This includes both circumcision prior to the eighth day and artificial insemination. Three responsa ("Masonic Rites in Temple," "Funeral Rites of Fraternal Orders," and "Marriage of Negro Man to a Jewish Woman") reflect the increased social integration of American Jews. Five ("Carillon Music [Carillon Tower on a Synagogue]," "Walking Across Religious Symbols," "National Flags at Religious Services," "Card-Playing

Table III: CCAR Responsa Committee Questions Submitted, 1940–55

Year	Author/s	Question	Category
1941	Israel Bettan	Predetermination of Sex	*Medical ethics*
1943	Israel Bettan	Marriage of Cohen to a Divorcee Prohibited	*Forbidden relations*
1946	Israel Bettan	Masonic Service at a Funeral	*Jews and gentiles*
1946	Israel Bettan	Divorce (Get)	*Forbidden relations*
1947	Israel Bettan	Rabbi Officiating at a Funeral of a Jew in a Non-Jewish Cemetery	*Jews and gentiles*
1950	Israel Bettan	Euthanasia	*Medical ethics*
1952	Israel Bettan	Sabbath Observance	*Sabbath*
1952	Solomon B. Freehof	Artificial Insemination	*Forbidden relations*
1953	Israel Bettan	Carillon Music [Carillon Tower on a Synagogue]	*Jews and gentiles*
1953	Israel Bettan	Time of a Bar Mitzvah	*Synagogue/ liturgy*
1953	Israel Bettan	Transplanting the Eyes of Deceased Persons	*Medical ethics*
1953	Israel Bettan	Walking Across Religious Symbols	*Synagogue/ liturgy*
1953	Israel Bettan	Refusing a Jew Membership	*Synagogue/ liturgy*
1954	Israel Bettan	Bat Mitzvah	*Synagogue/ liturgy*
1954	Israel Bettan	Funeral Rites of Fraternal Orders	*Jews and gentiles*
1954	Israel Bettan	Circumcision on a Day Other Than the Eighth Day of Birth	*Synagogue/ liturgy*
1954	Israel Bettan	Physician Keeping Truth from Patient	*Medical ethics*
1954	Israel Bettan	National Flags at Religious Services	*Jews and civil society*

Year	Author/s	Question	Category
1954	Israel Bettan	Marriage of a Negro Man to a Jewish Woman	*Jews and civil society*
1954	Solomon B. Freehof	Kaddish for a Unitarian Sister [=*RRR* #28]	*Jews and gentiles*
1955	Israel Bettan	Card-Playing in the Social Hall of the Temple	*Synagogue/ liturgy*
1955	Israel Bettan	A Proselyte Reciting Kaddish for Deceased Parents	*Jews and gentiles*
1955	Israel Bettan	Placing of Piano in Front of Ark	*Synagogue/ liturgy*
1955	Israel Bettan	Observance of Yahrzeit By Widow Who Has Remarried	*Death and mourning*
1955	Israel Bettan	Propriety of Using Discarded Practices in Reform Services	*Synagogue/ liturgy*

in the Social Hall of the Temple," and "Placing of Piano in Front of Ark") reflect the construction of new suburban synagogues, in which religious activity usually took a back seat to social and cultural activities, and where decisions on building design were often made by individuals with more money than Jewish learning or good taste. Finally, three responsa ("Time of a Bar Mitzvah," "Bat Mitzvah," and the crucial statement "Propriety of Using Discarded Practices in Reform Services") reflect the struggle over the reappropriation of traditional practices in Reform congregations as the movement's demographics changed.

The responsa listed above are only those that the Responsa Committee chairmen submitted for publication to the *Yearbook*. Unfortunately, they did not see fit to save their responsa correspondence, so there is no way of knowing either the full range of questions submitted to them or the total number. Freehof did note many years later that Lauterbach must have received "hundreds" of inquiries.[53] Nevertheless it is reasonable to suppose that the committee chairmen chose to address the most significant contemporary issues in print, and that the record is therefore an accurate barometer of CCAR concerns.

Although after the first few years the Responsa Committee always had five or six members in addition to the chair, genuine consultation between the chairman and the committee members was slow and difficult until the advent of email in the 1990s. The existence of occasional dissenting opinions from the Kohler, Lauterbach, and Mann years indicates that these men shared at least some questions with the committee. Bettan occasionally asked his friend Freehof for his opinion, or to write a responsum, but apparently the other committee members in his day were content to let him do the work. The Responsa Committee chairmen essentially functioned as solo authorities, often not even sharing routine inquiries with the committee. Freehof recalled that when he served two years (1922–24) on the Responsa Committee under Lauterbach, "being on the committee simply meant that before he turned it into the Conference, he sent it to you to say yes!"[54]

Conclusion

Responsa as a genre disappeared from nineteenth-century Reform discourse in both Europe and America as Reform moved away from the text-centered community of rabbinic Judaism and thus became less concerned with precedent. To the extent that Reform rabbis were concerned with precedent, it was in the context of historical-critical inquiry, and carried no authority as such. Through the early twentieth century, Reform leaders on both sides of the Atlantic were confident that scientific study of the tradition would reveal which elements of Judaism were eternal and had to be retained and which were contingent and could rightly and safely be jettisoned. Synods or rabbinical organizations would then translate these scholarly findings into agreed-upon programs for practical reform. Under the chairmanship of Kohler and then Lauterbach, the "responsa" produced by the Responsa Committee "addressed practical needs in a form that was in essence an academic essay."[55] Naming Jacob Mann and then Israel Bettan to head the Responsa Committee shows that the CCAR leadership conceived of the committee's task as a scholarly one but not necessarily one that required extensive expertise in rabbinics.

It is impossible to know how widely the decisions of the Responsa Committee were consulted or accepted prior to World War II. When

Kohler presented his responsum on burial of non-Jewish wives to the 1914 convention, he carefully noted that it was only his individual opinion, but expressed his hope that CCAR members would continue to consult the Responsa Committee so that it would become "the clearing house for all important ritual and theological questions."[56] This did not happen. After the Kohler and Lauterbach years there were years in which no responsa appeared in the *Yearbook*, a clear indication of the committee's lack of importance in the eyes of the rabbis. The CCAR accepted the vast majority of responsa that the chairmen did present, and even requested one for its own guidance. But the rabbis continued to make their major decisions without consulting the committee, and explicitly voted in 1922 to reject Lauterbach's responsum opposing women's ordination. The postwar years, however, would see a dramatic change in the committee's prominence, due primarily to the activities of Solomon B. Freehof.

2

How Freehof Became the Reform *Posek*

Solomon B. Freehof has been called the first genuine Reform *posek*, i.e., "a rabbi who emerges as a responsa authority on the basis of his own personal qualifications."[1]

His emergence as such was the result of the intersection of three factors: the evolution of Reform Judaism's attitude toward ritual observance and the ongoing debate over a code of Reform practice; Freehof's own considerable personal prominence in the CCAR; and the expertise he acquired as a writer of responsa for the military chaplaincy during and after World War II. Very simply, he was the right person at the right time.

The Revaluation of Ritual in Interwar Reform Judaism

The desire to restore some ritual to Reform Judaism is evident as far back as the 1890s. It was evident to many classical Reform rabbis that their people had forsaken ritual observance more completely than almost any Reform leader had advocated or foreseen, and that it was necessary to rectify this situation.[2] However, classical Reform ideology valued ceremony only if it was edifying, pointing the worshipper to some great ethical truth. As Kaufmann Kohler had insisted, "[I]n order to have a positive religious value and significance, ceremonies must either directly or symbolically express thoughts and feelings that appeal to us while elevating, hallowing and enriching our lives."[3] The interwar Reform revaluation of ritual was shaped by different intellectual and theological paradigms and located in greatly altered social conditions.

The early twentieth century witnessed the growing importance of the social sciences in American thought and a general revolt against the rationalism, historicism, and formalism of nineteenth-century thought.[4] New approaches to the study of history and philosophy and the new social sciences of anthropology and sociology undermined the intellectual paradigm within which classical Reform had taken shape. While contemporary intellectual life continued to threaten the authority of traditional religious belief, nevertheless the zeitgeist simultaneously expressed a yearning for the warmth and power of religious forms which had appeared irrational only a few years earlier, as numerous rabbis would remind their colleagues at CCAR conventions throughout the 1920s.[5]

In addition, the demographic makeup of the Reform movement was changing. To most classical Reformers Jews were both a religious community and a group defined by common descent, though many preferred to emphasize the former and downplay the latter, especially as it became entangled with American tensions about race.[6] However, they strenuously resisted the idea that there was a particular Jewish culture.[7] To the east Europeans this was palpably incorrect. That the east Europeans were characterized more by an ethnic "Jewishness"—*Yiddishkayt*—than by a commitment to Judaism as a strictly religious system is a truism of American Jewish history. As they came to dominate American Jewry, so did the self-perception of Jews as an ethnic group with a distinct culture.[8]

From 1900 on, east Europeans constituted the overwhelming majority of students entering HUC; during the 1920s upwardly mobile east European Jews began joining Reform congregations in significant numbers, constituting about half of the members of Reform congregations in the eleven largest centers of Jewish population by 1930.[9] Any east European Jew who was comfortable in a Reform temple in the 1920s had to be quite acculturated; nevertheless, the 1930 survey of Reform congregations found that foreign born Jews were more likely to own Jewish ritual objects and prayerbooks and that they observed "ceremonials" more frequently than did native born Jews.[10] Whether as rabbis or as congregants, they also brought to Reform an affinity for a cultural/ethnic Jewish self-definition and a concomitant sympathy for Zionism, if not a firm ideological commitment to political Zionism.[11]

Finally, the reappropriation of ritual became one of the explicit goals of Reform congregational life, chiefly through the efforts of R. Jacob D. Schwarz at the UAHC's Bureau (after 1935, Commission) of Synagogue Activities. The Bureau was originally established to help synagogues weather the Depression through better programming and financial planning, but Schwarz was a strong advocate of the reintroduction of traditional practices into Reform Judaism, and he soon branched out into strengthening synagogue life in general, including encouraging the reappropriation of ritual. From 1936 on he wrote a regular column on Jewish observance in the Commission's newsletter, which the UAHC soon collected and published in book form.[12] At his initiative the Commission created a Sub-committee on Ceremonies, which became the UAHC-CCAR Joint Committee on Ceremonies in 1939. The new body's explicit purpose was "to stimulate experimentation in the congregations for the revival of old and the introduction of new ceremonies and actually to create ceremonial materials and make them available to the congregations for experimentation."[13]

These trends are evident in the *CCAR Yearbooks* from the interwar decades. The rabbis' debates reveal a growing desire for ritual observance, a conscious rejection of the universalist language of "religion" employed by the classical Reformers in favor of a particularist Jewish vocabulary, and the explicit or implicit influence of religious thinkers such as Martin Buber, Mordecai Kaplan, and Rudolf Otto. One of the opening salvos in the fight for change was a 1923 paper titled "Shall We Teach Ceremonies in the Religious School?" that criticized Reform as too "intellectual" and called for a more emotional Judaism. "[I]t is sometimes to be wondered whether that pious old patriarch in his ramshackle tenement, who speeds the parting Sabbath on its way with prayer and melody and symbol while the very gates of heaven open up before his enthralled spirit, has not more of genuine Jewishness in him than can be found in some entire congregations of our knowing." The author advocated teaching "[d]evotions, public and private, prayers before and after meals, Sabbath-eve customs and holyday symbols and practices" and anything else with obvious "spiritual potentiality."[14]

The 1926 convention heard the results of a questionnaire sent to the membership. "There is no doubt that the trend is away from the rational to the emotional and the mystical. The weakness of Reform has been its over-emphasis on the rational; the swing is now on back to the emotional . . . There is a craving for something warm, definite, concrete,—that appeals to the heart, that grips the soul. That there is a return to the customs and ceremonies in home and Synagog is evident on every side," along with a desire for even more ceremonies: Kiddush, Seder, Hanukkah candles in the home, Sukkot, and Simḥat Torah. The responses emphasized "Jewishness" and the need for Reform to retain its connection to the rest of the Jewish world.[15] Even David Philipson confided to his diary that "[m]ore attention will be paid to the retention of ceremonial usages that have the power of appeal and have beauty of sentiment and memory to back them. . . . Reform has been too rationalistic . . ."[16]

Many laypeople shared the rabbis' concern. In 1935 the National Federation of Temple Brotherhoods asked the CCAR "to urge the reintroduction of ceremonials into Jewish life."[17] The January 1937 UAHC Council approved a resolution calling for including "traditional symbols, ceremonies, and customs" such as a cantor, an all-Jewish choir, only Jewish music, and Kiddush in Sabbath services.[18] At the same convention a speaker asserted that "there is great need today for more beauty, more mysticism and more drama in our synagogue ritual in order to infuse a more spiritual content into our prayer language. Ceremonies occupy an important place; those introduced or reintroduced should be adjusted to the spirit of the times."[19]

What all these calls for increased "ceremonials" had in common was the emergence of a new model of spirituality: not edification, but emotional connection—whether to God, the Jewish people, their families, their own sense of self, or some combination of all those. It was a desire to be "more Jewish."

The Guiding Principles which the CCAR adopted in 1937, known as the "Columbus Platform," demonstrated that Reform Judaism had left behind the Pittsburgh Platform and joined the new American Jewish mainstream in rooting its Judaism in its Jewishness, beginning with the opening sentence: "Judaism is the historical religious experience of the Jewish people." The document also adopted a new favorable stance toward the rabbinic tradition and ritual observance, as evidenced by its division into three sections: Judaism and Its Foundations, Ethics, and Religious Practice. The penultimate paragraph of the section on Religious Practice stated: "Judaism as a way of life requires in addition to its moral and spiritual demands, the preservation of the Sabbath, festivals and Holy Days, the retention and development of such customs, symbols and ceremonies as possess inspirational value, the cultivation of distinctive forms of religious art and music and the use of Hebrew, together with the vernacular, in our worship and instruction." In other words, it deemed four elements *essential* to distinctively Jewish religious behavior, in addition to adherence to the moral law: 1) celebration of the festivals of the Jewish religious calendar; 2) such old and new "customs, symbols and ceremonies as possess inspirational value"; 3) Jewish religious art and music; and 4) the use of Hebrew along with the vernacular in the liturgy.[20]

While the Columbus Platform retreated from classical Reform's stark differentiation between the moral law on one hand, and ceremony as edifying ancillary on the other, the difference was one of emphasis and tone, not a fundamental conceptual change. However, under the influence of the new religious thought it did offer a significantly less rigid set of criteria for deciding what made a ritual meaningful. Its chief author, Samuel S. Cohon, rejected the classical Reform view that the purpose of prayer and other ritual was *Erbauung,* "edification."[21] As Cohon wrote elsewhere, "Ceremonies represent the poetry and the drama of religion translated in forms that are universally understandable. They speak to the emotions, and invest life with holiness."[22] It did not matter if a ritual had a didactic value or not, as long as people found some significance in its performance.

Interest in the creation of some sort of guide to Reform ritual practice paralleled the increased interest in ritual practice. Among the earliest calls for guidance was a 1914 article by Rabbi Max Heller in the *HUC Monthly*, a student publication edited that year by his son James, Abba Hillel Silver, and Solomon B. Freehof. Heller criticized Reform's antinomianism and disdain for the rabbinic tradition, and called for guidelines. While agreeing that it would be a bad idea for Reform to codify religious observance rigidly, he insisted it could not simply leave everything up to the individual. He concluded with the suggestion that a good first step would be the collection of all German and American Reform rabbinical opinions. Such a collection would create "a species of Reform Responsa which constitute a valuable factor in the history of the Reform movement: they relate to such subjects as the liturgy, the rite of circumcision, the organ in the Synagogue, the covered head, cremation and the like; a collection of these would throw much light on the principles and progress of the Reform movement."[23]

The next public call for guidelines for Reform practice came a decade later. At the 1925 CCAR convention Louis Binstock demanded that the CCAR formulate "mandatory dogmas that shall regulate uniformly and universally the religious belief and practice of every rabbi and layman in Reform Judaism." Though Binstock muddied the waters by calling for Reform "dogmas," including clarification of views on God, the afterlife, and so forth, in fact his focus was on the lack of rules and the consequent chaos in Reform Jewish ritual observance.

> What I should like to know is what does Reform Judaism . . . teach authoritatively today regarding the religious necessity for communicants of our faith to keep their business houses closed on the ימים נוראים. . . . Members of our congregations who are constantly admonished in vague general terms to observe the Sabbath have a right to know exactly what Reform Judaism . . . teaches regarding proper Jewish worship and practice on the day of rest. . . . [While] all these matters seem very trivial—only matters of ceremony and not belief—matters of form, not of spirit, . . . [nevertheless] they puzzle the layman and often destroy respect for Jewish tradition and practice, the neglect of which we rabbis have lately begun to lament. . . .[24]

Serious momentum for some code or guide to Reform practice came in the late 1930s, spurred by Felix A. Levy, who also was the driving force behind the 1937 Statement of Principles. In his 1937 President's Message he called for a radical revision of the Reform attitude toward observance to complement the new platform's revision of Reform doctrine. Levy, who had become a Zionist and an advocate of more Hebrew and traditional practices following a 1922 trip to Palestine,[25] argued that the chaotic state of Jewish life made it essential for Jews once again to become a people united by Torah. Reform's task was to rejoin "catholic Israel" (he used Schechter's famous phrase) by acknowledging the reality of Jewish peoplehood and bringing its patterns of religious observance back to closer correspondence to the rest of Jewry.

> The unique feature of Jewish life is Torah, and the most strik-
> ing element in Torah is the Halachah. . . . I am not prepared
> to say how we can recover the abandoned ground and go back
> to some form of Halachic authority and practice. . . . I rec-
> ommend however that a committee be appointed to follow
> the work of the Committee on Principles that dealt with the-
> oretical questions, and that this committee draw up a code of
> rules for guidance in practice.[26]

Levy was quick to add that such a code would not be "final or even obligatory," but merely a "guide" that would create some uniformity in Reform practice and help the rabbis teach their congregants that Reform was about observance and not merely negation. However, this was cer-tainly only a sop to a certain segment of his audience, for the rest of his argument only makes sense when read in reference to some sort of au-thoritative code.

Levy's views were, in any case, far out of the mainstream of thought within the CCAR, but it did not help him that the Committee on the Pres-ident's Message, a large *ad hoc* committee constituted annually to trans-late the President's recommendations into resolutions, Executive Board decisions, and the like, was heavily weighted with older, classically-oriented members that year.[27] They did not endorse the idea of a code of Reform practice, but merely expressed cautious approval for "intensi-fying . . . ceremonial and ritual practice" to the extent that the Joint Com-mission on Synagogue Activities was already doing so.[28]

The question of a code of practice returned to the convention floor the very next year, in the report of the Committee on Synagog and Com-munity, whose mandate was "to consider methods and projects for mak-ing this principle [of the primacy of the synagogue in Jewish life] vital and effective in the life of the Jewish communities of America."[29] The four young members of this committee included one JIR graduate and one former member of a secret fraternity of HUC rabbinic students ac-tive in the last decade of Kohler's presidency who were committed to certain traditional forms of observance,[30] so it is not surprising that they managed to include in their report both an endorsement of Zionism and "the adoption of a code of Reform Jewish ceremonial observance."

> Thoughtful liberal Jews are becoming increasingly dissatisfied with the colorlessness and emptiness of much that constitutes Reform Jewish religious life. The feeling is now almost universal that too many warm, colorful helpful ceremonies and disciplines were discarded by the former generations of Reform Jews. . . . Many Rabbis and Congregations have reintroduced and recreated ceremonials. These attempts, however, have been sporadic and the work of a few individuals. The time has come for the responsible leaders of Liberal Judaism to formulate a code of observances and ceremonies and to offer that code authoritatively to liberal Jews.[31]

With no public discussion the convention referred their report to the Executive Board. In 1940 that body recommended that "as soon as practical, a paper be placed on the [convention] program . . . to be devoted to the feasibility and advisability of drawing up a Code of Practice."[32] That is how it came about that at the 1941 convention Solomon B. Freehof addressed his colleagues on the subject of "A Code of Ceremonial and Ritual Practice."[33]

A Reform Code of Jewish Practice and Reform Jewish Practice and its Rabbinic Background

When the CCAR leadership called upon Freehof in 1940, they knew him well. His old friend James Heller was the Conference's vice-president, and he himself was serving a term on the Executive Board in addition to his chairmanship of the Liturgy Committee and active membership on the Joint Commission on Education. His friends and colleagues knew of his interest and expertise in halakhah, even though his main scholarly contribution to the CCAR's activities prior to this had been as a liturgist. Classmates and former students were already turning to him for guidance in Jewish practice.[34]

Furthermore, Freehof was indisputably Jacob Lauterbach's chief protégé. (The two were also close friends until the latter's death in 1942.)

He had served on the Responsa Committee under Lauterbach in 1922–24. Among the very sparse documentation of Freehof's career prior to 1940 is a letter from Lauterbach answering a question on the halakhah of burying an amputated limb.[35] In 1963 Freehof would write that he had been a member of the Responsa Committee for about forty years.[36] (Though not listed as such in the *CCAR Yearbooks*, this letter and informal correspondence with Israel Bettan show that he did correspond with at least two of the committee's three chairmen on committee business.)

Freehof also absorbed much—but not all—of Lauterbach's views on the nature of halakhah and its place in Reform Judaism (see Chapter 3). His friends in the CCAR leadership doubtless knew, when they selected him to speak, that, unlike Lauterbach, he was opposed to creating a code of Reform practice. Indeed, he opened his 1941 paper by reminding his colleagues that the desire for an authoritative code went back to the early days of the movement in Germany, but that no Reform synod or body of rabbis had ever succeeded in creating one, and he quoted approvingly the comment of Dr. Nehemiah Bruell of Frankfurt at the 1871 Augsburg Synod: "'We regret that the fluid word of the Talmud codified in the Shulhan Aruch has become fixed and we would not like to see a new edition and revision of this book, a proceeding which could only be injurious to the development of Judaism.'"[37]

Freehof explained that there were several obstacles to creating a Reform code of practice. First was the fact that Reform Jews didn't care whether a particular practice had legal authority or not, because they viewed ritual as changeable *custom* that they were free to adopt, modify, or discard. Alluding to the ongoing work of the Commission on Ceremonies, he noted that Reform was now experimenting with ceremonies to see what was "effective," rendering the notion of a code particularly inappropriate. The issue, he emphasized, was not whether Reform Jews observe a particular practice or not; the issue was the *nature* of praxis. "The difference between us and [Orthodoxy and Conservatism] is that they consider these ritual or dietary matters as law even when they do not observe them while we consider them as custom even when we do observe them. We therefore have no desire to put these customs upon an authoritative basis by having them solemnly promulgated as authoritative by any synod."

Second, he insisted, any code would have to be comprehensive, including Jewish ritual practices that Reform Jews generally neglected, such as Sabbath observance and dietary laws. These two areas, encompassing such a significant amount of daily Jewish living, were the most obvious areas of halakhah in which Reform practice deviated from tradition and on which Reform had been unable or unwilling to offer guidance to its people. A Reform code of practice would only make the situation worse, Freehof bluntly pointed out:

> What could we say about [kashrut]? Should we describe the actual practice as it has developed among us or should we modify it? Should we say formally that the mixture of meat and milk dishes is no longer to be prohibited, that meat need not be slaughtered by a *schochet* [ritual slaughterer], that we should have no bread in the house during Passover but that we need not go through the ceremony of searching for *hometz* [leaven]? And what about Sabbath laws, the laws of work and rest? We dare not omit them from any full code of Jewish practice. What shall we permit and what shall we prohibit?

Furthermore, any code produced by the CCAR, even a non-authoritative one, would be regarded by the people as authoritative by virtue of its publication, and would place the Reform rabbinate on the horns of a terrible dilemma. If a code was seen by Reform Jews as authoritative, that would imply that these matters of ritual practice were *law*, and that Reform Jews who did not observe according to the code were violating Divine law—a notion that contradicted the very essence of Reform. But a code that described actual Reform practice in diet and Sabbath observance would "bitterly offend" the Orthodox, who would accuse Reformers of simply legislating their neglect of the law. The inescapable conclusion was that a code of Reform practice was an impossibility.

Freehof agreed that the motivation behind the idea of a code was a good one: "It would surely be helpful if people could be guided to a knowledge of the observances and if there were some ceremonial norm which all more or less would follow." What he then proposed was essentially an expanded version of Kohler's "Halakot." The "danger" of appearing to promulgate an official code could be obviated by having just one member of the Conference write his personal judgment of what constituted appropriate practice. This, he reminded his audience, was what Maimonides, Karo, and the other great codifiers had done.

The one desideratum he could see stemming from a guide was increased uniformity in Reform practice. Just as the CCAR's adoption of a prayerbook had led, without compulsion, to broad uniformity in Reform liturgical practice, so an equally non-compulsory guide to Reform practice in other areas "would find its way into the hearts of our people and gradually assume the authority of honored practice," though uniformity of practice was neither possible nor necessary. He therefore proposed that his colleagues adopt a taxonomy of Jewish practice with six rubrics, each rubric to be treated differently depending on its content and its place within the realm of Reform practice:

1. The dietary laws: About these the movement should do nothing, for reasons already given.
2. "Ritual ceremonies": These also should not be systematized in written form. The Joint Commission on Ceremonies was in the process of experimenting with all sorts of new "pageants and observances," and it was far too early to know which of them would work. These should continue to circulate freely and individually.
3. "Existing synagog observances": These were already systematized in writing: "Our Prayerbook is, in effect, a code of synagog practice." Since it underwent revision about every twenty-five years, a way already existed to provide for "new or revived" liturgical practices.
4. "Existing non-synagog observances": By this he meant home and cemetery rituals and practices. Since the Liturgy Committee (which he chaired) had a mandate from the CCAR to publish a book which would include all of these it would be a simple matter to add explanatory notes and directions, similar to what was done in annotated Orthodox prayerbooks.
5. Responsa: Freehof recycled and expanded Max Heller's proposal of twenty-seven years earlier:

   > *Our responsa* are all answers to practical questions involving the harmonizing of Jewish law with modern practice. We should publish all our responsa to date in a

well-indexed volume and every ten years should issue a new edition including the responsa to date. These responsa are not law but are learned opinions. We publish them as such. In a sense they constitute our oral law, an equivalent to the Talmud as it developed. This booklet will serve as a guide to us, particularly if we make full use of our Committee on Responsa and address more and more questions to them.

He noted that this was similar to what the CCAR had actually done in its very first *Yearbook*, when it collected and published the decisions of all nineteenth-century European and American liberal rabbinical conferences and synods. He also noted that when the CCAR made this decision in 1890, it explicitly refrained from endorsing any of the earlier decisions—even the Pittsburgh Platform—as binding or authoritative.[38]

6. "Marriage laws": The CCAR's efforts over the decades to arrive at a comprehensive treatment of this topic had still not borne fruit. Freehof stated unambiguously that the rabbis had to write "a clear-cut code which shall have the effect of law for us [concerning] . . . marriage, divorce, and conversion." Like Kohler and others who had tried to produce definitive Reform standards in marriage and divorce, Freehof's insistence in this area derived from the need to reconcile Jewish practice with the laws of the state. The CCAR, he concluded, needed to make these crucial decisions and publish them.

Freehof's six rubrics constituted an original and uniquely Reform taxonomy of Jewish practice that reflected the experience of the CCAR in its half-century of existence. His opposition to any guidelines for non-liturgical ritual observance accorded with its consistent reluctance to arrive at any conclusions in this area. Liturgy, on the other hand, was historically the focus of Reform activity, and was the CCAR's greatest area of success in terms of defining a uniquely Reform mode of observance. That his last rubric included conversion—a religious matter of no concern to the state—underscores the extent to which his taxonomy shared Reform's general *ad hoc* approach toward questions of observance. Common sense required that there be a way to define who was or was not a Jew, and there was no other rubric under which to place it.

Doubtless Freehof hoped that with this paper he had uttered the final word on the subject of a guide to Reform practice. The minority of rabbis who wanted an authoritative Reform code and a commitment to halakhah would see that it was, indeed, an impossibility, and stop agitating for it. The minority of rabbis who opposed any code of practice would hear him saying that there was no need for one. The majority, rabbis who wanted some sort of guidelines, would learn that, like the *bourgeois gentilhomme* who discovered he had been speaking prose all his life, they already had all the requisite provisions for ritual guidance, and that to the extent that they lacked it, it was because the movement itself was still in flux and could not provide it even if a code were to be written. Thus Freehof's paper reveals his genius as a conciliator and a consensus builder. None of the actions he recommended the Conference take—publication of a guide to home and life cycle rituals, regular collection and publication of responsa, and a final resolution of personal status issues—were new. All were reiterations of proposals the Conference had heard and endorsed years earlier, but had never carried through. In one area of Jewish practice where Reform practice was unclear and inconsistent, kashrut, he recommended doing nothing; with regard to many traditional practices then being introduced "experimentally" by the Joint Commission on Ceremonies, he similarly recommended inaction. In other words, in Freehof's opinion—and contrary to that of Lauterbach, who disagreed vehemently with Freehof's aversion to a guide to Reform practice[39]—the CCAR did not need to do anything about ritual practice among Reform Jews other than what it had already set itself to do.

There was no controversy following Freehof's presentation. The Conference's grand old man, David Philipson, endorsed his ideas; the Executive Board voted to establish a committee to consider his recommendations and report to the next convention on how to carry them out. Israel Bettan chaired the committee; Freehof himself and Samuel Cohon served on it.[40] Its 1942 report, which the CCAR adopted, reads as if Freehof wrote it himself with *Reform Jewish Practice and its Rabbinic Background* (*RJP*) already in mind:

> Your Special Committee . . . wishes to submit to the Con-
> ference a plan of action, which, while embodying the essen-
> tial features of Dr. Freehof's proposal, bids fair to meet the
> demands of many of our members. We take it that those who
> have been asking for a code of observances and ceremonies
> are actuated by a sincere desire to obtain authoritative guid-
> ance for themselves and for the congregations they serve.
> Surely, they are not anxious to submit their life's conduct to
> a fixed and unalterable legal code. What they really want is
> not a code of laws, but a manual of religious practices, in-
> formative rather than coercive in character. In such a man-
> ual, the customs and observances to which the liberal
> synagog [*sic*] subscribes, together with the conclusions of
> many pertinent responsa, would find their proper place. . . .
> To be sure, some theoretical questions will continue to claim
> our attention. Shall we, for example, number some dietary
> regulations among current religious practices? Shall we deem
> certain restrictions observed in some quarters on the Sabbath
> Day as necessary and fit subjects for further exposition and
> emphasis? But these and similar questions can be profitably
> discussed while the manual is being prepared.[41]

There is no record of how or even if it was decided to charge Freehof
with actually compiling the guide. He had delivered his paper in June
1941; by the time the CCAR gathered for its next convention in February 1942, the world war had overtaken them.

Despite heavy wartime responsibilities (see below), in 1944 Freehof
managed to publish *RJP*, to which he added a second volume in 1952.[42]
The book hewed closely to his 1941 proposal. At that time he had called
for a compendium of Responsa Committee decisions, since these "constitute[d] our oral law, an equivalent to the Talmud as it developed."[43]
Using the responsa for guidance would be the equivalent of the CCAR's
1890 decision to include the decisions of all nineteenth-century rabbinical conferences and synods in its first yearbook while denying them
any binding authority.

The "chief purpose" of *RJP*, as he stated in the Introduction, was "to
describe present-day Reform Jewish practices and the traditional

rabbinic laws from which they are derived."[44] There were four chapters: Public Worship, Marriage and Divorce, Naming of Children and Circumcision, and Burial and Mourning. (Volume II covered The Synagogue Building, The Synagogue Service, Marriage and Conversion, and Death, Burial, and Mourning.) Thus the book dealt only with public worship and life cycle events, the areas of Reform practice he had characterized in 1941 as having enough consensus to be describable. Each chapter was divided encyclopedia-style into a number of entries. For the most part each entry consisted of one practice or category of observance in which Reform practice differed from traditional practice. For each entry Freehof first briefly described the Reform practice and then described the traditional practice. He usually explained why the Reformers had decided to differ, and what justification they found in Jewish sources. Wherever there were Reform precedents (e.g., nineteenth-century decisions; CCAR resolutions, responsa, individual papers in the *Yearbook*, especially those of Kohler and Lauterbach; Moses Mielziner's book on Jewish marriage law;[45] the notes to the 1928 *Rabbi's Manual*) he incorporated them into his text to provide the most accurate description of a Reform consensus, where there was one. He cited existing CCAR resolutions as definitive, since these represented the official will of the assembled Reform rabbinate; otherwise he generally weighed the other sources according to the degree of consensus they represented, though in compiling his sources he also interpreted them to reflect his own views.

In the chapters other than those on marriage and conversion, most of the entries are leisurely discourses on various *halakhot* and *minhagim*, sometimes with no clear conclusion as to what should constitute current Reform practice, or else with only a descriptive reference to what Reform congregations commonly do. The following is a representative example:

> DATES FORBIDDEN FOR FUNERALS . . . *Funerals are not held on the Sabbath, on the Day of Atonement, or on the main days of the festivals.*
>
> Orthodox law, although prohibiting the burial of the dead on the Sabbath and the Day of Atonement (Sh.A. Orah Hayyim 526 #3), permits burial on the main day of the

festivals. . . . [Here follows a brief summary of the halakhah regarding burial on a festival.]

This law, permitting burial on the holidays, is, of course, based upon the law which prohibits keeping a body overnight. Among Reform Jews, where the practice of burying the body on the same day is not so strictly adhered to, bodies are not buried on the first day of holidays. In the year 1922 the Central Conference of American Rabbis (*Yearbook* XXXII, p. 80) adopted the following resolution:

"Although in the codes of Jewish law there is no express prohibition of conducting funerals on the festivals, yet in deference to Jewish custom and sentiment, your committee is of the opinion that members of the [CCAR] should abstain from conducting funerals on these days except where public health demands."[46]

The chapters "Marriage and Divorce" in *RJP* and "Marriage and Conversion" in *RJP* II are significantly different, in keeping with his 1941 paper. Here he focused on Reform precedents in order to deduce rules for Reform practice. (See Chapter 4.)

Continuing Debates over a Code of Practice

The publication of *RJP* did not put an end to the troublesome question of a code of practice; after the war, the CCAR returned to it. In 1946 Freehof delivered another paper, "Reform Judaism and the Halacha,"[47] in which he acknowledged the changed zeitgeist within Reform and tried to reinforce the desire of a growing number of his colleagues for a serious engagement with the rabbinic legal tradition, while simultaneously resisting the call for any sort of code of Reform Jewish practice. (See Chapter 3.)

Eight of the nine responses recorded in the *Yearbook* enthusiastically supported some degree of guidance for Reform Jews. The ninth was a tangential comment, not a criticism. Some respondents spoke of the need to teach their people how to live a Reform Jewish life; others of the need for something that would show people that Reform Jewish life was not contentless. Samuel Cohon criticized Freehof sharply for his "timidity" and emphasized the need to demand observance from Reform Jews.

> Nothing is ultimately binding in religion save that which we
> ourselves accept and to which we give our souls. We must
> first accept the yoke of the Divine Kingdom, and then the
> yoke of Mitzvoth. If men accept Judaism as a way of life,
> then we have a right to come to them with the claim that that
> way of life calls for a particular line of action. In this regard
> I disagree with Dr. Freehof completely. I am not afraid of re-
> ducing our usages to writing despite all the difficulties in-
> volved and I know they are many. We need a small Hayye
> Adam if not a Shulchan Aruch, written for the average man
> and woman . . . I am not afraid that people will call it the
> minimum of Judaism, because now the minimum is zero.
> Whatever you add to it will be a gain.[48]

Frederic A. Doppelt, arguing for a code, declared himself "in agreement
with Freehof's analysis and . . . Cohon's conclusion." He had been using
RJP as justification for introducing certain practices to his community;
when his congregants asked why, he told them:

> "Because it is the will of the Central Conference of American
> Rabbis. Here it is, compiled in book form. It is binding upon
> me as a member of the Central Conference to promote and
> further its recommendations and conclusions concerning Re-
> form Judaism." And I have found, Dr. Freehof, either because
> of your personal prestige or because of the prestige of the
> Central Conference that when I tell them that my authority is
> not in me personally but rather in a higher authority—that it
> is, as it were, in "Halacha l'Moshe Mi'Sinai," it is generally
> accepted by my people in the congregation. They respect au-
> thority, and certainly on matters pertaining to Reform Ju-
> daism this body of rabbis is the highest authority.[49]

Freehof, however, continued to insist in his final comments that a code
would not be of use. Referring to his Orthodox father's attestation of the
decline in observance in his community, he said, "If a fixed code were
a panacea, Orthodoxy would be vitally alive."[50] There the discussion
ended.

In subsequent years Freehof reiterated his opposition to a code at
every possible juncture.[51] Ironically, his determined opposition to a code

of Reform practice contributed to his becoming the premier arbiter of Reform practice. As he became more actively involved in writing his responsa for the CCAR, at least some of his colleagues were able to satisfy some of their desire for guidance in ritual matters by directing questions to him. Meanwhile individual members of the CCAR issued their own guides to Reform practice. The CCAR did not produce any such volumes until the 1970s.[52]

Freehof's Personal Prominence

In the late 1940s Reform rabbis Abba Hillel Silver and Stephen S. Wise, the outspoken and fiery heads of the American Zionist movement, were undoubtedly the most widely known rabbis in the United States. But within the Reform rabbinate itself, there was no figure more widely known, liked, and respected than Sol Freehof. Many members of the Conference knew him and remembered him fondly from their student days, when he had been one of the most popular members of the Hebrew Union College faculty.[53] During the 1940s, the peak years of his activity within the Conference and the movement, he made significant contributions to the CCAR's organizational development and to the intellectual and spiritual growth of Reform Judaism. He chaired two important committees, the UAHC-CCAR Joint Commission on Jewish Education and the CCAR Liturgy Committee. In the former capacity he wrote two well-received and widely circulated textbooks for use by children and adults.[54] He had chaired the CCAR Liturgy Committee since 1931; its years of labor finally bore fruit with the publication of the greatly revised *Union Prayerbook* in 1940 and 1945.[55] During the war he served on the CCAR Committee on Chaplaincy and chaired its Emergency Committee on Placement, which had the crucial and delicate task of recruiting members of the Conference for the military chaplaincy. He served as vice-president and president of the CCAR from 1941–45, one of the stormiest periods of the Conference's existence, when the controversy over the "Jewish Army Resolution" at the 1942 convention[56] led to the founding of the American Council for Judaism. Freehof, who despite his known Zionist inclination was a personal friend of men on both sides of the issue, was deeply involved in the unsuccessful effort to prevent the division of the Conference and came away from it apparently with little damage to his own reputation in the eyes of either side.[57] He acceded to the CCAR presidency in 1943, just in time to face the rebellion of the classical Reform congregations. When Houston's prestigious Beth Israel Congregation adopted new by-laws explicitly reaffirming the Pittsburgh Platform and rejecting the legitimacy of the Columbus Platform, several other congregations followed suit, raising the possibility of a schism in the movement.[58] Freehof's widely-acclaimed public response to Beth Israel's broadside captured the essence of post-Columbus Platform Reform: "It is only an Orthodoxy which dares not depart from 'classic' patterns laid down by past generations. . . . The same liberal principles which gave the Reform pioneers the right to change the venerable customs and prayer texts of Orthodoxy give us the right to change practices and modify doctrines of the pioneers. . . ."[59]

Finally, in addition to all of this work, Freehof was actively involved in overseeing the religious life of the Jewish military chaplaincy. Having served as a chaplain in 1918–19,[60] he now served not only as one of the CCAR's chosen representatives to the Jewish Welfare Board's Committee on Army and Navy Religious Activities (CANRA), but as chairman of its Responsa Committee. The Report of the Committee on Chaplains to the 1943 convention pointed out, "It is with pride that we record that one of the CCAR group, Rabbi Solomon B. Freehof, is the Chairman of the sub-Committee on Responsa. He has worked zealously and most efficiently with a representative of the Orthodox and of the Conservative group. The opinions on matters brought to the attention of the Committee on Responsa are first written by Rabbi Freehof and are based on the Halacha."[61] No member of the Reform rabbinate hearing that report would have failed to be impressed that one of their own was functioning in such a capacity vis-à-vis more traditional rabbis.

Freehof's Responsa Expertise

Freehof acquired his extraordinary expertise in the responsa literature largely through his own efforts in the service of the Jewish military chaplaincy, and he continued to develop it subsequently out of sheer interest in and love of the literature. The mandate of CANRA's Responsa

Committee was to "investigate into and conduct research on problems of religious ceremonial and observance, with which chaplains are faced as a result of the contingencies of army life. It is to be the policy of this Sub-Committee to render its opinions in as general a manner as possible."[62] The members of this Responsa Committee, as it was known, were Freehof, Orthodox Rabbi Leo Jung, and Conservative Rabbi Milton Steinberg.[63] Freehof became the chairman because, as he later recalled, "When the Chaplaincy Committee was organized, it seemed less (politically) trouble to have me as the Chairman of the Responsa Committee than either Jung or Steinberg."[64]

He proved more than equal to the task. His earliest letters to Steinberg and Jung are strikingly amateurish, both in their lack of depth with regard to halakhic citations and in their lack of concern for traditionalist sensibilities. But as the war progressed he became more and more adept in his use of the rabbinic literature, while developing his own style in the responsa he drafted for the committee.[65] His genius as a compromiser and conciliator enabled the committee to function smoothly; by the end of the war he had established a cordial and mutually respectful relationship with Jung and also with David Aronson, who replaced the ailing Steinberg. Most importantly, he had gained enormous knowledge of the responsa literature and experience as a decisor.

A library was, of course, a necessity. Freehof, always a bibliophile, began collecting responsa in earnest during the war. For his CANRA work the JWB purchased for him about $1200 worth of books—at a time when a complete edition of the Babylonian Talmud cost under $50— and when the war ended, he persuaded the organization to let him keep them all.[66] He also enlisted the help of overseas chaplains, writing to them to ask them to find certain responsa titles for him or send him unwanted or unclaimed books.[67] Later in life his library also grew through the efforts of his brother Louis, who regularly collected unwanted Hebrew books from dying inner-city synagogues and sent them on to him.[68] When he eventually donated his collection of responsa to the Hebrew Union College in Cincinnati, it numbered over 3,000 volumes.[69]

Freehof Becomes the Reform Posek

Although Freehof claimed that Jacob Lauterbach received "hundreds" of inquiries during his tenure as Responsa Committee chairman, it is undeniable that the phenomenon of widespread interest in responsa within the Reform movement dates to the postwar years, especially after Freehof's accession to the committee chairmanship. Freehof himself credited his CANRA work for his later immersion in Reform responsa,[70] but this only begs the question. Why, indeed, did his colleagues send him so many questions? What accounts for the apparent explosion in interest in halakhah and its bearing on Reform practice in the CCAR in the postwar years?

One scholar has tried to attribute this phenomenon to a sense of collective guilt over the European genocide and a desire to preserve some of the traditions destroyed by the war,[71] but there is no evidence for this theory. Another supposition is that many inquiries came from former chaplains, since they had become accustomed in the military to having to consider questions of Jewish practice from a halakhic perspective and also to adopting some traditional practices.[72] But Table IV, which shows that Freehof received 80 inquires from CCAR colleagues between 1942–1955, proves that was not the case. Of those, only 19 were from present or former chaplains or CANRA personnel, while 61 were from other rabbis, meaning that chaplains accounted for 24% of the questions he received from CCAR colleagues during a span of years when 23% of CCAR members served as military chaplains.[73]

What Table IV does show is that the increase in the number of inquiries was directly related to Freehof's increasing reputation among his colleagues as an authority on halakhah. In the six years from 1942–47 he received a total of seven inquiries. In the eight years from 1948–55, however, he received seventy-three inquiries. 1947 was the turning point—because it was the year when his CCAR colleagues saw his expertise at work.

In 1947 the JWB published *Responsa in War Time*,[74] a collection of CANRA responsa edited by Freehof, with a preface identifying him as the military Responsa Committee's chairman. This small volume allowed the Jewish public to see the committee's work and confirmed Freehof's status as an halakhic authority in the eyes of his Reform col-

Table IV: Questions Freehof Received Prior to His Appointment as CCAR Responsa Committee Chairman (excluding those sent to him for CANRA/DRA Responsa Committee consideration)

FROM	active duty chaplains	former chaplains	other CCAR members	other individuals
1942	1			
1943	1			
1944*	1			
1945			2	
1946		1		
1947†			1	
1948		3	3	
1949		2	3	1
1950		2	4	
1951		1	1	
1952		1	5	1
1953		1	12	3
1954			7	1
1955		5	15	2
TOTALS	3	16	53	8

*   Publication of *Reform Jewish Practice and its Rabbinic Background*

†   Publication of *Responsa in War Time*; Freehof presents Report of CCAR Committee on Intermarriage

leagues. More importantly, however, 1947 was the year the CCAR adopted the recommendations of a special committee on mixed marriage and intermarriage chaired by Freehof.[75] In accordance with the sixth rubric of his 1941 taxonomy of Reform practice, the committee report provided definitive guidelines for rabbis to follow, cited the traditional sources upon which these guidelines were based, and explained how and why Reform practice diverged from traditional halakhah. (See Chapter 4.) Thus, the entire CCAR membership had the opportunity to see Freehof's halakhic expertise and the way in which he was able to use that expertise to derive conclusions for Reform Judaism.

Conclusion

The apparent increased interest in responsa among Reform rabbis beginning in the late 1940s was actually the continuation of a process interrupted by the war and brought to fruition by the unique prominence and achievements of Solomon B. Freehof himself. The war interrupted an intense discussion within the CCAR on guidance for Reform practice and the relationship between Reform and halakhah, in which he played an important role. Indeed, during the war he managed to furnish the movement with a *de facto* code even while proclaiming his opposition to any such thing. At the end of the war, when the discussion resumed, he had the central role. He was well-liked and respected by his colleagues. Finally, all his colleagues knew about his growing halakhic expertise, while the 1947 report showed its use in a Reform context. When Israel Bettan stepped down as chair of the CCAR Responsa Committee in 1955, Freehof was his natural successor. Over the next thirty-three years his scholarship and creativity would bring the Responsa Committee to a level of unprecedented prominence within the Reform movement, as he answered hundreds of queries in accordance with his own methodology, which he named "Reform responsa."

3

FREEHOF ON REFORM OBSERVANCE, HALAKHAH, AND RESPONSA

Solomon Freehof loved the halakhah with a deep and abiding passion. To study it was his deepest joy. His life's crowning achievement was his responsa, in which he integrated his love for the halakhah with Reform Judaism. His conviction that Reform Judaism needed guidance from the halakhah, which he absorbed from Jacob Lauterbach, was an unchanging and essential element of his concept of Reform, and underlay his entire responsa enterprise. Yet despite his love for the rabbinic legal tradition, he had no desire whatsoever to move Reform Jewish life closer to a traditional pattern of observance or to create standards for Reform practice, nor did he live a more observant life than was the norm among his colleagues. (Indeed, he sometimes violated standards of behavior in ways that surprised his colleagues. Hosting a younger colleague and his wife in Pittsburgh during Passover, the Freehofs took their guests to the city's Jewish club following the morning service on the seventh day. There were rolls on the table. Freehof took one, made the blessing, and ate. Seeing his colleague's astonished reaction, Freehof smiled and said, "Oh, as far as I am concerned, as soon as the morning service is over, Passover has ended."[1]) As the Reform movement changed in the interwar period he negotiated a unique personal path, fully committed neither to the classical Reform of Kaufmann Kohler nor to the new Reform of the Columbus Platform, but rather to an idiosyncratic synthesis of the two. One cannot fully understand Freehof's stance as a decisor without understanding his distinctive approach to the complex question of the nature and role of "ceremony" in Reform Judaism.

Freehof on "Ceremony" in Reform Judaism

Immediately after the CCAR adopted the Columbus Platform, the UAHC commissioned Freehof to write a pamphlet explaining Reform Judaism.[2] A new account of Reform was needed that would incorporate the new perspective while reassuring Reform Jews unsettled by the new focus on ceremonies and Hebrew. Freehof's exposition of Reform in this pamphlet reveals essential elements of his own approach.

He set the history of Reform within the historicist framework he had learned from Kaufmann Kohler:[3] Organized religion is inherently conservative; progress in religion, therefore, comes from non-establishment figures. Thus, the movement for religious reform in Judaism was started by laypeople, who could see as a practical matter that Jewish tradition had to be modified.[4] This is Freehof's cardinal principle, that popular creativity is the real engine that propels religious life. The idea that progress and creativity in religion *always* come from the people would become the basis for his theory of the relationship between Reform Judaism and the halakhah.

When rabbis became involved in religious reform efforts in the 1830s, he continued, they "guided" the new movement. "They could not lightly sanction changes simply because such changes seemed desirable. . . . Therefore, the great aim of the rabbinate . . . was to evolve a Reform practice rooted in tradition."[5] Through their scientific scholarship they learned which elements of the tradition were permanent and which were not. Always a centrist, Freehof wrote the radical reformers out of this history: Geiger and his colleagues opposed the changes proposed by Holdheim and the other radicals because there was no justification for them in a "scientific understanding" of the tradition.[6] This is Freehof's second fundamental principle with regard to Reform and halakhah: The rabbis' function is not to lead the people to, or demand from them, new observances, but merely to regularize what they do, by studying the tradition to make sure that the popular changes do not stray too far from its essential content.

He allowed that the earlier Reformers were overly rational and had too negative a view of ceremonies; but, he insisted, they never claimed that their decisions were set in stone. Kohler himself, asserted Freehof, led Reform away from that earlier rational trend in 1907, when he emphasized the indispensability of ceremonial practices in religious life and called on the rabbis to develop beautiful new practices that would "appeal to our emotional nature" and "impress us with the holiness of life much more than abstract truth can."[7] As a result of this changed mood, Freehof concluded, Reform was now trying to create new ceremonies "on the basis of old practices." This change was not a betrayal of Reform, because a core principle of Reform is that "[e]ach generation has the right to change the outward observances of Judaism whenever such change is necessary to preserve its inner spirit." The crucial issue for a Reform Jew is not whether or not one observes this or that practice, but whether or not one believes that practices are *law*. "The man who believes that the ceremonies are helpful and useful, and if no longer helpful may be changed, is a Reform Jew even if he observes them all. The man who believes that the ceremonials of Judaism are *law*, a mandate which may not be changed, is in principle an Orthodox Jew even if he neglects them all."[8] (We saw that he said the same thing to his colleagues in 1941.) This is his third fundamental principle: Ceremonies are only a means to an end, not an end in themselves.

In crediting Kohler with steering the movement to its new openness to ceremonies, Freehof glossed over an inconvenient truth. For Kohler a ceremony was the means to an end, intended to stir the emotions of the one performing it and thereby move him or her toward a cognitive understanding of his or her duty to act as a moral being in the world. Theoretically, every ceremony had to be "scientifically" evaluated according to strict criteria before it could be deemed appropriate for current Jewish use. During his tenure as HUC President he rejected the students' desire to have a say in how services were conducted, reminding them that "ritual is not a matter of committee legislation, but the result of a process of historic growth along definite lines. The arranging of a ritual must therefore always be left in competent and duly authorized hands."[9] But between the wars, as we saw, rabbis and congregants increasingly expressed a desire for ritual because of its "mystic and emotional appeal,"[10] not because it was an edifying reminder of some ethical truth. While the rabbis who reshaped Reform Judaism between the wars continued to assert that the purpose of ceremonies was to make real the great prophetic ideals of Judaism, they didn't feel compelled to demonstrate rationally which observances were "meaningful," and why. Hence the

Commission on Ceremonies was given wide latitude to "experiment" with ceremonies. In restoring old rituals or creating new ones there was really only one standard: Did it "work," i.e., did people find it "meaningful?"—which is to say, would Reform Jews choose to practice it? For example, when the CCAR debated including Kol Nidre in the revised *Hymnal*, one rabbi said:

> I thoroughly disagree with the theology expressed in the Kol Nidre as every one of us does. However, in many of our congregations Kol Nidre is sung on Yom Kippur eve. Kol Nidre has a certain emotional force that no other song can convey to our people. Even in Orthodox synagogues they do not translate it and do not subscribe to its meaning, but use it out of pure sentiment.[11]

Another concurred; his congregation had introduced the Kol Nidre melody with new words, and he found that "the congregation gets something out of the singing of that Kol Nidre that it does not get out of the singing of 'O Day of God.'" But this was precisely what Kohler had explicitly condemned in 1907: "Romanticism which only loves ancient practices because they are picturesque representations of a dead past is not religion," he admonished his colleagues.[12]

Freehof eliminated this contradiction with brilliant sleight-of-hand: He reconciled Kohler's views with those of the new era by insisting that the essential element of Reform was only to agree that ceremony was merely a means to an end. What constituted appropriate ceremony, and what was an appropriate end—matters that were of supreme concern to Kohler—he declared secondary, mere functions of the zeitgeist. Kohler had his standards, determined by the rationalist thought of his era; contemporary Reformers had their standards, determined by the "psychological" zeitgeist of their era. Future generations, in turn, would adopt still other criteria. As late as 1978 he was still saying this:

> But we can adopt whatever sends us—provided we know that we are adopting it. And if we know that we are adopting it, and if it ceases to have meaning we can again drop it, then we are Reform Jews. . . . My sole criterion of what makes us Re-

form Jews is not how many ceremonies we observe or we don't, but our judgment of our ceremonies. . . .[13]

By affirming that Reform Jews could perform any ritual, provided they knew that it was merely custom, Freehof staked out a position as a centrist within the movement. On the one hand, he supported the new Reform of the Columbus Platform against those who insisted that only classical Reform was authentic Reform. On the other hand, he resisted the small but growing number of colleagues who were attracted to thinkers like Mordecai Kaplan,[14] Martin Buber,[15] Franz Rosenzweig,[16] and Rudolf Otto,[17] all of whom challenged in one way or another the basic Reform idea that Judaism consisted of an essential core of ethical monotheism plus ritual practices that were in some way "inspirational," to use a term from the Columbus Platform. Freehof never gave any evidence, in speech or writing, of having been influenced by any twentieth-century religious thought, Jewish or non-Jewish.

In sum, Freehof was generally supportive of the reappropriation of ceremonies in the spirit of the Columbus Platform, and found a way to reconcile his support for this reappropriation with what he had learned from Kohler and Lauterbach. Nevertheless, the sense one takes away from his writing is that he had found his personal comfort zone as a Reform Jew during the Kohler years at HUC and never felt any need to change.

Jacob Lauterbach's Influence on Freehof

While Kaufmann Kohler did not denigrate the rabbinic tradition to the extent that many reformers did, neither was he particularly interested in it other than as material from an earlier stage of Israel's existence, to be examined historically. As President of HUC he reduced the number of hours of Talmud in the curriculum from what it had been under Wise.[18] It was Jacob Lauterbach who shaped Freehof's thought on the importance of the rabbinic legal tradition and its role in Reform.

Jacob Zallel Lauterbach (1873–1942) served as Professor of Talmud at HUC from 1912 until his death. A native of Galicia, he was ordained at Esriel Hildesheimer's Rabbiner-Seminar für das Orthodoxe Judentum in Berlin and held a Ph.D. from the University of Göttingen. He had come to New York in 1903 as a staff member of the *Jewish Encyclope-dia*, in which capacity he authored numerous articles. After serving as rabbi of two traditional congregations he then became rabbi of a Reform congregation, a move reflective of his own evolution. From there Kohler brought him to HUC. It was from Lauterbach that Freehof learned to value the halakhic literature as a source of ethical guidance, as he noted on more than one occasion.[19]

At the 1913 CCAR convention Lauterbach delivered his seminal paper on "The Ethics of the Halakah." In classic Wissenschaft fashion, he argued that the rabbis believed the ritual law to be of divine origin only because they lived too early in human history to know better. Despite this limitation, he argued, they created a superbly ethical system. His central insight was that the halakhah was the rabbis' way of apply-ing prophetic ethics to daily life. In Lauterbach's reading of the tradition, the Pharisees became proto-Reform Jews. He argued that for them "all the laws of the Torah were merely the means to an end, [which was] the prophetic ideal of a Messianic era, when peace and brotherly love will prevail among all people." He cited Talmudic passages to prove that the rabbis distinguished between ritual and ethical laws and regarded the ritual laws as arbitrary, lacking inherent significance and serving only as a means to ethical perfection. For that reason they believed that all rit-ual laws would lose their force in the messianic era. Furthermore, since the rabbis believed that ritual law was less important than ethical pre-cepts, they believed that they were free to modify or reject ritual in order to preserve the "spirit" of the law. Lauterbach asserted boldly that "[i]t rests with the teachers of each generation, according to the Talmud, to determine whether the cause of Judaism will be furthered by the aboli-tion of certain ritual or ceremonial laws."[20] Nevertheless, he insisted, modern Jews, who know scientifically that the ritual law is not of di-vine origin, can still derive ethical guidance from the rabbis' halakhic pronouncements without having to accept their actual practices. There-fore, he concluded, Reform rabbis should not disparage the halakhah, but should study it for its ethical insights and guidance.

Despite their closeness, even Lauterbach found Freehof's opposition to any sort of Reform code problematic. Freehof sent him a draft of his 1941 CCAR paper, "A Code of Ceremonial and Ritual Practice"; he re-ceived back a friendly but scathingly critical letter rejecting every one of his arguments. Lauterbach faulted his friend for being content to "let things drift" when what was needed was guidance: "After all, I believe that the majority of our rabbis do want to abide by Jewish practices and customs, and if they violate them, it is in most cases due to ignorance and confusion, for they do not know how far Reform should go and where it should stop." He pooh-poohed Freehof's concern that a code issued by the CCAR would be regarded as law, countering that the Conference could easily state clearly and explicitly "that it is not a Code of Laws but merely a listing of customs, practices and ceremonies to which we have no objections, which we even recommend and, for the time being, approve." He saw no need for Freehof's caution that any sort of guide could only be written by an individual and not produced with the imprimatur of the Conference: Since not even the *Union Prayerbook* was accepted by all Reform Jews, why worry that this guide would be regarded as binding? Furthermore, Lauterbach pointed out, even in the Shulḥan Arukh Isserles had noted that some customs were observed in some places and not others; why couldn't the CCAR do the same? He could not understand why Freehof was content to let the Commission on Ceremonies invent all sorts of new ceremonies and rituals when, with a little information and guidance, there were existing ones that could be reappropriated, with or without modification. Nor did he accept Freehof's argument that a code had to be all or nothing; he countered with a list of codes that covered only certain parts of the halakhah. Finally, he observed that a guide could help reduce the division between the Reform and Conservative-Orthodox camps by "giving information and direction about the prevalent Jewish practices and ceremonies which do not outrage our sense of justice nor violate our aesthetic taste and which therefore can *and should* be observed by us in common with כלל ישראל the Orthodox and Conservatives, thus avoiding unnecessary division שלא ירבו מחלוקות בישראל"[21]

Freehof was not persuaded at all, replying, "You are thinking of the average young rabbi and the help and guidance which such a compendium would give him and I am thinking of the Conference as an official body and of the inevitably 'compulsive effect' which such a compendium would actually have. . . ."[22] Ironically, this was exactly the same argument Samuel Schulman had used in 1906 to torpedo Kohler's attempt to add "Halakot" to the Minister's Handbook.

Freehof's Concept of Minhag

Freehof was by nature a conciliator, preferring consensus and compromise to open controversy; but when he felt that principle was at stake, he was unmovable. His genius, as he demonstrated in *What Is Reform Judaism?*, lay in being able to combine compromises and principles into a seamless whole. *Reform Jewish Practice and its Rabbinic Background* was simultaneously a compromise, in that it provided guidance in Reform practice for those who wanted it while not straying from the principle that ceremonies were not properly matters of law; but it was also a statement of principle, in that it rejected the desire of some members of the CCAR to set actual standards of Reform observance.

The Introduction to *RJP* furnished the theoretical basis for his exposition of Reform practice. In this short but crucial essay Freehof propounded an original theory concerning the relationship between Reform Judaism and traditional halakhah. His goal in *RJP* was to demonstrate how specific Reform practices were rooted in traditional practices; in the Introduction it was to demonstrate that the very process by which Reform developed its distinctive practice was identical to the process by which all Jewish practice had always developed. If Freehof's identification of this process was correct, then both the old radical reformers who denied the importance of ceremonies as well as the new radicals who thought they could "declare that certain rituals and ceremonials are to be used,"[23] were wrong in their understanding of Reform. The Introduction, therefore, was a rebuttal not only to critics of Reform Judaism who saw it as not authentically Jewish, but also to colleagues within the movement, on both right and left, who disagreed with him concerning the nature of ritual practice in Reform.

Freehof's central thesis was that throughout Jewish history, flexibility in the law came not from the rabbis but from the "creative power" of the people, which he identified as minhag, "the raw material which the law took up and shifted, rearranged, justified, and embodied as the legal practice. The law itself did not create. The people created and the law organized."[24] In times of catastrophe it was the people who made the transition from one form of Jewish practice to another, not the leadership. This was partly because no legal system changes quickly, but mostly because Jewish law is particularly inflexible: Since the end of the Sanhedrin there has been no way to legislate new laws, so Jewish law has been limited to reinterpreting the old. This was true in the past and it has been true in modern times as well, since Emancipation destroyed the autonomous community for which Jewish law was developed and intended. In the modern age as in the past, in the absence of rabbinic adjustments to the law, popular creativity is stepping into the breach, creating new *minhagim*. Reform Judaism is the result of this process in the current era. In Reform Judaism "[t]he rabbis have expressed certain principles, certain theological ideals, but the people themselves by their rejections and their acceptances, by their neglects and their observances have largely determined their own religious practices. . . . It has arrived for the present at least at a definite form."[25] Those areas of Reform practice that have evolved into a definite form can be described, but nothing can be written about areas of Jewish law in which Reform practice has not yet evolved definite forms, such as dietary laws or Sabbath observance.

> What is Reform Jewish practice at present? What is observed? What is neglected? What new practices have developed? The purpose of this book is to describe this practice as a matter of interest to all who are concerned with the present-day problems of Jewish religious life.
>
> Only those traditional laws and customs are given which are connected with actual prevalent Reform practice. Thus, those branches of traditional law which have left very little mark upon present-day life of the Reform Jew are not dealt with. . . .
>
> It is not the purpose of this book to be, even in the humblest way, a modern Shulhan Aruk. It does not aim to lay down the norm of practice, except in two or three disputed situations where some preference must be made. Its chief purpose is to describe present-day Reform Jewish practices and the traditional rabbinic laws from which they are derived.[26]

To prove that minhag had always been the driving force behind Jewish religious life, Freehof relied on six examples drawn from the halakhic literature:[27]

(1) B. Berakhot 45a: Abaye decides which of two contradictory Tannaitic teachings is authoritative by saying, "Go and see what the people do." (*puk ḥaze may ama devar*)

(2) B. Pesaḥim 66a: Hillel resolves the dilemma of carrying the slaughtering knives for the Pesaḥ lamb to the Temple on the Sabbath by saying, "But leave it to the children of Israel [to know what to do], for if they are not prophets, they are the children of prophets (*Ela hanaḥ lahen leYisrael, im en nevi'im hen bene nevi'im hen*)."

(3) Y. Yevamot 12:1 (12c): The residents of a town insist that their local custom for performing *ḥalitsah* would be correct even if Elijah were to forbid it, because "custom overrides the law (*minhag mevatel halakhah*)."

(4) Y. Bava Metsia 7:1 (11b): Workers are supposed to be treated according to certain standards, but if a locality has slightly different conditions it is acceptable, because "custom overrides the law (*minhag mevatel halakhah*)."

(5) Shulḥan Arukh OH 690:17: Concerning various customs related to reading the *megillah* (OH 690:17) Isserles states, "But one should not abrogate a single custom or mock it, for it was not established without reason (*ve'en levatel shum minhag o lil'og alav, ki lo le-ḥinam hukba*)."

(6) Shulḥan Arukh YD 376:4: Isserles, describing different behaviors of mourners at the cemetery, writes, "and the custom of our ancestors is Torah (*minhag avotenu Torah*)."

Regarding (5) and (6), Freehof wrote that Isserles' hundreds of appeals to the durability of custom were evidence that "the rabbinical authorities appreciated the fact that the creative material in Jewish law which the official law could only analyze, sift, and organize, was the true basis of the continued vitality of Judaism." The great emphasis on custom, he asserted, proves that practice was not a "mood" imposed by the rabbinate, "but . . . a mass reaction, a mass creativity which produced practice and observance whenever Judaism needed to adjust itself to new conditions."[28]

Minhag is certainly a recognized rubric in halakhah, but Freehof's use of these examples entails serious methodological problems. First, (1) is a dubious case of popular creativity: The people merely follow the ruling of one rabbi or another. (4) demonstrates only that within certain parameters the law allowed local customs to prevail. Furthermore, this is a case of *mammon* (monetary matters), a realm of law in which historically a great deal of latitude was allowed in order to give maximum flexibility to meet changing commercial conditions.[29] (2), (3), (5), and (6) are, indeed, good examples of popular creativity, but all fall within the area of ritual and liturgical practice, also an area of halakhah in which enormous latitude was historically given to local practice.[30] But Freehof was not citing these examples merely to justify Reform liturgical and ritual changes, such as prayer and sermons in the vernacular. He was using them also to justify reforms such as the abolition of the *get*, the elimination of all considerations of *kohen* status, cremation, and conversion without *milah* and *tevilah*. Those are all matters of *issur*, the realm of halakhah where custom hardly ever overrides the law.

There is a logical reason why the power of custom to override law would be limited in the realm of *issur*. In the words of R. Simeon b. Solomon Duran: "Obviously, if we may repeal a prohibition on the basis of custom, then all prohibitions may be repealed one by one; and the Torah, God forbid, will be abrogated."[31] In other words, from the perspective of the halakhah, no matter how normative it may become in any Jewish community to eat lobster or to allow a woman to remarry without a *get*, such "customs" can never override the laws which say that the lobster is *treyf* and the woman and her new husband are actually adulterers.

Menahem Elon explains that the Hillel story (2) is, indeed, an example of "the creative force of custom," but notes that popular custom is a valid arbiter of law in this and similar instances only because "there is a presumption that the people . . . base their conduct on the halakhah [and] intend their practices to be true to its spirit."[32] For Freehof and all other reformers, it was axiomatic that they acted out of a desire to be true to the spirit of Judaism, but not that they based their conduct on the halakhah. How, then, could Freehof use this as a proof text to justify violating Torah prohibitions? As a halakhist he knew better.

The answer is that he read the halakhah not as a halakhist, but as a Reform theorist. From his academic interest in the development of the liturgy he was certainly familiar with many instances where local custom prevailed. Doubtless he was also familiar with numerous instances where codifiers and decisors wrestled with the tension between halakhah and local custom. He may have thought he was doing the same. Nevertheless, the assumptions he brought to his work made it quite different. He viewed the halakhah as an historical phenomenon, created by human beings, whose life span was limited to the period when civil governments accorded a separate legal status to the Jewish community. Since Emancipation it had lost any binding force. Minhag was different. This popular creativity was the constant substratum from which Jewish religious life emerged, and as such, it both pre-dated and post-dated the halakhah in determining Jewish religious observance. During the period when halakhah governed Jewish life, that creativity was recognized and accorded a formal role in the legal system as minhag. However, minhag was now outliving the halakhah, since the halakhah as a functioning system was inexorably disappearing in the post-Emancipation world. Reform Judaism was the result of the leading edge of that historical process, but the proof of the demise of the halakhah was evident in the fact that even for Orthodox Jews most of the halakhah had ceased to function. "A few generations ago the law governed life. Now the study of the law is intellectual exercise and pious self-absorption."[33] Popular creativity as the driving force in religious life was an absolute; from this perspective, Freehof was under no obligation to pay attention to restrictions placed on it within a system that had lost all its binding force. His six examples were thus, for him, paradigmatic examples of the role of custom in any and all aspects of Jewish religious life.

Freehof's Introduction to *RJP* barely touched upon a difficult issue that arose perennially in CCAR discussions: What was to be done in situations where the rabbis disapproved of what the people were doing or not doing? Most of Kohler's and Lauterbach's responsa, for example, were not responsa in the traditional sense but scholarly essays intended to demonstrate why the people should stop adhering to certain practices (bar mitzvah, saying Kaddish for only eleven months, breaking a glass at weddings, covering the head, etc.). Freehof did not directly address the question whether his theory of the interplay between popular minhag and rabbinic formalization gave the rabbis the right to tell the people that they should cease to follow certain customs. He did acknowledge, presumably out of the same concern that R. Simeon Duran had expressed, that not every popular custom could be allowed to abrogate any law. It had to be the custom of "respected people."[34] Who were the "respected people" and exactly what that meant, he did not explain. (However, he relied on this principle implicitly in many of his responsa, as will be seen.)

Freehof's theory of popular creativity implies that if the people have ceased to practice something, it means that a particular ceremony or ritual has outlived its useful life. But there was a difference between, say, abandoning adherence to the thirty-nine categories of prohibited activity on the Sabbath and ignoring the Sabbath, or between abandoning the legal fiction of selling *hamets* before Passover and not holding a Seder. Reform was about eliminating obsolete practices, not ignoring the essential elements of a Jewish religious life. Reform rabbis from the 1890s on had actively tried to bring their people back to the observance of the Sabbath and holy days as well as to regular prayer. Even in Reform Judaism there was a presupposed baseline of observance—the Sabbath, the festivals, daily prayer—that implied that if Reform Jews were not observing these, then their religious lives were deficient. When confronted with people's failure to lead a Jewish religious life, then, how did Freehof distinguish between lack of observance that proved that certain ceremonies were outmoded, and lack of observance that constituted a failure to lead a Jewish religious life? If Jews were not lighting Sabbath candles, did that mean that the custom had outlived its usefulness, or that they should be encouraged—or expected—to light them?

To this question he had no clear answer. His struggles with it emerge in his responsa, particularly in the responsa on Sabbath observance (see Chapter 6). In the Introduction to *RJP*, however, he explained that the book dealt only with actual Reform practice and thus excluded the dietary laws and the Sabbath, adding, "To put it bluntly, there is, unfortunately, as little observance of the dietary laws among Reform Jews as there is among millions of other modern Jews and also as little observance of the traditional laws of Sabbath rest."[35] By 1946, however, he was concerned about this issue and attempted to address it.

Reform Jewish Practice Reconsidered

During the war years the CCAR had more pressing concerns than a code of Reform practice. It appears, however, that the question remained a live one despite the publication of *RJP*, for at the very first postwar convention Freehof delivered a paper titled "Reform Judaism and the Halacha."[36] This paper recapitulated his 1941 paper and added to it his fully developed concept of minhag, but it also included some significant additions.

First, he addressed directly the central vulnerable spot of Reform Judaism—the accusation that it was not "authentic" Judaism. Orthodoxy, he said, by virtue of its antiquity and its claim to an unbroken chain of authority reaching back to Sinai, possesses a sense of authenticity that Reform lacks by virtue of its birth as a revolutionary break with tradition. The usual Reform response to attacks of this sort was to insist that ethical monotheism was the real essence of Judaism, that the law was merely the shell protecting that kernel, and that the error of traditional Judaism had been to take the law too seriously. Freehof himself did not disagree with this view, but he refused to let himself or his colleagues off so easily. "Reform Judaism cannot long refrain from adjusting itself to the fact that the Orthodox wing of Judaism claims a unique authenticity, a divinely ordained legality which Reform Judaism is said to lack. Judaism is a religion which was formed by law and has lived by law. It is clear that Reform Judaism must come to an understanding with the law or at least must define clearly its own relationship to it."[37] He personally admired traditional Judaism and "the magnificent consistency of Jewish law and the deep learning which sustains it." It had been "an immense success," propounding "a theory of Jewish law whereby the life of the individual in almost all its phases was conscious of the will of God," and enabling the Jews to survive and be creative for hundreds of years under terrible conditions.[38]

This was far more than just rhetoric from one who retained a lifelong respect for his parents' Orthodox way of life and nostalgia for the way he had been raised.[39] By the time he delivered this paper, he had been writing military responsa for four years, working closely with Orthodox and Conservative scholars. Participation in the process of halakhic decision making had clearly led him to ponder the implications for his own movement of what he was doing, and this had acquired urgency for him. In his call to his colleagues to confront the legal character of their tradition if they wanted to be "authentic," one can hear his own need for clarity on the issue.

The growing desire for more observance in Reform made it essential to engage the legal tradition, he continued. "Must we not revive the concept of *Mitzva*, of *Torah*, and thus attain orderliness and consistency and authority in our Reform Jewish life? . . . We cannot discuss Halacha, or Torah, or Mitzva, without evaluating the environment in which these concepts flourished." Proponents of a code of Reform practice must have been delighted to hear this, but they were quickly disappointed. His CANRA Responsa Committee experience had not changed his views one whit on the ultimate viability of the halakhah. It was still obvious to him that in the absence of either a revived Sanhedrin or the rise of courageous Orthodox authorities, the law was "unchangeable and unusable." Traditional Judaism had once been creative, but had then "petrified into changeless, despairing Orthodoxy." The creativity that it had once possessed belonged now to Reform, and Reform had to be careful not to destroy that creative power by trying to codify itself "prematurely."[40]

Still, he took a giant step toward the would-be codifiers. "What *we* seek," he continued, "is a legal philosophy which shall be in harmony with our actual practice, and simultaneously, we aim to develop a religious practice consistent with an acceptable theory." In *RJP* Freehof had envisioned only a legal philosophy in harmony with actual Reform practice. Now he acknowledged that Reform also needed to cultivate religious practice in the context of a new theory of Reform practice. He recognized that his colleagues wanted something more than the old Reform insistence that "[t]he only God-given law is the moral law. All the rest is dubious commentary."[41]

> When our Columbus Platform declared that the concept of Torah was essential for us and in the general description of Torah included ritual and ceremonial observances as well as ethics, the Platform meant to express our sense of the increased validity of the ritual practices within Judaism. *They are not quite law but they do have a certain authority.* . . . To declare that practice has some religious validity and to seek to establish a suitable foundation and structure for it is our concept of the present duty of Reform. [emphasis added][42]

In 1941 one of his objections to a Reform code had been the impossibility of claiming for it either divine or human authority, but five years later he was not so dismissive. He struggled to articulate a basis for that "increased validity," arriving at the conclusion that the rabbinic literature was not divine, but it had importance as "inspiration." "They [i.e., rabbinic texts] are divine only to the extent that somewhere in the mazes of these vast material [*sic*] we find God speaking to the hearts and minds of Israel; and we and our conscience must make the decision of what, in all these materials, we consider binding or meaningful for us." As always, he appealed to multiple streams within the movement: The term "binding" was for those who wanted a code; "meaningful" was for those who did not.

Revealed or not, he continued, for "practical purposes" one could say that "those observances which, inspired by the past, are accepted by Israel in the present or become acceptable to Israel, can serve us as a description of the content of Torah."[43] In other words, new or revised ceremonies adopted by Reform Jews now or in the future will constitute a Reform version of Torah. Displaying once again his ability to assert commonality in disparate ideas, he thus identified the desired end of the would-be Reform codifiers with his own notion of minhag. Reform's approach to practice is popular creativity in action; Reform Jews are in the process of developing a system of practice that they will regard as "binding or meaningful"; when they attain it, it will be the functional equivalent of the old system of halakhah, insofar as any system can be authoritative now.

However, Freehof would not concede an inch to the desire for a Reform code in the present. A code could only be the end result of a lengthy process. "We have a great deal of thinking, debating and selection to do before we can presume to say what is God's command and what is mere experiment. We must take a great deal of time to work out general categories as to which observances . . . are of religious moment." Ethics was, of course, first and foremost; then "the duty of public and private worship must be rebuilt into an intensely felt mitzvah," and then "the duty to study Jewish law and literature must certainly be rebuilt into a mitzvah."[44] It would be a huge and delicate task. As in the past, so in the present the people have made decisions that were wrong. The rabbis have to resist them and persuade them to do otherwise.

It is far from sufficient for us to declare that certain rituals and ceremonials are to be used. We must judge the mood of our people. We must change the mood of the people. Otherwise our listing of Mitzvoth will seem meaningless and even ludicrous to them. . . .

When we will have arrived at a general agreement as to what categories of action we can in conscience regulate, then we must develop systematically the growth and the encouragement of specific minhagim. This will involve a wider interest on the part of many of us in the whole mass of Halachic literature which, besides being an evidence of the tremendous mental alertness of Jewish scholarship, is also a repository of Jewish ceremonial creativity.[45]

In other words, Reform could not have a code *now*, but it was theoretically possible that it could have a code in the future. All that was necessary was for the rabbis to decide which elements of Jewish life could legitimately be governed by a code and then educate the people as to why those elements were important. Then, after the people internalized this message, the power of popular creativity would start to generate *minhagim* in these areas, which the rabbis could then formalize as Reform practice.

In the meantime, Freehof concluded, there were some things the rabbis could do already—the same things he had said could be done five years earlier. They must avoid dealing with the dietary laws, lest they raise them to the status of law; but they could continue to experiment with ritual ceremonies and could include newly accepted ones into the prayerbook each time it was revised. They could produce a home prayerbook with annotated ceremonies such as Sabbath and Ḥanukkah lights. They could collect the responsa and make them available. Finally, they could fix and codify the marriage laws. However, if this process was to succeed, it was essential that there not be a premature codification of Reform practice.

In the end, then, Freehof's practical recommendations were exactly the same as the ones he had previously offered. The process he outlined as the necessary precursor to such a code was really only a more elaborate description of what the rabbis were doing anyway—trying to explain to their people why it mattered that they live a Jewish religious life, and what that entailed. However, there were two significant differences between the papers. First, in the later paper he explicitly acknowledged the increased importance attached to ritual observance in contemporary Reform, and second, he accepted the idea that a code of Reform practice was not by definition an impossibility, though within his paradigm of evolving minhag, it was a very long way away and, in any case, was only to be undertaken by an individual and should never be an official act of the Conference.[46] This is the position Freehof held to for the rest of his life, reiterating it numerous times in individual responsa, the introductions to his published volumes, and elsewhere.[47]

The historian of Reform Judaism, Michael A. Meyer, credited Freehof with revolutionizing Reform by reversing its earlier emphasis on belief rather than practice. He wrote, "With Freehof's work, practice ceased to be the clothing for ideas—as it was still in Kohler's theology—and entered the substance of Reform Judaism."[48] When considering the entire history of Reform Judaism very broadly, Freehof's work is certainly a turning point, but he was not responsible for the rejection of the earlier Reformers' concept of practice; this had already happened and was enshrined in the Columbus Platform in 1937. Freehof both satisfied and fueled the growing interest in practice through his extensive writing about it during the 1940s: two CCAR papers, *RJP*, the 1947 Report on Intermarriage, and his earliest responsa. Although few people outside the CCAR have probably read his paper on "Reform Judaism and the Halacha," it was, indeed, a revolutionary statement—the first time a leader of the movement had said that ceremony could have more significance in Reform than "mere custom." Ironically, however, when Freehof said this he was not expressing his own views, but what he perceived as a consensus among his colleagues. Speaking as an individual, he always insisted that ceremony was nothing more than a handmaiden to the ethical laws. As he told his congregants in 1949:

> . . . [I]t is a principle of our Reform Jewish life that God does not command us [to perform ceremonies] . . . It may be desirable, but we will never believe that it is a religious mandate. We believe that the essential of the worship of God is

the ethical mandate and that the ceremonial is incidental, if anything. . . .

. . . These ceremonials are . . . drama. . . . We should have more of this splendor of Judaism, not in the Orthodox sense that it is our duty to observe rituals, but in the Reform sense that they are beautiful, that they aid in creating a spiritual mood in the home.[49]

Thirty years later he was still saying the same thing: "In other words, what's essential in Judaism are its great doctrines and its tremendous intellectual tradition. . . . Oh, beliefs, attitudes, these are sacred. It's only ceremonies that are to me secondary. . . . I don't consider ceremonies more than an emotional auxiliary to the ideals of the religion. . . ."[50] To the extent that he revolutionized the notion of practice in Reform Judaism, he was an accidental revolutionary.

Defining the Responsa Committee's Role

Agitation continued within the CCAR into the 1950s over the extent to which the Conference should regularize, guide, or direct Reform practice. The 1954 convention included a Workshop on Reform Jewish Practice at which several papers were presented on the desirability of some sort of code; those in attendance adopted resolutions calling for a discussion of "the Shabbos as it relates to Reform Jews" at the next convention, and for the CCAR to create the institutional infrastructure for creating a guide to "Reform Jewish Living."[51]

Meanwhile, the debate expanded to another front when the CCAR began publishing a quarterly journal in 1953. The first seven issues of the *CCAR Journal* included eight responsa by Israel Bettan, only one of which had been reported to the CCAR prior to publication.[52] The *Journal* published letters objecting to Bettan's rejection of bat mitzvah and to his insistence that *brit milah* take place on the eighth day regardless of medical and insurance obstacles, but these were just the tip of the iceberg of evident disagreement over Bettan's responsa. Indeed, Responsa Committee member William G. Braude officially recorded his dissent from Bettan's responsum on "Propriety of Using Discarded Practices in

Reform Services" when it was presented in 1955. That year the CCAR Executive Board voted to prohibit prior publication of responsa in the *Journal*, and at the convention the rabbis voted to establish a committee to re-examine the role of the Responsa Committee, to report back the following year.[53] Publishing responsa in the new periodical had raised anew the old question of the committee's authority.

Freehof, who had succeeded Bettan as Responsa Committee chairman after the 1955 convention, was a member of this *ad hoc* committee. He argued forcefully against altering the Responsa Committee's function in any way. It fulfilled three purposes, he explained. Two were merely informational, requiring only expertise in the rabbinic texts: to let younger colleagues know what the law is, i.e., to look up answers in the codes for those who lack the skills to find them; and to answer new or complex questions by consulting and evaluating the rabbinic sources. Its third and most important purpose, however, was to arrive at a *"Reform* attitude on certain legal questions." This involved not only gathering and evaluating the sources, but "re-apprais[ing them] from the Reform point of view." Echoing his 1941 paper, he argued that the committee should *not* have increased authority, because historically, decisors were accepted or not on their own merits. A Responsa Committee decision should *not* be authoritative for the Conference unless it was specifically adopted as such. *Ad hoc* committee members Israel Bettan, Leonard Mervis, and Norman Diamond agreed with him, though the latter feared that too much autonomy in the Conference might "lead to chaos."

Frederic Doppelt, who had argued so vehemently for a code in 1946, did not agree. Deploring the "chaos and confusion in Reform Judaism," he called once again for a guide to observance. To that end, he wanted the Responsa Committee to become a standing committee of the Conference, meaning that the plenum could make its responsa authoritative by voting to adopt them. Eugene Borowitz suggested a middle path: Increase the size of the committee and make it truly representative of the Conference, thus virtually guaranteeing diversity of opinion, and let it present majority and minority reports on every issue, with rabbis free to follow one or the other.

The report was referred to the Executive Board, and that was the last anyone heard of this committee. Freehof's view thus prevailed, and he continued to act on it for the next two decades and beyond.

Conclusion

Freehof offered a coherent, centrist conception of Reform Judaism. He forged a synthesis of older and newer versions of Reform in which ethical monotheism remained a constant, while attitudes toward, and rationales for, ritual observance changed with the zeitgeist. Applying to Judaism an historicist perspective according to which all progress in religion comes from outside the establishment, he concluded that Reform was merely the latest manifestation of a process that, he asserted, has always operated within Jewish history: When circumstances change radically, it is always the people, not the leadership, that develop coping mechanisms to continue Jewish religious life, since it is the people who are most immersed in the changed world. He identified this popular creative force with the halakhic rubric of minhag, and saw in Reform's emergence a classic instance of minhag at work: The people acted, and the rabbis later merely recognized what they had done by finding ways to harmonize it with earlier Jewish tradition. Thus he initially opposed the very notion of a CCAR-generated code of Reform practice as contrary to the natural evolution of Judaism and contrary to the nature of Reform, which denied the divine authority of ritual observance. Subsequently he moderated his opposition, however, recognizing that in the newer era of Reform a sense had emerged that ritual observance had some significance despite having no divine mandate. He then proposed the theory that popular creativity would eventually yield a commitment to certain observances that was strong enough that, within a Reform context, they could have a quasi-legal status. That, however, would be in the far future. In the present, the rabbis were to restrict themselves to offering guidance to the people as they sought it. That was the role of the responsa, and for that reason, Reform Jews needed to study the halakhah.

In his responsa Freehof applied to real life all his theories about the relationship between Reform Judaism and the halakhic tradition, minhag, and the creation of norms for Reform practice. The years of his Responsa Committee chairmanship coincided with the years of American Judaism's most spectacular growth as well as with dynamic changes within American Jewish life. These two processes in turn generated a host of questions for which he was the arbiter of choice among Reform Jews and, for much of the rest of the Jewish world, the authority on the Reform perspective.

4

MARRIAGE AND DIVORCE

When he rejected the notion of a Reform code in 1941, Freehof named marriage, divorce, and conversion as the exceptions. Since "[t]he state has definite marriage laws . . . we too must have clear-cut laws which govern us. . . . We must decide them definitely and publish them that all may know our decisions."[1] In the chapter on Marriage and Divorce in *RJP* he began this process. The individual entries he included in this chapter were (in order): Forbidden Degrees of Marriage; Mixed Marriage and Intermarriage; Conversion; Forbidden Dates for Marriage; Double Weddings; Marriage of Mourners; Visit to Rabbi and Synagogue; Home or Temple or Hall; Procession; *Minyan* and Witnesses; *Ḥuppah*; Plain Ring or Jeweled; Ring Finger; *Ketubah*; and Civil Divorce. He intermixed serious questions of *issur* with minor questions of minhag with no distinction, since all were equally questions of "practice."

Although a researcher writing in 1946 found only a small rate of exogamy among American Jews (the highest local rate he found was 7%) and no evidence to assume it would increase,[2] nevertheless a wave of concern over mixed marriage swept the CCAR after the war, doubtless because of the very visible incidents of Jewish servicemen forming romantic attachments with non-Jewish women they met while stationed far from home.[3] A comprehensive restatement of the Reform position on mixed marriage therefore became a desideratum for the Conference, which turned to Freehof (and a committee of two, though it is doubtful that either of them had any significant input) to produce it. He presented the "Report on Mixed Marriage and Intermarriage" to the 1947 convention.[4] It addressed conversion for the purpose of marriage; civil and common-law marriage between Jews; civil and common-law marriage between Jews and gentiles; two Jews married in a Christian ceremony; a Jew and a non-Jew married in a Christian ceremony; conversion of children; status of children born to a mixed marriage; and gentile children of a Jewish parent. It was formally adopted by a vote of the CCAR and remains the North American Reform movement's most comprehensive authoritative statement on matters of personal status.

In this chapter we examine the standards Freehof articulated in *RJP* and in the 1947 Report with regard to marriage and divorce, and compare them with his later responsa.

Forbidden Marriages

With regard to "forbidden marriages," Freehof stated in *RJP*: "The Biblical list of relatives who are forbidden to marry each other as well as the rabbinic amplification of that list, is strictly adhered to, but the special laws referring to the marriage of priests are no longer held to be binding."[5] He relied on Lauterbach's notes in the 1928 *Rabbi's Manual*, which in turn relied on Moses Mielziner's 1884 summary of Jewish marriage law.[6] However, he had no binding Reform precedents for reconciling the three most troublesome differences between Jewish and civil definitions of consanguinity. First, the Torah permits marriage between uncle and niece but prohibits marriage between aunt and nephew as incestuous. Both the double standard and the modern distaste for an uncle-niece relationship were disturbing to Jews who still felt the need to defend Judaism's rationality and high ethical standards. Second, Jewish law permits marriage between first cousins. This did not appear odd in Europe, where many among the elite regularly practiced it; but in the US, cousin marriage came to have negative associations with poverty and low class behavior, with the result that most states voted to prohibit it in the latter half of the nineteenth century.[7] For Reform Jews, to whom bourgeois respectability was an integral element of their Judaism, this was deeply embarrassing. Third, Reformers had been unable to decide what to do about marriage between a widow (with or without children) and her brother-in-law. Ashkenazic halakhah had come to require *ḥalitsah* rather than levirate marriage, in effect prohibiting all marriages between widows, with or without children, and their brothers-in-law, but nineteenth-century Reformers in both Europe and the United States had declared the ritual unnecessary.[8] They and their successors were deeply divided, however, over whether such marriages were now forbidden in all cases, or permitted in all cases. Isaac Mayer Wise set off a huge controversy in 1872 when he officiated at the marriage of a widow and her brother-in-law, justifying it on the grounds that the woman was childless and this was a valid instance of *yibbum*. Reformers lined up in opposing camps with or against Wise,[9] and the issue remained unresolved. Additionally, the absence of any stricture against a widower marrying his sister-in-law created another instance in which Jewish marriage law appeared to include a double standard.

In 1907 the CCAR established a committee to produce a comprehensive guide to Jewish and civil marriage law. After more than a decade it produced only Kaufmann Kohler's survey of the issue, which called for a reconsideration of all Jewish marriage law because it was pervaded by the "oriental" view of women as chattel. Kohler advocated creating complete consistency between Jewish practice and civil law by expanding consanguinity to prohibit marriage between uncle and niece and between first cousins, and ignoring the Torah prohibition on marriage between a widow and her brother-in-law.[10] The rabbis declined to vote on his recommendations, however. The committee—of which Freehof was a member—sputtered along for several more years, no doubt hampered by Kohler's declining health, but also by the rabbis' own lack of clarity on where they stood. In 1924 the whole project was scrapped.

Meanwhile, questions of prohibited marriages continued to vex the CCAR. In 1917 and 1923 the Responsa Committee unanimously denied permission for a marriage between a man and his half-aunt. In 1923 David Philipson asked the Conference for a definitive ruling on the marriage of a widow and her brother-in-law after he lost a member over this very issue, who had then found another Reform rabbi to officiate.[11] In response, Samuel S. Cohon wrote a *de facto* responsum, "Marrying a Deceased Brother's Wife," on behalf of the not-quite-moribund Committee on Marriage Laws. He concluded that the desire for consistency could not overcome the "feeling of repugnance" toward this type of marriage, and urged his colleagues not to separate themselves from *klal Yisra'el* by deviating radically from traditional marriage law.[12] In the ensuing discussion Lauterbach and Philipson supported him, but another rabbi stated that he would not abide by Jewish law and would officiate at such marriages. The elderly Samuel Schulman stated the obvious: Unanimous compliance was impossible within the CCAR. Once again the rabbis declined to vote on the question.[13]

In *RJP* Freehof approached the question of forbidden marriages by explaining the biblical prohibitions and then the rabbinic additions, referencing modern studies of the law in addition to the Talmud and codes. He briefly surveyed similarities and differences between Christian, European, and American consanguinity laws and Jewish law. Rather than address any of the difficult issues directly, however, he simply cut the Gordian knot by concluding, "In all these cases of discrepancy between Jewish law and state law the practice of Reform rabbis is to follow the stricter law." He did state explicitly that "we do not officiate" at the marriage of a widow and her brother-in-law, but duly noted Kohler's divergent view.[14] Since the focus of the 1947 report was mixed marriage, there was no need for him to address this issue.

By his own logic, however, he could not avoid it forever. In 1948 when he asked attorney Eugene Strassburger, a prominent member of his congregation, for information on American and British law regarding marriage to a brother- or sister-in-law, he explained:

> The problem which concerns me, since I know that someday I will have to write a paper on it, is the problem of *Reform* Jewish practice on the matter. To what extent should the forbidden degrees affect us when our present feeling has changed? With English law it is quite easy to settle such a question because the legislature can change a law . . . ; but with religious law it is not quite so easy to change. That is why we have a Reform movement.[15]

He never did write the paper, but his subsequent answers to this question show that he also never made up his mind. In several letters he underscored the severity of the Torah prohibition and expressed his reluctance to reject it unilaterally, even while admitting that he saw nothing morally objectionable in such a liaison.[16] He told one correspondent that such a marriage was absolutely forbidden, since the Bible considered the relationship "incestuous"; he permitted another to officiate only because the widow was not Jewish when she was married to her late husband.[17] He advised yet another to "follow your own conscience since many states do not prohibit it and since, as I said before, it is a matter of affinity rather than consanguinity."[18] In one instance he actually changed his mind in print. The editor of the quarterly *CCAR Journal* asked him to answer a number of questions of concern to many rabbis, among which was the case of an elderly widower and his childless widowed sister-in-law, who desired to marry; when an Orthodox rabbi had refused them, insisting that they perform *halitsah* instead, they came to a Reform rabbi and asked that the marriage be validated as a levirate marriage. Freehof responded that *halitsah* was essentially a form of *get* and Reform had done away with the *get*, and therefore "we would not hesitate to marry that couple any more than we would hesitate to remarry a woman to her first husband after she had been married to a second one."[19] However, when he reprinted that article in *CuRR* six years later, he added a number of references to the halakhah of *yibbum* and *halitsah* and pointed out that the marriage was less objectionable because the widow was childless, but then ended on a cautionary note entirely missing from his original response: While it was "possible" that a Reform rabbi "might officiate" for this couple, "[n]evertheless one should hesitate before officiating at a marriage to which most of the Ashkenazic authorities would be opposed."[20] He also frequently opined that he believed the majority of the CCAR would not officiate at such marriages. However, at least one correspondent reported back to him that no one—even the couple's Conservative rabbi, who could not officiate—had objected to his officiation, and expressed confidence that Freehof was a minority within the CCAR.[21]

Freehof did publish an extensive responsum permitting one type of marriage prohibited by the Torah but never addressed by the CCAR. The "Woman Returning to Her First Husband"[22] was another instance in which modern ethical sensibilities differed from biblical law. "Of course, we should always be cautious about abolishing or disregarding an old law, especially in questions of marriage. Yet, if there is some way in which we can do what, according to our conscience, is justice, we should do it whenever we can. Let us, therefore, look into the old law and see its reason and its extent."[23] His analysis pointed to three relevant facts: first, medieval commentators struggled to explain the Torah prohibition; second, the halakhah narrowed its application by not barring a man from remarrying his ex-wife if she had sexual relations with a man to whom she was *not* married;[24] and third, the halakhah clearly weighed violations of this prohibition less heavily than other *arayot*, because the children of such a marriage are not *mamzerim*.[25] He concluded that while earlier rabbis were compelled to adhere to the law despite their obvious sense that it was illogical, "[t]his is clearly a case in which we must mitigate the law. . . . Of course, such remarriages should not occur indiscriminately, since the law is there in the Shulchan Aruch. But wherever the human situation requires it, we should be frank enough and brave enough to be humane and just."[26]

Freehof's moral sense of the two cases was the same: The halakhah was unfair; the just and moral course of action was to allow the woman to marry. However, in the former, he was unwilling to contravene the Torah unilaterally when the halakhah expressed no doubt about it. In the latter, however, he found evidence that the rabbinic authorities had reservations about the Torah law, and he considered this sufficient grounds on which to reject the Torah law. These decisions are completely consistent with his view that the law was to be read for its ethical guidance.

His modern ethical sensibility did not extend, however, to acceptance of homosexuality. When the gay liberation movement emerged in the early 1970s he was nearly eighty years old. He considered homosexuality abnormal and could not countenance the Reform movement's support for it or for the fledgling gay/lesbian synagogues.[27] In a published responsum he insisted that "[i]f Scripture calls it an abomination, it means that it is more than a violation of a mere legal enactment; it reveals a deep-rooted ethical aversion. . . . Therefore homosexual acts cannot be brushed aside . . . by saying that we do not follow Biblical enactments. Homosexuality runs counter to the sancta of Jewish life."[28] Astonishingly, he actually advised a rabbi to breach a young man's confidence and inform his parents that their son was gay, since "it may be the type of homosexuality which is amenable to psychiatric treatment; and if it is an incurable type (I do not know that there is such a thing) then they must adjust their lives to it."[29]

Mixed Marriage

In *RJP* Freehof wrote, "Reform Judaism disapproves of mixed marriages (i.e., between a Jew and an unconverted Gentile), but intermarriage (i.e.,

a marriage between a Jew and a convert to Judaism) is of the same status as any other Jewish marriage."[30] This seemingly simple sentence was
carefully calibrated to reflect Freehof's own lifelong position, which he
wanted to present as the Reform position: that rabbis did not officiate at
mixed marriages, but could and would welcome and facilitate the conversion of gentile fiancé(e)s prior to marriage.

Indeed, no Reform leaders had ever advocated mixed marriage, and
only a small radical fringe had regarded it with equanimity. The 1844
Brunswick Conference did adopt a resolution acknowledging that
"[m]embers of monotheistic religions in general are not forbidden to
marry if the parents are permitted by the laws of the state to bring up
children from such wedlock in the Jewish religion," but the issue was
moot, since there was then no civil marriage.[31] In the United States, by
contrast, the lack of strong Jewish communal structures, the relative absence of antisemitism, and the general openness and mobility of American society all made interfaith romances easier, while the absence of
significant antisemitism also enabled American Reform rabbis to voice
their opposition to interfaith marriage more strenuously than could their
European counterparts.[32]

Still, a minority of American Reform rabbis did officiate at mixed
marriages. In 1909 two prominent members of the CCAR offered a resolution "that a Rabbi ought not to officiate at a marriage between a Jew
or Jewess and a person professing a religion other than Judaism, inas-
much as such mixed marriage is prohibited by the Jewish religion and
would tend to disintegrate the religion of Israel." After heated debate it
was rejected, 18-28. While only one participant admitted to performing
such marriages, many expressed reluctance to take a stance critical of
other rabbis' behavior, and all agreed that no resolution would stop anyone from officiating. In its place the CCAR voted 42-2 for a resolution
stating only that "mixed marriages are contrary to the tradition of the
Jewish religion and should therefore be discouraged by the American
Rabbinate."[33]

Freehof had always opposed officiation at mixed marriages, heartily
endorsing David Einhorn's famous characterization of it as "the nail in
the coffin of the small Jewish race."[34] In 1930 he wrote,

> My reason for refusing to officiate at intermarriages [i.e.,
> mixed marriages] is this: if two groups are involved it would
> be wrong for a Lutheran or for a Jew to officiate because in
> either case the religious principles upon which the marriage
> is based would be meaningless to one or the other of the par-
> ties. . . . That is why we have civil marriage. Hence, I don't
> so much object to Jew and Gentile marrying for it is to a large
> degree a private matter, but I object to *my* marrying them.[35]

As chairman of CANRA's Responsa Committee, he readily joined his
more traditional colleagues in prohibiting military chaplains from officiating at mixed marriages, on the grounds that the 1909 resolution did,
in fact, mean that rabbis were not to officiate.[36] (Other Reform rabbis
who opposed officiating at mixed marriages read the resolution the same
way over the decades.[37]) Significantly, in contrast to his reference to
Kohler's position on forbidden marriage, on this issue he chose not to include an alternative view in *RJP*. On the contrary; he insisted that "marriage between a Jew and an unconverted Gentile cannot be considered
Jewish marriage and a rabbi *cannot* officiate. [Emphasis added]"[38] To
convince his readers that civil marriage was a substantive alternative to
a Jewish ceremony, and that mixed couples should choose it, he cited an
Orthodox ruling that a Jewish couple married in a civil ceremony required a *get*, just as they would from a religious marriage. It appears that
when he was writing *RJP* he was unaware that this responsum was not
an Orthodox affirmation of the value of state authority, but rather part of
a stringent trend, especially in Ashkenazic halakhah, requiring a divorce
for any Jewish couple known to have been living together as a couple.[39]
By the time he wrote the 1947 Report, he knew differently. (See below).

The distinction he drew between *mixed marriage* and *intermarriage*,
which sounds quaint to contemporary ears, had its own history. Ever
since the Assembly of Notables furnished its responses to Napoleon,
modern Jews have been at pains to explain that the Jewish preference for
endogamy stems neither from hostility toward gentiles nor from a sense
of superiority, but from the importance of home and family in Judaism.
In like manner, Freehof began his discussion of mixed marriage with a
ten page apologetic clarifying and defending the Jewish attitude toward
exogamy. He took great pains to explain that Judaism opposes only *re-*

ligious exogamy; that any gentile who chooses to convert is recognized fully as a Jew with no limitations (following the precedent of the 1869 Leipzig Synod, which invalidated the traditional restrictions on marriage between female converts and *kohanim*[40]); that Judaism regards Christians and Muslims as Noahides and therefore already "half-proselytes" (as Lauterbach had written);[41] that Judaism recognizes the validity of civil marriage; and that Judaism does not consider the offspring of an interfaith marriage as illegitimate in any way. In short, he overemphasized those elements of the tradition that express open, friendly, and respectful attitudes toward gentiles, and ignored or dismissed as insignificant laws and sentiments which might appear to confirm the hateful accusations. His typical reader, however, was not the non-Jew desiring to learn about Judaism, but the Reform Jew, especially the Reform rabbi. In this section Freehof was providing ammunition for the rabbi to resist the pressure to officiate at a mixed marriage. Confronted with a young interfaith couple, the rabbi could give the non-Jewish partner every assurance that she could convert and be fully welcomed into the community. There was another possible subtext: At a time when tensions between religious and secular definitions of American Jewish communal identity were still alive, Freehof's language subtly reminded any lay readers that religion and not nationality or ethnicity was the central element of Jewish life.

In addition to arguing that there is no such thing as a Jewishly valid marriage between a Jew and a non-Jew, Freehof repeated the modern era's two most common arguments against mixed marriage. First, he asserted that Judaism, as a minority religion, must "guard against disintegration"—a phrase also found in the rejected 1909 draft resolution—or as he later stated more forcefully: "Our concern is the maintenance of the Jewish community which is small and subject to attrition all the time."[42] (He later referred to co-officiation with Christian clergy as "slow suicide."[43]) Second, he warned that partners from different religious backgrounds would not have a happy marriage. This argument would gradually disappear from his responsa correspondence, no doubt because as time went on it became increasingly obvious to everyone that there were, indeed, many happy marriages between people of different religious backgrounds, although divorce rates have remained higher in religiously mixed marriages.[44]

Freehof included much of the language about mixed marriage from *RJP* in the 1947 Report. He inserted his own point of view by stating that Reform does not bar civil marriages, but "it should be clear that the fact that [a] couple is already married by civil law does not obviate the necessity of conversion of the Gentile party before the Jewish marriage services can take place."[45] Not wanting to reopen a controversy, however, he also included a recommendation that the CCAR not strengthen the 1909 resolution, asserting that rabbinic officiation at mixed marriages was only a rare response to unusual circumstances, and that to address it in a resolution would imply that it was more common than it actually was.[46] Many of his colleagues did want a stronger statement, and there was a heated debate; but in the end the motion failed narrowly, 74–76, after which the rabbis unanimously reaffirmed the existing resolution.[47] Years later Freehof attributed that failure to the generational divide: "[T]he younger people wanted us to prohibit any member from officiating at a mixed marriage, [but] the older men insisted that there are times when it is far preferable to do so. Therefore, because of the influence of the older men, the former regulation of the Conference was reiterated . . . "[48]

During the postwar decades, the pressure on Reform rabbis to officiate at mixed marriages grew exponentially, as more and more Jews formed romantic attachments outside the community.[49] Some colleagues wrote to Freehof asking whether they could officiate, while others wrote to ask how far they could go in incorporating Jewish liturgical elements into a ceremony they had already decided to perform. He always urged the former to stand firm and resist the pressure. Certain that mixed marriage was destructive to the Jewish community, he believed that rabbinic officiation normalized it and, conversely, that rabbis could help prevent young Jews from marrying out by their refusal to officiate. "I have had to endure the resentment of one family every now and then; but I have helped every other family in the community . . . By refusing to marry such a couple, you are helping every other family in your congregation."[50]

Nevertheless, he sympathized with, and even consoled, those who felt that they had no choice but to give in, delicately offering them a way to maintain their self-respect. For example, prominent congregants wanted their rabbi to participate in their son's wedding; the bride's father was a national celebrity and the son had agreed to be married by a Catholic priest in a church. The rabbi wanted to know what would be the justifiable minimum of participation on his part. Freehof replied that there was no such thing, that on the contrary, the rabbi needed to be even firmer and tell the parents that because this was a celebrity wedding, what he did would be known and would make it that much harder for other rabbis to refuse. His own preference, he then observed, would be that the family not invite him to the ceremony or to the celebration—but if they insisted, he would attend, and would even make a *motsi* and "add a word of benediction for the couple...(reluctantly)."[51]

However, he offered no leniency in any circumstance that would make it seem that the ceremony had Jewish religious legitimacy. To a colleague facing a similar situation Freehof sent a similarly sympathetic answer. But when the rabbi then wrote again to ask whether it was permissible to co-officiate with the priest in a church if there was no mention of the Trinity—basing himself on Freehof's responsum permitting a rabbi to conduct a burial service for a Christian[52]—the reply was definitively negative. " . . . [W]e are in duty bound to bury the dead of Gentiles. But we are not in duty bound to officiate at their marriages or at a mixed marriage. The burial of the Christian dead is a Mitzvah for us; this is not."[53] Yet another colleague asked if he could bless the couple during services in front of the ark rather than co-officiate with Christian clergy. Freehof's reply was firm: "It is pathetic the way in which our members, with their children caught in an intermarriage, want to give it the semblance of Jewishness. . . . If you will bless the couple before the open ark, you are telling all these couples that it is all right to intermarry, the rabbi approves of it. . . . The most I would do under these circumstances would be, if I were a guest at the wedding dinner, to bless the bread and, incidentally, bless the couple." He reiterated that he would not give a blessing at a ceremony performed by a minister or priest; he would not permit the marriage on temple premises; and he would not give the couple a religious blessing in front of the ark or anywhere else.[54] He was certain that if more rabbis took his position, there would be fewer mixed marriages.[55]

Nevertheless, as the decades passed and the rate of mixed marriage increased, he reached a *modus vivendi* with the new reality. He eventually came to admit the value of rabbis who officiated at mixed marriages in retaining for the community the minority of intermarried Jews who wanted to retain a connection to the Jewish community: "I am not one of them and I could not be, but I am glad that those colleagues are available. There is some justification for the argument that at least we can, perhaps, influence their future more than if the couple had been met with outright refusal. . . . "[56] He even advised one colleague that, given the 1947 debate, he would not be acting against the "spirit of the Conference" by making an exception for an elderly couple, one of whom was not Jewish.[57] However, he cautioned, it should only be a last resort, if the man absolutely refused to undergo even a very undemanding conversion. He himself, he noted, had once done a *pro forma* conversion for an older man, "but that was because they were old and not likely to have children."[58]

During the 1960s a renewed debate over mixed marriage swirled within the CCAR as the rabbis became aware that not only was the incidence of mixed marriage on the rise, but more and more members of the Conference were officiating at these marriages, whether willingly or because of what they felt was irresistible pressure from their members. Particularly controversial were the small minority of rabbis whose officiation crossed religious boundaries in egregious ways: co-officiating with non-Jewish (usually Christian) clergy; officiating in churches; officiating on the Sabbath and Jewish festivals. In 1963 a special committee called on the Conference to soften the 1909/1947 resolution, proposing a new resolution that rabbis "do everything within [their] power consistent with the principles of liberal Judaism to discourage mixed marriage," and to be sure that mixed couples received a thorough grounding in Judaism prior to marriage.[59] The resolution did not pass, but it launched the CCAR into a decade-long debate over mixed marriage.

During this decade Freehof, too, was reconsidering the CCAR's position. On one hand, dismayed to learn that the majority of Reform rabbis on Long Island were officiating at mixed marriages, he wondered whether the Conference should take a stronger negative stand.[60] On the other, writing to a colleague who favored officiation, he wondered if the CCAR had a duty to those who did officiate to provide more guidance as to what the ceremony should be—"not as a statement of the official position of the CCAR but perhaps as a creative, liberal approach to this most painful problem."[61] Significantly, however, he never published a responsum to provide such guidance, either in a Responsa Committee report or in one of his own books, though he was asked many times. Since he did not believe that rabbis should perform mixed marriages, he was not about to help colleagues do so by offering either the CCAR's or his own imprimatur.

The only responsum he published on mixed marriage, therefore, was on an issue not addressed in 1947, but which arose subsequently as families shopped around for willing officiants, playing rabbis off against each other: Could a mixed marriage be held on the synagogue premises if the congregation's rabbi did not officiate? He used this responsum as an opportunity to reiterate all his arguments against rabbinic officiation and concluded by suggesting that his colleagues adopt the rule in use at his own congregation, i.e., that no wedding could take place in the synagogue unless one of the synagogue's rabbis was an officiant. "In this way the rabbi does not brush aside a specific family with its specific request, but he says 'no' because he is guided by a rule of the congregation of which he approves. . . . [W]e must avoid hurting decent people, and yet maintain our responsibility as to the maintenance and strengthening of Judaism."[62]

When Freehof published this responsum in 1971, the CCAR was about to reconsider the 1909/1947 resolution. The committee charged with submitting a report to the 1972 convention consulted with him extensively. They felt themselves pulled in both directions: On the one hand, Reform rabbis were under enormous pressure from their congregants to be more accommodating to mixed marriage; on the other, the committee had met with some liberal Orthodox rabbis who were requesting "certain . . . changes in practice" in order to lessen tensions between Reform and Orthodoxy and make it possible for liberal Orthodox rabbis to associate more closely with their Reform colleagues without incurring the wrath of the Orthodox right wing. Should the CCAR relax its opposition to mixed marriages or strengthen it? Reach out to mixed-married couples or reach in to more traditional Jews?

Freehof contributed a resource paper to their deliberations titled "The New Marriage Problem," but he refused to have it published or to take any public role in the deliberations. He urged them not to yield on the mixed marriage question, even though this stance made rabbis appear, in contrast to Christian clergy, "uncomradely, unecumenical, and hidebound."[63] He also urged them not to change anything for the sake of relations with the Orthodox because, he assured them, without complete Reform capitulation to Orthodox demands, no rapprochement would succeed. (See Chapter 7.) In the end, he advised the committee to recommend that the CCAR stay with its current policy as long as the social situation was in flux and there was no evidence to show what policy would be better. The only suggestion he contributed to easing the mixed marriage dilemma didn't address the heart of the problem: If the non-Jewish partner converted before the marriage, Freehof offered, then the officiating rabbi could invite the in-laws' clergyperson to deliver a blessing at the ceremony, since according to the halakhah one is allowed to respond *Amen* to a blessing by a gentile.

Marriage and Divorce as Jewish Legal Institutions

In *RJP* Freehof emphasized the validity of civil marriage in order to persuade mixed couples to marry civilly. In the 1947 report, however, he wrote that "while we consider civil marriage valid, it is certainly not adequate."[64] Here he was more thorough in his discussion of the halakhah, noting that traditional authorities were divided on the validity of civil and common law marriages between Jews.[65] The CCAR had not yet taken a definitive stand on the question. He therefore proposed, and the CCAR adopted, a resolution stating that civil marriage is valid but lacks sanctity, and such Jewish couples should have a religious ceremony. The rabbis also adopted a resolution affirming the Report's language that "it should be clear that the fact that [a] couple is already married by civil law does not obviate the necessity of conversion of the Gentile party before the Jewish marriage services can take place."[66] He affirmed this position in his responsa correspondence.[67]

The status of Jewish marriage in the post-Emancipation context was problematic for reformers. In response to Napoleon's question on divorce, the Assembly of Notables had declared that "[i]t is a principle generally acknowledged among [us] that, in every thing relating to civil or political interests, the law of the state is the supreme law," and that since the Revolution, "the functions of Rabbis, wherever they are established, are limited to preaching morality in the temples, blessing marriages, and pronouncing divorces . . . "[68] But what did "blessing marriages" mean? Jewish marriage—*kiddushin*—is effected by means of *kinyan*, a contractual transaction—a "civil" act. It is not effected by anything the rabbi does; the rabbi's presence is only customary. This challenged the reformers' neat separation between religious and civil matters. (In the post-Emancipation context reformers uniformly considered the *ketubah* superfluous, since the laws of the state now protected Jewish women.[69])

In 1843 the radical reformer Samuel Holdheim argued that because traditional Jewish marriage was a civil act, it now properly belonged under the control of the state in accordance with the Talmudic principle of *dina de-malkhuta dina* ("The law of the land is the law"). The state, not the rabbis, had the right to determine the laws of marriage. Among the implications of this position was that nothing prohibited a rabbi from officiating at a mixed marriage. In rebuttal, Zacharias Frankel argued that the *kinyan* of marriage was qualitatively different from other forms of *kinyan* because of the religious and moral dimension integral to *kiddushin*.[70] In the US, Frankel's argument was adopted by Mielziner, Kohler, and Lauterbach. No one wanted to cede control over marriage to the state. As Lauterbach wrote: "Marriage comes under the aspects of both civil and religious law, of both *dina* and *issura*. Accordingly, on purely spiritual grounds, Judaism retains the right to determine which marriages it considers proper, and which marriages it condemns as improper."[71]

However, Reform rabbis were generally not concerned with whether the *kinyan* was being done according to halakhah. Many nineteenth-century Jews wanted the bride to take a more active role in the ceremony, as they had seen in Christian marriages, both by giving a ring and by saying something. At the 1869 Leipzig Synod, Joseph Aub proposed that the bride have the option of giving the groom a ring and stating something such as *Ani le-dodi ve-dodi li* ("I am my beloved's and my beloved is mine"). At the Augsburg Synod in 1871, he rejected as "sophistical" the argument that an exchange of rings would nullify the *kinyan* (though that argument is, in fact, part of the standard modern Orthodox opposition to double ring ceremonies with mutual declarations[72]). The synod, however, cautiously allowed the bride only to give the groom a ring and to say "a few appropriate words" if she so desired.[73] While sexism doubt-less played a part, the synod was apparently reluctant to contradict the halakhah so explicitly. By contrast, the 1869 Philadelphia Conference, attended largely by radical Reformers,[74] ignored halakhic considerations, mandating both a double ring ceremony and a mutual declaration, with both parties asserting that they were marrying according to "the law of God" instead of the law of Moses and Israel.[75]

At the first convention of the CCAR, Moses Mielziner introduced a marriage ceremony in which the groom made the traditional declaration in Hebrew and the couple then said to each other, "Be thou consecrated to me as my wife/husband according to the law of God and of man." Mielziner explained that he retained the traditional Hebrew formula out of "regard for the prevailing custom among our fellow-believers in all countries of the world," though the result, probably not unintentionally, was also a ceremony that sounded quite universal yet preserved the ha-lakhic *kinyan*. Though not officially adopted by the Conference, the cer-emony was widely used.[76] However, the 1917 *Minister's Hand Book* moved leftward by eliminating the Hebrew declaration and having the couple say to each other only, "Be thou consecrated unto me with this ring as my wife/husband according to the faith of Israel and the law of God," with or without a second ring.[77] The 1928 *Rabbi's Manual* was a compromise between traditional and radical Reform. Its marriage cere-mony assumed that the double ring option was standard, but included the single ring option. First, the groom recited the English declaration which originated at Philadelphia, "Be thou consecrated unto me with this ring as my wife, according to the faith of Israel," and then the traditional He-brew. The bride repeated the English formula, with or without mention of a ring, as appropriate.[78] Whether the ceremony included a halakhi-cally valid *kinyan* was irrelevant, but retaining the traditional declaration of *kiddushin* and having only the groom say it in Hebrew imparted a tra-ditional feeling to the ceremony.

Freehof was therefore in the mainstream of Reform practice when he wrote in *RJP* that Jewish marriage had no legal standing and there-fore the old halakhic stringencies were unnecessary. All these—the pres-ence of a *minyan*, valid witnesses for the *ketubah* and the *kiddushin*, the type of ring—flowed, he explained, from the Jewish marriage laws' for-mer function as "the sole legal safeguard of the wife, husband, or children." Today, however, when the state provides the legal safeguards, the "religious marriage is primarily the spiritual and moral side of the marriage," and Jewish legal forms are dispensed with. Thus there is no need for a *minyan*, qualified witnesses, a *ketubah*—which is "merely a civil property document"[79]—or a plain ring.

He received very few questions about marriage. Not surprisingly, those he did receive were about non-Jewish participation. In one of these he had a hard time explaining why the witnesses to the *kiddushin* and the signatories to a Reform wedding certificate (not a *ketubah*) had to be Jews, given the Reform insistence on the non-legal character of marriage. In this instance he could only assert that "marriage by the rabbi is Jewish religious marriage and it is not proper for a non-Jew to be a signatory of this document, attesting to its validity."[80]

The other question he received, however, entangled him in a thicket of contradictions regarding the legal nature of *kiddushin*. Asked whether it was appropriate for the bride's sister, who had become a Christian, to stand under the *huppah* as an attendant, he advised the questioner:

> A Jewish wedding is legal if the husband proposes to the wife and gives her an object of value, and she accepts in the presence of witnesses. Here the apostate sister is not necessary as a witness. There are other witnesses present, and so there can be no legal objection to her participating in the wedding. . . .
> Nevertheless it would be wise not to have her there if it is a very small wedding. If there are more people present who are considered the legal witnesses . . . then there can be no legal objection to her presence.[81]

He could have answered simply that Reform Judaism does not regard marriage as a legal act and does not require the presence of a *minyan* or kosher witnesses, so it doesn't matter who stands under the *huppah* with the bride and groom. Instead, he seems to have forgotten this point and answered with a halakhic muddle. The halakhic norm is that women cannot be witnesses, except in certain extraordinary circumstances, and an apostate can never be a witness.[82] In an halakhic context the sister could not be a witness; in a Reform context, she was not needed as a witness. The answer is a jumble. In fairness, this responsum was published in

1980, when Freehof was already in his late eighties; the responsa from these last years of his life all suffer from a marked lack of depth and thoroughness when compared to his earlier work. The fact that the question involved an apostate probably also colored his answer.

Although Freehof had insisted in *RJP* that Reform marriage had no legal character, his responsa show his unwillingness to take the step that would render the *kinyan* halakhically invalid, i.e., to make the exchange of rings fully equal. In 1966 he was actually asked if a reciprocal exchange of rings and a reciprocal declaration would not invalidate the entire marriage. He replied that Reform wanted to assert the principle of gender equality in the ceremony, but that "this act of justice runs counter to the entire legal tradition in the matter. Therefore you will notice that the Rabbi's Manual in the bride's formula put the words 'By this ring' in parenthesis, thus avoiding a direct (although morally justified) contravention of the law." He explained to his correspondent, "In my own practice, I avoid having the bride recite a Hebrew formula and have her say merely, 'Be thou sacred to me as husband, according to [the] law of God.'"[83] In other words, he chose not to openly break with the traditional understanding of the halakhic character of *kiddushin* rather than take the "morally justified" but non-halakhic course that would affirm the equality of women.

A few years later he answered a similar inquiry with a lengthy disquisition on all the ways in which Reform changes to marriage and divorce laws had created halakhic difficulties, and then pronounced, "Yet we brush all these laws aside without hesitation because there is a matter of conscience involved. We insist upon the equal status of men and women, and are willing to put aside a large section of the law and face possible unpleasant consequences [in terms of our relationship with Orthodoxy]." Still, he maintained his practice of not having the bride recite the traditional formula. "I myself, in many hundreds of weddings (and I believe most of my colleagues too in their marriages), make no attempt to use a Hebrew Halachic-sounding formula . . . Thus we are not troubled by sounding Halachic when we are really in this case contra-Halachic."[84]

Freehof was more comfortable with some forms of gender equality than with others. As the years went on and changes permeated the larger society, his views also changed to some extent, though an old fashioned paternalistic attitude frequently appeared in his writing, as when he referred to a woman who refused to accept a *get* as a "stubborn girl."[85] As a young HUC faculty member, he was in the minority that opposed allowing Martha Neumark to take a High Holy Day pulpit, expressly because he did not think that women should serve as rabbis.[86] However, asked in 1970 about the propriety of having religious school girls come up for *aliyot* wearing *tallitot*, he expressed no objection and commented, "Besides, in our Reform Movement, where special emphasis is placed upon the religious equality of men and women, there can be no real objection to young women putting on the *Talit* when they participate in the service."[87] Doubtless, however, his favorable view was colored by his view that wearing the *tallit* was simply a ceremonial practice that earlier Reform Jews rejected as meaningless but that contemporary Reform Jews, acting within a changed zeitgeist, found meaningful. (See Chapter 8.)

Divorce

"Reform congregations recognize Civil Divorce as completely dissolving the marriage and permit remarriage of divorced persons."[88] The longest single section in *RJP* is the section on divorce, because Freehof included a thorough discussion of why Reform Judaism had opted for civil divorce in place of the *get*. He surveyed the history of the *get* in the context of rabbinic efforts over the centuries to mitigate the inferior legal status of women, the insurmountable halakhic obstacles to eliminating women's disadvantage with regard to the *get*, Reform attempts to deal with the *get*, and the reasons why opting for civil divorce was the preferred course. He explained that American Reform, following Samuel Holdheim, included divorce among all the other elements of Jewish civil law which were now superseded by the law of the land according to the principle of *dina demalkhuta dina*. "Besides, it is the true function of the rabbi to solemnize marriage and not to break it. Divorce should . . . be under the control of civil law and the rabbi should have nothing to do with it."[89] The chaotic condition of American law in the nineteenth and early twentieth centuries, however, had made it inadvisable for the rabbis simply to adopt the civil standard. The 1869 Philadelphia Conference decided that rabbis should decide on the acceptability of civil divorces before remarrying someone, a view that Kohler later endorsed. "In theory the Reform rabbi would like to review civil divorces and officiate at second marriages only if they approve, but they have not been able to put this into practice. In actual practice, the civil divorce is simply accepted as final," and he later advised a colleague to accept it as such.[90]

Freehof admitted that Reform acceptance of civil divorce had created problems in the movement's relationship with Orthodoxy and Conservatism. He cautioned that although the CCAR had not yet decided whether a Reform rabbi should officiate at a marriage for a Conservative or Orthodox Jew who did not have a *get*, Reform rabbis should definitely not officiate at the marriages of individuals whose own rabbis refused to officiate based on their religious standards. However, he would not subject a Reform Jew to the stricter traditional standards. A colleague wrote asking for his approbation for refusing to officiate at the marriage of a civilly divorced female congregant who adamantly refused to accept the *get* her ex-husband in Israel wanted to give her; Freehof disagreed. By Reform standards the woman was free to remarry. She could still accept the *get* at any future time. "In other words, I would have done as you did, made every effort toward a *Get*. Though you failed, this stubborn girl is *still* entitled from the Reform point of view, to be remarried."[91]

Conclusion

Freehof's work in the 1940s gave American Reform rabbis and laypeople a coherent and easily accessible exposition of Reform standards for marriage and divorce. In the ensuing decades, however, he received few questions on any of these issues aside from mixed marriage.

Why did rabbis feel the need to write to him to ask about mixed marriage when they knew that as Reform rabbis they had the right to make decisions for themselves and that the 1909 resolution did not prohibit them from officiating? The answer is obvious from the tone of the questions. Those rabbis who wanted to officiate simply did so, without consulting Freehof. Those who wrote him were those who were personally opposed to officiation and wanted either a statement against officiation from a source more "authoritative" than their own opinion, or a statement that would justify some limited ceremonial participation in order to satisfy a family. In short, Freehof "codified" Reform practice regarding marriage and divorce, and thereafter primarily answered questions on the issue for which social conditions raised problems.

5

CONVERSION AND JEWISH STATUS

In 1941 Freehof had stated that the CCAR needed "a clear-cut code which shall have the effect of law for us . . . in the field of marriage, divorce and conversion . . . [because t]he state has definite marriage laws and we too must have clear-cut laws which govern us."[1] The state, of course, did not care who was a Jew, though the rabbis most certainly did. Opposed to any sort of Reform code for any other reason, however, Freehof used a little sleight of hand and included conversion here. It was logical, since the question arose most frequently by far in relationship to marriage. For the same reason, his 1947 report to the CCAR on marriage and intermarriage also included a section on conversion. A question he did not address at that time was the Jewish status of apostates or their children; he later received many inquiries on it, also usually in connection with marriage. In all questions of Jewish status Freehof balanced an open and welcoming attitude with the need to resist blurring the boundaries between Jewish and not Jewish.

Conversion in Reform Judaism

In creating conversion guidelines Freehof had comparatively few precedents upon which to draw. The Augsburg Synod did vote to accept female witnesses at the *mikveh* (ritual bath) in consideration of an increase in the number of Christian women converting before marriage, but this was irrelevant in an American context where the *mikveh* was declared unnecessary.[2] In the United States, the rate of mixed marriage was high when the Jewish community was tiny or when Jews lived in isolated locations, but otherwise there were relatively few mixed marriages, and even fewer converts for other reasons.[3] Rates of mixed marriage and conversion to Judaism remained low in the United States and Canada prior to World War II.

Any consideration of conversion required addressing circumcision. Many nineteenth-century Jews internalized the dominant Christian Euro-American view of circumcision as a primitive and alien practice. Jews refrained from circumcising their sons to render them less identifiable in the non-Jewish and increasingly antisemitic social milieux to which they had won entry.[4] Radical Reformers on both sides of the Atlantic advocated abandoning the rite of *brit milah* on principle, either because of its "primitive" character or because it unnecessarily distinguished between Jews and gentiles. Even Abraham Geiger referred to it privately as "a barbarous, bloody act."[5] Both the Philadelphia Conference and the Augsburg Synod adopted resolutions affirming that the uncircumcised son of a Jewish mother is no less a Jew. While this was the halakhah, the conferences were using it to turn the exception into the rule. It is fair to say that circumcision would have disappeared completely from the lives of liberal American Jews had it not been adopted by the larger society in the twentieth century as a hygienic practice.[6]

The 1885 Pittsburgh conference resolved not to require *brit milah* for converts.[7] In 1891 the new Central Conference of American Rabbis heard two lengthy papers and reviewed a number of shorter opinions on the same question; the following year they approved, 25-5, a resolution proposed by Isaac Mayer Wise eliminating the need for any ritual whatsoever in conversion. Any rabbi, together with two "associates," could now "accept into the sacred covenant of Israel . . . any honorable and intelligent person, who desires such affiliation, without any initiatory rite, ceremony, or observance whatever; provided such person be sufficiently acquainted with the faith, doctrine and religious usages of Israel . . . " The convert was to pledge verbally and in writing to commit herself or himself to worship God alone; to be governed in life by God's laws; and to adhere to "the sacred cause and mission of Israel." The "associates" did not have to be rabbis, since it was not always possible to bring together three rabbis, and in any case, the halakhah had not required three rabbis but only a court of three. Of the CCAR's leading scholars, only HUC Professor of Talmud Moses Mielziner objected to the resolution.[8] In 1914 the CCAR rejected the draft of a new conversion ceremony requiring the convert to promise a *brit milah* for any sons. Kaufmann

Kohler argued that since the ritual was not "absolutely indispensable" and "had no sacramental character at all in Judaism . . . , to ask the convert whether he will have his children circumcised is to be more Popish than the Pope himself." Stephen Wise chimed in, "There may be some people who want a *Milah* service, but that does not compel the whole of Jewry to do the thing they do not believe in."[9] The 1917 *Minister's Hand Book* was a compromise, probably helped out by the growing advocacy of circumcision by the medical profession.[10] It asked not only whether the prospective convert agreed to raise her/his children as Jews, but also, "Do you also agree to have male children circumcised?" However, the convert's formal pledge included only a promise to raise the children as Jews, with no mention of circumcision.[11]

After 1892 the CCAR did not reconsider conversion until 1947, while only one published responsum addressed the subject. Asked about a child's religious upbringing when a Jewish husband's pregnant gentile wife reneged on her promise to convert, Kohler observed in passing that "when raised as a Jew, the child could afterwards, through Confirmation, be adopted into the Jewish fold like any proselyte."[12]

Freehof's Conversion Guidelines in RJP *and the 1947 Report*

In *RJP* Freehof summarized the existing Reform conversion procedure, saying that the candidate received instruction "in the doctrines and observances of Judaism" and then at the rabbi's discretion "he or she is accepted into Judaism in the presence of three men, if possible three rabbis."[13] He explained that the section on conversion was in the chapter on Marriage and Divorce, since most conversions were for the purpose of marriage.[14] He acknowledged the Talmud's ambivalence about such conversions before continuing on to a brief exposition of the traditional ritual requirements for conversion and then the CCAR's revision of those requirements. He did not address the question of conversion of children at all.

In the 1947 Report, presented with the opportunity to create authoritative standards for Reform Judaism, as he had envisioned in 1941, he addressed as many elements of the knotty issues of conversion and Jewish status as he could.

1. Conversion for the sake of marriage: The Report bears witness to Freehof's experience as CANRA's Responsa Committee chairman. Military chaplains were frequently asked to convert a non-Jewish fiancée and then to officiate at the marriage; in the course of the committee's deliberations on this question Freehof's Orthodox colleague, Leo Jung, introduced him to two responsa on which he would rely in subsequent years, one by Jung's teacher David Hoffmann (1843–1921) and the other by Frankfurt rabbi Marcus Horovitz (1844–1910).[15] In contrast to the restrictive attitude of most Orthodox decisors, these two men decided that it was preferable to keep the households in question closer to the traditional ambit than to reject them and have them go to Reform rabbis or sever their ties to the Jewish community completely.[16] As Jung wrote to Freehof, if a couple was already married civilly and "the Rabbi is convinced that the would-be Ger [male proselyte] or Giyoreth [female proselyte] is an intelligent and responsible person, then a Rabbi (a Mussmach [Orthodox ordinee]) could undertake a conversion," using the authority granted him by the Shulḥan Arukh to "rely on his own judgment—lefi r'oth eynov."[17]

   In addressing the question of conversion for the sake of marriage in 1947, Freehof took time to defend the Reform position from attack. The rabbis of the Talmudic era, he insisted, would have approved the Reform practice of accepting converts for the sake of marriage; rejection of the practice by subsequent authorities represented a narrowing of perspective due to historical circumstances.[18] The early rabbis, Hoffmann, and Horovitz all upheld the principle that had long guided Reform, that of *"hakol l'fi r'os bays din . . . ,* it all depends on the judgment of the court" when evaluating the motivation of a prospective proselyte.[19] In other words, American Orthodox (and Conservative) rabbis who criticized Reform for being too willing to accept converts were wrong. The CCAR adopted the resolution he proposed: "The CCAR considers all sincere applicants for proselytizing as acceptable whether or not it is the intention of the candidate to marry a Jew."[20]

2. Conversion of children: Freehof restated the halakhic precedents
   which Reform had always accepted: Children have their own status and must have their own conversion; the status of the child
   follows the status of the mother, meaning that the child of a Jewish mother is a Jew, but the child of a gentile mother is a gentile
   and requires formal conversion to Judaism.[21] Any confusion about
   this stemmed from the fact that Reform had no ritual for conversion. "[W]ith us, where . . . only the ethical and intellectual [ele-
   ments] are considered prerequisite, how are we able to convert
   young children or even infants?" He answered his own question
   by proposing that the CCAR adopt these guidelines, derived, by
   inference, from Kohler's single offhand sentence:

   - The declared intent of the parents to raise an infant as
     a Jew is "sufficient for conversion," in keeping with
     the normative halakhic interpretation of B. Ketubot
     11a, that either parent may present a child to the
     court for conversion.
   - Listing the child's name in the religious school Cra-
     dle-Roll[22] could serve as "impressive formality," if
     some formal acknowledgement was wanted.
   - School age children require no special ceremony but
     should simply be enrolled in religious school. The
     Confirmation ceremony "shall be considered in lieu
     of a conversion ceremony."
   - The Talmud gives the minor child the right to reject
     its conversion upon reaching the age of majority.
     Therefore a child beyond the age of Confirmation
     should not be converted without its own consent.
     Such a child should undergo regular instruction and
     have a "regular" conversion ceremony.

It may surprise modern readers, accustomed to the contemporary Reform emphasis on "appropriate and timely public and formal acts of identification with the Jewish faith and people,"[23] to
see no mention of either *brit milah* or naming, but neither the
commandment nor the custom was as important to Reform Jews

then as they have since become. By 1947 virtually all sons of Reform Jews were circumcised, though usually only as a medical procedure, sometimes followed by a naming in the synagogue, a reality to which Freehof accommodated himself.[24] As he explained to one correspondent, it was sufficient to enroll a child with a gentile mother in religious school because "of course, all boys are circumcised."[25] The *Rabbi's Manual* contained a naming prayer to be said by one or both parents on their first visit to the synagogue following a child's birth, with no reference to the sex of the child, though ritual namings for girls were even more unusual.[26] Insistence on ritual *brit milah* for converted infants would have implicitly raised the difficult question of its importance for born Jews.

3. The conversion process in a Reform context: Freehof offered his colleagues a clear and concise summary. Whereas the traditional process included both ritual and "ethical" elements, Reform dispensed with the rituals and substituted a "ceremony of declaration and prayer," to be preceded by an investigation of motive and "a period of instruction in which we emphasize the principles of Judaism in the words of Maimonides: 'Modiin oso ikre hadas [They make known to him the essentials of the religion].'"[27] The specific content of preparation, he emphasized, could not be uniform but had to be appropriate to the person's age and station. Young people, for example, would need to be questioned in particular concerning their motivation, while older people who had been involved in Jewish life for some time might need less instruction. The important thing was to adhere to the rabbinic principle that it is up to the discretion of the court.

The CCAR adopted all the Report's recommendations. Subsequently, therefore, when Freehof received questions concerning conversion, he was able to rely on authoritative decisions of the CCAR which he himself had shaped. As a result, though he received many inquiries concerning conversion, none of his responses deviated significantly from the 1947 guidelines. A responsum he published in 1974 reads almost exactly like the 1947 Report.[28] However, he received numerous questions that the guidelines did not address. His responsa also reveal some modifications and refinements to his positions in response to changes in social circumstances.

Freehof on Standards for Conversion

Not surprisingly, most questions Freehof received on conversion involved marriage. The prospective converts were usually women and were either engaged or married to Jewish men; his responses always presumed that the most important consideration was how to create and strengthen a Jewish family.

Typical of these inquiries was one that reached him in 1955 from El Paso: A Jewish doctor in Juarez from a family that "leaned to" Orthodoxy had married a Catholic woman, who was now pregnant. The in-laws wanted her to convert, but when the Orthodox rabbi refused, the couple had come to the Reform rabbi. The woman spoke no English; the inquiring rabbi spoke very little Spanish and had no books on Judaism in Spanish. He wanted to know if it would suffice that he tell her in Spanish to accept Judaism and reject her former faith, to raise her children as Jews and send them to religious school, and to promise to worship as a Jewess, i.e., only the few essentials mentioned in the *Rabbi's Manual*. Given the high rate of mixed marriage and assimilation in the Mexican Jewish community, the rabbi continued, he wanted to "salvage as much as I can."[29]

Freehof replied in the affirmative: It was appropriate "to convert a Christian wife of a Jewish husband in order to strengthen the religious unity of the marriage."[30] There was no set course of instruction, he pointed out. While the Orthodox would teach her how to keep a kosher home, we teach "the principles and doctrines of religion and morality." The rabbi's proposed questions were all that the Talmud required, but the most essential element was to be sure of her "willingness and sincerity in taking this serious step and her full awareness that she is joining a minority group which is sometimes subject to persecution." As long as he was certain of this—by using an interpreter—he could convert her after asking those few questions.

From today's vantage point this is a disturbing responsum. The woman's profile emerges from between the lines: probably less educated than her husband, possibly of lower social class, almost assuredly expected to take the traditional role of wife and mother and to allow her husband to make all the family's significant decisions. If his family wanted her to become a Jew, how free would she have been to refuse? Under these circumstances—and with a language barrier to boot—how could a rabbi possibly evaluate the sincerity of her motivation? Indeed, on another occasion that was precisely the problem. Freehof was asked about the Jewish status of a child whose Catholic mother had converted to Judaism "unwillingly," to please her husband's parents, and then had the child baptized without the father's consent. He reassured his correspondent that the conversion was valid no matter how unwillingly undertaken, though he was glad that at least one rabbi tried to delay the conversion. Nevertheless, his chief concern was that if rabbis hesitated too much over converting the gentile partner prior to marriage, it might make a conversion after marriage even less likely.[31] He never expressed any concern about unwonted pressure from the Jewish family on the gentile fiancée.

Using the same reasoning he approved the conversion of a woman who had already married her Jewish husband in a Catholic ceremony, and of a divorced mother to obtain custody of her Jewish children.[32] He did, however, refuse to approve conversions in certain instances: when the prospective convert clearly had expressed reservations; when performing the conversion could lead to tensions with the Christian community; when there was evidence of mental instability; and when the prospective convert's spouse and children would remain Christian.[33] He also maintained that an atheist could not be accepted as a convert. While acknowledging that the classical authorities were divided on the question of whether belief in God was a mitzvah, he argued that "if it is well known, especially from his own avowal that he does not believe in God, then he does not believe in the *mitzvos* which we (with varying degrees of selectivity) believe are God-given. Since he cannot accept the *mitzvos*, he cannot be converted."[34]

He insisted that conversion to Judaism was "more than being converted to a religious doctrine; it also means sharing the world lot of the Jewish people. You can well say that this, too, is part of our religion, because the role of the Jewish people, whether interpreted in the Orthodox or Reform way, is a part of our religion."[35] This consideration of kinship led him to hesitate, through the 1970s, concerning the conversion of non-Caucasians:

> As to converting for marriage a person of a different race, Negro, Chinese, etc., I have always avoided this as much as possible. It is, of course, quite true that Judaism is not racial and any individual who is worthy and sincere may be accepted by Judaism. *Nevertheless* we should always bear in mind that conversion to Judaism is essentially different than conversion to Christianity. . . .[W]ith us a convert is a "new-born child." He becomes an intimate part of our personal family. Therefore my personal hesitation about converting a Black or Chinese is that it is very difficult—almost impossible—for them to become a part of our daily family life. It is better to dissuade them; they will be happier eventually.[36]

By the standards of his time Freehof was not a racist; he tolerated no doubt concerning the Jewish status of black converts.[37] His response simply reflects the unconscious ethnocentrism typical of American Jews of his generation.

Freehof's standards for conversion were flexible; aside from insisting that the convert disavow all other religious attachments[38] and promise (if appropriate) to raise her/his children as Jews, he adjusted the standards to the individual situation, never asking more of a convert than of an average congregant. He took seriously the language of the Talmud and the codes that conversion should not be a difficult and rigorous process.[39] A rabbi had promised congregants with a prospective gentile son-in-law that he would meet with them, but had not guaranteed that he would convert the young man; the parents had then turned to another rabbi who met the couple once, converted the fiancé, and performed the wedding. The first rabbi, furious, wrote to Freehof, seeking his agreement that there should be standards for Reform conversion. Freehof sent him a *laissez-faire* reply: The other rabbi was wrong, but the CCAR could not impose standards on its members. While rabbis should be as careful as possible with young people, "[t]here should be some leeway. . . . When we are marrying a widow of sixty-five to a widower of like age, and there is no prospect of children, we can somewhat simplify the preparations for conversion."[40] According to the principle of *hakol lefi r'ot ene bet din* ("All is according to what the court deems right"), a rabbi always had the right to decide who was a suitable candidate for conversion and how much preparation was required.[41] Indeed, he himself performed conversions with virtually no instruction prior to marriage when the couple involved was past the age of procreation. "I had a similar problem about ten years ago. Also an elderly couple was involved. The man was Christian, though not particularly devout. I asked him whether he was willing to consider himself a member of the Jewish community and to maintain his household as Jewish, and he said he was. I considered that avowal in this case as equivalent to conversion." It was the Reform equivalent of the Orthodox *kabbalat ol mitsvot* ("accepting the yoke of the commandments"), because "[t]o us the Mitzvos do not mean observing all the details of ritual law, but what we would call loyalty to Judaism, a home that considers itself Jewish and attendance at services, as much as our own born Jews do."[42]

Nevertheless, he defended the integrity of Reform conversions as opposed to Orthodox ones, often comparing Reform's emphasis on instruction in the "principles" of Judaism with what he characterized as the Orthodox focus on the rituals of circumcision and immersion. "I, who respect the Halacha, nevertheless am convinced that our Reform conversion is more thorough-going than the Orthodox conversion which tends to become a ritual formality."[43] Elsewhere, to underscore the seriousness of Reform conversion, he reported with evident pride that rather than requiring merely a ceremony, Reform required at least a month of instruction.[44] Whatever ceremony a Reform rabbi used to mark a convert's entry was merely a formality, and not the essence of the conversion process. A pregnant woman who studied for conversion but missed the conversion class's formal ceremony when she went into labor, and then had a second child before she returned to ask about completing her conversion, was a Jew—as were her children—because the learning and commitment to living a Jewish life were the essential elements of her conversion.[45] As Reform rabbis began more and more often to encourage or require *tevilah*, Freehof remained indifferent, consistent with his views on the reappropriation of discarded rituals. (See Chapter 8.)

Conversion of Children

The guidelines the CCAR adopted for the conversion of children in 1947 seemed straightforward. Following Marcus Horovitz, there was firm halakhic precedent for converting the children of Jewish fathers and gentile mothers. Just as the Talmud allowed a parent to present a child to the court for conversion, so Reform Judaism required that the parents indicate a commitment to raising the child as a Jew. There was no need for ritual immersion, and instruction could be carried out through the ordinary religious school. The child had only to be entered into religious school and continue through Confirmation. Freehof reiterated these points in both published responsa and correspondence.[46]

The inherent difficulty in the guidelines as Freehof wrote them, however, is that they are teleological. Taken at face value, the conclusion is that a valid conversion can only be judged after the fact, since a valid conversion is one that produces a young adult who has been raised and educated to live a proper Jewish life as defined by Reform Judaism. The guidelines presupposed stable families affiliated with synagogues, making decisions at the time of their children's birth to raise them as Jews, and keeping them in religious school through age sixteen. When that sequence was interrupted for any reason, many rabbis were uncertain how to proceed. Freehof, too, made contradictory and inconsistent decisions when trying to weigh something as inherently vague as parental intent.

For example, he advised that a boy with a Jewish father, approaching the age of bar mitzvah but given no Jewish education or upbringing, was not eligible to begin bar mitzvah training, but could still be converted. "Even from our Reform point of view, you see, the boy has not gone to our schools and the parents have not hitherto indicated in any way that they desire the boy to be Jewish. Therefore on the basis of Halacha, Orthodox and liberalized Halacha of Reform, there is no ground for admitting this boy for bar mitzvah." However, he continued, echoing Horovitz, we do not close the doors to repentant individuals. Give the father an opportunity to demonstrate that he sincerely wants his son to be a Jew.

> Does he really wish the child to be a Jewish child; in other
> words, to raise the child as a Jew? Then clearly he must

demonstrate it to you, because he is asking you to do something contrary to Jewish tradition. How can his sincerity be proved? He ought to join the congregation. This is indispensable. If he wants his boy to be Jewish, he must want the institutions of Judaism to be maintained. The fact that his mother who is a Gentile already belongs to the Sisterhood would indicate that the request that the father join the congregation might not be resisted too much. Secondly, the boy should receive a proper preparation for his bar mitzvah and, thirdly, it might be well if you made the parents and the boy promise that after bar mitzvah he would stay in the school until Confirmation.[47]

Three years later, however, he decided that a young woman who had *voluntarily* attended religious school from age ten through age fourteen was a gentile, because

[w]hat the Conference has in mind is a Jewish couple or a half-Jewish couple wanting the child to be formally Jewish, with the understanding that it will live in a Jewish family. In other words, the child will be taught by us as Jewish and raised by them as Jewish. But this girl had no Jewish environment at home and even now is married to a Gentile. Therefore we cannot consider that she has been converted by her brief Jewish education. If she is now to be Jewish, she will need to be converted.[48]

Freehof acknowledged that waiting until Confirmation to determine a child's Jewish status was absurd. He therefore advised correspondents that parental intent was sufficient to confer Jewish status. "Here we are at a disadvantage with the Orthodox, since we do not have a fixed ceremony which marks the time of conversion of a child. Surely the Conference did not mean that we have to wait fifteen years before the child is a Jew. If the child is entered into the Cradle Roll of the congregation, which indicates an intent to raise it as a Jew, I am sure that it was the intention of the Conference to consider that child Jewish. That is what I think we should do in such cases."[49] Even a minimum of education was sufficient to establish parental intent. "In Orthodox law this little girl would be dipped in the Mikva and that would be enough. Surely the intention of raising the child as Jewish and one complete year of Jewish education is as significant as one dipping in the Mikva."[50] He came to regard parental intent as the most significant element in determining a child's Jewish status.

Neither the Talmud nor the Shulḥan Arukh demanded a parental commitment to raising the child as a Jew as a precondition for *brit milah*—not because earlier generations were extremely lenient, but because for them the commitment was implicit in the request. The changed conditions of modern life made it possible for Jewish men both to have gentile wives and to request that their sons be brought into the covenant in the traditional fashion. Freehof was personally in agreement with Marcus Horovitz's approach: The request for *brit milah* was an opportunity to bring the household closer to the Jewish community and to a proper Jewish way of life. If a Jewish father requested that his son have a *brit milah*, the rabbi should agree, as long as "the parents . . . promise that the child will receive a Jewish education and be raised as a Jew."[51] Untangling the relationship between parental intent to raise the child as a Jew and parental desire for a *brit milah* or naming, however, proved too complex for Freehof to demonstrate consistency.

In a 1952 military responsum he and his committee ruled that a chaplain could arrange a *brit milah* "if the father clearly indicates that it is his intention to induct the child into the religion of Israel and to raise the child as a religious Jew," but they also noted that even if the father expressed no intention of raising his son as a Jew, "there is no clear prohibition to having this child circumcised by Jewish rites."[52] However, Freehof never relied on this lenient precedent in his responsa correspondence. Indeed, he actually encouraged his colleagues to refuse *brit milah* or naming in situations where it seemed clear that the parents had little or no intention of giving the child a Jewish upbringing. Thus in 1956 he praised a colleague: "So you did exactly right in refusing to give a religious service at a circumcision in which there was no commitment to raise the child as a Jew."[53] A few years later a rabbinic student arranged a *brit milah* only to learn after the fact that the mother was gentile and that the ritual had been only done to please the observant grandfather in Israel. Freehof expressed anger at what he considered deception: Had the student known beforehand, he would have had no right to participate in "a ceremony which in a roundabout way pretends that it is a Jewish child being circumcised." Nevertheless, he wrote, if the student believed that the father would raise the child as a Jew, "then you may consider that this child can now be looked upon as a convert. . . . Circumcision depends on the father's desire to raise the child as Jewish. There is debate in Jewish law as to whether his promise is trustworthy, but certainly to us it would be considered acceptable if we believe it."[54] Trying to apply this principle *ex post facto*, however, led him to articulate an absurd double standard to which he was, apparently, completely oblivious. The adult daughter of a gentile mother and Jewish father, with no Jewish upbringing, was not a Jew and the questioner should not officiate at her marriage to a Jewish man. Her brother, however, *was* a Jew because he had had a *brit milah*, and this was sufficient indication of his father's intent to raise him as such![55]

Ab initio, however, if a father was not motivated to raise his son as a Jew, Freehof felt no obligation to "reward" him with an isolated life cycle ritual to which he had a sentimental attachment. Refusal to rely on a lenient halakhic precedent was an exception to his own judicial methodology, but for Freehof this refusal was both a tactic of resistance to mixed marriage and a defense of the Reform view of conversion. Jewish upbringing and learning made a Jew, not a ritual performed on an infant. For the same reason he expressed reservations when an unaffiliated Jewish woman, married to a gentile man, wanted her daughter named in the synagogue. Although the child was definitely Jewish, he assured the questioner that "we have the right to ask of the Jewish mother why she insists upon this ceremony," for which there was no requirement.

> If she is asking us to conduct this ceremony in order to please her parents, we have no objection, provided she means to raise the child as a Jewess. But if she does not intend to raise the child as a Jewess, but *merely* wishes to please her parents and possibly even delude them thereby, we must not be a party to such an unworthy purpose. But if we are convinced that it is the sincere intention of the parents to raise the child as a Jewess and that the naming ceremony is, in effect, a public announcement of that intention, then we should certainly help her and conduct the ceremony.[56]

On another occasion he discouraged naming a girl in synagogue when the father was not Jewish: The child was Jewish anyway, most people don't even bother with naming girls, and in any case a family with a non-Jewish father shouldn't do it because "the father is usually called up for the reading of the Torah."[57] The deprecatory language that permeated his correspondence on mixed marriage sometimes appeared in his writing on conversion as well. Asked on another occasion about naming the child of a Jewish mother and gentile father, he sent a delayed reply with an apology: "I suppose I sidestepped it because it reveals such an unhappy situation which is now widespread over the country."[58]

Nevertheless, Freehof was not quite able to reconcile his resistance to reducing the conversion of children to a ritual matter with his recognition of *brit milah* as the essential conversionary act (traditionally followed by *tevilah*, of course) for the son of a gentile mother. As a result, his treatment of the status of these circumcisions was inconsistent. In 1963 he went against the codified halakhah by advising a rabbi that "the child is legitimately circumcised as a convert" but that he could use the regular blessing instead of the one for converts, since "'To bring him into the covenant of Abraham our father' applies to Gerim [proselytes] also." The rabbi could, if he chose, add the blessing for the circumcision of converts, but it was not necessary.[59] In a published responsum that year he avoided completely the question of which blessings to say, but equated the ritual with conversion: "The implication is that this religious circumcision will make the child a Jew; in other words, it is intended, in effect, to be a ceremony of conversion. . . ."[60] However, he then downplayed it, insisting that "the ceremonies involved are secondary," and that sincerity and instruction were the "essential prerequisites." Therefore "[w]e would ask the parents to promise that the child will receive a Jewish religious education [through Confirmation] and be raised as a Jew. If both parents agree to that, we should consider this sufficient, since, at all events, the ritual circumcision of such a child is permitted by the law, and the conversion of such a child is permitted by the Talmud."[61] In a later published responsum, he again insisted that a rabbi should only participate in a *brit milah* ceremony if the parents have made the commitment to raise the child as a Jew, but also added at the end, "Since this circumcision is a *conversion* circumcision [emphasis original], the child must be named as the child of Abraham," and not as the son of the natural father. (In contrast, in the same responsum he advocated ignoring the halakhah and using some equivalent or transliteration of the gentile father's name in naming the child of a Jewish mother.)[62]

In 1983, at the urging of Rabbi Alexander Schindler, President of the Union of American Hebrew Congregations, the CCAR adopted a controversial resolution stating that "the child of one Jewish parent is under the *presumption* of Jewish descent [emphasis added]," but that the Jewish status of such a child must be "established through appropriate and timely public and formal acts of identification with the Jewish faith and people," such as "entry into the covenant, acquisition of a Hebrew name, Torah study, Bar/Bat Mitzvah, and *Kabbalat Torah* (Confirmation)."[63] Both proponents and opponents of the decision pointed out that this was already the *de facto* procedure for children of Jewish fathers; indeed, in that sense the resolution was merely a restatement of the 1947 guidelines. Motivated, however, not only by a desire to retain the loyalties of the growing number of mixed-married households but also to apply egalitarian principles in all possible areas of Jewish life, American Reform rabbis essentially split the difference between the treatment of children of Jewish mothers (no longer fully Jewish by birth) and those of Jewish fathers (no longer requiring conversion). Neither was Jewish by birth, and neither required formal conversion. All became Jewish by virtue of being raised as such.

Freehof, then ninety years old, was not actively involved in the debate, but privately expressed his dismay. In all of his published responsa and unpublished correspondence, he had consistently held to the traditional standard that the status of the child follows the status of the mother in determining Jewishness.[64] Although he applauded the desire to reach out to the children of Jewish fathers, he called the idea of according Jewish status to children with gentile mothers "dangerous," because of the divide it would create between (American) Reform Jews and everyone else. "If the Reform movement insists upon counting as Jewish such people as the rest of Jewry counts as Gentiles, it will indeed make a great separation between us. It will go deeper than our differences in [conversion] ritual." He also considered it unnecessary. "The Conference has long decided that we will not go through formal conversion ritual for infants and young children. If the parents want them to be Jewish, they need only normal time in our Sunday school and we accept the willingness to raise the child as a Jew as sufficient justification for our accepting him as such."[65]

RJP *on Apostates*

Although Freehof did not specifically mention it in 1941, the need for clear guidelines in conversion was part of the larger question of who is a Jew. Defining apostasy means answering the question, When is a Jew not a Jew? The overwhelming consensus of the halakhah is that a Jew never ceases to be a Jew, but one who has adopted another religious tradition is barred from participation in most elements of Jewish religious and communal life. In *RJP* Freehof addressed the subject in a most unusual way, with an entry on Christian Scientists in the chapter on Burial and Mourning: "If the family of a Christian Scientist of Jewish birth asks to have him buried in the Jewish cemetery, is such permission to be given?"[66]

Christian Science had attracted a number of Reform Jews in the early twentieth century. Some of these individuals cut all ties to Judaism, but many who became practitioners did not consider what they were doing as conversion to Christianity.[67] Freehof cited a firm CCAR precedent, a 1912 resolution affirming that accepting Christian Science constituted a definite rejection of Judaism, i.e., apostasy. However, characteristically, he wanted to erect a firm wall of religious separation while minimizing the emotional impact of that separation on families. Following Kaufmann Kohler, he provided a loophole for families and rabbis who may have needed one by stating that individuals who were "merely experimenting with a new medicine for their ailments" were not necessarily apostates.[68] He then devoted a full three pages to citing halakhic sources affirming that an apostate does not cease to be a Jew, but is considered, rather, a Jew who has sinned and whose Jewish marriages and divorces are still valid. While one does not observe mourning rituals for them, he cited the Shulḥan Arukh to assure his readers that an apostate could be buried in a Jewish cemetery and that "[t]here can be no objection to a rabbi officiating at the funeral since it is permissible for him to officiate even for pagan idolators,"[69] but all burial rituals and grave markings had to be exclusively Jewish.

Apostasy and Jewish Status in Freehof's Responsa

Freehof received numerous inquiries about the Jewish status of individuals raised as Christians, often in the context of a prospective marriage to a Jew. With no Reform decisions to rely on as precedents, his decisions reflected his own priorities of maintaining and strengthening Jewish family life within the context of affiliation with a Reform synagogue, and not blurring the boundary between Judaism and other religions. Therefore he consistently decided strictly with respect to adults who demonstrated by their own actions that they did not want to be part of the Jewish community, but leniently with respect to apostates' offspring who wanted to claim their Jewish status, though he also admonished correspondents to make sure, if marriage was the issue, that these latter would live as Jews.

A case in his first published volume is representative of his approach.[70] The daughter of a Jewish mother and gentile father had been baptized as a child in Germany for her protection; did she require a formal conversion before marrying a Jewish man? Freehof spent fully half of the responsum demonstrating that a child born to a Jewish mother and non-Jewish father was, indeed, a Jew. With respect to the Jewish status of the daughter, Freehof represented the law accurately. The consensus of the tradition is that Jewish status, acquired either through birth or through conversion, is irrevocable, and can neither be relinquished nor removed.[71] He was asked about this many times and always gave the same answer.[72]

In the second half of the responsum in *Reform Responsa* he insisted that no formal ritual was necessary for this young woman to be recognized as a Jew. He stated that Moses Isserles held that "by cautionary law (m'd'rabbanan) it may be that he *should* bathe and promise in the presence of three to be obedient to the law. . . . However, [the Magen Avraham] . . . is careful to remind us that this requirement is not strict law. As a matter of fact, most of the leading authorities would not require it at all."[73] As proof of this latter statement he cited a responsum of R. Solomon b. Simeon Duran regarding the returning Marranos, and one by Rabbenu Gershom about a penitent *kohen*, neither of whom required any formal ritual of return. He concluded, therefore, that the young woman needed no formal ritual. Though this would be "against public policy,"—i.e., it would appear that the rabbi was conducting a mixed marriage—nevertheless it was sufficient that "she *declares* [emphasis original] her willingness to be Jewish . . . She must be accepted as a Jewess without any ritual of conversion, and the marriage ceremony may be performed without any doubts."[74]

The return of an apostate Jew to Judaism was an act of personal *teshuvah*, but some Rishonim insisted that it also required public acknowledgement, some formality whereby the returnee could acknowledge his renewed acceptance of the responsibilities of Jewish life and the community could indicate that it was re-embracing him.[75] Moses Isserles codified this requirement in the Shulḥan Arukh: "An apostate Jew who repents does not need to immerse [according to the Torah]; only by rabbinic law he must immerse and accept upon himself *divre ḥaverut* [a formal indication of re-affiliation] before a court of three."[76] Modern authorities, however, have felt free to apply it more or less stringently, depending on the circumstances.[77] Given that Reform did not require immersion for any reason, Freehof's position here is no more lenient than that of Orthodox authorities. However, to justify his decision, he translated Isserles' statement rather freely, making it appear as an advisory opinion and not a requirement. His appeal to the responsum of Rabbenu Gershom as precedent was odd. The question was whether a *kohen* who had returned to Judaism should enjoy all of his priestly honors; R. Gershom answered in the affirmative, writing that the *kohen* "had returned in penitence; therefore he returns to his holiness."[78] But the responsum made no reference to the process by which the man had returned in penitence, so including it here proved nothing.

In this responsum Freehof relied heavily on a responsum of R. Solomon ben Simeon Duran of Algiers (1400–1467) on the Jewish status of the *conversos*. He included this text in his 1962 *Treasury of Responsa*, an anthology of sixty-three responsa he deemed especially interesting or significant, with original translations and introductions. (This volume was preceded by *The Responsa Literature*, his 1955 introduction to the vast corpus of responsa literature with chapters on its significant characteristics, the major respondents, examples of responsa as a source of social history, and more.)

Freehof called Duran's responsum a "'leading case' in Jewish Law," meaning it was a broadly recognized legal precedent.[79] Duran ruled on the basis of B. Sanhedrin 44b ("a Jew who has sinned remains a Jew") that the conversos arriving in Algiers who sought to return to Judaism did not require conversion. As long as the individual in question was born to a Jewish mother, he or she retained complete Jewish status. "Therefore children of these apostates (the marranos), as long as their mother is of Israel, even over many generations and even if it was a Gentile man who married this apostate Jewish woman, are, to the end of all generations, Jewish."[80] Thus they were not to be treated as prospective converts, but rather welcomed back into the people of Israel. They required no immersion, and the uncircumcised men were to recite for themselves the blessings that a father recites for his son's circumcision, not the blessing for the circumcision of a convert.

Freehof concluded, "This legally sound and nobly motivated responsum became the standard opinion as the status of the marranos in all the centuries that followed."[81] This observation was not completely accurate. As he himself later noted on a number of occasions, eventually many authorities became more reluctant to assume Jewish status for Marranos, because the more generations since the original forced conversion, the less certain was their Jewish ancestry. Some authorities also expressed reservations about the Jewish ancestry of Marranos whose families could have emigrated from Spain or Portugal when restrictions were lifted, but chose not to. Nevertheless, he invariably relied on Duran's responsum to affirm the Jewish status of virtually all returning apostates or offspring of apostates.

Freehof's use of Duran's responsum illuminates his own learning process. He had received his first inquiry on this topic in 1947, when a chaplain wanted to know if he could marry a Jewish soldier to a baptized woman whose Jewish mother had been baptized prior to marrying a Christian man. He answered in the affirmative, though CANRA's executive director, Chaplain Aryeh Lev, opined at the time that it bothered him that "'En Sof Ladovor [There is no end to the matter].' It would mean that every daughter in succession could be considered as Jewish irrespective of baptism in every generation." Freehof was then obviously unfamiliar with Duran's responsum, because he responded, "As far as I can discover, there is no responsum which discusses the question directly, as to how many generations would retain this Jewishness. . . . It is an interesting question, but I do not believe there is any discussion of it anywhere."[82] Perhaps there would be, he offered, in sixteenth- and seventeenth-century responsa about long-term Marranos. He answered similarly over the next decade,[83] grounding his response on laws presuming the Jewish status of "the child captured by idolators" and a gaonic responsum. Sometime in the late 1950s he discovered Duran's responsum and relied on it thenceforward.

Rabbis continued to send questions on the Jewishness of the children of apostates to Freehof. Often the inquiring rabbi had already reached a tentative decision, but wanted confirmation from Freehof, e.g.: "I interpret the candidate's status to be legally Jewish. Her mother left Judaism of her own volition, but I believe could always return to her former faith without a conversion. Therefore, at least K'din [according to the law], she would still be considered a Jewess. Since the child of a Jewish mother is a Jew, I believe that her daughter is also legally Jewish."[84] Freehof's answers remained consistent. First, a Jew who severed ties to the Jewish community and either attended worship at, or formally converted to, another religion, was an apostate—e.g., a Jew who quit the synagogue and joined the Unitarian church; or a Jew married to a Catholic, who attended a Unitarian church and gave nothing to Jewish causes.[85] Second, an apostate was still a Jew. "In spite of her conversion, the mother is Jewish. Judaism does not acknowledge baptism. How can it? As the Talmud says: 'Although sinning, still a Jew.'"[86] Third, although apostates were technically Jews, and were considered such in matters of marriage and divorce, they were not to be included or honored within the Jewish community. They should not be called to the Torah or allowed to light the Shabbat candles in the synagogue. A rabbi who refused to officiate at the marriage of two apostates was absolutely correct (though had he done so, the marriage would have been valid).[87] Fourth— and on this he received numerous queries—the child of a female apostate was still a Jew, as were all descendants in the female line. Jews accorded no validity to baptism.[88] The Duran responsum was his favorite proof text. "The classic answer on this question was by Solomon ben Simon Duran . . . who says definitely that they are Jews as long as their maternal parent is Jewish. They are Jews through all the generations, ad sof kol ha-doros [to the end of all generations]."[89]

However, one may discern a gradual shift in his attitude regarding the need for returning apostates to make formal re-affiliation. He first suggested in 1960 that Isserles' insistence on *divre ḥaverut* "could well be accepted by us as a cautionary action. We should ask the person involved to promise to maintain a Jewish home. This, at the most, is all that is necessary."[90] However, it was still only an option. In 1964 he wrote that if Duran did not require any formalities for ex-Catholics whose Jewish descent was certain, then certainly none were required for a young woman raised as a Unitarian by a Jewish-born mother.[91] The following year, however, asked about the daughter of an apostate mother and a Christian father, he cited Duran but then continued, "Of course, in later years, the rabbis grew somewhat stricter and would require at least a promise of Chaverus; and it would not harm if you asked this person to pledge his [*sic*] loyalty to Judaism, even though legally a ceremony of conversion is not required."[92] That same year he was asked about a man who had formally registered as a Christian in pre-war Vienna in order to survive. Most of the man's family had been killed, the rabbi wrote, and "this forsaking of his identity and faith have preyed on his conscience. He desires to be formally readmitted to Judaism. He came in from New York especially for such a ceremony . . . [and] I performed it before the open Ark in our Chapel." The rabbi wanted to know if Jewish law required anything else in such a situation and whether there was any "special ceremony" to be performed. Freehof referred him to his 1960 CCAR responsum and merely added, "The man is a Jew and no ceremony is *required*, but if he desires some impressive ceremony, there is certainly no objection to it."[93]

Then in 1966 he was asked about a prospective convert whose maternal grandmother was Jewish but whose mother was raised, and in turn raised her, as a Catholic. On this occasion, though he cited Duran to confirm the woman's Jewish status, he added: "However there is also a rule that if a Jew apostatizes and then returns, he should make a promise of Chaverus, that is to say, loyalty to Judaism. In this spirit, I would suggest that you give her instruction; explain to her that this is not to convert her, but simply to confirm her resolution. Then have her state her desire to be loyal to Judaism."[94] The following year, again after referencing Duran, he advised a questioner that "when a person has been raised as a Christian . . . he or she must promise Chaverus; in other words, loyalty, henceforth to Judaism." He did not, however, mean that a formal ceremony was required. The young woman in question was apparently under some emotional strain relating to her religious identity and Freehof did not think asking her to make a formal declaration was the best way to "bring her into Jewish life." He advised his correspondent to tell her that she did not need to convert but only to learn about Judaism, and to let her wait to decide whether to join a synagogue. "If she will marry a Jewish boy she will establish a Jewish home and that will be a good time for her husband and her to join the congregation. She needs to do nothing other than learn a little about Judaism."[95] Marriage to a Jewish man, followed, presumably, by keeping a Jewish home and joining a synagogue, was an equally valid way to demonstrate her loyalty. Here, as in his decisions regarding marriage and conversion, the ultimate proof of Jewishness was the creation of a Jewish home.

Gradually the recommendation of *haverut* came to be a regular element of his answers regarding returning apostates. In a 1969 published responsum he wrote that while not absolutely a requirement, "it was generally customary to let them go through some ritual, or at least to promise '*chaverus*'; that is to say, to be loyal to Judaism. . . . Therefore in the case of this young lady . . . we would ask her to study and declare in some way her desire to be loyal to the Jewish faith."[96] Though he continued to cite Duran to affirm the Jewishness of children of apostates, he also emphasized the need for something that would indicate the individual's intention and commitment. Sometimes he cautioned his correspondent that later rabbis, less certain of the descent or the motivation of returning conversos, advised *haverut*; on other occasions he cited Isserles. ". . . [T]ell the young woman that she is Jewish by birth, but since she has lived as a Christian we ask her now (perhaps in the presence of three people) to promise to live as a Jewess and maintain a Jewish household."[97] As with all topics on which he received numerous questions, as time went on his responses became more and more similar, as he settled on language he liked. As his responses became semi-formulaic, the later ones also tended to be less complete than the earlier ones. Sometimes his letter to the correspondent was very brief but he included with it a fuller answer on the same topic that had been written for someone else.

Finally, however, an unusual question led him to a significant reconsideration of Duran's responsum. The question was whether any special procedure was required for a Jew who had become a nun and now wanted not only to return to Judaism but to teach in a Jewish school. For the first time Freehof reflected on the historical circumstances that shaped the halakhah on returning apostates, noting that "it would seem that in those countries where there was comparatively little experience with mass conversion and, therefore, with mass reconversion, the rabbis tended to be stricter than in those countries where it was important to encourage the great mass of ex-Jews to return to the parental faith."[98] Therefore, he commented, Isserles took a stricter view than Duran or Karo. But he noted that none of the Spanish cases addressed specifically the reconversion of former priests, monks, or nuns, or anyone who wanted to become a teacher, or a *kohen* who wanted to exercise his special sanctity. Rabbenu Gershom had addressed this last, however, and declared it permissible, which Freehof interpreted to mean that there was no bar to this former nun becoming a teacher. Nevertheless, he refrained from his accustomed leniency. The old responsa, he explained, reflected the rabbis' compassion for persecuted Jews. But this woman chose to become a nun, so she must have acted out of deep conviction. Was she now demonstrating equally deep conviction or instability? Caution was necessary. "This young lady is a person who has been deeply impressed with ritual procedures, and so it might be well therefore in her case to follow the counsel of Isserles, who suggests some ritual to impress the reconvert. . . . [I]n the presence of three, she should declare *divre chaverus*. She should make a statement under rather solemn circumstances that she will devote her heart and mind to the faith of her fathers." Then, he ruled, we may "follow the mood" of Rabbenu Gershom and allow her to take on the "sacred and priestly function of Jewish instruction."[99] (Again, his reliance on this responsum appears ill-founded. In Rabbenu Gershom's case the returning apostate had special status as a Jew, not as a Christian; and his status was inherited, not chosen as a religious career. Freehof could only make it applicable by conflating priest and teacher in a most un-traditional sense.)

Freehof's Attitude toward Apostates

Questions concerning apostates were usually family matters, involving relationships between Jews and their relatives who had adopted another faith. Freehof generally tried to decide leniently to accommodate the emotions of the Jewish relatives. He found halakhic authorities permitting the recitation of Kaddish for an apostate relative, while making clear that it was discouraged or prohibited by most authorities. A woman who converted to Catholicism in a concentration camp could be buried, without Catholic ritual or symbols, with her parents in a Jewish cemetery. A rabbi could officiate at an unveiling for the grave of a Jewish apostate in a Christian cemetery because she had been buried as a Christian and her parents needed this ceremony, which had no legal standing in any case. The son of an apostate woman and a Christian father should be ritually circumcised because he was a Jew. While a practicing Christian Scientist should not be allowed to serve on the Sisterhood board, Freehof advised that the woman could retain her membership in the congregation because "any sort of sinner has the right to be a member of the congregation."[100] This last is surprising, coming from a man who fought a losing battle for years against allowing gentiles to be synagogue members, but as he showed in *RJP*, he was considerate of family ties. He probably reasoned that a Jewish woman in a small Midwestern city who was active in the temple Sisterhood but also a practicing Christian Scientist was very likely from a family rooted there, socially well integrated into the tight-knit Jewish community and probably related to other Jewish families. The young rabbi would have had a major controversy on his hands had he tried to expel her. By the 1950s, when Freehof received this inquiry, the popularity of Christian Science among Jews was clearly on the wane; his letter gives no indication of concern that her presence might influence others. As he later wrote, "If, of course, apostasy would increase greatly, . . . then the apostate would be a constant danger to us and our attitude might then be justifiably sterner. Unless that occurs, then . . . we do not reject [the harmless apostates] altogether. The door is always open for their return."[101]

Apostates who proselytized Jews, however, made him very angry. An Alabama rabbi turned to him when some of his congregants disagreed with his decision to refuse to sell ritual objects from the temple gift shop to an apostate who was actively proselytizing. Freehof did not mince words in his response. While he recognized that the congregants in question might fear a public backlash, "in this case . . . we must take a stand and risk some unfavorable publicity. . . ."

> . . . [W]hen a man openly abandons our faith for another and, indeed, actively tries to persuade fellow Jews to leave the Jewish faith, he is an active enemy and belongs to that long and miserable list of apostate Jews (meshumodim) who have persecuted our people through the ages.
>
> Dear colleague, you are absolutely right in your action. Anyone who knows the melancholy history of the hurt that such apostates have done our people in the past, would without hesitation act in the same way.[102]

This gut-level abhorrence of apostates, virtually universal among Jews until recently, is reflected also in his answer concerning a *brit milah* at which a rabbi recited the ritual while the physician, an apostate Jew active in his new church, performed the circumcision. Freehof scrupulously noted the split among earlier authorities over whether this was a valid *milah*, and then concluded that "it is the sign of the Jewish covenant, and it is certainly poor taste to use as circumcisor one who has repudiated Judaism consciously and openly. If, as the questioner indicates, he *flaunts* his apostacy [*sic*], then he is close to being a Mumar l'hachis [one who apostasizes from conviction] whom none of the authorities would permit to circumcise." After the fact, however, he advised against questioning the validity of the ritual.[103]

Significantly, he chose to publish his response to a former HUC student who asked him, "In these days of ecumenical mood, religious groups are rethinking their attitude toward each other. Should we not, therefore, also rethink our attitude to those Jews who have abandoned Judaism for Christianity?" In response, Freehof explained the halakhic difference between "hostile" or "provocative apostates" (*mumar lehakh'is*), i.e., those who act from conviction or then take action against Jews and Judaism, and "non-destructive" or "for their own benefit" apostates (*mumar lete'avon*), i.e., those who are motivated by personal gain and do not then become persecutors of Judaism. Most of the apostates today in the United States, he continued, fall into the latter category: They have converted for marriage or to further their careers or social standing. "Of course, we cannot have any respect for them because they have abandoned our embattled Jewish community for the sake of their own ease or wishes. . . . Yet although we do not respect him, it is nevertheless clear from the general mood of Jewish law that we do not cast him off. . . . He still has bonds with Jewish family life, according to Jewish law. . . . Besides, it well may be that he or his children may return to Judaism."[104] In other words, he warned his questioner, the traditional boundaries are quite proper and we should not lower them any further than we already do by reading the traditional sources charitably.

Freehof adhered to the traditional view that one could not be simultaneously a practicing Christian and a member in good standing of the Jewish community because belief in the Trinity constituted what the rabbis termed *shituf*, "adding" to the one God other entities as objects of worship. This did not suffice, however, when considering Jews who attended Unitarian churches. The issue was not merely unitarian as opposed to trinitarian theology, he told the minister of a local Unitarian church who inquired about a Jewish family. If it were, there would be no objection to Jews becoming Muslims. But "in Judaism it is not merely the theology, it is also the fellowship." Being a Jew meant being part of the Jewish community and the Jewish people. Even if no *shituf* was involved, a Jew who joined another religious community and also cut himself off from the Jewish community was an apostate. Lest he sound too harsh, however, Freehof made allowance, as he had with Christian Science, for the dabblers. "Of course, if . . . his purpose in joining is merely to aid a good group of people in their work, and if he does not mean by that to leave either Jewish faith or Jewish fellowship, there cannot be too much objection to that."[105]

Conclusion

Freehof's views on conversion and Jewish status followed from his concern with mixed marriage and reflected his desire to maintain a strong community of committed, synagogue-affiliated, Jewish families. Though he was stringent in insisting that converts sever all ties to their former religion, he also insisted that preparation for conversion not be an obstacle course, and that the level of Jewish knowledge and practice demanded of the prospective convert should not be set higher than what was expected of the average Reform congregant. If there were going to be children who could be raised as Jews, the right thing to do was to support the creation of a Jewish home, rather than run the risk of losing a family to the Jewish community. Rabbis should try to persuade the gentile partner to convert to Judaism before the marriage, or at least before any children were born. The parents' willingness to convert the children to Judaism was the last best hope, but that meant a commitment to raising and educating them as Jews. The conversion guidelines for children that he developed for the CCAR, however, were often difficult to apply in practice, since in place of the rituals of *milah* and *tevilah* they substituted the vague criterion of a Jewish upbringing, which presumed a long-term synagogue affiliation that was not the reality of many families' lives. His answers to questions concerning the Jewishness of the children of gentile mothers, therefore, were highly situational and sometimes inconsistent, illustrating the difficulty in establishing a definitive Reform practice in this area. However, he consistently recognized the Jewish status of returning apostates and their children, though he came gradually to advocate some equivalent of the halakhic requirement for a formal declaration.

6

SHABBAT AND KASHRUT

Aḥad Ha'am famously observed, "More than Israel has kept the Sabbath, the Sabbath has kept Israel." Nothing so profoundly separated Jews from the peoples among whom they lived as a distinctive calendar—and a distinctive diet. But emancipation brought Jews into social contexts where Saturday was a weekday. Living and working as full and equal members of society while remaining completely Sabbath observant required a level of commitment that increasingly secularized laypeople generally lacked. Meanwhile, Reform rabbis increasingly questioned the theological premises upon which rested the mass of rabbinic law concerning Sabbath observance. Already in 1846 the Breslau rabbinical conference recognized the need among contemporary Jews to restore the Sabbath to its honored place. It criticized the overly restrictive rabbinic laws as impediments to real observance of the day and eliminated them, and called for efforts to make services more "solemn" and "to further the sanctity of the Sabbath in the homes."[1] This declaration essentially defined the parameters of all subsequent Reform discussion about Shabbat: The traditional laws were too restrictive, but in their place the rabbis could offer only vague platitudes about bringing people back to a recognition of the sanctity of the day at home, and the need for inspiring worship in the synagogue.

Shabbat and Kashrut in American Reform Judaism

In 1840s Germany, Samuel Holdheim proposed moving the Jewish day of rest to Sunday, arguing that the concept of rest was more important than adherence to a particular day; but his Berlin congregation was the only European one to take the radical step of worshipping on Sunday instead of Saturday. The 1869 Leipzig Synod called for a critical study of marriage, Sabbath, and dietary laws in order to determine to what extent they should still be observed. Two years later the Augsburg Synod voted to allow riding to synagogue, if distance or age made walking impossible, and for performing charitable, educational, or recreational activities if necessary.[2] Early Reform congregations in the United States tried to enforce Shabbat observance, but the combination of economic pressure and lack of conviction proved irresistible. Faced with Saturday morning services where the congregation consisted of women and children and a few old men, American Reformers responded by introducing both the late Friday evening service and the Sunday morning service. Kaufmann Kohler introduced the latter at Sinai Congregation in 1874 as a weekday service held in addition to the regular Saturday morning service; his successor, Emil G. Hirsch, made Sinai the only American synagogue to eliminate the Saturday service in favor of a Sunday service. Even the radical Hirsch, however, did not go so far as to declare Sunday the Sabbath.[3]

Kohler turned against the Sunday service in the 1890s. "It may crowd temples to overflowing," he declared, "but . . . [i]t destroys or undermines the Sabbath, [and] fails to build up a Judaism loyal to its ancient institutions."[4] Nevertheless, a Sunday morning service featuring a lengthy sermon and an abbreviated weekday liturgy was a practice that many Reform congregations adopted and maintained well into the twentieth century, including Rodef Shalom throughout Freehof's tenure. The practice guaranteed a large weekly attendance, but it did not address the question of what to do about the fact that most modern Jews largely ignored Shabbat.

Some Reform rabbis wrote Shabbat manuals or held classes to teach people how to observe Shabbat at home,[5] but by 1902 the members of the CCAR were in a quandary concerning the virtual disappearance of the Sabbath from the lives of their congregants, and they commissioned two papers for consideration. In the first, Jacob Voorsanger starkly confronted the problem in a lucid presentation that identified three reasons—spiritual, economic, and cultural—why Reform Jews ignored Judaism's central holy day: Neither the rabbis nor the laity believed any longer that the Sabbath was divinely ordained; the six-day work week and the blue laws compelled Jews to work on Saturdays; and American Jews had adopted the prevailing equation of rest with leisure, and no longer found meaning in traditional Sabbath rest.[6] Voorsanger opposed the Sunday Sabbath, however, lest Reform become a sectarian movement. He wanted the CCAR to take counsel and issue a firm statement of what constituted appropriate Sabbath observance in a Reform context.

In contrast, Hyman Enelow argued for a Sunday Sabbath. He asserted that modern biblical scholarship had proven that the fundamental purpose of the Sabbath was not rest, but the worship of God. All the biblical laws mandating rest were merely means to that end; rabbinic Judaism had, unfortunately, confused ends with means. Since worship and not rest was the true purpose of the Sabbath, it could and should rightly be celebrated on whatever day people were free from work, which in the modern world, where Christianity prevailed, was Sunday.[7]

While the CCAR did reject Enelow and voted to endorse the "historic [i.e., Saturday] Sabbath," much fruitless debate and several annual committee reports ultimately produced only a toothless statement of pious sentiments about what that meant. The rabbis agreed to encourage Jews to revive home observances such as candle lighting, Kiddush, blessing the children, and gathering for a family meal; to organize Sabbath Observance Leagues; to publish helpful literature; to appeal to Jewish businessmen at least to allow observant employees, if not themselves, to keep the Sabbath; to persuade congregational leaders and religious school teachers to observe the Sabbath; to ask parents to avoid private lessons for their children on Saturdays and Jewish private schools not to hold Saturday classes; to encourage guests at summer resorts to observe more Sabbath rituals; and to attempt to obtain legal exemptions from Sunday business restrictions for Sabbath-observant Jews.

The committee that produced these tepid recommendations admitted frankly that they had been unable to decide what constituted Sabbath observance in a Reform context.[8] They still faced the formidable obstacles Voorsanger had identified. He had insisted that the people needed authoritative guidance on practice and not a mere restatement of Judaism's ethical teachings, and he had wanted the rabbis to "define, if possible, the spiritual authority that guides and directs the religious practice of our people."[9] Authoritative guidance with respect to praxis, however, was precisely what a large segment of the CCAR was philosophically opposed to providing.

Max Heller's 1914 article calling for authoritative guidance in Reform praxis (see Chapter 2) also made reference to the Sabbath conundrum, observing unhappily that "it is a fact that Reform means a complete license to use the Sabbath according to one's whim or convenience."[10] He, too, wanted authoritative decisions from the CCAR. Was it permitted to hold formal classes in "religion" or any other subject on the Sabbath? Could one spend Saturday afternoon preparing for a charitable event that night, rehearse the synagogue choir after services, go on a picnic, attend a matinee at the theatre? He himself ventured to set forth three fundamental principles of Reform Sabbath observance. First, a good deed involving a great deal of toil should not be done on the Sabbath if it could be done at another time. Second, traditional practices which had become meaningless could be dropped or changed. Third, Reform Jews should value Friday night as family time and should not schedule meetings or attend entertainment then.

Neither rabbinic nor lay Reform bodies were interested in tackling this vexing question, however. Over the next several decades discussion of Sabbath observance in movement-wide settings was limited to liturgical matters as part of the trend to "reintroduce . . . traditional symbols, ceremonies, and customs" to the Friday evening service.[11]

While Reformers lauded the Sabbath as one of the crowning glories of Jewish religiosity—its message of rest from toil conveying a central value of ethical monotheism—from the 1880s on they rejected the dietary laws as outmoded ritualism or as a now superseded hygienic practice. Indeed, it was not until the turn of the twenty-first century that American Reform Jews began to reconsider kashrut. However, many American Jews, including Reform Jews, avoided pork for what were, in the 1800s, genuine hygienic reasons, and later, for some combination of hygienic considerations and sentiment.[12]

Freehof's Position and Postwar Questions

In his seminal 1941 paper Freehof argued that one of the reasons Reform Judaism could not and should not try to produce a code of practice was the difficulty of addressing Shabbat and kashrut.

> What could we say about [the dietary laws]? Should we describe the actual practice as it has developed among us or

should we modify it? Should we say formally that the mixture of meat and milk dishes is no longer to be prohibited, that meat need not be slaughtered by a *schochet* [ritual slaughterer], that we should have no bread in the house during Passover but that we need not go through the ceremony of searching for *hometz* [leaven]? And what about the Sabbath laws, the laws of work and rest?...Whatever we say on these matters in any type of a code of practice will, first of all, bitterly offend the Orthodox who will consider that we are legalizing our negligence and then will offend our own conscience because we will be giving to customs the status of law and, indeed, what is more, virtually the status of the law of God.[13]

We have seen that Freehof was never afraid to defend Reform deviations from Orthodoxy when he believed that principles were involved. His concern for Orthodox opinion here reflected his reluctance to defend Reform practices arising from indifference and convenience rather than principle. Surely he had in mind his teacher Kohler's 1885 admonition to his fellow Reformers in Pittsburgh, that they had to create a coherent statement of principles to show that their abandonment of traditional observance was rooted in principle, in contrast to the many Jews who were abandoning Shabbat and kashrut out of indifference.[14] Reform as yet had no coherent principles with regard to either the Sabbath or the dietary laws, and therefore could not go public on them. For that reason neither volume of *RJP* addressed these two issues. As he explained there:

> Only those traditional laws and customs are given which are connected with actual prevalent Reform practice. Thus, those branches which have left very little mark upon present-day life of the Reform Jew are not dealt with. To put it bluntly, there is, unfortunately, as little observance of the dietary laws among Reform Jews as there is among millions of other modern Jews and also as little observance of the traditional laws of Sabbath rest. Hence, these branches of Orthodox law are not dealt with.[15]

Prior to 1950 the Responsa Committee reported only one question on Shabbat observance in a Reform context, whether a non-Jewish contractor building a synagogue could work on Saturday. In the postwar era, however, the question flared up, prompting Responsa Committee chairman Israel Bettan to write a comprehensive statement proposing principles of Reform Shabbat observance that he urged the CCAR to adopt. Some rabbis, he wrote, were "irritated by the widely accepted [Shabbat] restrictions" that were preventing them from "improv[ing] temple attendance or expand[ing] its recreational program." For example, could a synagogue sponsor a teen dance on Friday night after services, rather than lose its teens to the high school dances on that night? Could a synagogue baseball team practice on Saturday afternoon? Others found Shabbat observance too constricting with respect to their participation in the larger community: Could a rabbi take part in "public ceremonies" on a Saturday when invitations were extended to "representatives of the three faiths?" Others wanted to know what sorts of synagogue committee meetings could take place on Shabbat.[16] The questions clearly reflect the changed circumstances of postwar Jewish life.

In his response Bettan tried to pick up where Voorsanger had left off half a century earlier, criticizing the CCAR for "willfully turn[ing] away from the opportunity that was ours to bring the institution of the Sabbath under the searching light of liberal thought." It was time to recognize that the thirty-nine categories of forbidden work (*melakhot*) did not reflect the contemporary situation, and to reject the rabbis' "countless precautionary regulations . . . in the interest of a saner observance of the Sabbath." Implicitly rejecting the Sunday Sabbath argument, he reaffirmed that the Sabbath was the distinctive Jewish day of rest, and that its central purpose was "to let go of the toil which occupied our energies during the week"; but in the modern era, he asserted, Sabbath observance should not be restrictive. "In an age like ours, when we have come to view sports and games of all sorts as proper forms of relaxation on rest days, to hark back to the puritanical rigors of the Rabbinic Sabbath is to call in question the relevancy of religion to modern life." Though the responsum performed a great service for the movement by articulating for the first time what most serious Reform Jews had instinctively practiced, the CCAR still did not take up the challenge of providing guidelines until 1972, when it published its *Shabbat Manual*.[17] (See below and Chapter 9.)

Between 1952 and 1972, and even after, Freehof answered numerous questions on Shabbat observance. His decisions generally accorded with Bettan's conclusion, though he never referred to his responsum as a precedent. This was not for lack of respect for Bettan; the two men had been friends and colleagues since their student years. But the CCAR had expressly decided that a committee responsum was not an authoritative precedent. Consistent with what he had written in 1941, Freehof had no authority to declare what the Sabbath should be in a Reform context, but could only offer his own informed opinion as to whether popular practice was in keeping with precedents found in the tradition. More importantly, in expressly advocating a new basis for Shabbat observance in place of the traditional thirty-nine *melakhot*, Bettan went beyond what Freehof was willing to do. In 1946 he had agreed that *eventually* Reform Jews would evolve a new set of norms of ritual observance that could be codified, but he insisted that it was far too soon to begin even to think about what such a codification might include. Bettan's responsum took a significant step in that direction. Freehof preferred not to theorize, but to let the people's minhag evolve. Accordingly, he limited himself to answering questions as he received them, addressing himself specifically to the issue at hand.

In adhering to his principles, however, he faced another problem. His concept of minhag meant that Jewish practice was ultimately what evolved out of the people's daily lives in their current social context— but Reform Jews were ignoring the Sabbath completely, a reality that he could not possibly countenance. A unique dynamic therefore underlies most of his Shabbat responsa: He treated the day as if it were an endangered species in need of preservation.

> Reform Judaism never told anyone to violate any Sabbath law. However, it faces the fact that Sabbath laws in the western world are largely neglected and tries to rescue the *spirit* of the Sabbath as much as is possible. . . . The best that we can do in this vague situation (whose vagueness we did not create but life created) is to judge by the feeling of the particular community. . . . We respect whatever Sabbath observing sentiment is present, provided it is genuine, as far as we can. . . .
> There is a principle in Jewish law which says, "Every-

thing is according to the place and the time." Of course, they did not mean it to apply to whether the Sabbath is to be observed and how much, but we apply it in this realistic circumstance in this way.[18]

Freehof saw modern life inexorably destroying the traditional Sabbath of the sort he had lived growing up. All rabbinic attempts to resist this natural historical process by fiat could only be futile and unrealistic gestures. His task, therefore, was to preserve and nurture whatever "spirit of the Sabbath" remained—as long as it was "genuine." (That caveat provided him with a large loophole through which to dismiss what he regarded as hypocritical selective insistence on traditional practices.) Deciding just what constituted the "spirit of the Sabbath," however, required him to deploy additional criteria.

Shabbat Observance in the Synagogue: Prohibited and Permitted

Freehof's respect for popular minhag did not preclude his taking a strong stance even in the absence of Reform precedent. He consistently opposed anything involving monetary transactions on the Sabbath. A responsum he published on whether the Sisterhood could operate its gift shop on Shabbat afforded him an opportunity to air his views about Reform Sabbath observance. He restated the original question in these words:

> The congregational Gift Corner provides books and Prayerbooks, candles and candlesticks, Chanukah menorahs; in other words, it serves a religious purpose. Should this fact not justify keeping the Gift Corner open on Friday night? It is only on Friday night that large numbers of people coming for the Sabbath service can conveniently make use of the Gift Corner.[19]

He replied that while the halakhah prohibited any such activity, Reform standards were still uncertain, because social reality was causing most Jews to ignore the Sabbath. Reform had rejected the Conservative approach of vainly trying to force people to return to Sabbath observance, and was instead trying to face reality. "Generally we feel that those observances that are gone cannot now easily be restored. The effort to restore them would require an overemphasis on ritual matters. However, what we can preserve, and without too much overemphasis restore as a natural mood of the people, that we should endeavor to do." This meant that synagogues needed to be held to a higher standard than individuals. Gently heading off a possible accusation of hypocrisy, he pointed out that "people recognize that certain types of celebrations or observances which they follow elsewhere are not appropriate in the temple."

Having established the parameters of the issue, he surveyed the halakhic sources to show that there was no precedent that might be stretched to justify opening the Gift Corner on Shabbat. While the law allowed the auctioning off of *aliyot* during the service on the grounds that it was communal business, and it allowed making money calculations on the Sabbath for the purpose of a mitzvah, it never allowed actual monetary transactions. While the Gift Corner raised money for the synagogue and was clearly in business for the benefit of the community, conducting actual monetary transactions would be "violative of the mood of the Sabbath, especially in the synagogue." Acknowledging that the question was doubtless a divisive one in the congregation, and that in the absence of definitive Reform guidance the solution depended on "the mood of the particular congregations involved," he suggested a compromise that would avoid handling money on the Sabbath, or even record keeping: Keep the Gift Corner open, but manage it differently than on weekdays. Let people come and select what they want and make arrangements for payment at another time, just as they do in department stores. It was unlikely, he commented, that business would be so extensive or complex that the women would be unable to keep everything in their heads. He concluded by emphasizing the Jewish educational benefit of drawing such a distinction between weekday and Sabbath procedures: "This distinction between the Gift Corner's procedure on the Sabbath and on weekdays would rather tend to strengthen the consciousness of the Sabbath in the lives of our people. It would serve to remind them of the Sabbath traditions and perhaps influence them to do less purchasing in general on the Sabbath, whenever such self-restraint is practical."

In 1962, a rabbi who clearly wanted help ending the planned event asked about a Sisterhood rummage sale on a Saturday. Freehof furnished him with as much ammunition as he could muster. He pointed out that Jewish tradition considered it a sin and then added that for a synagogue to do it was a "a violation of the Sabbath b'farhessya, in public, and to do that in behalf of a congregation is also very ugly (m'shum miyuss)." While he could only offer his own feelings in the absence of any liberal halakhah, he emphasized that his feelings were those of "an experienced rabbi of a large, historic congregation. It is my conviction that it should not be done; that it is especially improper for a synagogue to do it; and worse that it is done in public."[20]

Two years later he objected to a congregational fundraising activity on a Sabbath. The plan was to sell tickets in advance for a Saturday afternoon children's show with an emcee, clowns, and cartoon films. The rabbi wanted to know 1) was it proper for the synagogue to be doing this on the Sabbath? 2) could tickets be sold at the door? 3) could they sell refreshments? 4) could they sell refreshments if the selling was not handled by congregants? Freehof responded that there was no objection to entertainment on the Sabbath, but that any actually selling, regardless of who was doing it, was "contrary to Jewish law and contrary to the spirit of modern Judaism."[21]

In that same year a rabbi wrote him to say that while his board had backed him—barely—in blocking a Sisterhood proposal to open the gift shop on Friday nights, both he and his congregants wanted to know what the Reform approach to Sabbath observance actually was, and if it was stated anywhere.[22] In response, Freehof opined that perhaps it was time for the CCAR to discuss the issue again. "There is no sense in insisting upon observances which our people will not follow, but there may be good sense in urging them about certain observances of the Sabbath which they may be persuaded to follow."[23]

Weddings were another activity he considered an unacceptable violation of the Sabbath. In *RJP* he stated that "Weddings are not conducted on the Sabbath or on the main days of holidays," cited the Mishneh Torah and the Shulḥan Arukh as proof, and then went on to explain that while R. Moses Isserles permitted it in case of emergency, he intended only rare exceptions such as the famous case when he married the orphan girl whose Friday afternoon wedding was delayed due to quarreling over the dowry.[24]

He received his first question about marriage on the Sabbath in 1950, when one CCAR member wrote to complain that a colleague had officiated at 4:00 on a Saturday afternoon that was also the eve of Passover, angering many people in the community. The officiant argued that "there is no prohibition in Reform Judaism against writing on the Sabbath, and that a wedding ceremony is essentially a religious act which should not be prohibited on a holy day." In reply Freehof alluded to Isserles' exception, but stated categorically that "no Orthodox or Conservative rabbi would do it, and no Reform rabbi would. . . . We often feel that what our people *do cherish* we should help them cherish. As far as I am concerned and I am sure the overwhelming number of our colleagues, I would never officiate at a wedding on the Sabbath."[25]

Always concerned for the good name and image of Reform Judaism in the community, he used that as another argument against officiation on Shabbat in a published responsum about a Saturday night wedding scheduled to take place before full dark. Such things happened "every now and then" with regard to summer weddings, he observed, when a rabbi realizes that he consulted his Jewish calendar to set the time for the ceremony but forgot to add an hour for daylight saving time. Weddings on Shabbat were definitely forbidden. Rabbenu Tam had approved it after the fact in an exceptional situation, and Isserles had relied on him to do it on one very unusual occasion, but these were exceptional. One could say now that with all the preparations made, officiating before it was quite dark could fall under Rabbenu Tam's exception, and the "the sin of officiating would not be so very great." Doing so, however, would "create antagonism, particularly from Orthodox rabbis." The wiser course, for the sake of *mar'it ayin* ("as the eye sees," meaning performing a permitted act in such a way that it could lead unwitting witnesses to conclude that something forbidden was actually permitted) was to avoid it. When the wedding was scheduled before full dark, "it would be wise to delay as long as possible."[26]

As popular pressure mounted on Reform rabbis to officiate at Saturday night weddings prior to sundown, however, Freehof grew worried. There was a significant difference between occasionally fudging the time a bit and regularly holding weddings in broad daylight. In 1969 he told a colleague, "I advised Bernstein that if it is not quite dark, it is not too serious, but I will say to you that if we openly hold Saturday weddings, it would not only shock the Orthodox . . . , but even more importantly, would speed the fading of the Sabbath from our lives, which would be a tragedy."[27]

Two years later CCAR Executive Vice-President Rabbi Joseph B. Glaser turned to Freehof after he received a complaint from a Conservative rabbi about a local Reform rabbi who agreed to officiate at the home of Conservative congregants at 2:00 on a Saturday afternoon.[28] While Glaser had assured the other rabbi that it was not the policy of the CCAR to officiate at weddings on the Sabbath, in fact, there was no policy, and he wanted Freehof's advice as to whether he should tell the Reform rabbi in question not to go ahead with the wedding. All Freehof could recommend was to bring the complaint and the responsum to his attention, because the CCAR had no authority to discipline him. Marrying a couple on the Sabbath was not, strictly speaking, against halakhah "but it certainly is against Jewish tradition and Jewish feeling.... Especially we Reformers who are not bound by Halacha should pay close attention to the feelings of our fellow Jews."[29]

In 1963 Freehof allowed that in those few accidental cases of not-quite-dark one might use Rabbenu Tam's exception as a fig leaf. By 1976, however, it was clear that many Reform rabbis had no compunctions about officiating on the Sabbath. Some CCAR members wanted the convention that year to adopt a resolution specifically condemning rabbinic officiation at marriages on the Sabbath and festivals or with non-Jewish clergy (see Chapter 10). The rabbis voted to refer the question to the Responsa Committee, to Freehof's dismay. Any responsum he wrote would have to include the permissive exceptions of Rabbenu Tam and Moses Isserles, with "harmful" results, as he explained: "While the permission was meant only for real emergencies, any officiant wanting to marry a couple on Saturday would find it easy to persuade himself that it was an emergency. In other words, the law as it actually exists could well lead to great abuse if it were well known." His reluctance, he noted, was rooted in the Talmudic principle not to publish easily abused permissions.[30] He preferred that the CCAR take another tack. "If the Conference, as its resolution indicates, means to fight against marriages on the Sabbath and co-officiating with Gentile ministers, it cannot well fight the battle on *halachic* grounds. It must be fought on social, psychological, and communal grounds."[31]

Freehof had already published two references to Moses Isserles' opinion and one to Rabbenu Tam's. Both of those, however, represented only his personal opinion and, after all, were in books that rabbis had to buy (and *RRR* was already out of print in 1976). Decisions of the Responsa Committee were not binding, but they did at least carry the imprimatur of a CCAR committee, and they were distributed to every CCAR member, in the *Yearbook*. He did not want to be the agent of promoting behavior in the CCAR which he opposed. Yet his resistance in this case also meant that the Responsa Committee would not be fulfilling its mandate of providing guidance to those rabbis who requested it. This might have been an opportunity for Freehof to use the Responsa Committee as his bully pulpit in the way that Kohler and Lauterbach had—but he had a different vision.

Preserving the "Spirit" of Shabbat

The questions Bettan addressed in 1952 were the beginning of a trend. Rabbis hoped to draw congregants to the temple on the Sabbath by offering various social and leisure activities. In deciding what was or was not appropriate for the synagogue, Bettan and Freehof appealed to the "spirit" or "mood" of Shabbat. This was not a uniquely Reform argument. The Conservative *Guide to Jewish Religious Practice* shows the difficulty in defining activities consonant with the spirit of Shabbat even "where no other violation of the Sabbath is involved."

> In the case of social amusements that may take place at home or in the synagogue, we can only suggest the following as a guide: "The Sabbath is a sacred day and there are certain kinds of enjoyment which by their very nature, are out of harmony with its inherent holiness. Participation in them on the Sabbath is like a sudden intrusion of a shrill street organ on a beautiful melody sung by a lovely voice. It is difficult, almost impossible, to lay down a definite rule on this point. . . . The matter must be left to the individual conscience . . . " As an illustration, we would suggest that playing poker on the Sab-

bath, even without money, would be considered unseemly; playing chess would not. Attending a poetry reading would be permissible; attending a wrestling match would not.[32]

Nevertheless, with no halakhic criteria on which to rely, Freehof could only fall back on his sense of the "spirit" of Shabbat to decide what activities were or were not appropriate in the synagogue. (Tellingly, he never received a single question asking what individual Reform Jews should or should not do at home as part of their own Shabbat observance.)

Propriety and taste were the operative principles on which he based his opposition to temple New Year's parties in years when December 31st fell out on a Friday. In 1965 a questioner asked whether the temple should sponsor a New Year's dance after the Friday evening service, and whether it would be improper for the people to attend the service dressed for the dance. Freehof replied that it would be improper for any Jewish organization and doubly so for the temple. He urged the rabbi to stand firm. "I am sure that many people will resent it, and the status of the Temple will be hurt. . . . I think a large number of the congregation will respect you all the more if you simply omit the dance this year."[33] To a similar inquiry a decade later he replied that "a large party with . . . the traditional hilarity of New Year's Eve, would certainly be contrary to the spirit of Jewish life and of our Jewish religion and would certainly create shock all through the community. What individuals may do . . . is *their* affair, but for two congregational organizations to give a wild New Year's Eve party on a Sabbath should, in my opinion, be strongly resisted."[34]

Card playing was also unacceptable. In 1966 a rabbi asked him if bridge lessons could be offered in the temple building and sports in the temple parking lot on the Sabbath. He replied that card playing was "objectionable." The tradition saw it as "unworthy," even if no gambling was involved. "The Sabbath is meant to be a day of spiritual joy, and if there is any study to be done on it, it should be some form of study of Torah. To use up time which might be devoted to sacred study and apply it to the study of card playing and have that teaching go on in the Temple itself on the Sabbath, seems certainly violative of the spirit, if not of the letter, of Judaism. Sports, however, are another matter."[35] Why mastering a complex game of strategy constituted a greater *bittul Torah* than throwing a ball through a hoop probably had as much to do with Freehof's love of sports and his estimation of card playing as déclassé, as with any halakhic associations of card playing with gambling or the existence of a Renaissance-era responsum permitting tennis playing on Shabbat.[36]

Freehof's Sabbath most definitely included sports. A lifelong baseball fan, he frequently attended Pittsburgh Pirates games on Shabbat. (Purchasing tickets or refreshments was not an issue; he sat in a box with the team's owner.[37]) In 1950 Abram L. Sachar, president of the new Brandeis University, came under fire from some segments of the Jewish community for allowing the Brandeis football team to play on Saturdays.[38] Three years later on a visit to Pittsburgh he asked Freehof about the halakhic issues involved. The latter replied that there were ample grounds in the law for allowing ball playing, but noted wryly that the issues of traveling and using money were "of course another question."[39]

Freehof's Sabbath also included dancing, at least initially. He received his first question about orchestral music at a Saturday afternoon bar mitzvah reception in 1958 and replied that these were permitted, citing a responsum that reported that gentile musicians played on Shabbat during the week of wedding festivities.[40] A bit later he wrote a responsum permitting his own religious school to hold a teen dance with recorded music on a Saturday afternoon. There he traced the issue through the halakhah, showing that from the Mishnah to the Shulḥan Arukh, rabbinic authorities declared dancing on Sabbath and festivals forbidden, even while they acknowledged that the people were doing it. "[T]here was not enough basis in the law itself for resisting the universal preference of the people." He concluded that there was no reason to prohibit it now.[41] He included in his 1962 *Treasury of Responsa* a "puritanical" responsum of R. Joseph Steinhardt (1720–1776) that prohibited dancing on the Sabbath, commenting pointedly on it, "The very fact that a number of responsa voice stormy objections to the habit of people of dancing, even men and women together, is an evidence of the fact that the rabbis were fighting against an irrepressible impulse."[42] That same year he told a lay leader in a congregation whose members were fighting over smoking and dancing on the Sabbath that dancing was permitted, and sent him a copy of the as yet unpublished responsum.[43] (See the discussion of smoking below.)

Reading between the lines of that inquiry, however, it is obvious that the man was asking about dancing with a band or DJ at a bar mitzvah—exactly the sort of excess that Freehof despised. Once he realized the import of such questions, his attitude changed completely. Asked whether it was "proper to have a dance band play at the Bar Mitzvah reception after the service, in the Temple building," he acknowledged that "from the point of view of the *Sabbath* law," there was no problem with having gentile musicians play for Jews. "But this is a dance band, and the music will be 'twist' and 'cha-cha,' etc., and it is definitely wrong." A bar mitzvah reception was, according to Solomon Luria, a *se'udat mitsvah* (religiously mandated meal); the party, therefore, had to be of a "religious nature." He sympathized with the local rabbi. "This is the spirit of tradition, but whether or not you can resist the coarseness of modern communities is a question which I cannot decide. Certainly your feeling is right that it is contrary to the spirit of Bar Mitzvah."[44] Subsequent inquiries concerning dance bands at bar mitzvah parties received the same increasingly unrealistic answer: Gentile musicians were perfectly appropriate, "providing, of course, loud dance music is not played."[45]

Shabbat Observance in the Synagogue: Matters of Taste and the Mood of the Congregation

With no official Reform guidelines for Sabbath observance and popular awareness of the "Sabbath spirit" variable, Freehof necessarily recognized a vast grey area in which observance depended on the sentiment of the local congregation. If a majority was offended by a violation of traditional observance, then they should refrain from doing it; if not, it was acceptable.

Smoking on the Sabbath fell into that grey area of what Freehof called matters of "taste." For example, in 1959 a layperson in a congregation of mixed Reform and Conservative inclinations asked if Reform Judaism demanded anything other than "the belief in the oneness of God and social justice. I would like to know," the irate questioner continued, "the minimum commitment for a Jew affiliated with a Reform congregation. Does such commitment include abstaining from smoking on Fri-

day nights at an ONEG SABBATH [*sic*] meeting?" Freehof replied that
the question was difficult to answer because "Jewish ceremonial practice is not *central* to our thinking and feeling as Reform Jews. Therefore
we have not yet been impelled to clarify our relation to Jewish law, or
our adherence to certain specific elements in it." This applied also to the
Sabbath, though Reform would never, for example, decide to prohibit
driving to the temple, and probably would not take a stand on smoking.

> However, we certainly are concerned with the religious
> feelings of our fellow Jews. If, for example, your congrega-
> tion is such that people would be offended at some members
> smoking on the synagogue premises on the Sabbath, we
> would consider it wrong to violate their loyal memories. If it
> is a congregation of such a mood that it does not mind it, we
> do not consider the smoking, *in itself*, a sin. Your answer,
> therefore, depends upon the mood of your congregation and
> your rabbi.
>
> This is about as specific as it is possible for Reform Ju-
> daism to be on this matter. In brief, to smoke on the syna-
> gogue premises on Friday night is *not* forbidden by Reform
> but it may be in bad taste, this latter depending upon the
> mood of the congregation.[46]

In 1965 Freehof received an inquiry from his old CANRA friend, Philip
Bernstein; so many Conservative Jews were visiting his congregation
regularly for bar mitzvahs that his Board was proposing to issue the following statement: "To maintain the spirit of the Sabbath, and to make it
a day with its own distinctive atmosphere, smoking in the Temple building on the Sabbath is firmly discouraged. It is hoped that all members of
the congregation will cooperate with this decision and make it known to
their guests who are in the Temple on the Sabbath." Since it was controversial, Bernstein wanted Freehof's input. He suggested a substitute:
"'Because of the feelings of some of our members and many of our
guests, we would ask guests and members to refrain from smoking on
the Temple premises on the Sabbath.' In other words, I would agree to
urge refraining from smoking as an act of politeness and consideration,
but I would not prohibit it as if it were a religious law. It is a matter of
taste . . . "[47] He showed his own taste in the matter, however. In a letter

supporting the action of a rabbi who had asked a congregant to go out in the hall to smoke right after the meal during a congregational Seder, Freehof also commented, "Likewise, in the synagogue itself on the Sabbath, it would destroy certain respect [*sic*] if a man smoked on the premises."[48]

What sort of organizational activities could proceed on the Sabbath was likewise a matter of "taste," dependent on the reservoir of Sabbath sentiment in the congregation. In 1960 he published a responsum on holding a congregational meeting on the Sabbath.

> The question comes from a congregation that until recently was Orthodox and now is more or less Reform. The congregation is planning some improvement to its facilities. It has proved difficult to assemble a congregational meeting except on Friday evening after services. The congregation is divided on the question of whether it is proper to have a business meeting on late Friday evening.[49]

As in the question of the Gift Corner, he reviewed the halakhah regarding discussion of money matters on the Sabbath, to show that discussing money matters for the good of the community was generally permitted, but no handling of money or writing down records was allowed.

The crucial factor was the community's sentiment. This was true even in Orthodoxy; "it is a well-established principle in Orthodox law not to make any decision to permit something (even though it may actually be permitted) if to the people it will appear to be a strange decision (since they all believed it to be prohibited). In other words, even Orthodox law hesitates to run counter to popular notions." If people felt strongly enough about not violating the Sabbath, he pointed out, they would make it their business to come to a weekday meeting. Since they haven't done so, they are obviously not really Orthodox. Nevertheless, in deference to the sentiments of the traditionalists, let them meet on the Sabbath to discuss congregational business, as permitted by halakhah, but let them not keep written records or go into too much detail regarding actual finances. Preparing on the Sabbath for fund raising activities on Saturday night was similarly a matter of local taste and sentiment.[50]

The mood of the congregation was also determinative in the case of the non-kosher caterers coming into the synagogue on the Sabbath to prepare food for a Saturday night party. The halakhah, Freehof explained, prohibited a gentile contractor from performing work on the Sabbath in a Jewish street because of *mar'it ayin*, i.e., it would appear that either a Jew was working or had ordered work to be done on the Sabbath. He thought most congregations would refrain on that basis, but "there are some congregations that might not mind it. . . . If the congregation would not object to it, I do not think the rabbi should raise an objection."[51]

On the other hand, sharing procedures he had developed at Rodef Shalom could be a gentle way to offer guidelines. Asked what a gentile custodian could do on Shabbat, Freehof described his procedure, which "suits my feelings: We have a Christian employee who is given the schedule early in the month, and she herself knows what is needed. So we are spared even having directly to order something on the Sabbath, since by law telling a Gentile to do something is forbidden. If the Gentile does it of his own accord, that is another matter."[52]

The Reform Sabbath in the Larger Community

Freehof's strenuous defense of Reform's legitimacy (see Chapter 8) included fighting to open Jewish Community Centers on Shabbat. This required him to balance traditional notions of rest with modern notions of leisure. His suggestion was to avoid "flagrant" violations of the Sabbath, recognizing that each possible activity would have to be judged individually. He proposed that the Centers be closed until 1:00 on Saturdays in order not to interfere with service attendance, and that "thereafter all activities proceed except those which can especially be proved as violative of Sabbath laws, such as writing and painting, etc." The Orthodox could "get around" the issue of staff "if they wanted to," for example, by considering staff activity on Saturday as volunteer time not included in their salaries.[53] Just as he hoped his Orthodox counterparts would rule leniently in order to make such a consensus work, so he was willing to be correspondingly stricter. "But I make a distinction between what we do in our own environment and what we do in an environment . . . which would represent all of American Jewry. . . . I believe we owe a duty to the sensitivities of those more observant. That is why I would permit dancing and would not permit writing; but that applies to the 'Y,' not to our Temple."[54]

Always sensitive to the way the rest of the community regarded Reform Jews, he appears to have withdrawn a lenient opinion on one issue. In 1961 he was asked whether a temple youth group could work at renovating houses in a slum area if the only time it could be done was Shabbat. He sent a meandering reply that reads as if he were weighing the issue even as he dictated. It would be a bad idea if the group included Orthodox youth, a YMHA should not do it, don't do things like painting and scraping, don't do it if it's in a Jewish neighborhood—but it's certainly a mitzvah that would create goodwill for the Jewish community, so "If it is not a Jewish neighborhood, try it out. After all, we are in a vague area of decision here. . . . [U]se your judgment, considering the locale and the group, etc."[55] The questioner reported back to him that the reply had silenced his critics and the teens had gone ahead with the project. However, at a subsequent regional youth meeting, the group had debated the issue and voted that it should not be done in the future. In fact, the teens were disturbed by the fact that Reform had no conception whatsoever as to how the Sabbath should be observed, as was the questioner.[56] Perhaps as a result of this exchange, when Freehof received a similar question the next year, he answered very differently. Since Reform had no firm guidelines, he wrote, "I can only tell you how I would feel about it. I would not permit a youth group to work in public on the Sabbath, especially a youth group which works under the direction of the synagogue. I could tell you my various reasons, but you can guess at them. This answer, therefore, is not an answer that can be satisfactory. I am simply saying that I would not have my youth group do public work on the Sabbath."[57]

As ready as he was to stand up to Orthodox pressure when matters of Reform principle were at stake, so he equally tried to avoid controversy on other occasions. In December 1971 an editorial in the Detroit Jewish newspaper criticized a local Reform congregation for its Men's Club's social action project, filling in for local Christian hospital workers on Christmas—which fell on the Sabbath that year. Editor Philip Slomovitz actually sent Freehof a copy of his column, along with a clipping from a local newspaper titled "'True Christian' Spirit Shown By Local Jews," and challenged Freehof to issue a responsum on the question, "Is the good deed of substituting labor for Christians sacred and justified when it simultaneously calls for the desecration of one's own Sabbath?"[58] At almost exactly the same time Freehof received a letter from R. Richard Hertz of the congregation in question, with another copy of Slomovitz's editorial, asking for advice.[59]

Freehof was then seventy-nine years old and retired, and spent his winters in Florida. He responded to both Hertz and Slomovitz upon his return to Pittsburgh in March. To the rabbi he sent a formal responsum[60] arguing that there is no halakhic objection to associating with Christians, who are not idolators, on their holidays; the Talmud obligates Jews to perform "social services" for non-Jews as well as Jews for the sake of goodwill; it is not a violation of the Sabbath to help the sick; therefore what the Men's Club did was permitted. To the editor, however, he wrote that he had written a responsum for Rabbi Hertz, but would not share it with him. "[S]ince I do not like to get into any dispute with Orthodox or Conservative rabbis, I would not like to have published what I have written without the statement that the responsum is for the guidance of Reform. In that way, there can be no occasion for the Orthodox or Conservative to say that I have presumed to speak for them. Rabbi Hertz has the responsum and if he wishes to give it to you, that is up to him."[61] Slomovitz did print the responsum, and Freehof did come under criticism from Orthodox rabbis, but other Reform colleagues whose congregations did the same thing were eager to have copies of it. R. Bertram Korn, for example, wrote, "I am in complete agreement with you, and authorized our Men's Club to engage in this kind of practice. More than 200 of our people were involved. It was a great and very meaningful service. I am sure the leaders of our Men's Club who were under attack by other rabbis in the area who disagreed with us would be pleased to see a copy of your answer to this question."[62]

Like Bettan, Freehof received a number of questions from rabbis uncertain about the limits of participation in non-Jewish public functions on the Sabbath. Freehof, who valued his own prominence in Pittsburgh civic life for the opportunities it gave him to create good will toward the Jewish community, tended to be very generous in his answers. In 1955, for example, a rabbi in a small community asked whether he should accept the invitation to speak at the local high school graduation on a Friday night at the very hour when he regularly held services. He had originally declined, for which the Conservative rabbis in the nearest large community had praised him. His Reform colleagues there, however, had told him that "the question of the honor to the position of Rabbi and the Jewish community was more important," and he should go.

Freehof's judicial methodology of always consulting the halakhic sources first led him to formulate an odd response: Halakhically the late Friday night service was just as objectionable as the high school graduation, since the Sabbath was being ushered in late, candles were being lit after dark, and people were being encouraged to violate the Sabbath by driving to synagogue. Therefore, from a traditional perspective, he would do no worse by going to the graduation. And from a modern point of view,

> [t]he opportunity to speak at a high school graduation, in a school where there are few Jewish children, is an opportunity to spread a knowledge of Jews and Judaism at an effective place, at a time when general American democratic idealism has its strongest appeal. There is hardly an occasion in American life where the noble American ideals are more to the front than at a high school graduation. Therefore, you have the opportunity to achieve something of the virtue of Kiddush Ha Shem, of bringing honor to the name of God, and doing a service to us all. . . . I, myself, would participate in the high school graduation.[63]

Freehof could have answered that ordinarily the proper thing for the rabbi to do would be to attend services on Friday night and to spend the rest of the evening at home with his family, but that in this case, the public good he could do by appearing at the graduation outweighed the fact that he would be missing the Friday night service and going someplace he normally wouldn't go on the Sabbath. Why didn't he say that? He can hardly have intended to delegitimate Reform practice as this answer implies. He may have replied carelessly and in haste; but his answer may reflect, once again, his reluctance to create standards where there were none.

A Shift in His Attitude

The 1965 CCAR convention devoted an entire day to the absence of Sabbath observance among Reform Jews. W. Gunther Plaut's keynote address suggested provocatively that making the Friday evening service the main focus of Reform Sabbath observance was the core of the problem. He called for re-educating congregants to observe the Sabbath at home on Friday night, to attend synagogue on Saturday morning, and to make the Sabbath last through sundown—and to do all that by creating standards of Sabbath observance.[64] Plaut was then named chairman of a new CCAR Committee on the Sabbath. In 1968 the Committee proposed a plan to publish a Sabbath manual, including standards for Sabbath observance.[65]

This sort of activist attempt to return Reform Jews to modes of observance they had abandoned ran completely counter to everything Freehof believed. Yet he was not immune to the concern over the disappearance of "Sabbath spirit" among Reform Jews. In private he allowed that perhaps it was time to give it a try. In a letter to Plaut he noted that although a Reform code could not possibly have any authority, nevertheless, "[p]erhaps it is possible to explain that what we are recommending is in no way claimed to be the word of God, but the consensus of judgment of members of the Conference. . . . I suppose there is no harm in trying, except the harm of futility; and I know that many members of the Conference agree with you that what we need is a Code."[66] This was, in effect, what Lauterbach had said to him back in 1941. He likewise gave cautious approval to the Sabbath Committee's 1968 proposal, again writing to Plaut:

> Let me congratulate you on the work of the Sabbath Committee. You know well that I have always been opposed to any attempt to make a code of practice for our people. . . . My chief reason is that we cannot, in conscience, declare certain ceremonial action [*sic*] a mitzvah, a devine [*sic*] command. Therefore, our codes would be ignored by the people and more harm than good would be done by them.
>
> . . . [I]t is my belief, that mitzvahs will gradually develop among us, beginning as observances of choice and then gradually becoming rooted as mandate. . . .

> Your report is exactly in this spirit. You suggest valuable
> and worthwhile procedure and you hope that they will grow
> gradually into mandate.[67]

The CCAR published a guide to Shabbat observance in 1972. In substance it contained nothing that contradicted anything Freehof had written in any of his responsa, except that it characterized its guidelines as "positive and negative *mitzvot*,"[68] which probably distressed Freehof greatly. Significantly, he never referred to this book in any of his subsequent responsa on Shabbat questions. Nevertheless, relinquishing his opposition to a CCAR guide to observance was a major shift in his stance.

Kashrut

Freehof's stance on kashrut in the few inquiries he received on the subject closely resembled his stance on the Sabbath: Whatever sentiment remained should be respected; the synagogue should be held to a higher standard than the home; we Reform Jews should be considerate of the reaction our actions will cause in other Jews—but we will not consent to adhere to practices we have largely abandoned for legitimate reasons. He himself ate shellfish, which he discovered growing up in Baltimore, but not pork.[69]

A 1962 letter sums up his attitude, which remained consistent throughout the years.

> We Reform Jews go on the principle that the ritual prohibitions of food, etc., are not vital to Judaism, but that does not mean we are not considerate of our own parents and our friends who are more observant. What makes the problem more difficult is that people nowadays are absurdly inconsistent. They will insist upon the wearing of a hat at a wedding, which has almost no status in Jewish law. They will insist on the breaking of the glass, which is more a superstition than anything else. Then they will eat, blatantly, trefe food at the wedding dinner.
>
> What is served or not served at the Temple is a conspicuous matter. When we consider the horror that it would awaken

in many fellow Jews that pork, etc., should be served at the Temple, it is simple Jewish decency not to do so. In other words, the whole basis should be our respect for the feeling of others and, also, what our feelings are too. I do not think, for example, that shellfish is as annoying to most Jews in America as pork would be, but judge by the feeling of your congregation.[70]

Rabbis were now asking him frequently about what to serve at the temple, he told another colleague two weeks later. "I believe it is a symptom that accompanies our Bar Mitzvahs. Bar Mitzvahs bring grandparents, and since our movement has grown, we are now connected with a quarter of a million grandparents, Orthodox or semi-Orthodox, over the country."[71] Nevertheless, while it was usually wildly inconsistent in context, he did not dismiss the people's concern as completely unworthy. Many Reform Jews still regard the biblically prohibited animals as forbidden, he noted in his only published responsum on the subject. "This, certainly, if not religious, is reverential, and the synagogue should not discourage it by bad example."[72]

Although he could express great sympathy for people's "sensitivities" regarding the dietary laws, in fact, his primary concern was the public image of Reform. It looked bad for the movement when forbidden foods were served in Reform synagogues or at Reform-sponsored events. It was not necessary to advertise Reform deviation from tradition if no principle was involved. Thus he was very upset that one Reform temple sponsored an annual "Crab Feast," but his advice was only that they stop *advertising* it, not that they actually stop doing it. "[I]t is one thing to proclaim an anti-halachic attitude because of moral conscience and another one to proclaim it because of appetite. It is not morally important what we will eat and what we will not eat, and we ought not to make a fuss about it. . . . Why does not your congregation have an annual 'Fish Fry' instead of a 'Crab Feast?' At your 'Fish Fry' you will not have a mashgiach [kashrut supervisor] to see whether the fish have fins and scales."[73] Similarly, a Sisterhood should not publish a cookbook with recipes that included forbidden foods. The Rodef Shalom Sisterhood's recent cookbook, he pointed out, excluded not only *treyf* meats but even meat and milk combinations. "Besides, . . . [w]e have no right to hurt our Orthodox brethren, as they would be hurt if they saw such a publication. . . . It is not a question of *halacha*, but of decent consideration."[74]

He was, therefore, not sympathetic to a request to make kosher food available at the UAHC summer camps. UAHC President Maurice Eisendrath turned to him for advice on this issue after being informed that some children at the camp in Massachusetts, who came from homes where kashrut was observed, felt alienated at the camp. The complainant asked that the camps make special provisions for anyone who observed kashrut. UAHC Vice-President Jay Kaufman, however, thought that the issue was not really kashrut but only the serving of forbidden foods. He noted that both rabbis and laypeople had complained recently when shrimp was served at a Reform Jewish Appeal dinner on Long Island and recommended only making sure that pork and shellfish were not served at the camps or at Reform movement events.

Freehof responded with his customary rant that while he didn't want to offend anyone's sensitivities, he also did not want to be "forced into Kashrus" as the Orthodox were now doing at public Jewish events. Let kosher food always be available for those who want it at Jewish communal affairs, but in a Reform setting, we should only avoid serving forbidden foods, "even though I am told that there is hardly a bar mitzvah without shrimp in our congregations." Further than that he would not go, because to be genuinely kosher would mean bringing Reform kitchens under Orthodox supervision. "I would absolutely never yield to having a Mashgeach to see that the food is absolutely kosher." Furthermore, the Orthodox were in a perpetual game of one-upsmanship over whose kashrut standards were stricter. Therefore "I might add that you will never be *absolutely* kosher even if you were weak enough to bow to the demand. It is the unfair technique of new Orthodox groups to declare the meat of their predecessors in the country to be trafe. . . . I would resist, therefore, all attempts to accede to the principle that what is not absolutely kosher is not Jewish. I believe that all our affairs should be not manifestly trafe."[75]

Conclusion

Although Freehof adhered to his conviction that both Sabbath observance and the dietary laws were areas in which Reform should not make fixed rules, he did possess a set of personal standards on which he relied in answering questions. The Sabbath, in his view, required protection from the corrosive effect of modernity; to the extent that Reform Jews retained any attachment to traditional observance or sensibilities, therefore, he generally supported it. With warm memories of his own traditional upbringing he possessed a powerful sense of what constituted the "spirit" of Shabbat, and tried to protect and strengthen it in a Reform environment. He had no personal or philosophical attachment to the dietary laws, but he believed that Reform Judaism should not be blatant about its rejection of them by serving forbidden foods in synagogue and organizational settings, or at least should not advertise doing so, since there was no real principle involved. Such open disregard for traditional sensibilities on an issue that was merely a matter of "appetite" served no purpose. Acutely sensitive to the differences between Orthodox/Conservative and Reform observance and concerned for the good name of Reform, he strove simultaneously to assert Reform's legitimacy and to avoid controversy over its deviations from traditional practice. In the absence of clear Reform principles or guidelines concerning Shabbat and kashrut, however, and faced with the reality that most Reform Jews ignored these practices (especially kashrut) for reasons of convenience rather than conviction, the only way to achieve that end was to urge his correspondents to use good taste and judgment and avoid having the synagogue or its constituent groups engage in blatant violations of the halakhah.

Activities he expressly and absolutely opposed on the Sabbath were any sort of commercial transaction, which he condemned in the strongest possible language, and weddings. Pork and shellfish in the synagogue also distressed him greatly. Everything else was negotiable, depending on the "mood" of the particular congregation, but whenever he could, he advised correspondents on how they could act in a manner that showed greater sensitivity to the Sabbath. Selecting items from the gift shop but not shopping; listening or even dancing to genteel music but not to rock bands; dancing but no "wild" popular dancing; playing sports but not playing cards—these and other details add up to an outline of the Sabbath as a day of worship and of leisure free of vulgarity, exactly as Israel Bettan had written in 1952.

7

LOOKING OUTWARD:
THE BOUNDARIES OF JUDAISM

One of the primary motivating factors in the creation of Reform Judaism was the desire for a Judaism that demanded less segregation from the larger society and that appeared less alien in the context of the majority Euro-American Christian culture. As Israel Jacobson said at the dedication of his *Tempel* in Seesen, at the very dawn of reform, "Let us be honest, my brothers. Our ritual is still weighted down with religious customs which must be rightfully offensive to reason as well as to our Christian neighbors. It desecrates the holiness of our religion and dishonors the reasonable man to place too great a value upon such customs; and on the other hand, he is greatly honored if he can increasingly encourage himself and his friends to realize their dispensability."[1] The Pittsburgh Platform famously rejected all rituals "such as are not adapted to the views and habits of modern civilization."[2] Creating a Reform Jewish lifestyle was never merely a matter of abandoning and recreating ritual, or even of adopting ideas such as the mission of Israel or the messianic era. As in other Jewish religious reform movements, it was also about the acquisition of *Bildung*—the civic, cultural, and aesthetic behaviors of the modern citizen. This was equally true on both sides of the Atlantic, and remained true long after the Reform pendulum began its swing back from the extreme rejection of ritual.

Arnold Eisen has written that "the decisions made by Jewish individuals, movements, and groups throughout the modern period to maintain, alter, or discard distinctive Jewish observances, have, in addition, ultimately represented decisions about the *marking of difference,* and thereby served to effect a greater or lesser degree of *separation from Gentile neighbors and fellow citizens.*"[3] All forms of modern Judaism have sought to define a lifestyle that is simultaneously sufficiently Jewish and sufficiently part of the larger culture. Thus it is not surprising that Freehof received an enormous number of questions asking him to "mark the difference" between Jew and gentile. He was proud of the Reform willingness to wrestle with the consequences of living in an open society. "All these are new questions, the product of modern life. Orthodoxy brushes them aside. Reform Halacha faces them and deals with them."[4] Indeed, many of these questions had nothing to do with halakhah or even long-established minhag; what underlay them, rather, was the need to articulate what Freehof referred to as the "spirit of Judaism." While Reform Jews sometimes found it difficult to set limits, he himself had no such difficulties. He possessed a very clear sense of what that "spirit of Judaism" was, and did not hesitate to say so. Above all, it meant not blurring the boundaries between Judaism and Christianity (or any other religion, though in the years he was active, Jewish social interaction with non-Christian religions in the US was virtually non-existent).

Gentile Participation in the Synagogue

In the pre-modern *kehillah*, standing as a voting member of the community was restricted to male heads of household at or above a certain financial level. In the modern era, synagogues as voluntary organizations at first extended membership to households, with voting rights going to the male head of household. Women in American Reform congregations gradually acquired membership rights beginning in the late nineteenth century, and full voting rights after the ratification of the Nineteenth Amendment in 1920, but the unit of membership was still most commonly the household.[5] The social upheavals of the 1960s and later would eventually change that, but as new synagogues formed in the immediate postwar years, the most immediate problem—at least the one that led Reform rabbis and laypeople to consult Freehof—was what to do about households in which one spouse was not Jewish. Could they have a "family membership?" Could the non-Jewish member of the couple vote on synagogue business or be elected to positions of governance?

The prospect of non-Jewish synagogue members appalled Freehof. "Anyone who is a member [could] presumably become elected to office. The thought is unbearable that a Christian woman who never ceased to be a Christian and still believes in the Trinity, etc., should become a President of a Sisterhood or of a congregation." Dismissing the idea that denying membership was unfair to Christian spouses, he pointed out that Orthodox synagogues would not even extend membership to a Jew with a gentile spouse. "It is not an injustice to a Christian wife to say to her: '. . . We permit [your husband] to become a member and you are welcome to become a member too if you accept the doctrines of Judaism.'"[6]

He vehemently condemned a model temple constitution drafted by the UAHC that recommended allowing memberships for mixed couples, publishing a strongly worded responsum that indicated his displeasure not only with it, but with the general lowering of boundaries between Jews and the larger society that gave rise to it, especially mixed marriage. Judaism historically opposed mixed marriage, he explained, because of its potential for drawing Jews away from Judaism. The very question now being asked would have "astounded" earlier generations and therefore is not even discussed in Jewish law, so there is only the "spirit" of the law to offer guidance. While the present lack of hostility toward Jews and Judaism is good,

> it is not a good sign that people who do not believe in Judaism at all would be quite willing to join a Jewish congregation and that a Jewish congregation would consider admitting them. This attitude reflects the general indifference nowadays as to the unique nature of the respective religions. People tend to feel that all religions are alike, that all exist merely to teach the Golden Rule or the Ten Commandments, so that it makes no difference to which you belong. . . .
>
> Jewish congregations consist of Jews by birth or conversion. . . . [W]e cannot allow the transformation of a Jewish congregation so that it ceases to be the family, the brotherhood, of Israel. . . .
>
> . . . [If such mixed couples] could all be admitted without the conversion of the Gentile partner, this policy would diminish the motivation for conversion.[7]

Rabbis and lay leaders continued to ask Freehof about the issue, and he continued to respond in the same way. "[A] Temple membership is a fellowship of Jews for the maintenance of the Jewish religion. The mem-

bership becomes meaningless if non-Jews are admitted membership."
[*sic*][8] The question was sufficiently vexing that he published a second responsum on it thirteen years later, when a rabbi asked him about his
board's plan to revise its constitution to allow membership to any "individual . . . whose spouse is of the Jewish faith." The issue needed re-ex-
amination, he wrote, because so many Reform congregations were
extending membership rights to non-Jewish spouses. After enumerating
all the ways in which Reform Judaism had tried to accommodate gentile
spouses, he again reiterated his concern that an unconverted gentile could
not possibly be a sincere member of a religious institution whose beliefs
s/he did not share. He suggested that the congregation in question adopt
a by-law specifying that in cases of mixed marriage, "the family as a
whole becomes a member and the membership shall be in the name of the
Jewish spouse." He continued to advocate this position long after most
Reform congregations had extended membership to mixed couples.[9]

Rabbis whose congregations extended membership to gentile
spouses sometimes wrote to Freehof asking for clarification of the limits of their participation in congregational life. In 1970 a rabbi sent this
inquiry: His congregation had non-Jewish choir members and soloists,
granted membership and burial rights to non-Jewish spouses, and allowed "deserving" non-Jewish members to open the Ark for the Adora-
tion (Alenu). The rabbi, who also allowed women to light the Shabbat
candles before they completed their conversions, did not want to change
these current practices, because it would alienate his non-Jewish members, whom he referred to as "yir'e shamayim [God-fearers]." Recently,
however, a gentile member who was not a regular attendee opened the
Ark for Alenu and wore a *tallit* while doing so.

> Since we have an influx of a few conservative members
> a storm broke out which is threatening the unity of the con-
> gregation. I realize that according to Reform practice Gen-
> tile participation in our services is not permitted. I personally
> cannot understand why exceptions like the above ones should
> not be permitted and even desirable. What is the difference
> between a sermon, delivered by a Christian clergy man [i.e.,
> a sermon delivered by a guest minister or priest], and any of
> the above mentioned rituals?

He wanted Freehof's opinion before making his decision.[10] The incident evidently caused quite a stir in the congregation, because Freehof also received a letter about it from a distressed congregant,[11] to whom he responded diplomatically that he would not take sides between a rabbi and a congregant—though he then referred her to a printed responsum with his own views opposing such participation.[12] (In a letter about the situation to a friend he wrote frankly that he agreed with the congregant, but "since my opinion is that she is right and the rabbi wrong, I do not want to tell her so."[13])

Another rabbi asked whether a gentile member who "has reared two children as Jewish and kept a Jewish home and worked with great devotion for the temple" could be elected president of the sisterhood. Freehof chose to publish this responsum also. The congregation should thank this woman for her devotion, he said, just as the halakhah made provisions for gentiles to offer gifts to the Temple when it stood. But the Talmud and codes also required that all communal officials be Jews. Whatever this woman's reason for not converting after all these years, it has practical consequences now: In a period of rising numbers of mixed marriages, a non-Jewish sisterhood president "would be an obstacle to one of the important goals of the congregation," i.e., encouraging gentile spouses to convert to create unified Jewish families.[14] He opposed using the defunct halakhic category of *ger toshav* for gentile spouses or individuals involved in the congregation who did not consider themselves Christian but refrained from formal conversion to Judaism, or for non-Jewish custodial parents who continued to send their children to religious school, lest these appear to be an acceptable alternative to formal conversion.[15] He also opined that a man with a gentile wife should not be nominated as the congregation's vice president because officers were supposed to represent the congregation's ideals, and "if this man were in a position of leadership, his very presence would be an encouragement to young people in the congregation to feel that mixed marriages are just as good as all Jewish marriages."[16]

Freehof's restrictions on gentile participation in the service show that he took seriously the halakhic difference between the obligatory liturgy and other acts of prayer and devotion. A gentile could not lead the service, but could read a biblical passage, such as a psalm, if there was a desire to include him or her in the service; could not be called up for an *aliyah* and recite the traditional blessing, but could take the Torah scroll from the Ark; could have a parent's name on the Kaddish list and recite Kaddish for a parent, but could not recite any blessing with the phrase *asher kideshanu bemitsvotav vetsivanu* ("who has sanctified us by Your commandments and commanded us").[17] On this last he was adamant. Gentile spouses were Noahides. No matter how committed they were to raising their children as Jews or to supporting the temple, they were not party to the Sinai covenant and could not honestly recite that phrase. Therefore they should never take any ritual part in a Jewish service.[18] (The special case of pre-converts was the only instance on which he changed his mind. Early in 1965 he had advised that in the case of a conversion class participating in the Friday evening service, a woman who had not yet converted should not recite the candle blessing at all.[19] Four years later he published a responsum allowing it.)

In practice the question of ritual participation was usually linked to bar/bat mitzvah. In postwar synagogues, both Reform and Conservative, it became customary to honor the bar mitzvah boy's parents on Friday evening by having his mother light the candles and his father lead Kiddush. Fathers, of course, were also typically called to the Torah at the morning service. As the number of mixed couples affiliated with Reform congregations rose, the pressure on rabbis to allow participation of gentile spouses increased. The tension over a non-Jewish parent's participation was especially acute in the Reform context due to the absence of halakhic norms.

Adding to the confusion was the context within which bar mitzvah was being reintroduced. In its classical phase Reform had eliminated not only bar mitzvah but also such time-consuming and "oriental" practices as *aliyot* and Torah processionals through the congregation. A son's bar mitzvah was the only occasion on which a man might expect to be anywhere near the scroll. Indeed, most Reform congregations had no regular Saturday morning service; now a morning service was scheduled only for a bar mitzvah. There was no regular congregation present, but only the family's invited guests. Inevitably people came to regard the event as their son's "bar mitzvah service," a private family celebration, with the bar mitzvah boy and his parents as the "stars" of the show. (Many Conservative Jews also shared this attitude, but most congregations in that movement had at least a nucleus of regular worshippers on

Shabbat mornings that established some communal context, and ha-lakhah set some limits.) Naturally people came to expect that a parent, regardless of Jewish status, would play the "customary" parental role at "their" son's bar mitzvah service.[20]

It is thus no surprise that the overwhelming majority of questions sent to Freehof about gentile participation were specifically about women lighting Shabbat candles and men being called to the Torah. His earliest responses on the subject merely said that gentiles could not participate in specifically Jewish rituals, for the reasons explained above. However, he eventually realized that "just say no" was not an adequate response to the pressure, and began to offer a way for his colleagues to allow gentile parents to participate. As he explained to one correspondent:

> The question . . . has become . . . more and more urgent in re-cent years, first because of the increase in mixed marriages and then because a Gentile second husband will adopt the child of the first husband and his Jewish wife will demand that he take the father's role at the Bar Mitzvah.. . . . If I were still in active service in these difficult days, and I would find it very difficult to refuse a Gentile second husband the right to come up to the Torah at the Bar Mitzvah of his adopted son, I would write an English prayer which a Gentile could sincerely voice.[21]

In response to numerous inquiries he suggested that a gentile mother could light the Shabbat candles or a gentile father be called to the Torah, as long as they said something other than the regular blessing.[22] Thus on one occasion he suggested that the gentile father be called to the To-rah and recite, "Heavenly Father, in gratitude for Thy law which is given for the guidance of the children of man, we read the sacred words and ask for Thy continued guidance and blessing." In a published respon-sum on the subject he offered a more traditional-sounding alternative: "Praised be Thou, Lord our God, King of the Universe, Who has given His sacred law unto all his children that we may learn, observe, and serve him in righteousness."[23] However, he continued there, a gentile father or stepfather may not recite the *barukh shepetarani* blessing,[24] because as a gentile he is not commanded to teach his son Torah. Either the Jewish grandfather or the rabbi, acting as the court, should recite it.

In these responses Freehof was at pains to explain that Jewish particularity did not mean that non-Jews had a lesser status. He took exception when Jews demanded the exclusion of gentiles from ritual participation on the basis of ethnic chauvinism rather than religious considerations. " . . . [T]hose of your members who say not to allow them to participate in the service . . . , declaring them to be 'second-class citizens,' . . . are mistaken. . . . A Christian is not a second-class human being in the eyes of Judaism. Her sincere faith is accepted as valid for her. . . . We are under the covenant of Sinai. She is under the covenant of Noah. . . . "[25] As always, foremost in his concern was Jewish *religious* distinctiveness.

While Freehof was willing to make concessions to parents who had demonstrated that they were raising their children as Jews, he was not as flexible before the fact. His final published responsum on gentiles called to the Torah, from 1990, is reminiscent of his opposition to baby namings and circumcisions when parents have not committed to raising the children as Jews. A rabbi—who was not going to officiate at the marriage—asked whether a Jewish woman's gentile fiancé could be called to the Torah on Friday evening for an *ufruf.* Freehof's response presumed that the primary concern was the bride's parents' desire to have the rabbi "give the couple some semblance of Jewishness so that there will be hope that the future grandchildren will be raised as a Jews." First he reaffirmed (contrary to the CCAR resolution adopted seven years earlier) that the children of this Jewish woman would be Jews regardless. Then, characterizing having an *aliyah* as a "well established custom" to which a bridegroom had "'rights' established by custom," he noted that a minor halakhic work, the *Shaare Efraim,* the "well known handbook on Torah reading," referred to the "obligation" to call a bridegroom for his *ufruf.* On that basis, Freehof concluded, "we are making a serious gesture when we call the Gentile partner . . . to the Torah. Doing that seems to me to be more than we can properly do to allay the understandable grief of the Jewish parents."[26] The decision was based on the slimmest of reeds, and ran counter to his entire theory of how minhag was supposed to operate, but Freehof resisted, as best he could, the blurring of boundaries in the synagogue.

Gentiles' participation in other life cycle events (aside from marriage, of course) was far less emotionally and halakhically fraught and produced far fewer queries. To the few inquiries he received about the role of the gentile father at a *brit milah*, Freehof always replied that it was not possible for him to recite the father's blessings and that the rabbi, acting as the *bet din*, should recite them in his place.[27] Gentile bridesmaids, maid of honor, and groomsmen were perfectly acceptable, since having them was merely custom.[28]

Not surprisingly, death, burial, and mourning generated a sizeable number of questions (even allowing for the many questions on funeral and burial customs that came from Freehof's brother Louis, a funeral director). Here Freehof had some authoritative Reform precedents. The CCAR had departed from halakhah when it voted in 1891 to permit cremation. The most pressing question regarding burial—whether a gentile spouse could be buried in a Jewish cemetery—had been answered in the affirmative by Kaufmann Kohler.[29] Both cremation and mausoleum burial had at least some biblical precedent,[30] and the inclusion of non-Jewish spouses was logical and compassionate within a Jewish community where mixed marriage was tolerated. All of these decisions had been reached in the movement's classical era and were thus part of the body of Reform practice that Freehof considered sufficiently "crystallized" in the 1940s to include in *RJP*, though he noted there that since the body did not come in contact with the earth, mausoleum burial "[did] not accord with the spirit of Orthodox law."[31]

In the 1950s and 1960s he received additional questions regarding burial of non-Jews, often from congregations whose members reflected a range of observance. He assured them all that it was permissible to bury any of one's gentile relatives in one's family plot in a Jewish cemetery, since the plot is considered one's own property. A rabbi could officiate at the funeral of a non-Jew since the commandment to bury the dead includes the gentile dead, but there could be no non-Jewish rituals in the burial or symbols on the gravestones.[32] He had no objection, however, to military gun salutes or Masonic rituals at Jewish funerals.[33] It was appropriate to mourn a gentile who was devoted to the synagogue and raised Jewish children by reciting Kaddish, holding services at the home during the week of shiva, and putting up a *yortsayt* plaque.[34] But a gentile should not receive the honor of a funeral held in the synagogue, since that is something traditionally reserved for great scholars or other distinguished individuals who are role models for the community. (In fact, he opined, it would be inappropriate to extend that honor even to a Jew married to a non-Jew.[35])

He was careful not to make permissive decisions that might further reduce the separation between Jews and gentiles. For example, disinterring a Jew from a grave to be reinterred with a gentile spouse in a mausoleum in a gentile cemetery was absolutely unacceptable. Not only was earth burial traditionally preferable to mausoleum burial "even in the *same Jewish cemetery* [emphasis original]," but "to remove a Jew from Kaver Yisroel [a Jewish grave] to bury him in a Gentile cemetery can in no way be permitted. It is against the entire spirit of the law."[36] While using common era dates on a tombstone was acceptable, even to Orthodox authorities, inscribing "Suffer no more, dear," on a stone was "somehow Christian." He wrote his troubled colleague on this occasion, "So I could not point to a specific rule against the inscription, any more than you can, but I have a strong feeling it is not Jewish in its mood."[37]

On one occasion he complained about Reform Jews eliminating mourning rituals. It was being proposed in Pittsburgh that synagogues and funeral homes agree on a simple, inexpensive standard funeral package instead of requiring grieving families to meet with the funeral director to negotiate the arrangements. Freehof found the proposed simplicity insufficiently respectful of the dead. From this mild criticism, however, he launched into a tirade. The idea was indicative of a "harmful tendency" to eliminate mourning rituals in general. People no longer observed shiva; in some communities, he had heard, they buried the body separately and held only a memorial service. He was "seriously concerned that this deritualization of funerals should not be encouraged. . . . A certain amount of mourning, a certain amount of 'doing something' for the departed dear one, is not only required traditionally, but is wholesome for psychological health."[38]

Rabbinic officiation in non-sectarian cemeteries was not a problem, but Jews who chose to be buried in Christian cemeteries were, in Freehof's eyes, indicating their desire to cut their ties to the community, or at least setting a precedent that would encourage other Jews to separate from the community; rabbis should try to discourage such arrangements.

"In general, I would prefer not to officiate in a Christian cemetery, and I would make an effort to persuade the family to bury a Jew in a Jewish cemetery. . . . However, in an emergency, I would do it, provided it is not a separate grave, but is part of a lot owned by the Jew or his family, and provided it is not in a crowded part of the cemetery in the near proximity of Christian symbols."[39] If such separation could not be assured, the rabbi should officiate only at the funeral home.[40] Under no circumstances should a rabbi co-officiate with other clergy. "I would officiate in a nonsectarian cemetery alone because, after all, a Jewish communal cemetery has not a firm foundation in Jewish law. A person may be buried in his own property. . . . But to officiate with a Christian minister anywhere would clearly result in confusion and breaking up of the sense of unity in the Jewish community."[41] A quarter-century later, he expressed himself even more strongly: "You were absolutely right in your refusal to officiate [at the burial of a Jew] in the Christian cemetery with a Christian minister. . . . If you had consented to bury this Jew in a Christian cemetery, you would have been committing a sin, when you consider what effort is made all through Jewish history to bring scattered bodies of Jews to Jewish burial (Al Kever Yisroel)."[42] None of these decisions required him to take an unusual stance in relation to the halakhah.

In contrast, he did once find halakhic grounds to allow a colleague to co-officiate with a minister at the funeral of a Christian personal friend, asserting that Jews have a "religious duty" to help bury the non-Jewish dead.[43] In contrast to his strictness in helping rabbis enforce boundaries in congregational settings, he knew he could be lenient in this personal setting (especially for an old friend who generally shared his views).

"Gentile Practices"

Beyond questions of halakhah and minhag, the modern battle over Jewish distinctiveness has been fought in the realm of culture ever since traditionalists condemned the use of vernaculars other than Yiddish. Freehof received a large number of questions that fell loosely within the rubric of *ḥukkot hagoy*, "gentile practices." This halakhic rubric is an inherently subjective one. The Torah states, "You shall not copy the practices of the land of Egypt where you dwelt, or of the land of Canaan to which I am taking you; nor shall you follow their laws [*uveḥukkote-hem lo telekhu*]" (Lev. 18:3) and "You shall not follow the practices of the nation [*velo telkhu beḥukkot hagoy*] that I am driving out before you" (Lev. 20:23). In the biblical context it was clear that the Israelites were not to adopt the idolatrous practices of the nations around them and thus deviate from the service of YHWH. In the Tannaitic period, defining an acceptable separation between Jews and the Greco-Roman pagan envi-ronment was significantly more complex. Rabbinic prescriptions took into consideration not only pagan rites but also styles of dress and stan-dards of modesty and morality, laying the foundation for what became an ongoing and ever-expanding effort on the part of Jewish leaders to de-fine appropriate standards of Jewish distinctiveness and separation from the majority within a variety of non-Jewish contexts.[44]

While the issue was generally framed as one of avoiding religious syncretism, the underlying anxiety was the blurring of boundaries that could come from easy social interaction. In the modern period the two concerns fused for traditionalist opponents of religious reform. Every-thing the reformers did was, in their eyes, a violation. In fact, reformers of all stripes, no less than their traditionalist opponents, were intent on maintaining what they considered appropriate boundaries between Jew-ish and non-Jewish. They just drew the boundaries in radically different places. The real difficulty for Reform Judaism was setting criteria for boundary markers in the absence of halakhah or any unanimous agree-ment concerning the basis for arriving at norms of praxis. Freehof's re-sponsa, therefore, reflect his subjective view of what constituted proper Jewish sensibility within the boundaries of Reform precedent. His an-swers demonstrate an approach consistent with the previous discussion: Nothing should be done to blur the boundaries, but where the bound-aries are clearly understood, we accommodate the needs of the individ-ual. For example, there was no problem with allowing a convert to donate Torah ornaments in memory of her father, since there were ha-lakhic precedents allowing gentiles to donate funds for the construction of a synagogue.[45] But a synagogue organ should not have chimes on it. "However, there is always an avoidance of imitation of that which is characteristically Christian. It is therefore a matter of feeling whether bells sounded in the service awaken Christian associations rather than

Jewish. Since it is only a matter of feeling rather than law, I can only tell you my feeling in the matter. If there were bells or chimes on our organ, I would never permit them to be played."[46]

The criteria are obviously subjective when an organ in the synagogue does not arouse Christian associations but its chimes do; indeed, Freehof's responses to questions of this sort were all subjective. Asked whether using a trumpet rather than a *shofar* on Rosh Hashanah was not a "gentile practice," he allowed that "the sound of [the *shofar*] is . . . deeply ingrained in our religious consciousness...[and] would be preferable," but there are few trained *shofar* blowers, and in any case the trumpet is not a "gentile practice" because the Mishnah attests to the fact that in the Temple they used trumpets along with the *shofar* on Rosh Hashanah. (He conveniently neglected to mention, however, that the same *mishnah* explains that the commandment of sounding the horn is fulfilled through the *shofar* and not through the trumpets.[47]) Asked about celebrating holidays such as New Year's Eve or Valentine's Day in the synagogue, he noted first that there was no point in trying to prohibit people from celebrating them outside the synagogue. "Often in the rabbinic legal literature when the people follow certain dubious customs, the rabbis say, 'Let them alone.' The reason for letting them alone is that if they forbid them to follow these customs, they will do it anyhow; and then, added to whatever sin is involved in following the custom, is now the sin of direct disobedience." But bringing them into the synagogue was essentially advocating that Jews observe them, an entirely different matter. "The New Year party in a Temple, I would tolerate because it is almost entirely forgotten as 'the feast of the circumcision [of Jesus].' Valentine Day is still spoken of as Saint Valentine's Day and I would do nothing *active* to foster it."[48] In other words, a holiday that still had a Christian name attached would blur the boundary; a holiday that seemed secular would not (though a New Year's party on Shabbat raised other issues, as we saw).

He had no objection to Jewish children trick-or-treating on Halloween or even participating in school Christmas pageants, but he opposed having them recite a non-denominational blessing before their meals in the public schools since it might cause them to use it as a substitute for the *motsi*, which would be an unacceptable usurpation. Having them recite the Lord's Prayer was also absolutely unacceptable; the

"Lord" in question was Jesus, and "it is a general rule that such prayers which non-Jews use greatly as indispensable are for that very reason of the association not to be used by us if possible. . . . Finally, this prayer is so associated with Christian worship that for that reason it is not usable by us."[49]

What about a Sisterhood gift shop selling Christmas cards for Jews to send to their Christian friends? Freehof noted permissive halakhic precedents: Christians are not idolators and it is permitted to send them gifts and greetings, and the law has become lenient with regard to selling religious goods to Christians. But, he continued, it is one thing for individuals to do it and another altogether for the *synagogue* to do it. Having the cards for sale will encourage Jews to send them to each other and thus signal that it is acceptable to celebrate Christmas, which is wrong. Therefore the gift shop must not sell Christmas cards.[50] The temptation to celebrate Christmas, to blur the boundaries, made it essential that the synagogue not do so. Furthermore, because the synagogue represents proper Judaism, it must not appear to be sanctioning celebrating a Christian holiday even if the reality is completely innocent: A synagogue has the right to ask its live-in custodian not to display his Christmas tree in a window that is visible from the street because of *mar'it ayin*.[51]

Freehof cited halakhic precedents to decide that a synagogue may rent its facilities to a church for classes and services, since Christian worship and symbols do not render the premises unfit for Jewish use, though the Jews might prefer to rent specifically to denominations that do not require crucifixes to be present for their worship. It does not matter that they are teaching a trinitarian interpretation of Scripture; Jewish authorities have long recognized that they are monotheists. But a synagogue must not share a jointly owned building with a church—especially a Unitarian church, since so many Jews who leave Judaism find it easier to become Unitarians than trinitarian Christians. "It is certainly unwise, therefore, and even dangerous on our part, so to blur the distinction between Jews and Unitarians, as this suggested proposal would do, and thus tend to encourage those unfortunate defections from our faith and our people."[52] Jewish services could be held in a church as long as no Christian symbols were displayed; interfaith chapels were acceptable as long as no religious symbols were permanently displayed.[53]

Again, he demonstrated greater restrictiveness where the danger of blurred boundaries was greater.

Another question demonstrated that his modern commitment to respect for all religions did not negate an aversion to some of Christianity's historical manifestations. A Jewish man was to be made a Chevalier in the Order of Cyprus by a Catholic bishop and wanted to hold the induction ceremony in his synagogue's sanctuary during a Friday evening service. This was originally an order of Crusader knights, though as Freehof noted, membership is now accorded to anyone on the basis of humanitarian achievement.[54] His outrage is almost palpable in his response, which lacked even a single reference to any Jewish source, halakhic or not. The Order, he explained, originated during the Crusades, a period with "horrible associations in Jewish history," because of the massacres in the Rhineland and also the massacre in Jerusalem, when "the streets were awash with Jewish blood shed by [the Crusaders]." He continued,

> It is highly doubtful whether a Jew can comfortably be a member of a crusading order, no matter how much it has 'ecumenized' itself but that, of course, is Mr. Heiman's personal business . . . [b]ut certainly to have one of the crusading orders induct a Jew into its membership in a Temple would be embarrassing to all who know Jewish history. . . . [H]e should be asked, for the sake of the tragic associations of the Crusades with Jewish history, to withdraw his request to have the induction take place in the Temple.[55]

The rabbi followed Freehof's decision and sent him a copy of the honoree's furious protest against what he considered narrow minded anti-Christian prejudice. Freehof replied resignedly that in an era of increased ecumenism, sometimes Jews must inevitably appear "narrow and provincial," just as when a priest is happy to marry an interfaith couple and the family cannot understand why the rabbi will not co-officiate. "But," he reiterated, "it is embarrassing to a synagogue for a Crusader organization to conduct a ceremony within its premises."[56]

Law, custom, and aesthetics intersected in questions of synagogue design. There was nothing on the subject in *RJP* I, but in 1952, with the postwar synagogue building boom underway, Freehof included a full chapter on the topic in *RJP* II. Its implicit purpose was to defend Reform synagogues against Orthodox criticism by providing halakhic justification for landscaping, diversity of architectural style, orienting the building and the Ark in directions other than east, placing the *bimah* at the front, using stained glass windows, and depicting human figures in stained glass windows. However, the building boom also led to some unusual questions, as some lay leaders had more money than Jewish sensitivity. In one egregious example, Responsa Committee chairman Israel Bettan rejected the idea of "a Memorial Tower from which would be played at festival times hymns out of the Jewish background" on the basis that it was a "glaring imitation of the church."[57] As noted above, Freehof similarly opposed the use of the chimes on an organ. On at least three occasions he vehemently rejected the "curious suggestion" of placing human ashes in the cornerstone of a synagogue building. It was "gruesome" and according to halakhah, no *kohen* would be able to enter the building.[58] In 1977 he published the question originally addressed to him in 1959 and stated categorically that "there is no doubt at all that deliberately to put the residue of a Jewish body in the cornerstone of a synagogue would be repugnant to the spirit of Jewish law."[59] The "spirit of Jewish law" was essentially the only criterion he could fall back on, since Reform had rejected all laws relating to ritual purity and the special status of the *kohanim*. He also advised against erecting a statue of the former rabbi on the synagogue lawn and a statue of Moses in the building itself. "Being Reform Jews, the Jewish legal statutes do not always govern us, [but] . . . we are also concerned with the impression which a certain action might make on our fellow Jews and the community. Certain things may be permitted and yet, nevertheless, not done, 'mipne maaris ayin,' because they *look* bad." A portrait or a bust of the rabbi would be "less objectionable" than a full statue, and a statue of the rabbi would be less objectionable than a statue of Moses. But if they insisted on having a statue, at least let them put it inside and not out in front where it would look like a Catholic saint.[60]

He considered invocations at dinners not in "the spirit of Jewish tradition"; to stand for them was "un-Jewish" because the Jewish practice was to sit while making the *motsi*. Valentine's Day parties should not be held in the synagogue because the holiday was of Christian origin.[61] While there was no prohibition against Jews extending good wishes to their Christian friends at Christmas, nor against Jews earning a living by selling Christmas decorations or other merchandise, nevertheless "our feeling, if not the letter of the law," says that it is wrong for a Sisterhood gift shop to sell Christmas cards, "if only M'shum miyoos, 'because it is ugly.'"[62] However, although he once commented that a Jewish Mason would have to be guided by his own conscience as to how far he could ascend in degrees, he himself conducted Jewish funerals and then allowed the Masons to append their rites, since they were "harmless."[63] (This had precedent in a 1946 committee responsum by Bettan, which declared that "[t]he funeral rites of fraternal organizations . . . are harmless pageantry."[64]) He objected to other practices on other grounds. He urged a colleague to "resist to the last inch against violating Jewish sentiments" by burying a pet animal in the cemetery, warning, "Otherwise, in these sentimental days you will get more and more such requests," and wrote a responsum vehemently opposing honoring deceased pets with rituals used for people.[65]

Conclusion

The questions Freehof received in the areas of gentile participation in the synagogue and adoption of gentile practices reveal the constant pressure on rabbis to blur the boundaries in a movement that valued openness to the larger society and that included more and more intermarried couples as the decades passed. In the absence of strict social, legal, or halakhic boundaries between Jews and gentiles, American Reform Jews needed help in determining where the boundary stood, and why. Freehof's responsa show him determined to mark it firmly by keeping individuals, families, and synagogues authentically Jewish. Over a span of almost forty years his positions were largely unchanged, reflecting a set of strongly held principles. The rights and responsibilities of a Jew were covenantal and therefore of the essence of Judaism; the integrity of Judaism could not be compromised by bestowing them on one who was not party to the covenant. Within those limits, however, the Jewish community was to be as welcoming as possible to gentile spouses in order to encourage their conversion, and gentile parents raising Jewish children also deserved appropriate acknowledgement. The synagogue itself as an institution had to model an appropriate separation from gentile customs and mores. True to his dictum that the halakhah provided "guidance, not governance," he appealed as need be to halakhah, to minhag, and even to a vague "spirit of Judaism" to keep any hint of the majority religion out of the religious lives of Reform Jews and their synagogues. Although he welcomed and celebrated the full inclusion of Jews in the larger society, his responsa, published and unpublished, show his insistence on maintaining the exclusive Jewishness of the Jewish community and his resistance to anything that might threaten what he always saw as "our embattled Jewish community."[66]

8

LOOKING INWARD:
THE BOUNDARIES OF REFORM
JUDAISM

Freehof was largely correct in 1944 when he stated in the Introduction
to *RJP* that Reform practice had crystallized to the point where it could
be described. However, the postwar era tested the limits of Reform
practice and challenged the very definition of the Reform synagogue.
The progressive acculturation of the east European Jews and their influx into Reform congregations lowered the cultural and socioeconomic
barriers between Reform Jews and the rest of the American Jewish community. This and the growth of Conservatism and Orthodoxy renewed
questions about the relationship between Reform and more traditional
forms of Judaism. Freehof's responsa reflect the tensions within American Reform Judaism and the centrist course he attempted to chart for
the movement.

Reform Ritual Practice

As we saw in Chapter 2, during the interwar period Reform Jews began
to reappropriate previously abandoned rituals. In 1937 R. Jacob D.
Schwarz, head of the UAHC's Commission on Synagogue Activities,
described a Friday evening service typical of this new direction: "The
service is held after the evening meal when both men and women may
attend. Sabbath candles standing in large candlesticks on the altar are
kindled. The Rabbi or Cantor chants the Kiddush ceremony. The choir
sings the Lechah Dodi and other music based on traditional Jewish
melodies. The remainder of the ritual and the sermon are retained in their
usual place."[1]

Schwarz nurtured a gradual and orderly process of careful adaptation of traditional practices to dignified new versions suitable for the decorous Reform context. However, ritual innovation in Reform synagogues of the postwar era was anything but orderly. Between 1943 and 1964 the UAHC added over 350 new congregations, overwhelmingly in new suburban areas of settlement, and with membership overwhelmingly derived from the population of second-generation American Jews of east European origin.[2] For most of them, their childhood exposure to Judaism consisted of High Holy Day attendance at an immigrant Orthodox synagogue, with—for the men—the minimum amount of Hebrew education necessary to be called to the Torah as a bar mitzvah. Beyond a more or less kosher kitchen, their home and personal observance had been somewhere between inconsistent and nonexistent. Although—or because—their Jewish identity was primarily ethnic, they attached enormous importance to certain practices which to them represented "proper" Jewish behavior, appearance, or aesthetics. In a synagogue men covered their heads and wore *tallitot* at morning services; obvious *treyf* (pork and shellfish) did not make an appearance in the synagogue kitchen; one did not smoke on synagogue premises on Shabbat; a wedding ceremony ended with the breaking of a glass; and boys became bar mitzvah.

For classical Reformers these same practices had possessed an equally symbolic, though diametrically opposite, importance: They epitomized the "oriental" Jewish behaviors Reform was committed to discarding. The fact that neither side distinguished between halakhic mandates and custom constitutes powerful evidence that conflicts over head coverings, breaking the glass at weddings, children's names, *tallit*, bar mitzvah, and other questions were battles in the ongoing war over defining Jewish identity in the American context. A crucial question sent to Israel Bettan in 1955 captured this tension perfectly.

> In the area in which my temple is located, we increase our membership by attracting men and women from Orthodox and Conservative homes. The new members, when principals in a wedding ceremony, will often ask that the older forms to which they are accustomed be retained in the service. These include the covering of the head by all par-

ticipants, the reading of the traditional *Ketubah*, and the breaking of the glass.

Similar requests come at times from the parents of a Bar Mitzvah. To please an older member of the family, they would have the boy wear *Talit* and skull-cap during the Bar Mitzvah ceremony.

The members of our Ritual Committee take the stand that the rabbi of the Temple, when acting as officiating minister, must conform to the practices of Reform Judaism. They likewise insist that the Bar Mitzvah ceremony as conducted in our Temple must be viewed as a form of initiation into the ways of Reform Judaism, and should therefore present no feature that is glaringly inconsistent with our established practice.

What do you think of the position taken by the Ritual Committee?[3]

Although Bettan had already gone on record with a cautious endorsement of the renewed presence of bar mitzvah in Reform congregations,[4] his response was an encouragement to stand firm against the particular encroachments which he viewed as challenges to the very essence of Reform. "There is an erroneous impression abroad," he observed drily, ". . . that while the undevising traditionalists are ruled by a sense of loyalty to Torah, we who have espoused the principle of Reform are guided by such motives as personal convenience and temperamental preference. . . ." He explained that Reform had eliminated the *ketubah* because the changed circumstances of Jewish life had rendered it meaningless as a legal document; that it had discontinued breaking the glass because it was a "crude" custom; and that it regarded the covering the head, a custom of dubious origin, as "an act of willful and useless self-isolation" in a social context where baring the head was a sign of respect. He praised the inquirers' "firm" stance, noting that it "augur[ed] well for the continued stability of our Reform religious practices."[5]

When Freehof read the draft of this responsum he wrote his friend, "I have your responsum . . . and I could not possibly agree more completely with you. You have my wholehearted concurrence."[6] Indeed, he later published a responsum urging Reform rabbis to oppose the occasional request from "tradition-minded families" to break a glass at the wedding. There he summarized the findings of Lauterbach's classic article. Citing contemporary Orthodox authorities lamenting reactions of hilarity rather than solemnity to the glass breaking, he concluded that even the few Reform rabbis who might like the custom would be dismayed at such "shouting and . . . laughter and . . . snickering" when the glass is broken. Most Reform rabbis, he asserted, had appropriately negative feelings about the custom because of its origins. He concluded, "If a ceremony of dubious origin becomes noble, it might in its new guise be admitted into our worship. But if even a noble ceremony has become ignoble, it should be firmly set aside."[7] As he wrote privately and more pithily to a colleague, "Now, with regard to marriage, no matter how much I am urged to, I never have a Chuppah or break a glass at any marriage where I officiate. I am not going to let ignoramuses tell me what is essential to the Jewish ceremony."[8]

He found the inconsistencies in the traditionalist aesthetic of his east European brethren both amusing and bemusing. In response to a 1963 inquiry concerning the propriety of wearing a *tallit* but not a *kippah*, he observed:

> A case could be made for wearing the tallis and not the hat . . . However, this would be artificial. In actual Jewish life for the last ten centuries, a hat was as sacred as a tallis. I cannot understand why we have the tallis altogether and not the hat, and why any of them, but there we are in the realm of sentiment. Why do our people shudder at pork chops and eat ham and bacon? What is the principle? . . .
>
> Somebody ought to make a study of the psychological basis for the strange choice of the people, and this applies to Orthodox Jews too in America, as to what they will observe and what they will not observe. . . . However, all I can say to you is that this is a choice based upon popular feeling, and I can see no more logic in it than you can.[9]

Sometimes he was more sarcastic: "The descendants of eastern European immigrants have made of the Yarmulke the outstanding sanctum of Judaism and the breaking of the glass the evidence of the validity of a marriage."[10] Nevertheless, he never took a strong stance about wearing a *kippah*, since it was "hardly a question for legal decision, but rather a question of taste and emotional reaction." He even advised a rabbinic student that it was his "duty" to wear one when participating in an interfaith event in a church.[11]

In practice, however, Freehof's stance in the postwar decades was far less rigid than what Bettan had articulated in 1953. Indeed, most of the time he had no trouble accommodating many of the changes within his definition of Reform. In 1953, the same year he approved Bettan's responsum, he explained to a Reform readership that the prevailing "religious mood" had changed, among Christians as well as Jews. The previous generation was more "doctrinal"; the present one, more "ceremonial." Thus most Reform temples now had candle lighting and Kiddush on Friday nights, and many were reintroducing bar mitzvah. "A generation ago the majority of our people would have said that none of these ceremonials has any modern significance for the religious-ethical life. Nowadays there seems to be a genuine eagerness for some form of these traditional observances. Our people have changed." However, he hastened to reassure his readers, Reform was not thereby being false to itself. Reform is about change, but it possesses an historic permanence despite these changes.

> What is it that makes us Reform? Basically, it is the conviction that what matters most in Judaism is its religious-ethical content. . . .
> Second and consequently, Reform believes that each generation has the right to modify Jewish law and observance in order to find the proper vehicle for its basic aim....We take it upon ourselves to say that that which does not inspire us we do not observe. . . . Therefore, we use the great treasures of our Jewish past selectively. . . . The difference between us and our predecessors is that we are perhaps more inclined than they to include the Talmudic and legal literature as the mine in which to find inspiration. But we are both Reform because we both presume to select from tradition on the basis of judgment and conscience.[12]

He had used the same argument about the relationship between permanence and change in defending the Columbus Platform in 1937 and in defending the legitimacy of Zionism in a Reform context in 1942.[13] An Orthodox rabbi who insisted that a Jewish wedding required a *ḥuppah* was an "ignoramus"; but if the "ladies" of Rodef Shalom "embroidered a magnificent *ḥuppah*" for use at temple weddings, there was no harm. It was merely a reflection of the change in "mood" in Reform as times changed "from the age of the philosophical to the age of the psychological." As he explained in 1978, "In other words, we're in a period where we need pictorialization of Judaism again and it might as well be the old ones. But only if we understand that we have adopted them, and not that it's *Torah miSinay*."[14]

However, despite his general tolerance of the reappearance of ritual, he was personally more resigned than enthusiastic about it, and this attitude of resignation sometimes colored his responses. Asked whether it was appropriate to chant, rather than read, Torah at the Friday night service, he observed somewhat disparagingly that the answer involved a "change of mood" in the larger world and consequently in Reform. For example, his brother Louis, a funeral director, was asked whether someone could be cremated wearing a *tallit*. "How can a family which practices cremation be illogical enough to want the tallis on the body of the departed. [*sic*] The answer is simply that logical or not, it appeals to them!" The same was true of cantillation. "Friday evening is not the Orthodox legal time for reading the Torah and yet at this Reform observance somebody wants to have the most Orthodox custom of cantillation. It is illogical but this is the age of emotion. They simply like it, and that is enough for them." He concluded with a reluctant conditional consent. "Perhaps we have to make some concession to the spirit of the age and say to them that if somebody will study the cantillation and do it *perfectly* so as not to create irreverent amusement in the Congregation, we might try it out. That is all that I can say in such an illogical situation."[15] He was similarly skeptical concerning the incorporation of *tevilah* into Reform conversions. "People do not mind anymore any illogical inconsistency if the ceremony involved simply appeals to them. . . . I suppose we should not criticize these inconsistencies. They apparently do not matter in an age when the question no longer is 'does it make sense?' but, 'does it send me?' I am not sure whether my modern slang is still modern."[16] Despite his personal opinions, however, when he felt that no essential principle was at stake and that the behavior in question was not otherwise unworthy, he upheld the doctrine he had expressed in *RJP*, that the operative principle in Reform was the people's minhag.

Questions about such practices often afforded him opportunities to expound on the nature of Reform Judaism and to share his approach to adjudicating questions of ritual practice in a Reform context. Perhaps the best example of his principled acceptance of practices which he considered unnecessary was his response to a 1967 inquiry concerning observance of the second day of Rosh Hashanah. A congregant whose synagogue had recently changed its affiliation to Reform wanted to know if observing the second day of Rosh Hashanah "violate[d] the principles of Reform Judaism."[17] The similarity between Freehof's response on this occasion and his views of thirty years earlier reveals the consistency of his views. He gently explained to the questioner that "[t]he word 'commandment,' a mandate which must be obeyed under penalty of Divine displeasure, or also under human penalty, is no longer a concept which is generally held in Reform Judaism. The prevalent Reform attitude is that only the moral laws are accepted as God's mandate. All others are not Divine commandments but historical developments precious, in some cases, for their own reason or as being helpful towards the moral life." When Reform was in its earlier, more radical phase, some declarations were made rejecting some "ceremonial commandments." However, Reform is no longer as radical as it once was. "In general in modern Reform there is a desire to obey such commandments as are still meaningful and to consider the Jewish legal literature as guidance rather than as strict governance." Therefore one cannot say definitively that Reform either prohibits or commands any ritual practices. Rather, the question at hand is whether "it [would] be contrary to the general mood of Reform if this congregation should decide to continue to observe Rosh Hashono for two days instead of one day, as nearly all Reform congregations do." Quite simply, he advised, "whatever inherited observance appeals to the congregation as helpful to the religious and ethical spirit can with propriety be observed." He suggested a litmus test: If the members objected to sounding the *shofar* on Shabbat, they should observe two days—even though, as he noted elsewhere, he did not consider the second day "historically justified."[18]

He was similarly open to Reform Jews observing the commandments of *tallit* and *tefillin*, despite the fact that his own transition to Reform had included the abandonment of these practices.[19] In response to a rabbi who was clearly uncomfortable with the idea, he wrote, "[T]his is garb for every Jew and there can be no objection to it."[20] Indeed, he defended elements of tradition that he considered important and that Reform had never officially rejected. One of these was the *minyan*. Although Reform precedent explicitly rejected the need for a *minyan* for a wedding (and therefore Freehof supported a colleague's decision to officiate for a couple whose Conservative rabbi would not marry them in the absence of a *minyan*[21]), no Reform body had ever explicitly endorsed or rejected the requirement of a *minyan* for public worship. Asked about this in 1936, Jacob Mann had cited the precedent of the Palestinian Talmud of requiring only six or seven and advised, "While every attempt should be made to have a full Minyan, the importance of regular services in the Temple is such as to conduct them even when there are fewer than ten people present in accordance with the above-mentioned old Palestinian custom."[22] He did not specify, however, whether six or seven was the minimum required, or whether any number below ten was acceptable in time of need. Actual Reform practice varied, therefore, as rabbis and congregations saw fit.[23] Most Reform congregations ignored the issue; consequently many Reform Jews were unaware of the concept. Thus in 1963, a former congregant of Freehof's from Chicago asked rather confusedly about practices he had encountered at an Orthodox shiva: "And what in the world is a Minion . . . ? [When they couldn't find a tenth man] the poor man who had passed away had to go thru [*sic*] the night without the Minion???????" A decade later a colleague asking whether a *minyan* was required for a *pidyon haben* began his letter, "I know that we in Reform Judaism do not insist on the minyan . . . "[24]

Freehof, however, did insist on the *minyan*'s importance, declaring that "we count it as indispensable for public worship," and expounding on its importance for prayer and for Torah reading: "This constant effort [to have a *minyan*] in every community, large or small, indicates how precious this quorum was to the people of Israel. And to us it need be no less important, especially since we have always declared the religious equality of men and women and the quorum is easier for us to provide. So . . . every important public service does require it, and our people have always exerted great effort to provide it."[25]

He also opposed the practice common in smaller Reform congregations of celebrating holidays on the closest Friday night rather than on the day itself. Reform had made some changes to accommodate modern schedules, he noted, such as the late Friday evening service and the omission of the second day of the festivals. Only the radical Emil Hirsch, however, had changed the date of a holy day, by moving Sabbath services to Sunday, and that congregation had long since discontinued the practice.[26] Including Yizkor in the evening service was perfectly acceptable, however, because it was a logical consequence of the Reform practice of reading Torah on Friday night, which "is contrary to tradition, but we decided to do it anyhow because the actual facts of American Jewish religious observance required it."[27]

Occasionally Freehof's answers were simply inconsistent, indicating a lack of serious engagement with the question on his part. Asked whether it would not be more "convenient" to hold Confirmation—which doubtless would also have been the congregation's only Shavuot service—on the second night of Shavuot when the first evening fell on Saturday night, he reminded the questioner firmly that Reform had given up the second day of the festivals for very good reasons. He advised the rabbi just to admit that he was rescheduling Confirmation for convenience, rather than confuse matters by reopening the question of *yom tov sheni*. Only a few years later, however, asked about holding Confirmation on a Sunday regardless of when Shavuot fell, he advised trying to keep it on Shavuot—"but if there is strong desire in the congregation for Sunday, our Confirmation is not so deep-rooted in Jewish law that one cannot yield to it.... Frequently Shavuos does come out on Saturday, so the second day is Sunday. This year you could easily have Confirmation on Sunday."[28]

Freehof did not have to fight the battle over whether or not Jews should practice circumcision, because by 1950 virtually all male infants born in the US were routinely circumcised. In *RJP* he had written, "The ancient practice of circumcising a male child at the age of eight days, the first commandment given to Abraham our father (Genesis 17:11), is strictly observed."[29] This may well have been the case in 1944. When new mothers were routinely kept in the hospital for more than a week, it was a simple matter to have a Jewish physician perform the operation on the eighth day, with a rabbi present to recite the blessings. In the decade immediately after the war, however, hospital stays shortened. Among Jews, the question now became medical circumcision in the hospital or a traditional *brit milah*. Freehof received letters from around the country explaining that hospitals were now discharging mothers and newborns after no more than a week's stay, and rather than return on the eighth day, families were simply choosing to have a medical circumcision prior to discharge.[30] Complicating the issue was that middle-class Americans had been taught to value the modern, sterile medical environment. Having some untrained amateur perform a medical procedure in one's germ-ridden home was unthinkable, and going back to the hospital was inconvenient, expensive, and possibly dangerous for the baby in inclement weather.[31] The question was, therefore, whether it was permitted to perform the *brit milah* prior to the eighth day to accommodate the new reality.[32]

In 1954 Israel Bettan chose to take a strong stand for the Responsa Committee:

> The question, therefore, is not whether it is physically safe to perform the act of circumcision before the eighth day. . . .The real question for us to answer is whether it is wise in this instance to depart from the Biblical law which is universally observed by the Sons of the Covenant. . . . Shall we not be running the risk of converting a religious rite into just another surgical operation? . . .
>
> The slight inconvenience involved in returning the baby to the hospital on the eighth day . . . need barely enter into our consideration . . . No religious discipline could long endure were we to consult at every step our personal convenience . . .[33]

By contrast, when Freehof went into print with his own responsum[34] he took quite a different approach. He acknowledged the reasons behind the Reform trend: insurance-mandated shorter hospital stays; doctors' preference for performing the procedure in the hospital; and the reality that unlike the Orthodox, Reform Jews were just not committed enough to bring their infants back to the hospital on the eighth day. The question as he saw it, then—as with Shabbat afternoon bar mitzvahs—was how to accommodate the people's practice, even though it entailed a significant departure from Torah and halakhah. "What shall we do about this probable preference of the members of our congregations, which . . . will mean that most of the circumcisions will be before the eighth day?"

There was no possible precedent for altering the Torah's commandment, so Freehof created one. Citing several authorities who held that a child circumcised for medical necessity before the eighth day need not have *hatafat dam* on the eighth day, thereby implying that the original act was valid, he leapt to an astonishing conclusion: "It is clear that there is a considerable weight of authority that gives legal status to the pre-eighth-day circumcision at the command of a doctor, and in the present case it is clear that the doctors so desire it." He acknowledged that these were "liberal opinions . . . regarded as important 'to rely upon in time of need'" and were clearly "contrary to general Jewish practice." But "in case this hospital practice of sending mothers home early becomes permanent, and in case the parents insist upon the circumcision being performed in the hospital before the mother goes home, then we may have to face the fact." He advised rabbis not to be present at the medical circumcision, but to have the father recite the blessings and then be called to the Torah the following Shabbat for a naming, as for the birth of a girl. He also included a tepid call to rabbis not to give in too quickly to the new reality, but to advocate for longer hospital stays and try to persuade couples to return to the hospital on the eighth day. Ironically, the only factor he mentioned in favor of waiting until the eighth day was medical opinion, noting physicians' preference for doing the procedure later.

Nevertheless, he believed that he had not actually given his approval for circumcision before the eighth day. Four years after this responsum was published he wrote a colleague asking about the same issue, "I do believe we ought to stick to our insistence, or rather our strong recommendation that circumcision take place on the eighth day." A few months after that he insisted that although he had written about circumcision before the eighth day, he had "never permitted it outright."[35] In fact, his response was consistent with his concept of minhag and the relationship between popular practice and rabbinic regulation. In the face of overwhelming evidence that this was now popular minhag, he limited his response to what he believed constituted the proper rabbinic role, "regularizing" popular practice within the parameters—however widely drawn—of the tradition.

In the context of Freehof's generally *laissez faire* approach to "ceremonies" in a Reform context, his strident opposition to bar mitzvah—including his refusal to allow it at Rodef Shalom[36]—demands explanation. He did not have a rigidly ideological objection to bar mitzvah, though he did fear its spread would weaken Confirmation, which he regarded as one of the best examples of Reform innovation.[37] He recognized the emotional pull of bar mitzvah, admitting to a congregant, "If I had a son, I would want him to be Bar Mitzvah, but for family reasons, because it would hurt my father if his grandson were not Bar Mitzvah."[38] What he objected to was the excess associated with bar mitzvah celebrations, which were unlike "the modest affairs they were in my boyhood."[39] In this he was not alone, of course. Bar mitzvah celebrations, already lavish before the war among east European Jews who could afford it, grew progressively more outrageous after the war, provoking intense distaste, resistance, and anxiety among rabbis and thoughtful Jews across the religious spectrum.[40]

Bar mitzvah had never completely disappeared from Reform radar screens, though in the interwar period many who wanted it were more likely to take their sons to the Orthodox congregation down the street for the occasion than to insist that it be celebrated in their Reform temple.[41] But by 1953, the year in which Freehof received his first question on the subject, boys were celebrating their bar mitzvahs in an overwhelming 92% of Reform congregations, which rose to 96.4% in 1960.[42]

The very first inquiry he received asked whether a bar mitzvah might be held on a Sunday. Noting that "[t]he essence of the service is the reading from the Torah and I do not see how that can be done on a Sunday," Freehof mildly suggested scheduling the bar mitzvah for a Sunday in *ḥol ha-mo'ed* or on a *rosh ḥodesh*, or "[i]f no such occasion is available near the boy's birthday, then, if you wish, you might merely take the Torah out as a symbol and have the boy read from the printed Bible."[43] (A year later Responsa Committee chair Israel Bettan wrote a responsum opposing the idea of bar mitzvah on Sunday, though for a different reason. Reform, he explained, had replaced bar mitzvah with the far more satisfactory Confirmation. If a minority still continued to practice it, at least it was helping the "spirit of worship on the Sabbath Day." Moving it to Sunday would obviate even that bit of good.[44]) Enough variations on the same question continued to cross Freehof's desk after he assumed the Responsa Committee chairmanship that he grew disturbed, and in 1960 published a strongly worded responsum against holding bar mitzvahs on Sundays. He explicitly targeted "the unfortunate fact that the social celebration that accompanies the Bar Mitzvah has become so elaborate and so many guests are invited, that parents are eager to have it on Sunday, the day on which more people can attend." We have an obligation, he continued, to strive to maintain bar mitzvah as a religious occasion centered on the boy's participation in the Torah reading; it should, therefore, take place on Shabbat. The celebration should also take place on that day, according to traditional authorities. However, he continued, "it is much easier to keep the Bar Mitzvah service religious than to make the modern party spiritual. It would be wise, then, to make clear distinction between the ritual and the party. Let the ritual remain on the Sabbath where it belongs, and let the party be on Sunday, when the people seem to prefer it." If the rabbi is under great pressure to have a Sunday bar mitzvah, it may be scheduled on a Sunday when there is a Torah reading. "But to conduct a Torah reading where no Torah reading belongs, to recite the blessings of the Torah when none are due (Berocho L'vatolo), merely in order to make the religious service convenient to the social celebration, is to consent to an inversion of values, and should not be done."[45]

In private he was far more emphatic. He was appalled by the materialist values already inseparable from bar mitzvah: "[N]owadays, with the lavish child-worship by American parents, Bar Mitzvah observance has become a public disgrace." He observed that once some families start doing it, every child wants a party, and "no parent can then afford to deny it to his child, and Bar Mitzvah becomes universal in the congregation. When that happens, every Sabbath has a Bar Mitzvah, the regular Sabbath service is destroyed because the regular worshippers stop coming, and you have a different congregation every Sabbath. . . . I am glad that I never yielded to the Bar Mitzvah pressure; and I doubt whether any of my colleagues can accuse me of lacking traditional Jewish feelings."[46]

Nevertheless, the bar mitzvah juggernaut continued to roll on. In

1963 Freehof published a responsum endorsing bar mitzvah at Shabbat afternoon services for congregations that already had bar mitzvah, noting that it seemed a good way to revitalize a hitherto neglected service.[47] A colleague sent him a good-natured protest: "Oy vey iz mir! O naïve one, don't you realize that the motive for this kind of thing is as far removed from religion as it can be, but that it proceeds directly from a desire to go directly from the tfilah [prayer] to the cha-cha. We on the front lines are fighting this thing hard, for it means that people come to the service in their formal clothes & fancy dresses (or don't come at all), and presto, the party is on." Freehof's response was revealing:

> It is evident to me that I have much to learn about the realities of American Jewish life. Here I was in favor of Saturday afternoon Bar Mitzvah on Halachic grounds and also on practical grounds since I thought of diminishing the pressure on Saturday morning. And now you tell me that they come in evening clothes and from the Bar Mitzvah go directly to some cha-cha dance! I do not understand what Hillel meant when he said that if the Jews are not prophets, they are children of prophets. If that is what they have made of Bar Mitzvah, of which prophets are they the children?[48]

In 1968 he capitulated. In a responsum that year he reiterated all his criticism of Shabbat afternoon bar mitzvahs but then bowed to the inevitable. "It is evident that this arrangement fits the social wishes of the people, and if it is otherwise acceptable, will undoubtedly increase . . . Since, then, we are dealing with a situation which may well spread over the country, it is well to go into the matter in detail from the point of view of the Halacha, congregational welfare, and the mood of the community."

He therefore surveyed the halakhah regarding the latest proper time for *minḥah* and the earliest possible time for ending Shabbat, and found a passage in the Shulḥan Arukh[49] allowing one to pray the Saturday night *maariv* service and make *havdalah* (eliminating the candle) before full dark for the purpose of doing a mitzvah. Since Solomon Luria considered the bar mitzvah meal a *se'udat mitsvah*, Freehof concluded, "If, then, some words are spoken at the dinner table referring to the religious nature of the ceremony, this may be considered a *seudas mitzvah* . . .

and for that purpose a late *Mincha* service and a somewhat earlier *Havdalah* service (say at dusk, before the three stars appear) is permissible." He agreed with the questioner that these Saturday afternoon bar mitzvahs would weaken the Saturday morning service but saw no way to halt the process. Under the circumstances, "[w]hat must be done is to keep it within the decencies of tradition as much as possible." If congregations follow the guidelines he proposed, "[i]n that case, the new custom may be deemed quite acceptable."

By then Freehof knew that the mood of a Saturday night bar mitzvah party was completely at odds with any sense of religiosity, and that the likelihood of beginning the evening's affair with anything resembling words of Torah (other than, perhaps, the band leader dragging *zeyde* up to the microphone in his rented tux to mumble a *moytzi*) was between slim and none. Nevertheless, even here his response was consistent with his understanding of the relationship between popular minhag and rabbinic authority. The people were creating new customs around bar mitzvah; it was his role merely to regularize it. For Freehof this meant finding some halakhic precedent on which to rely, no matter how slim the reed, despite his dismay that bar mitzvah as the epitome of excess went on to become a staple of North American popular culture.

He opposed introducing bat mitzvah for the same reasons, but emphasized that allowing one required allowing the other, since "then you do not violate the Reform principle of the religious equality of men and women."[50] Similarly, he insisted that women be counted in the *minyan*.[51] However, he had been one of the HUC faculty members who voted against Martha Neumark's request for ordination,[52] and all his life he continued to evince concern for those who were uncomfortable with women's participation beyond the passive inclusion of mixed seating and being counted in the *minyan*. Asked about *aliyot* for women in 1957, he allowed that a congregation sufficiently modern could certainly call women to the Torah, "at least occasionally. I do not do it often, but if there is a special service, like a Sisterhood Service, or some other special occasion, I would not hesitate."[53] By the early 1970s he was more enthusiastic, but advised congregations to go slowly in introducing the practice.[54] While reaffirming that the Reform principle allowed a teenage girl to blow the *shofar*, he warned a questioner that older people might be uncomfortable about it because this was traditionally an honor given

to a pious man; and since *shofar* is one of the time-bound commandments from which women were exempt, "they would have considerable
justification" for their objections. "[W]e try, as much as possible, not to
contravene traditional law, especially not to contravene traditional custom to which people became very attached."[55] (In contrast, however, he
evinced no concern for traditionalists' discomfort when he decided that,
while a *shofar* was preferable, a trumpet was an acceptable alternative
and did not constitute *ḥukkot hagoy*.[56]) The comfort level of members
also mattered when it came to the question of employing a female rabbi.
In principle, Reform gave full rights to women; in practice, however, it
all depended on the "taste and feeling" of individual congregations.
Shortly before HUC ordained Sally Priesand, he wrote, "I would say
that if a congregation wants to separate men and women during worship, it is violating the spirit of Reform. But if it refuses to elect a woman
as cantor or rabbi, it has the right to its choice."[57]

The Reform Synagogue

The "German" vs. "Russian" demographic and cultural fault line in
American Jewry had persisted through the end of the Second World War,
with Reform Judaism still firmly in the "German" camp despite the extensive penetration of east Europeans into both leadership and membership. Freehof himself typified the mid-twentieth-century Reform
rabbinate. His father, Isaac Freilichoff, was a Ukrainian-born *sofer* and
mohel whose advertisement in the Baltimore Yiddish paper read, "*Makht
keyn misteyk ven ir broikht a moyl*" ("Make no mistake if you need a
mohel"); his mother Goldie piously read her *Tzena Urena* (the popular
Yiddish-language version of the Torah written for women) every
Shabbes. The Hebrew Union College had not only boosted his socioeconomic status by ordaining him and enabling him to receive a B.A.
from the University of Cincinnati; it had also ensured that he and his
peers adopt manners and mores suitable to social contact with their congregants. HUC President Kaufmann Kohler, for example, who spoke
with a thick German accent, nevertheless refused to assign students with
heavy Yiddish accents to student pulpits.[58] His successor, Julian Morgenstern, customarily invited seniors to his home for a meal at which he

served artichokes, to make sure that they knew how to eat this delicacy.[59] The College administration routinely "persuaded" students with egregiously east European-sounding names to change them to something less jarring to their future congregants' sensibilities—which is how Freilichoff became Freehof.[60]

The number of east Europeans in the Reform movement did grow in the interwar period, constituting half of the membership of large urban congregations by 1930.[61] But these individuals—who still represented only a fraction of the total number of east European Jews in the US—constituted a small, wealthy, and far more acculturated segment of that population. The postwar influx was different—largely native born and even less familiar with traditional Jewish life than their mostly immigrant parents. Although economically upwardly mobile, in educational level and cultural interests many of these people still differed significantly from the existing norm in Reform congregations. To put it bluntly, to many long-time Reform Jews the east Europeans still appeared crude and uncultured, the *Ostjuden* come to America. Not surprisingly, therefore—but ironically—Freehof sometimes applied his erudition to the defense of good taste.

Gambling and alcohol were cases in point. Asked whether it was permitted to gamble or play cards for money on the synagogue premises, he responded that his own Rodef Shalom permitted no liquor or gambling on the premises. He did not even like the fact that his Men's Club held a bridge tournament. Although no halakhah actually prohibited these activities in a social hall or similar space, nevertheless "the older Rabbinical authorities are right when they say, 'Whoever is strict, a blessing will come upon him.'"[62] Freehof was no bluestocking; he enjoyed his daily drink.[63] But gambling and the consumption of hard liquor in the synagogue building were simply déclassé.

Under no circumstances should a synagogue raise funds by gambling.[64] In 1963 he advised a Reform rabbi in a new suburb against having a gambling night to raise funds for the congregation. He acknowledged that a "terrific amount of gambling . . . goes on in New York, for example, in behalf of Orthodox congregations," but pointed out that while Orthodox and Conservative congregations did it, "Reform congregations hardly do it, though I can imagine that some smaller congregations must be using gambling in desperation." He suggested that if the congregation really wanted to have gambling, they could do it on Purim as part of a carnival.[65] He had the luxury of that position, of course, because Rodef Shalom Congregation could afford to rely on the generosity of wealthy donors and had no need to resort to raffles, lotteries, "Las Vegas nights," or bingo. In 1963 there was still an obvious socioeconomic gap in American Judaism: Reform had a disproportionate share of venerable, wealthy congregations like Rodef Shalom, while Orthodoxy was still largely the religious preference of the poorest segment of the community and Conservatism represented a rising middle ground. But most Reform congregations established after the war were virtually indistinguishable from their Conservative counterparts; membership in both was almost entirely young families, children of east European immigrants in the early stages of building their suburban dreams. They could not always be as fastidious as Freehof.

The east Europeans had brought with them to America ideologies of secular Jewish identity. The "German" vs. "Russian" split manifested itself, therefore, in yet another broad division within mid-century American Jewry, between those whose Jewish identity was rooted in religion (with or without peoplehood) and those whose Jewishness was ethnic and avowedly secular. During the interwar years some secularists advocated creating "Jewish Centers" (not to be confused with Mordecai Kaplan's "synagogue center"), where Jews could assemble for cultural and social activities, with no need for religion. Complicating this ideological divide was the dismaying reality that before World War II, most east European Jews were not evincing any commitment to any sort of Jewish affiliation, but were content with a non-ideological ethnicity solidly rooted in dense Jewish neighborhoods, Yiddish-English popular entertainment, and "kosher-style" gastronomy.[66] Freehof's answer to a 1953 question concerning congregational conflict on the suburban frontier reveals the intersection of class and aesthetics with this deep social and ideological division over the nature of American Jewry.

Dr. Frank Rosenthal, a scholarly graduate of the Jewish Theological Seminary of Breslau who had served pulpits in Germany and been interned in Buchenwald before coming to the US in 1940, was the rabbi of a new congregation in the Detroit area.[67] The members had just voted to build a synagogue, but there was not enough money to build the entire structure at once. As he explained to Freehof:

> One of the peculiarities of this congregation is that a very vocal minority originally joined for its social and cultural programs, and not for its religious activities. This group continues to stress its interests, and since our lay leadership is young and somewhat inexperienced it is confused as to whether we should build a chapel first or a multi-purpose room (social hall) which could be used for all types of activities including card playing and dancing. I am frightened at the spectacle that our congregation may be asked to decide between the building of a Beth Hamikdosh [sanctuary] or a dance hall. Rabbinical advice in the matter was not requested by the lay bodies which went ahead with their planning on the premise that it is the function of the Rabbi to concern himself with the 'religious aspects' of congregational matters (whatever that may mean) and that building problems should fall within the province of our lay leadership.[68]

He was therefore writing to Freehof for help. He wanted to know what religious activities could not take place in the proposed multipurpose hall, but he also wanted Freehof to weigh in on whether "the erection of a social hall as the first part of our building plan [would] be in keeping with our dignity as a Jewish community, and fulfill the spiritual needs of our membership, our children and our community as a whole."

Freehof shared Rosenthal's concerns completely and determined to help him take a stand. After protesting that he was too busy to respond in depth, he wrote two extensive letters to bolster the rabbi's position, subsequently publishing them virtually unchanged in his first volume of responsa.[69] He made his fear quite clear: An identifiably Jewish institution where Jews gathered apart from their Christian neighbors, but only for low-class amusements like dancing and playing cards, would spark antisemitism.

> The good name of the Jewish community is involved. It is, alas, sad that it must be so but it is important that we make it clear to our fellow Americans that we are not a strange, mysterious clan, but a religious faith and we build a house of

worship for our spiritual needs. This is not mere assimila-
tionist catering to Christian opinion. . . . It is a religious mandate for us so to conduct ourselves that whoever sees us will
say God is in their midst. It is, therefore, not only a legal duty
but a spiritual duty to build a sanctuary as soon as possible.[70]

He re-emphasized this point in his second letter. "The good name of
Jewry must be the concern of every Jewish group (Kiddush Ha-shem).
. . . If the only building which a congregation will have for a number of
years is a dance and a card hall, people will tend to consider the Jewish
group merely a pleasure-hungry clan."[71]

Though antisemitism tapered off rapidly in the postwar years, in 1953
Jews were not yet certain that the most antisemitic period in American
history was truly past. Freehof had had his own experiences with it. In
the early 1930s he had a lengthy correspondence with members of Phi
Delta Epsilon, the Jewish medical fraternity, about his proposal to reduce "the crowding of Jewish young men into the medical schools and
the law schools," which was "particularly dangerous today when pro-
pagandists are searching about for reasons to provoke antisemitism."[72]
During the war, he and his rabbinic colleagues on CANRA had coped
with antisemitism in the military and guided military chaplains accordingly. Now, in the new suburbs, Jews were living interspersed among
the gentiles in unprecedented numbers, allowing for far more visibility
and social intercourse. It is not surprising that he should share the anxiety of many American Jews in the postwar years: *"Mah yomru
hagoyim?"*—"What will the gentiles say?"[73]

However, in stressing the need to build first a structure exclusively
for worship, Freehof was taking a stance not merely about one synagogue but about the nature of American Jewry. The synagogue-center,
not invented, but fully realized, by Mordecai Kaplan, emerged onto the
American Jewish scene in the 1920s and spread throughout the country.
While Judaism had a central and essential role in Kaplan's synagogue-
center, in that same decade secular Jewish professionals formed a separate movement that also adopted the term "Jewish center." This group
"advocated a multipurpose . . . institution that could exist outside of, and
even without the synagogue. The implication was that Jewish religious
life was obsolete, in line to be replaced by the cultural and ethnic

Jewishness of the secular center." The result was a struggle between the rabbinic advocates of the synagogue-center and the social workers of the secular Jewish Center movement as "the religious and the social spheres of Jewish community [fought] for predominance. Both wanted to be at the 'center' of Jewish life." In the immediate postwar years, when Jews were building new communal institutions in suburbia, synagogues and Jewish Community Centers became rivals.[74] In writing that the "vocal minority" that so disturbed him had "originally joined for its social and cultural programs, and not for its religious activities," Rosenthal indicated his worry that the very nature of the new institution was at stake: Would it be a synagogue or a secular Jewish Center? The question wakened Freehof's fear of the slippery slope.

He was not opposed to bringing together religious and secular activities under one roof, even secular activities of questionable taste. Some large Reform congregations already functioned as synagogue centers early in the century and more expanded into centers in the 1920s.[75] Freehof's own Rodef Shalom certainly offered the usual complement of Sisterhood, Brotherhood, adult education, and youth activities in addition to services and Sunday school. Asked in 1955 about gambling in the synagogue (not for fund raising), he readily acknowledged the modern synagogue's dual identity. "We must assume . . . that American Synagogues, as the Talmud says of certain Babylonian synagogues, *were* built with the express pre-condition of not being sacred. It is clear then that we have two opposite moods:—considerable tradition of hilarious celebration in parts of the building, and on the other hand, care for the sanctity of the place of worship itself." The rabbi had to exercise good judgment in determining what was appropriate.[76]

Nevertheless, it was easy for Freehof to envision a Kaplan-style synagogue center degenerating into a secular Jewish center, particularly since he already despised Kaplan's notion of Judaism as a civilization. (Only a year before receiving this inquiry, he had written to a colleague, "But I want you to know that I have a prejudice against all these latkes and kreplach that are dragged into our reform ritual as if thereby we deepen the traditional spirit. I wrote to the source of all this idea, Dr. Mordecai Kaplan, in which, when he asked me in answer to his question, 'Why do I object to the Latkes?' I said I love latkes as a diet; I detest them as a doctrine."[77]) His classmate Abba Hillel Silver had already grown disillusioned with the synagogue-center twenty-five years earlier, because the secular activities caused people to lose sight of the institution's central sacred purpose.[78] Rosenthal's letter clearly sparked Freehof's fear that multipurpose facilities of the type proposed would undermine the primacy of religion in defining Jewish life. Indeed, a decade later he would frame the conflict explicitly: Asked whether a congregation should cancel its Shabbat evening service to join a community-wide celebration at the JCC he wrote: "[I]t is certainly contrary to the spirit of Jewish law to abandon the services in Mikdash Meat, 'the small sanctuary,' especially nowadays when the Jewish Centers often will vaunt themselves as *the* Jewish institution. It is necessary to affirm the status of the synagogue."[79] Faced, therefore, with a group who only wanted "social and cultural" activities in what was supposed to be a synagogue, he held the fort.

Holding the fort, however, required an extremely tendentious reading of the halakhah. For tactical advantage he defined the proposed multipurpose space as a purely profane space and characterized it in the most derogatory terms possible. Prayer and study were both "clear mandate[s] of Jewish law," but the law never even mentioned "a communal social hall." One could pray even in an inn with crosses in times of emergency, but the law did not allow the use of "banquet halls" for regular prayer.[80] "If, in spite of the requirement of Jewish tradition, the Chapel is not built first, then it must be understood that the Social Hall[,] which is used for card-playing and dancing, cannot possibly be used for worship. . . . Even for occasional worship it is questionable whether a place of amusement may be used for worship. . . . "[81] He applied similar deliberate tendentiousness to the Talmud, the Shulḥan Arukh, and a Hungarian responsum forbidding a mourner from assembling a *minyan* in a coffeehouse to recite Kaddish,[82] to conclude that

> [i]f the group insists on building this social hall first, and the presumption is that this will be the congregation's only building for a few years until more money can be raised, then they must also build a small, inexpensive chapel in which the Ark and Torah shall be housed and in which services shall be held. If, however, as Jewish tradition requires, the house of worship is built first, this sanctuary can be used, if necessary,

for meetings held for the benefit of the synagogue, congregational meetings, Sisterhood meetings, et cetera. Even so, these meetings must be conducted with the dignity due the sanctuary.[83]

Freehof's answer carried sufficient weight that when the congregation built their new facility, they built it with both a sanctuary and a social hall.[84] He, however, eventually made his peace with multipurpose spaces. They became so commonplace that questions addressed to him asked only about the propriety of given activities within them. In 1960 he confirmed that it was permissible to place an Ark in an area that would be used for other purposes besides prayer, as long as it was done in such a way that the Ark could be closed off when not in use.[85] In 1964 he advised against allowing popular dancing at a bar mitzvah party in a multipurpose room with a screened-off Ark, but the inflammatory rhetoric was gone. Since the synagogue in question had been built with "the understood pre-condition" that it was a multipurpose space, "certain social activities . . . such as dinners" were permitted, though "mixed dancing, particularly of the rather wild, modern kind, . . . [did] not comport with the mood of the building." He encouraged his correspondent to take a firm stance against dancing as a way to ensure that the congregation would build a proper sanctuary. Nevertheless, he admitted that the answer was only "a matter of taste, because Jewish tradition offers contradictory answers."[86]

By contrast, he had no reservations whatsoever about a synagogue fundraising production of *The Mikado* being staged in a multipurpose space, even without a partition in front of the Ark, because "Gilbert and Sullivan's operetta is charming and delightful, and there is nothing immoral in it. Besides, the fact that it aided in the maintenance of the synagogue and created good will in the community is certainly a justification for it and similarly decent operettas to be given there." The halakhic objection to music in the synagogue only "represent[ed] a puritanical attitude and a gloom of grief which can hardly apply to the mood of a modern congregation." Nor would the staging of a theatrical production affect the sanctity of the space; as Moshe Feinstein had ruled, we distinguish between "a place which is regularly used for unworthy purposes and a synagogue in which occasionally some unworthy act has occurred. The synagogue retains its sanctity," though he did allow that for the sake of those few members who objected, "it might be advisable for a rather extensive and opaque partition to be put up before the Ark." However, bringing a pig into the social hall for a production of *Li'l Abner* was going too far. There was no actual prohibition because such a question would never have occurred to our ancestors, but it should not be done "on the general basis of keeping disgusting things from the synagogue."[87]

The evolution of Freehof's responses reflect his accommodation of the new minhag, but that accommodation was made possible by the fact that by the 1960s the battle over American Jewish identity was apparently over. Synagogues and JCCs had learned to coexist.

Consistent with his opposition to secular Jewish centers, Freehof—who came from a strongly Zionist family background and was committed to Jewish peoplehood—believed that in the Diaspora Jews were properly a religious group. He explained himself in an unpublished responsum answering an inquiry about the status of gentile spouses who attend synagogue regularly, raise their children as Jews, and who "consider themselves Jews, not Christians." He told the questioner:

> When the Jewish state existed we could have a Ger Toshov [resident alien] because they were in relation to a community, to a state. They were not citizens, they were residents with a special right of residence in a state. If we were still a state, we could give such people residential rights, which did not make the recipient a Jew religiously. . . . But here in the diaspora we are not a state, but a religious community. A so-called or quasi-Ger Toshov asks to be given not residential rights of an immigrant, but religious rights of a semi-convert.[88]

This was consistent with the response he had given a decade earlier to Israeli Prime Minister David Ben-Gurion, who wrote him asking for advice on what to do about children of Jewish fathers and gentile mothers. The state was willing to register them as Jews but the Orthodox rabbinate opposed this. Freehof responded that in Israel, unlike in the Diaspora, one could again be a Jew both by religion and by nationality, and suggested that the state apply the category of *ger toshav* to those who were Jewish only by nationality.[89]

Reform Judaism as Authentic Judaism

Throughout his career Freehof walked a very narrow line, carefully balancing his love and respect for traditional Judaism with his insistence that the Orthodox community extend to Reform Judaism its due respect. With warm memories of his Orthodox upbringing and a deep and abiding respect for his parents' piety and his father's erudition, he was disposed to regard traditional Judaism generously. He particularly admired the traditional "democratization" of learning:

> How can we [Reform Jews] rebuild true, continuous adult education in our community? . . . It isn't Judaism without democratic learning. . . . This is the glory of Orthodoxy, that it can re-establish in the New World yeshivas and have boys devote their lives to it . . .
>
> . . . [W]e lack in general the whole system of adult education which is the heart of Judaism. Just think of the fact that at least in the last generation every Orthodox *shul* had a *ḥevra mishnayos* [Mishnah study group]. Some had a *ḥevra shas* [Talmud study group]. A hundred people in a *ḥevra tehillim* [Psalms study group]. . . . Everybody studied. That was the unique feature of Judaism that no other religion had. And when we lose that we lose our real identity, it seems to me.[90]

He saw Orthodoxy, however, as a tragic phenomenon. It was dying, he was certain. It was incapable of surviving in the modern world, which had removed the boundaries of Jewish communal autonomy that had enabled it to survive. In the absence of enforced separation, "life" was challenging "the law," and "life" was winning; the inevitable result was the wholesale abandonment of halakhah and the emergence of new minhag that differed from codified halakhah in the limited realms of life in which Jews still acted as Jews. Even self-proclaimed Orthodox Jews were part of this trend; for them just as for Reform Jews, the realm of religion encompassed only ethics, ritual, and life cycle, while the rest of their lives were guided by secular laws and courts. The Orthodox rabbinic leadership, however, refused to accept the inevitable. Perceiving themselves under attack by modernity, the response of Orthodox rabbis in the modern period was to become ever more stringent, in turn alienating more Jews.[91]

This had not always been so. In previous ages the rabbis had responded with flexibility and creativity to the radical changes in Jews' lives; now, however, petrification had set in.[92] Furthermore, the very structure of the halakhah meant that it lacked the flexibility to adapt to changed circumstances: In the absence of a Sanhedrin, there was no way to make the fundamental changes necessary to enable "the law" to survive the encounter with "life."[93] Reform had been a necessary development within Judaism because the tradition had lacked both the will and the capacity to respond to the needs of the times. Thus Freehof looked on developments within Orthodoxy with pity.

> One might think that men such as you and I, who have been brought up in an Orthodox home and revere it, would have nothing further that we needed to learn about the mood of the Orthodox; but there is a difference between the Orthodoxy in the home and the Orthodoxy in the organized Orthodox rabbinate. The Orthodoxy of our home was a natural, normal way of life. The Orthodoxy of the rabbinate is a beleaguered Orthodoxy in a state of siege, which they feel must be constantly protected against the encroachments of modern life. They may well be quite right about it.
> . . . Whenever there is a choice between a strict or a lenient version of the law, they feel it is safer, in the present beleaguered condition of Judaism, to advocate the stricter interpretation.[94]

Nevertheless, his personality and his scholarship enabled him to build bridges and even maintain warm friendships with Orthodox colleagues. He had close personal relationships with some of his Orthodox colleagues on the military chaplaincy board and valued their cross-movement cooperation. David de Sola Pool, Leo Jung, Joseph Lookstein, Emanuel Rackman, and other leaders of modern Orthodoxy respected his learning.[95] He enjoyed a cordial relationship and exchanged scholarly correspondence with Rabbi Wolf Leiter of Pittsburgh and

Rabbi Yitsḥak Gruenfeld of Columbus. He regularly read the ultra-Orthodox halakhic periodicals *HaPardes* and *HaMa'or*.[96] While he answered the occasional question from Orthodox correspondents, he referred inquiries on kashrut and *gittin* to Leiter, since he felt he had no right to rule on these matters for practicing Orthodox Jews.[97]

In the 1950s, however, Freehof's collegial relations with the Orthodox members of the chaplaincy board became strained as the latter came under pressure from right-wing Orthodoxy not to rule leniently and not to cooperate with non-Orthodox rabbis. His response was to be as flexible as possible in order to preserve the unity of the chaplaincy board.[98] He also made an effort to forestall any development that might make it more difficult for his modern Orthodox colleagues to continue their cooperation with representatives of Reform and Conservative Judaism. In 1953, when it appeared that the UAHC might reopen the question of a code of Reform practice, Freehof opposed it for all his usual reasons, and then added that "a code would be an open attack upon more observant groups of Judaism by officially declaring that that which we do not include is no longer God's will or never was God's will, and that the Orthodox are deluding themselves by their loyalties. It is unnecessary to make an official statement severing ourselves from them just at a time when we are achieving comradely relations."[99] Asked in 1954 for an interview for a news story about the Reform rabbi whose "knowledge of halacha was such that a good many Orthodox rabbis came to you with their problems," he flatly refused.

> Much of my work in the Halacha in relation to Orthodoxy has been for the last ten years due to my chairmanship of the committee on responsa of the Chaplaincy Commission. . . . Our friendly cooperation is due to the fact that there is no publicity, and thus we do not compel the Orthodox rabbinate to make public acknowledgement that they rely upon the responsa written by a Reform rabbi.
>
> Publicity in this case would do harm to a very important cause. Please be kind and take no notice of this work of mine.[100]

By nature conciliatory, he refused to be provoked into public controversy. In 1964 he received a letter from Bertram Schlein, director of a Jewish cemetery in Philadelphia. Schlein had advertised mausoleum burial in the Philadelphia *Jewish Exponent*, using an out of context quotation from *RJP* and Freehof's name to assert its Jewish legitimacy.[101] This had sparked controversy: The paper published a hostile letter to the editor claiming that comparing modern mausoleum burial to ancient cave burial was like calling something "kosher style," and that Freehof in any case was not a proper rabbinical authority for American Jews because he was a Reform rabbi. The letter writer was an insurance salesman with Orthodox rabbinic credentials of dubious provenance, Schlein informed Freehof. But the Philadelphia Rabbinical Council and the Rabbinical Assembly had just issued statements saying mausoleum burial violates Jewish law, Conservative rabbis in the area were in agreement with the letter, and local Reform rabbis were up in arms over the slur on Freehof. Now Schlein wanted to know what to do. Freehof responded mildly, "I presume you had quoted from *Reform Jewish Practice* i, p. 122. You will notice that I say it is not in accordance with Orthodox practice today; but as I have said, I do not want to be quoted as an authority for Orthodox practices, or even to express any opinion to Orthodox Jews about it—and certainly not to get into any controversy with them."[102]

He often advised Reform colleagues not to act in ways that would violate traditional sensibilities, e.g., not to perform weddings on Hoshana Rabba or Tisha B'Av.[103] Even as he strove to be conciliatory, however, he came to realize that the breach was real. What happened to the chaplaincy was happening everywhere in the community. The new reality grieved him. Concerning the refusal of an Orthodox *mohel* to circumcise the son of a Reform convert, he wrote:

> This is a sad situation for American Jewry because it involves a breakdown of slowly achieved brotherliness and an increase of bitterness. I, who find my chief intellectual interest in halacha, have naturally always had the feeling of affection, understanding, and considerateness to Orthodoxy, which is the chief source of the material I live with. Nevertheless, even I am convinced that the time has come to fight back. If we do not, they will push us mercilessly into unbearable situations.[104]

As Reform and Orthodox Jews interacted more and more in Jewish communal settings, he encountered more and more instances of Orthodoxy expecting that its standards should be communal norms. In 1957 a Reform colleague asked whether he should co-officiate at a wedding with an Orthodox rabbi when his participation would be limited to delivering a sermonette; Freehof took this opportunity to air his feelings about the new situation.

> This question is getting more and more troublesome by the year. The large immigration, chiefly into Brooklyn, of unyielding, Hassidic Orthodox rabbis have [*sic*] forced the more American Orthodox rabbis into increasing strictness and, we might say, fanaticism. . . .
>
> We are being subjected in the last two years to a mounting campaign of hate. . . . Up to about ten years ago it was easier to achieve some cooperation in wedding and funeral services with Orthodox rabbis. Now it is very difficult.
>
> You really are not asking a halachic question, but a question of policy, and I can only tell you what my feelings are in the matter. I read the rabbinic magazines constantly and see these embittered attacks as often as they appear. I have decided for myself, not to be bullied by them, although you know me to be easy-going in disputes and, in fact, to have a deep affection for Orthodox law and custom. But I have decided that we must consider our own self-respect and also must protect American Jewry against being overwhelmed by fanatics who always have the advantage of vehemence. . . .[105]

He stiffened his own stance on issues of cooperation, as he correctly perceived such conflicts as attacks on the legitimacy of Reform Jewish practice. In that same year he wrote:

> For example, we are constantly urged to have all charity dinners completely kosher. I used to be inclined to agree with it. I am no longer so inclined in the light of the campaign against us. I will advocate tables of kosher food for as many as will demand kosher food, but I will not allow, if I can help it, kashruth exclusively, for everyone at public dinners. I will not permit the attacking Orthodox to force me to eat kosher

food on the argument that it will not harm me to do so. It does violate my principle to force me to admit that kosher is so essential that no public dinner should occur without it. My religious principles teach me that kosher is incidental to religion, and I will not permit, if I can help it, a public declaration that my religious principles are an illusion. I will no longer be driven to the point where I admit by implication that my way of Judaism is publicly indecent.[106]

He continued to encourage Reform Jews not to allow Orthodox norms of kashrut to become the norm in Jewish communal life, though he also cautioned UAHC President Maurice Eisendrath to follow his own practice at Rodef Shalom and avoid serving pork and shellfish at Reform events, since it would "[hurt] the sensitivities of many fellow Jews, particularly since the tradition is on their side in this matter.[107]

Freehof likewise asserted the legitimacy of Reform Jewish practice with respect to activity on Shabbat at Jewish Community Centers. A 1960 request for guidance from a Reform member of the policy committee for the Detroit JCC gave him the opportunity to articulate his views. The matter, he observed, "involves the whole changing religious scene of American Jewry." As befitted a country that guaranteed freedom of religion, there was no central Jewish body to set religious standards. Orthodox and Reform Jews would have to compromise. "Clearly a class in painting is strongly violative of Orthodox sentiments. But I would like to see an Orthodox authority give me Jewish *legal* proof that playing basketball violates the Sabbath." He recommended "an American Jewish solution," that each and every possible activity be judged individually. "A demand . . . to stop *all* activity is not required by Orthodox law and is a *propaganda* demand, an attempt of one group of the community to dominate another. Such a decision must be resisted. But every *separate* activity of the Center should be judged, one by one, and those deemed a *flagrant* violation of the Sabbath laws should be abandoned."

Two years later in response to a similar inquiry he distinguished between "sentimental and emotional demands" as opposed to "the actual requirements and prohibitions of Jewish law," and pointed out that R. Eliezer Silver of Cincinnati, the honorary president of the Agudas Ha-Rabbonim, had proposed the same solution as he had, but was then attacked by his colleagues "because they wanted to make a *demonstration* of the triumph of complete Sabbath observance." Again he insisted, "It is about time that it be openly stated that the Jewish *public* is no longer an Orthodox public exclusively. . . . We cannot permit the public management of Jewish institutions to assert, by the manner in which the institutions are conducted, that only an Orthodox Jew is a true Jew."[108]

Nevertheless, asked in 1966 by a South African colleague whether he felt that an "unbridgeable gulf" existed between Orthodoxy and Reform, Freehof responded out of his native moderation: ". . . [I]f we . . . give vent to our most extreme opinions, then there can *develop* an 'unbridgeable gulf.' . . . But in actual fact, human beings . . . try not to be as extreme as their doctrines can possibly drive them to be; and people being reasonable, they manage to get along. . . . With us Jews the task is easier because, besides being followers of a doctrine, we are brothers of a family, and decent people among us always try to get along...."[109]

While Freehof had a sentimental attachment to Orthodoxy, he had little tolerance for Conservative Judaism, though he was always gracious and helpful when Conservative colleagues turned to him for halakhic guidance.[110] He regarded the Conservative attempt to carve out a distinctive halakhic path as "admirable" but fundamentally flawed, for two reasons. The first was "social-psychological": By acknowledging the authority of the halakhah, Conservatism was necessarily acknowledging the authority of the Orthodox rabbinate, but the Orthodox would never reciprocate by acknowledging their authority. "I think that we Reformers and Conservatives, who are both Liberals in Judaism, should decide what we want to do in every case according to our best judgment and conscience, knowing beforehand that nothing we do will make our movement[s] or our ceremonials acceptable to the Orthodox." The second was what he considered the fundamental reality that Conservatism was trying to ignore—that there was "no possible stretching of the law or liberalizing it that can enable it to roof over the realities of modern Jewish life."[111] Attempts by the Conservative rabbinate to forbid practices that were spreading throughout their movement were futile attempts to stem the tide of popular minhag.[112] Convinced of the truth of his understanding of the relationship between law and life, he was not interested in changing Reform practice to harmonize with Conservatism. When Freehof read a CCAR board member's public endorsement of a

Rabbinical Assembly proposal to the CCAR Executive Board, that American Reform and Conservative Jews align themselves with each other and with Israel by adding the second day of Rosh Hashanah in Reform and eliminating the second day of the festivals in Conservatism, he fired off a letter in protest. The Reform position was authentic and derived from the Torah; the second day of Rosh Hashanah was only a medieval import from the Diaspora. In any case, popular minhag was against it: "[O]ur congregations will vehemently object, or will vote against it by absenting themselves from the second day."[113]

He fought just as vehemently against Conservative denials of Reform legitimacy as against Orthodox ones. In 1961 a Philadelphia Reform rabbi turned to Freehof for support when the local Conservative rabbis attempted to enforce an agreement with kosher caterers not to cater any function on Shabbat at which there was photography, smoking, candle lighting, or playing of instrumental or recorded music (presumably in order to prevent dancing). The apparent intent was to put an end to violations of halakhah that had become common at bar mitzvah parties held outside the synagogue. However, the agreement also meant that either these caterers would lose their eligibility to serve at Conservative functions if they catered Reform bar mitzvahs, where these were not necessarily considered prohibited activities (see Chapter 6), or Reform Jews would have to adhere to Conservative standards of Shabbat observance.[114]

Freehof responded with outrage at this delegitimation of Reform practice, intended or not. He even argued that the Reform rabbis could easily have filed a civil court case against this "conspiracy . . . to hinder or prevent the Reform type of Bar Mitzvah observance [which was] surely a violation of freedom of religious conscience." His strongly worded responsum reaffirmed the authenticity of Reform observance by employing Orthodox arguments against the validity of Conservative halakhah. He ranted that Reform rabbis could have gone to the Jewish press to show that the Conservative point of view was merely a "pretense of piety" on the part of people who allowed "the public Sabbath violation of riding to the synagogue . . . as a matter of course." He observed snidely, "Those who permit or condone the public violation of the Sabbath (which sin is deemed to be equivalent to the violation of the entire Torah) can, alas, be described only as hypocritical if they try to force

Orthodox observances on others." He launched a series of pointed ha-lakhic barbs at the Conservative stance. First, just as a sinful *kohen* may still bless the people, we do not prevent Jews from fulfilling one mitz-vah (eating kosher food) just because they violate another (Shabbat); that in itself is a transgression. Second, their reasoning was inconsistent. Smoking is, indeed, a serious transgression; but though the Mishnah for-bids dancing on holidays, the texts show that the halakhah did not take this too seriously. "Why should the Conservative rabbinate of Philadel-phia take upon itself to be more strict than the Tosfos and Moses Isser-les?" Third, there was no halakhic basis for prohibiting non-flash photography. The Conservatives appeared to be guided by non-halakhic considerations. "[T]o lump the clear prohibition of lighting fire and smoking on the Sabbath with the two highly dubious prohibitions of dancing and photography, makes one wonder whether this whole enter-prise can be deemed to be Halachic at all." Fourth, the caterers them-selves drive their trucks to the synagogues on Shabbat, making them public Sabbath violators whose food is of dubious kashrut. Therefore even if the Reform congregations bowed to Conservative pressure, he observed sarcastically, "their weakness would be in vain, for they would not be getting truly kosher food in return." At least the Orthodox would make sure to close that loophole! Finally, their agreement with the cater-ers violated halakhah because, while one may make an agreement to be stricter than the law, one may not make an agreement to violate it—and "to gather and make a public agreement to perpetuate the Conservative system, which condones the violation of great sections of the law, is clearly a sin in the eyes of traditional law, and is to be described as 'mak-ing a condition against what is written in the Torah' (Masne al ma she-cosuv ba-torah, m. Ketubos IX, 1). The Orthodox rabbinate could well assure the caterers that such an agreement is null and void." In short, he concluded, "the Conservative rabbinate is trying to enforce . . . not true Jewish traditional law, but the selective Conservative custom, which per-mits certain things, or condones certain violations and emphasizes cer-tain other things. We would be the last to deny that they have a right as human beings to this selectivity...[b]ut they have no right to speak in the name of the legal tradition, and certainly not to force their particular sys-tem of selectivity upon others." He recommended that in the face of "this strange situation which is contrary to the essentials of Jewish law and yet which speaks in the name of Jewish tradition," the Reform rabbis should issue a public declaration insisting on their freedom of religion and committing to exercise it by doing business with other caterers—kosher caterers, if possible, or just Jewish caterers, or even gentile caterers, "since our people do eat in public restaurants," and agreeing to provide fish or other special dishes for the benefit of any Orthodox relatives present. "This will make our meals as kosher as most public meals are in the Jewish community . . . "[115]

The same issue of legitimacy underlay his resistance to the prospect of Reform rabbis altering Reform standards in personal status matters for the sake of communal unity. Though his objection was partly pragmatic—no matter what Reformers did, it would never satisfy the Orthodox[116]—there was principle behind it. Firmly convinced that Reform had done the right thing with regard to conversion, divorce, and marriage, he saw no need to change. Thus he wrote to support a colleague in a dispute over the conversion of an infant: "The Orthodox refuse to accept the validity of Reform conversion. We must not yield to their pressure. We cannot admit that our way of life is not Jewishly religious. If they do not wish to accept us, that is their business, not ours. . . . Please do not yield on this matter. Yielding would be tantamount to admitting that Reform Jewish practice is not Jewish."[117]

He insisted that Reform conversions were actually more thorough and meaningful than Orthodox ones. When an Orthodox day school refused admission to children of non-Orthodox converts, he criticized its rabbis for relying on a mere "technical justification as to non-Orthodox conversion." In reality a Reform conversion was "more thorough-going" than an Orthodox one, "which tends to become a ritual formality."[118] The argument was halakhically untenable, of course; he knew that the halakhah assumed that all Jews accepted *milah* and *tevilah* as norms. But he was defending Reform legitimacy. From within his ideological paradigm, the fact that Reform conversions did not include *milah* and *tevilah*, and that Reform's understanding of *kabbalat ol mitsvot* differed from the traditional one, was irrelevant. The stringency of the contemporary Orthodox rabbinate was a regular target of his ire; in this case, he argued, the halakhah itself prohibits casting doubt on the Jewishness of children even when the parent's own conversion is doubtful, and also

mandates that all Jewish families are to be presumed kosher.[119]There-
fore "[t]hese people of whom you speak are violating, if not the letter,
at least the spirit of the Halacha."[120]

He was adamant on the subject of the *get*. Asked about introducing
some form of liberal *get*, he responded with the classic Reform arguments he had offered in *RJP*, adding that the fact that the vast majority of Jews no longer cared about *gittin* was proof that the Reformers
had decided correctly. He also noted pointedly that the British Reform
get had not increased Jewish unity. "On the contrary, the Bes Din has
been infuriated at them and has recently issued a special pamphlet
against them for presuming to meddle in matters that do not concern
them." American Reform, therefore, should not change its practice.
"History is on our side. We represent the living facts of Jewish life."
He assured other colleagues that there was no need to be concerned
over this difference between Orthodox and Reform practice because
the *get* would inevitably disappear from Jewish life, and warned that
even if Reform did introduce some sort of *get* it would not be recognized by the Orthodox, who "[would] never be satisfied with less than
complete surrender."[121]

Only once did he put in print any direct challenge or response to Orthodox objections to Reform practice in personal status matters. In 1956
Moshe Feinstein issued his famous responsum invalidating all Reform
marriages, on the grounds that (1) the ceremony used by Reform rabbis
is not correct; (2) even if it were, there are no kosher witnesses at a Reform wedding; (3) *kiddushin* by intercourse is valid only when there was
already *kiddushin* but the couple had reason to suspect that it may not
have been valid, which couples married by Reform rabbi do not suspect;
and (4) even if a couple lived together subsequently as husband and wife,
we do not give them the benefit of the doubt of *en adam ose be'ilato*[122]
because we can only make this assumption in the case of observant Jews
who conduct themselves properly.[123] While Feinstein wrote his responsum to free an *agunah*, a purpose for which the most far-fetched lines of
argument are routinely employed, it was also an expression of deep con-
tempt for Reform Judaism. Nevertheless, it actually had few practical
ramifications, at least in the United States, where the decentralization
of Jewish religious life allowed all Jews to do as they pleased religiously,

and where Reform Jews were numerically sufficient to resist Orthodox pressure.

The situation was otherwise in Britain, however, where an Orthodox Chief Rabbinate controlled many aspects of Jewish religious life and where liberal Jews made up a much smaller percentage of the Jewish population. Three years after Feinstein wrote his responsum, Freehof received a plea for help from the rabbi of the West London Synagogue, the flagship congregation of the British Reform movement. Reform marriages were under "concentrated attack" by the "Orthodox authorities." Letters to the Jewish press, public comments by Orthodox rabbis, and a "whispering campaign which greatly disturbs people who otherwise would have been married in our Synagogues" were claiming that witnesses at Reform marriages were not kosher, that these were not valid Jewish marriages, and that the status of children of such marriages was in doubt even when both parents were born Jews.[124] Clearly the accusations were based on Feinstein's responsum.

Freehof's letters to Dr. Werner Van der Zyl became his lengthy responsum "Orthodox Aspersions Against Reform Marriages."[125] Although he never referred to Feinstein or his responsum, this was without a doubt a response to it and to what Freehof saw as all the other provocations on the part of the Orthodox. First he raised the question of what makes a marriage valid, concluding that while this was a contentious issue in the earlier halakhah, conditions of life in the modern period—particularly the advent of civil marriage—have led the majority of halakhists to conclude that a marriage's validity is ultimately not a matter of ritual requirements, but depends rather on whether the couple had lived together as husband and wife with public knowledge of that fact. He concluded that while there are also Orthodox opinions arguing that common-law and civil marriages are not valid, those decisors carry less weight than their opponents, and he demonstrated that authoritative decisors increasingly regard these irregular arrangements as valid marriages. Therefore, he argued, even if Reform marriages lack the rituals required by halakhah, according to respected Orthodox opinion these marriages are nonetheless valid because the couples live together with the knowledge of the community. "[T]he *wedding* ceremony may be objected to by the Orthodox, but the *marriage* itself is absolutely valid according to Orthodox law." An Orthodox authority who doubts the va-

lidity of a Reform marriage "is not only callous to human considerations, but ignores the main development and tendency of Orthodox
law."[126]

Next, as with conversion, Freehof argued that the trend of the halakhah itself is to rule in such a way as to maintain Jewish unity. "Jewish legal tradition on marriage is so complicated and is such a mélange
of laws and customs that it is only too easy to cast aspersions on the validity or at least the propriety of any marriage." For example, some authorities absolutely prohibit marriages within the synagogue; others
prohibit mixed seating; others insist on checking the kashrut of witnesses; yet there are Orthodox weddings held in synagogues, in the presence of mixed groups, and with witnesses of doubtful fitness, and these
are not challenged. The Rishonim even found ways to allow marriages
with Karaites. "This reluctance to exclude Jews from the family fellowship of Israel is a basic one in the Halacha"—so basic that even the *kiddushin* of a willful apostate is valid (i.e., a halakhically valid marriage,
which can only be effected if both partners are Jewish, can be effected
even if one of the parties is a Jew who has adopted another religion).
"Clearly, then, anybody or any group which seeks to declare another
group of Jews unfit to marry with according to Jewish law is violating
the basic tendency of the law." He concluded with a ringing statement
of the ultimate correctness of the Reform position:

> But the practical question is, How shall we react to those
> embittered people who, in the heat of controversy, would
> break the family unity of our people? . . . Those who *want* to
> exclude will find reasons for it. We may face them, however,
> in the confidence that they will not succeed. We are part of
> the Jewish people. We share its destiny. We join in every great
> Jewish cause. No legalists will succeed in persuading the ma-
> jority of Jews—Orthodox, Conservative, or Reform—that we
> must cease marrying with one another. We may leave the de-
> cision as to "Who is a Jew?" to the sound instinct of our peo-
> ple, which has expressed itself magnificently in the *spirit* of
> the Halacha: "Let the people of Israel alone [they will find
> their way]. If they are not prophets, they are certainly the chil-
> dren of prophets" (b. Pesachim 66a).[127]

Freehof was at his absolute angriest in a letter to R. Hayim Halevy Donin, who sent him a draft of an article bemoaning the problems caused by the Reform abandonment of the *get* and of halakhic standards for conversion. In so doing, Reform rabbis were "sowing the seeds of divisiveness as well as of untold human tragedies . . . especially to another generation of totally innocent children, who will grow up in the full belief that their Jewish . . . credentials are perfectly valid and universally recognized, only to traumatically discover at a crucial point in their lives that such is not the case." By failing to warn individuals of this reality, Reform rabbis were "[parties] to their deception." Donin's proposed "compromise" solution was to offer a suggestion made by Chief Rabbi Jacobovits of Great Britain: that to preserve Jewish unity, the Orthodox should offer a "truce" to the Reformers, by which all personal status matters would be handled by Orthodox authorities, who in turn would "close our eyes to their forms of synagogue services and religious education for the time being."[128]

Freehof was outraged. "If it were not that my honored friend Emanuel Rackman suggested that you send your article to me, I would not answer your letter at all." He heatedly rejected the accusation that Reform rabbis were responsible for increasing *mamzerim* and creating a division among the Jewish people. The situation was over 150 years old, he pointed out; did Donin really want to exclude "hundreds of thousands of Jewish families" from the Jewish people? Was he also going to write off people who had a Conservative *get*, and all the unaffiliated Jews who didn't obtain *gittin*?

> Orthodox rabbis in practice never even raise the question which you have raised. I have not known any Orthodox rabbi who has refused to marry someone from an Orthodox or Conservative family on the ground of the presumption of illegitimacy. Orthodox rabbis, quite sensibly, prefer to follow the example of Bes Shammai and Bes Hillel, at the end of Chapter 1 of Yevamos, where we are told that although they disagreed as to the validity of certain marriages, the families of the two schools never hesitated to intermarry.

After heaping scorn upon Donin's proposal by pointing to the impossibility of compiling accurate lists of all Jews, he then asked, "Is such a horrible enterprise possible at all? And if it were possible, which it is not, would you have the heart to do it? And if, God forbid, you had the heart to do it, who is it who would be dividing Jewry?" Disdainfully he recommended that Donin just follow the ruling of Moshe Feinstein, that Reform marriages are not valid.[129] Doubtless the exchange only confirmed for Freehof what he told any Reform colleagues who broached the subject of a Reform *get*: that Reform had good and cogent reasons for eliminating it, that there was nothing halakhically wrong with recognizing civil divorce—and that in any case, no matter what, the Orthodox would never accept any non-Orthodox *get*.[130]

Conclusion

The most commonly asked questions that found their way to Freehof's study were about the parameters of Reform Jewish existence, the markers of difference not only between Jews and the larger gentile world, but also between Reform Jews and other Jews, whether secular or more traditional. His responses hewed closely to the center of Reform ideology as defined by the Columbus Platform and expounded in his own work. Individual Reform Jews or congregations could adopt whatever rituals they chose, as long as they did not regard these as divine commands or laws. In opposition to the secular ideologies or minimalist ethnicity of large segments of the American Jewish community, he asserted Reform's commitment to religion as the central element of Jewishness. In opposition to Orthodox and Conservative Judaism, he asserted Reform's principled commitment to a different understanding of the significance of ritual and its principled and deliberate rejection or alteration of some rules and forms, particularly in matters of personal status. Consistent with what he saw as the historic dynamic between rabbis and laypeople in the evolution of Judaism, Freehof allowed Reform Jews to evolve their own practice with limited interference. At the same time, however, he drew a firm border around Reform Judaism, clearly demarcating its difference from other ideologies of modern Jewish life, to complement the other firm border he drew between Judaism and other religions.

9

THE SIGNIFICANCE OF FREEHOF'S RESPONSA

In 1955 Freehof received a comment on *Reform Jewish Practice and its Rabbinic Background* from colleague Steven S. Schwarzschild: "I sometimes have the feeling that you track down the *halachah* on a certain point most assiduously and revealingly—and then the 'reform' [*sic*] recommendation does not seem quite to follow from the *halachah* (which is, of course, not too surprising). The question must then inevitably arise: why bother with the *halachah* in the first place? Do you think my impression is mistaken?"[1]

Indeed, he was not the last to wonder why Freehof "bothered" with the halakhah when he had so little hesitation in disregarding it. Dan Cohn-Sherbok, the only other scholar who has attempted to analyze Freehof's decisions systematically, could only express dismay at the "inconsistency" he found in Freehof's adherence to, or deviation from, halakhah.[2] One of Freehof's successors as Responsa Committee chair, W. Gunther Plaut, observed that Freehof exercised great scholarship in detailing the decisions of the traditional decisors, and "took their advice on most occasions because he saw no particular reason not to take it; but when he did depart from it he rarely gave reasons that were grounded in any Progressive thought system. . . . The past was instructive, but not decisive, and Reform minhag was given pragmatic preference when the chips were down."[3] Arnold Jacob Wolf was less delicate: "Freehof?? Terrible!! We needed halakhah, and all he gave us was *minhag!*"[4] Wolf's desire for Reform halakhah was in keeping with similar earlier calls, against which Freehof had argued for half a century; he would not have considered it a criticism of his work, but an error in understanding the nature of Reform Judaism.[5] Similarly, while Cohn-Sherbok correctly pointed out that Freehof was not consistent in deciding whether to uphold or deviate from existing halakhah, Freehof would not have regarded that as a criticism, but as a fundamental misunderstanding of what he was doing. Indeed, Cohn-Sherbok either fails to take into account Freehof's concept of minhag or completely misunderstands it.

Nor did Freehof regard Schwarzschild's question as a criticism. He sent an amiable reply agreeing with him and explaining himself. He had written *RJP* the way he did, he wrote, because he liked the halakhic literature—"the most significant part of post-Biblical tradition"—and he wanted Reform Jews to get over their unfortunate alienation from it and like it as well; because he didn't want Reform Jews changing their practice "wilfully" [*sic*], but rather by using the halakhah as their guide; and because—well, *because*. He was not sure. "The central problem involved in our situation, and in a sense it touches our entire movement, is what is our relation to the Halacha. I have not yet made up my mind on a basic answer to that question. I am exploring. I am writing all these books partly to clarify my own thinking, and to bring the subject in [*sic*] the realm of interest of my Colleagues."[6] In the five years between writing that answer to Schwarzschild, however, and the appearance of his first volume of responsa, Freehof developed his theory of the relationship between Reform Judaism and the halakhah—or rather, he developed a theory about why he could continue to do what he did without the existence of an agreed-on theological understanding of the relationship between Reform and the halakhah. Critics may question its merit, but he certainly believed that he was working within a theoretical framework.

Freehof on the Relationship between Reform Judaism and the Halakhah

Plaut's criticism, however, would have stung deeply, because Freehof saw his approach to responsa as emerging organically from the very nature of Reform Judaism. Freehof was no Abraham Geiger or Kaufmann Kohler. He never wrote a scholarly exposition of his theory, never attempted to use the canons of critical-historical study to prove his conclusions and arrive at a comprehensive explanation of how Reform Judaism evolved inevitably out of earlier forms of Judaism. He was a generalizer and a popularizer, eliminating significant differences between conflicting ideas with rhetorical sleight-of-hand. He got away with it in part because he was such a good writer, but more importantly, because he created a theory of Reform Judaism and halakhah that legitimated his ability to offer guidance without answering the tough questions.

The tough questions were those that had plagued Reformers since the inception of the movement: If only the moral law is of divine origin, then what is the nature and function of the ritual laws? If, in the classic Jewish understanding, covenantal faithfulness requires obedience to the entire law, what does covenantal faithfulness require of the Reform Jew beyond ethical conduct? If Reform Jews hold that some "ceremonials" are essential to Jewish covenantal faithfulness, on what basis do they do so? Who decides what those ceremonials are, and on what basis do they decide? Who decides how those ceremonials are to be practiced, and on what basis do they decide?

Freehof asserted that these questions were *as yet* unanswerable. The answers, he insisted, could only emerge after a lengthy process of doing exactly what he was doing, i.e., creating an ongoing dialogue between Reform Jewish minhag and the halakhic literature—which, he believed, was the way Jewish life and the inherited tradition had always inter-acted. In 1960, in the introduction to his first responsa volume, he stated the central conundrum: Reform theology could not yet define the au-thority of the halakhah, but in the meantime, as a practical matter it could not avoid turning to that tradition for guidance.

> It is clear why halachic questions come up, but it is not clear what, in Reform, should be the basis of the answers. Is the Talmudic literature our *authority* in the legal sense? . . . The answer to the question of legal authority cannot be post-poned on the ground that religious authority is based upon the doctrine of revelation, and that doctrine still needs to be clarified for modern man. Even though the theoretical ques-tion must wait, it is nevertheless difficult to make even a sin-gle practical decision without having an attitude on the authority of the Halacha. . . .
>
> It is, of course, possible that by some future date our part of the tradition will grow first habitual, then legal, then au-thoritative.[7] But it is not authoritative now and cannot, and

perhaps should not, be declared so to be. If, then, it is not a God-given authority, what does the law mean to us? Why do we so regularly consult it, and how do we react to the answers that we receive?

He had no answer but to repeat what he had told the CCAR in 1946.

> The law is to us a human product. That does not mean that God does not somehow reveal Himself in the "language of the children of men." Perhaps He does, but if He does, His self-revelation is not so perfect nor so clear nor so final as to make the whole law His sure commandment. . . . Therefore we respect it and seek its guidance. Some of its provisions have faded from our lives. We do not regret that fact. But as to those laws that we do follow, we wish them to be in harmony with tradition.

Nevertheless, even with respect to "those observances that are still vital," the halakhah did not have binding authority. If we have good reason to decide otherwise, we may. "In other words, the law is authoritative enough to influence us, but not so completely as to control us. The rabbinic law is our guidance but not our governance."[8] In other words, Reform Judaism adhered to halakhic precedent—except when it chose not to. But while Plaut saw this as a meaningless tautology, Freehof saw it as a reflection of historical reality.

For Freehof, "ceremonials" were human products, and therefore always subject to the vicissitudes of history. This reality had been masked not only by belief in the divine authorship of the halakhah but also on the existence of a political system that placed the Jewish community under its totalizing control. Now historical and intellectual progress had made Jews into citizens of the states in which they lived, and had undermined belief in revelation. Not Reform rebelliousness, therefore, but impersonal, inevitable historical change, had rendered vast areas of halakhah irrelevant. *Reform Judaism had not* rejected *the authority of the law; it had merely* recognized *that the law no longer possessed authority as law.*

Freehof recognized the danger to Reform in this new situation. Like other forms of liberal religion, without a new definition of authority and revelation, "its form of Judaism would degenerate into a mere convenient construct of willfully chosen observances, where the will of God is only metaphorically present and where there is really no such thing as a commandment."[9] Nevertheless, he had no such new definition to offer. As a mediator between the halakhah and the people he could not mandate obedience but could only try to persuade them to accept the guidance of the halakhah during this transitional period. To persuade them, he offered three arguments.

First, the halakhic literature was the main compendium of Jewish creativity and wisdom; to ignore it was to cut oneself off from a central element of Jewish culture.[10] "[T]he Jewish spirit expressed itself in rabbinic literature *creatively* for almost two thousand years. Who can ignore it without being a Karaite?"[11] Second, as Lauterbach had taught, halakhah was human, but "nobly human"; it was the application of prophetic ethics to everyday life.[12] Nevertheless, as a Reform Jew himself, Freehof also reserved the right not to find it persuasive, e.g., with respect to the laws on the status of women.[13]

Third, he offered a number of arguments to show that the Reform rejection of rabbinic law was a function of its origins and in any case was never as extreme as some people thought. The early radicalism of Reform leaders was like a youthful break from an overly controlling parent; since the break was now accomplished, there was no need for continued "adolescent" behavior. Indeed, rabbis like Aaron Chorin had actually attempted to ground religious reforms in the law; only the obdurate inflexibility of traditionalist authorities had led them eventually to reject it so completely. Early Reformers preferred the Bible to the Talmud because it was "the common source of religion in the Western world [and] was idealistic and inspiring, while the rabbinical literature could easily be envisaged as merely legalistic pettifogging," but Isaac Mayer Wise had sided with Isaac Leeser against the radical David Einhorn because he understood, correctly, that "[o]ur life is inspired by the Bible, but organized by the Talmud." Furthermore, while early Reformers drew a sharp distinction between the divinely revealed Scripture and the human Oral Law, biblical criticism had undermined that clear distinction. Now that Scripture was seen to have a human element, it was easier to see that God could also speak through the rabbinic literature. The earliest reformers had all grown up in traditional homes and had a familiarity with and a personal connection to the tradition that prevented them from dismissing it, but this had not been the case among Reform Jews for several generations; hence an alienation arose, which was now vanishing with the influx of Jews from more traditional backgrounds into the movement.[14]

But the reason Freehof cited most frequently for the renewed Reform interest in rabbinic law was Reform's changed "mood." "A hundred and fifty years ago when the Reform movement started, the mood of the world was different from the mood of today. In those days the chief interest of intellectuals was philosophy; now the chief interest of intellectuals is psychology. In those days, therefore, doctrine was dominant. Today emotion is dominant. . . . Thus old rituals return for their emotional, for their psychological effect."[15]

Still, he urged caution upon those who wanted definitive standards of Reform observance. Personally he remained convinced that any such activity was contrary to the nature of Reform Judaism. The disappearance of the authority of the halakhah from the lives of individual Jews had been a gradual, unconscious process. The creation of a new rationale for observance in Jewish life, if one could be created, would be a similarly incremental process: "first habitual, then legal, then authoritative."[16] As he wrote to a colleague in 1961,

> You would prefer that we make decisions on the basis of doctrine, as to which observances we should follow. I would prefer that the social, psychological process of popular decision continue for a while and that we follow the Talmudic principle: "Let us see what the people do." I would not deprecate the search for a systematic principle, but I would say that any general principle is still premature, as long as almost *all* of Jewry (most of the self-styled Orthodox as well) are participating in a widespread, selective process of observance.
>
> This is what I mean by saying let the commandments take their chance. Some will die away in spite of any doctrine we enunciate. Some will become important in spite of doctrine. The essential thing is to recognize that we are in a process of dynamic change with regard to halacha, and by "we" I mean virtually all Jews.[17]

By writing responsa, therefore, Freehof believed that he was performing an essential role in the evolution of Reform Judaism.

Freehof's idea that patterns of observance would arise organically out of Reform Jews' lives was not shared by rabbis who worried about the disappearance of ritual observance in the daily lives of Reform Jews. The desire for a guide or code of Reform practice gained ground in the movement in the postwar decades. Frederic Doppelt, who had wanted the Responsa Committee to be given a more authoritative role, and David Polish pressed the case for a Reform code[18] and published their milestone guide to Reform practice in 1957. They framed their project in concepts and language taken from Freehof himself. "In the words of Rabbi Solomon B. Freehof: 'The foundation of Jewish religious life is Jewish practice upon which are built habits of mind and attitudes to the universe. . . . We do not begin with theology, we *arrive* at theology. This is the historic Jewish way.'" Reform had never intended to dispense with observance altogether, but "unbridled liberalism in religion" had made it appear so, and more recent generations had realized that this was an error. A Reform guide would not be "authoritarian thought-control"; rather, it "would help bring a greater degree of observance, self-disciplining commitment, and spirituality back into our religious life, because it is essentially a response to many who have long been seeking guidance." It would be a Reform guide because "what determines whether a custom, ceremony or symbol is either Orthodox or Reform is not its observance or non-observance; it is rather the right to change it when necessary . . . and to innovate when desirable."[19] However, unlike Freehof, who—despite his statement in the Introduction to *RJP* that *doing* would lead to *belief*—maintained a lifelong adherence to the classical Reform notion that "ceremonials" may "enhance" religiosity but are never its essence, Doppelt and Polish grounded ritual practice in covenantal obligation—an obligation to which, to be sure, the individual Reform Jew was free to choose whether or not to commit.

As we saw in Chapter 6, Freehof reluctantly went along with CCAR President W. Gunther Plaut's plans to strengthen Reform Jews' Shabbat observance. Plaut was named chairman of a new CCAR Committee on the Sabbath, which in 1968 reported back to the Conference its plan for a published guide including standards for Sabbath observance.[20] This it achieved in 1972 with *A Shabbat Manual*, although, as Michael A. Meyer points out, acceptance by the CCAR came only at the cost of "sometimes tortured language" that covered the "painful compromise" that eliminated any reference to the language of obligation, producing only an inoffensive manual for teaching Reform Jews how to make Shabbat at home.[21]

By the late 1960s Freehof and the proponents of a guide had essentially reached a compromise. Although they generally spoke the language of covenantal obligation and he still spoke the language of Kohlerian classical Reform, both theologies agreed that being a Reform Jew entailed more than ethical conduct, that it required a life of personal piety manifested in regular prayer and ritual, grounded in the historic Jewish tradition to the extent that it was still meaningful. As he wrote in 1969, there was a new "mood that has been working in the Conference in recent years to turn it in the new direction which may be described as pro-Halachic." This, he asserted, was still a vague feeling, and there were still too many things that Reform Jews could not possibly accept as divine to simply return to an acceptance of the law. Freehof carefully kept the responsa process separate from the issue of a code by insisting that Reform still required a lengthy period of evolution, experimentation, and education before it could settle on standards of ritual practice. Still, he continued,

> [w]e have long held that the ethical doctrines and ideas are a God-given mandate and that we are bound to obey them. May we not come to believe that the worship of God in the sanctuary is likewise a demand upon our consciences? That to worship regularly must not depend upon the attractiveness of the sermon or the choir but must rest upon a commandment which we have accepted and which we will obey?...
>
> Thus it may develop with us. Worthy actions may grow into religious duties, and so our Reform code will develop *mitzvah* by *mitzvah*, as each action achieves its sanctity. Some of these may be new *mitzvos*, but most of them will be rediscoveries of actions which our tradition has cherished. We will have to find out which elements in the Jewish traditional life-style we can truly accept as mandate and which will remain merely custom and therefore changeable. All this social psy-

chology must be explored and experienced before we can ever attain a clear-cut philosophy or well-defined ceremonial discipline.[22]

But how were Reform Jews, most of them now unfamiliar with much of the ritual of Jewish life, supposed to know what those "worthy actions" were, and how to do them, so that they could develop into mitzvot?

"What? Another book on Jewish practices from the Reform Movement?" So began the Foreword to the CCAR's 1983 *Gates of the Seasons: A Guide to the Jewish Year.* Yes, it continued, "[t]here has been an undeniable trend toward the reinstitution of traditional practices in Reform Judaism during the past decade. . . . [But i]t is our philosophy of Judaism that makes us Reform Jews. Particular ritual practices which, on the one hand, do not negate our philosophy and which, on the other, reinforce and enrich our Judaism are not only acceptable in Reform, they are desirable."[23]

The publication of *A Shabbat Manual* was a turning point for the CCAR, which for the first time was telling Reform Jews that a Jewish life had to include certain ritual as well as ethical behaviors in order to be authentically Jewish. Still, in deference to those who opposed anything resembling a code, it included language that Freehof himself might have used: The book was an "effort to recover Shabbat observance as *an enhancement of Jewish life*" [emphasis added]; the section detailing the positive observances of the day was titled "Catalogue of Shabbat *Opportunities*" [emphasis added] with the more directive "What to Do (Mitzvot Aseh)" relegated to the subtitle in smaller type.[24] The reader was repeatedly advised that it was not necessary to do everything, but that it was essential to begin with something, and to make it a habit.

The book's approach owed much to the work of Doppelt and Polish and addressed the long-standing desire of many rabbis for a commitment to the idea that Reform Judaism required more than ethical conduct. Though it avoided any language that might be construed to mean that rituals were obligatory, significantly, the *Shabbat Manual* used the word *mitzvah* rather than *ceremony,* explaining that a mitzvah "is what a Jew ought to do in response to his God and to the tradition of his people. . . . Mitzvah is, therefore, more than folkway and ceremony." In both the "What to Do" and "What Not to Do" sections, each individual rubric began with the phrase, "It is a mitzvah . . . ," e.g., "to recite or chant the Kiddush," or "not to perform housework on Shabbat."[25]

This volume was followed within a few years by *Gates of Mitzvah: A Guide to the Jewish Life Cycle*[26] and then by the above mentioned *Gates of the Seasons*. Both of these larger and more comprehensive volumes emphasized the necessity of ritual observance for Reform Jews to a greater extent than had the *Shabbat Manual*. Both opened by citing an excerpt from the CCAR's 1976 Centennial Perspective, the successor to the 1937 Columbus Platform. The 1976 statement of principles, reflecting the covenant theology of Eugene B. Borowitz, brought the Reform movement even closer to declaring that ritual was an essential element of Reform Judaism. Thus the excerpt in *Gates of Mitzvah* stated in part:

> Judaism emphasizes action rather than creed as the primary expression of a religious life, the means by which we strive to achieve universal justice and peace. Reform Judaism shares this emphasis on duty and obligation. The past century has taught us that the claims made upon us may begin with our ethical obligations, but they extend to many other aspects of Jewish living . . . Within each area of Jewish observance, Reform Jews are called upon to confront the claims of Jewish tradition, however differently perceived, and to exercise their individual autonomy, choosing and creating on the basis of commitment and knowledge.[27]

As editor Simeon J. Maslin stated explicitly in the introduction: "*Mitzvah* is the key to authentic Jewish existence and to the sanctification of life."[28]

Reflecting the CCAR's ongoing efforts to guide Reform Jews along the path of Shabbat observance, 1991 saw the publication of *Gates of Shabbat: A Guide for Observing Shabbat*. Not only did this volume offer more information about Shabbat observance, but it also included an innovative section titled "Establishing Definitions for Work and Rest on Shabbat." At long last the challenge laid down by Jacob Voorsanger in 1904—how to negotiate the tension between the Jewish value of rest and the American value of leisure—had been addressed.[29]

Gates of Mitzvah and *Gates of the Seasons* were intended to give Reform Jews all the guidance they needed in order to live their life cycle events and celebrate the holidays in a Jewishly appropriate way. To this end they provided clear guidance and extensive supplementary information. The extensive endnotes cite halakhic sources to offer fuller explanations and to show how Reform practice is rooted in the classical tradition. Where relevant, they also cite decisions of the CCAR. For example, one of the longer notes cites sources for the historic Jewish opposition to marriage with non-Jews, and also mentions the three CCAR resolutions on the subject.[30]

To illustrate what the CCAR considered appropriate in a "code of practice," consider as a representative example the section on birth in *Gates of Mitzvah*. It contains six rubrics: 1) the mitzvah of procreation; 2) birth control; 3) abortion; 4) the mitzvah of adoption; 5) the mitzvah of prayer after childbirth; and 6) the mitzvah of *tsedakah*. To understand how these books were intended to revolutionize Reform Jewish life, note that of the four acts identified here as mitzvot, only one (procreation) is among the traditional 613. (While taking in orphans was always regarded as meritorious, the modern notion of legal adoption is foreign to the halakhah.[31] Spontaneous private prayer is something the classical tradition would not have thought necessary to mandate; and while giving *tsedakah* is certainly a mitzvah, it is not particularly linked to childbirth.) The author and his committee were not concerned to demonstrate a link between their work and the traditional enumeration of the mitzvot. Rather, by designating actions as mitzvot, they intended to make the point that this was how a Reform Jew ought to sanctify his or her life. Thus these two volumes offered a genuinely Reform approach to observance.

As CCAR publications, they also carried more weight than responsa, at least in theory. Although these two volumes, intended for lay use, were not of substantive use to the Responsa Committee, once they were published their "official" status could be invoked as an additional argument to strengthen the committee's stance. This is evident particularly in responsa on Shabbat observance.[32]

The first of these two volumes, *Gates of Mitzvah*, was dedicated "with love and gratitude to מורנו ורבנו Solomon B. Freehof[,] whose devotion to God, Torah and Israel has been a source of enlightenment and inspiration."[33] No one saw irony in dedicating the CCAR's first code to a rabbi who had opposed such works throughout his career; rather, the dedication emphasized the extent to which Freehof's insistence that Reform Judaism must use the halakhic tradition for "guidance, not governance," had become normative.

Freehof's Approach to Halakhah

It is essential to understand that implicit in Freehof's understanding of the end of halakhic authority is a radically supersessionist attitude toward Orthodoxy. History had ended the sway of halakhah over the Jewish community. Orthodox legal theory might still assert halakhic control over all realms of life, including civil law, business law, and relations with gentiles; but the fact that the vast majority of Jews—even those who called themselves Orthodox—ignored Jewish law in those areas demonstrated that the Orthodox view of the law was no longer valid. In a futile reaction to this new reality, the right-wing Orthodox authorities issued ever stricter rulings that were accepted by an ever shrinking segment of the Jewish community.[34] (Like most of the non-Orthodox segment of the Jewish community, Freehof was slow to recognize the extent of the Orthodox and ultra-Orthodox resurgence.[35] One wonders what he would have thought about developments since his death.)

Even if one wanted to be governed by the halakhah, it was impossible. Jewish law no longer possessed the flexibility to adapt to new circumstances. All legal systems have two ways of making law, by legislating and by interpreting; in Jewish law, however, only interpretation is currently available. The law is believed to be divine, and only a Sanhedrin may alter it; since that will never happen, Jewish law remains a closed system that cannot possibly have the sort of flexibility needed to allow the law to accommodate to modern life, even in a Conservative context.[36] Indeed, he explained, Samuel Holdheim was the most radical of the early reformers precisely because he was the most learned; because of his great learning he knew the futility of trying to stretch the law to accommodate the needed changes.[37] The law, therefore, could no longer fulfill its historic role as law for the Jews. Nevertheless, as the primary repository of Jewish creativity and knowledge, and as the Jewish attempt to apply prophetic ethics to daily life, and as the source of most of the actual substance of Jewish religious life, it had to be consulted; but its proper role now was to offer "guidance, not governance."

He explained to his colleagues in 1956 that the questions he and the Responsa Committee received were of three types. Some required only a brief response referencing the codified halakhah and could be answered in a short note. Some required a more thorough investigation of the sources and required a more extensive summary. Some, however, demanded a "specifically Reform" answer, meaning that they touched upon areas in which Reform practice already diverged, or might diverge, from the codified halakhah on the basis of uniquely Reform considerations.[38] Of these last he chose one or two each year to circulate in draft form among the committee for their final approval for his annual report to the CCAR. (The paucity of substantive correspondence in his files from committee members indicates that this was usually a formality.) These last also constitute the type of responsa he chose to publish.

In 1978 Freehof explained how he arrived at his decisions. He began with the Shulḥan Arukh and its major commentators, then went back to the Tur and the Bet Yosef "to see the whole debate" (there was "nothing better" than the Bet Yosef, he commented), and then turned to "a modern classic," the Arukh HaShulḥan. Alternatively, he began with a Talmudic reference and followed the cross-references from there. Once he had found all the opinions, including the relevant responsa, it was time to make a decision. In a traditional context two factors governed a decision, he explained: the majority opinion and the opinion of the later authorities, since *halakhah kevatra'ey* (the law is according to the later decisors). However, he added,

> in a Reform responsum . . . we are interested in what is not in an Orthodox responsum. . . . Reb Yitsḥak in the Talmud says that you mustn't bother about *ta'ame hamitzvos* [the reasons for the commandments] . . . it's God's command, you follow it, but the Jewish philosophers in the middle ages, after all, did do that, see, so we are concerned sometimes with going back of the law and asking why they made the law. And we will apply what the Supreme Court would call the intention of the lawgiver. . . . That's *ta'ame hamitzvos*. So the decisions are as follows: first, the majority of opinion. Then,

> the latest opinions. And third, for a Reform responsum...the
> ethical purpose behind the halakhah. . . . An Orthodox scholar
> might say, you have no right to do that, even though they will
> do that, you understand? Orthodox scholars do it too, but they
> don't admit it. . . . [39]

Making explicit room for ethical considerations in the adjudicatory process is not a uniquely Reform approach. Orthodox rabbi Saul Berman, for example, has described his methodology as a six-step process in which the fifth step is evaluating his preliminary halakhic conclusion in the light of "meta-halakhic values"—e.g., *kevod habriyot* (respect for all people); *darkhe no'am* (peaceful relations); *hillul haShem* (profanation of the Divine Name); *mishum evah* (because of hatred)— in other words, what Freehof would call ethical principles.[40] The difference between the two, of course, is whether the decisor's idea of what is "ethical" may override the norms of the law. "Willful" change, to Freehof, meant not consulting the halakhah to determine the "spirit" of Jewish law or tradition, by which he meant the meta-halakhic values and attitudes implicit in the legal literature.[41] Disregarding the halakhah after consulting it, however, could be a principled stance, because meta-halakhic values were more important than legal norms, as he went on to explain: "So after I use the majority opinion, then I face the actual living and I say the moral intent of this halakhah is this and this."

But then he added a qualification: ". . . and I try to find, if possible, those who support this liberal interpretation."[42] The premise that a *sine qua non* of Reform responsa is finding the most *liberal* possible halakhic opinion was crucial to his responsa methodology, because

> [o]ur concern is more with the people than with the legal system. Whenever possible, such interpretations are developed which are feasible and conforming to the needs of life. Sometimes, indeed, a request must be answered in the negative when there is no way in the law for a permissive answer to be given. Generally the law is thus searched for such opinion as can conform with the realities of life. If no such answer can be found, it is so stated, and then the law must take its chance in the struggle with life.[43]

The rabbi's task, according to Freehof, was to organize and regularize popular practice, not to mandate or control it. When, therefore, current practice diverged from historic practice, the rabbi had to exercise great restraint before pronouncing the new practice unacceptable, because to try to resist "the realities of life" was misguided and futile. Finding some liberal precedent, on the other hand—as in the case of circumcision prior to the eighth day—enabled the rabbi to tell the people that they only had to "regularize" their practice.

However, historic practice had to be taken into account, as Freehof made clear in a surprising and significant criticism of the 1893 CCAR decision not to require adult male converts to be circumcised. To a British Reform colleague who inquired whether the decision had a halakhic basis, he responded,

> . . . [I]t was the tendency of the early Reformers to go back to origins. Therefore, it was of weighty importance to them that the Bible itself, and also the Mishnah, has no clear requirement of initiatory rites for proselytes. I believe that our standpoint is different. . . . The *total* tradition is vital to us as guidance, at least, if not as rigid governance. Therefore it is important to us that the Talmud and Maimonides and the *Shulchan Aruch* . . . have circumcision as firmly established law and that, therefore, it is the widespread practice of our people to circumcise proselytes.[44]

While he accepted the CCAR's decision as authoritative, he did not like the way it was reached.

Freehof's approach to the rabbinic texts was neither traditional nor historical-critical, though it incorporated both. Like a critical historian, he regarded the text as a human product and therefore shaped by social context, but unlike Kohler, for example, he generally avoided using social context as an interpretive technique. A significant exception to this rule, however, was his frequent dismissal of contemporary Orthodox rulings, which he characterized as motivated by an aberrant and politicized tendency to stringency in the face of social circumstances (e.g., "Orthodox Aspersions Against Reform Marriages, *RRR* #42). Like a traditionalist, he read the halakhah as an ahistorical source of precedent. Unlike a traditionalist, however, the precedent he sought was only *nomos* to the extent that it conformed to his meta-halakhic Reform hermeneutic.

The preceding discussion explains the general absence of close analysis of Freehof's approach to the halakhah in this study, with the exception of several instances where his tendentious use of halakhic precedent in order to reach a desired conclusion has illustrated the extent to which he did not feel constrained by it. He cannot be identified with any approach to halakhic jurisprudence or fruitfully compared to any Orthodox *posek*. He certainly had the ability to read the texts, and most of the time he read them in a straightforward manner, but if he thought that meta-halakhic considerations required an answer at variance with the codified precedent, or with the dominant view among halakhic authorities, he disregarded precedent or chose to use a minority opinion as a precedent.

There is some resemblance between Freehof's approach to the halakhah and the legal philosophy known as legal realism. This school of thought, which originated with Justice Oliver Wendell Holmes, Jr., rejected the idea of law as an abstract standard and saw it rather as "a practical question of social management," in which judges had great leeway to render decisions based on considerations such as the social impact of a decision.[45] Legal realism was popular between the wars, but unfortunately, since Freehof never referred to any works on the subject, it is impossible to know if he was directly influenced by it.

The Limits of Acceptable Reform Practice According to Freehof

Given Freehof's commitment to the primacy of popular minhag and the consequent obligation to decide liberally whenever possible, it follows that his own opinions and standards emerge in his negative responses. When he disagreed with popular practice, he revealed his own meta-halakhic values as well as the contours of the path he attempted to chart for Reform Judaism. This study has shown that he opposed popular minhag when it violated any one of four standards:

1) Practices contrary to official CCAR policy, e.g., officiation at mixed marriages.

2) Practices that blurred religious boundaries or undermined the integrity or dignity of the Jewish minority vis-à-vis the Christian majority, e.g., according synagogue membership to gentiles or allowing gentiles to participate in ritual that was properly exclusively Jewish.

3) Practices that reflected badly on Reform Judaism by flouting widely acknowledged traditional sensibilities, e.g., holding a synagogue rummage sale on Shabbat or serving shrimp in the synagogue.

4) Practices that were vulgar and tasteless, e.g., having a rock band play at a Shabbat afternoon bar mitzvah reception or raising funds for the synagogue by gambling.

Finally, he opposed any attempt to compel Reform Jews to adhere to standards of religious practice that undermined the legitimacy of Reform Judaism itself.

The Practical Value of Freehof's Responsa

Already in his 1941 paper Freehof had suggested that the collected work of the Responsa Committee could serve as a guide to Reform practice, an idea that had been floating around at least since 1914, when Max Heller suggested it in an article in the student publication *HUC Monthly*, of which Freehof was then an editor.[46] By the early 1950s he was planning such a collection as a complement to *RJP*. Tentatively titled "One Hundred Reform Responsa," it would be devoted to "specific questions such as artificial insemination, joint chapels in hospitals with the other two faiths, etc." He predicted that the three volumes together would answer "most of the questions in Jewish law which are likely to arise in our Reform experience these days."[47] When Israel Bettan asked him to take over the Responsa Committee, he actually hesitated at first, because he worried whether he would be free to include in the book responsa he would write as committee chairman. Then he hit upon a solution:

> [S]ince it is impossible to know always whether I am receiving the question as Chairman of the Committee or just as a rabbi, I will consider that only such responsa belong to the

conference as are read or accepted by the conference or mentioned to the conference by subject. All others I will assume belong to me as an individual. In other words, let us say that the *Yearbook* will have one or two responsa which the conference accepted; and I will keep the rest, if it is agreeable to you.[48]

In the end, however, he reprinted about three-quarters of the responsa that appeared in the *Yearbook* in his own responsa volumes.

As Responsa Committee chairman, Freehof exercised great discretion in choosing which responsa to submit for inclusion in the *Yearbook*, choosing those responsa he thought would be most helpful for his colleagues. In his first annual committee report, he explained that many inquiries were easily answered just by referring to the halakhic sources. What he would submit were one or two, occasionally three, that were "interesting in themselves" because they required "not only research but also a Reform decision."[49]

Table V shows that between 1956 and 1976 he submitted a total of thirty-one responsa. However, it appears that he exercised a certain discretion in choosing which ones to submit. Of these thirty-one responsa, eleven, or about 35%, dealt with medical ethics (#2, #3, #11, #15, #16, #18, #19, #20, #23, #27, #31); seven, or about 23%, dealt with funerals and burials (#4, #8, #9, #21, #28, #29, #30); and four, or about 13%, dealt with questions of Jewish status (#1, #5, #12, #14). The remaining 30% dealt with a wide variety of issues.

Some were clearly related to issues that were controversial at the time ("Woman Wearing a Tallit," "Substituting for Christians on Christmas," "Judaism and Homosexuality"), but it is difficult to imagine that others were causing large numbers of rabbis to lose sleep at night ("Unworthy Man Called to the Torah," "Marriage With Karaites," "The Hospital Chapel"). His published responsa volumes, by contrast, contain many responsa on some far more urgent or controversial topics, written during the same period, e.g., "Gift Corner Open on the Sabbath," "Circumcision Before Eighth Day," "Jew Joining the Unitarian Church," "Status of Apostates [Children and Adults]," "Marriage With Ethical Culturists," "Mixed Marriage on Temple Premises," and "Wedding Without a License." His unpublished responsa correspondence provides

Table V: Responsa Freehof Submitted to *CCAR Yearbook* as Responsa Committee Chair, 1956–76

1	1956	The Status of a Gentile-Born Child Adopted into a Jewish Family
2	1956	The Use of the Cornea of the Dead (=*RROT* #31)
3	1958	Abortion (=*RRR* #31)
4	1959	Funeral Service for a Suicide
5	1960	Status of Children of Doubtful Religious Background
6	1961	Collecting Synagogue Pledges Through Civil Courts (=*RRR* #44)
7	1962	Unworthy Man Called to the Torah (=*CuRR* #16)
8	1963	Non-Jewish Burial in Jewish Cemetery (=*CuRR* #39)
9	1964	Tombstone in the Absence of a Body (Cenotaph)
10	1964	The Expulsion of a Member from the Congregation (=*CuRR* #21)
11	1965	Anesthetic for Circumcision (=*CuRR* #27)
12	1965	Marriage with Karaites (=*CuRR* #46)
13	1966	Rabbinical Fees and Salaries (=*CuRR* #50)
14	1966	Bar Mitzvah for an Uncircumcised Boy (=*CuRR* #28)
15	1967	Freezing Bodies for Later Revival
16	1967	Using the Blood of the Dead (=*CuRR* #59)
17	1967	The Hospital Chapel
18	1968	Choosing Which Patient to Save (=*MRR* #36)
19	1968	Surgical Transplants (=*CuRR* #31)
20	1969	Allowing a Terminal Patient to Die (=*MRR* #35)
21	1970	Exchanging a Tombstone (=*CoRR* #53)
22	1972	Woman Wearing a Tallit
23	1972	Caesarean on a Dead Mother (=*CoRR* #48)
24	1972	Substituting for Christians on Christmas [on Shabbat] (=*CoRR* #29)
25	1973	Judaism and Homosexuality (=*CoRR* #4)
26	1974	Ownership of a Sefer Torah (=*CoRR* #22)
27	1975	Relieving Pain of a Dying Patient (=*RROT* #17)
28	1975	Two Coffins in One Grave (=*RROT* #20)
29	1976	Omission of Committal Services (=*RROT* #30)
30	1976	Mother's Name on Son's Tombstone (=*RROT* #24)
31	1976	Cosmetic Surgery (=*RROT* Inquiry #8)

copious evidence that he received and answered many more questions on controversial issues facing the CCAR than he chose to publish. Clearly, he consciously avoided submitting responsa on controversial topics. Ever the conciliator, Freehof had no desire to reignite controversy over the role or status of the Responsa Committee. Indeed, he had no reason to do so. He had won the fight in 1955 to maintain the status quo. (See Chapter 3.) Publishing an unlimited number of responsa under his own name, in books that could be easily purchased by people who had no access to the *CCAR Yearbook*, was a far more effective means of influencing Reform Jews and encouraging them to re-engage with the halakhic tradition.

His "one hundred Reform responsa" multiplied into several hundred in eight books published between 1960 and 1990. These were not official CCAR publications, though the Rabbinic Alumni Association arranged for all but the last volume to be published by the HUC Press. At least several dozen additional responsa remained unpublished, but he kept them on file and sent individual copies to answer subsequent inquiries as needed. He also sent letters with informal short replies. In some cases, after writing a short letter, he returned to the issue and wrote a full responsum. Often he chose to write and publish a responsum after receiving multiple inquiries on the same subject, indicating that it was a significant issue for Reform Jews. Altogether he answered upward of 2,500 inquiries.[51] In 1983 he selected 712 of the letters as a representative sample of his correspondence, spanning the years 1961 to 1983, and donated the collection to the American Jewish Archives in Cincinnati.

The largest number of those inquiries came from CCAR colleagues, though these were not evenly distributed, as Table VI shows. Despite the small numbers under consideration, three trends are clear. First, colleagues who were active in the years of his highest profile within the CCAR—particularly the 1940s, when he dominated the Conference as an officer and by his service on several high profile committees—were most likely to send him their questions. In other words, his personal stature influenced his colleagues' readiness to ask him for guidance. Second, the number of inquirers dropped off sharply beginning in the 1960s. Since his first volume of responsa appeared in 1960, this probably reflects the fact that rabbis could now find the answers they needed in his books. Finally, rabbis ordained at Stephen Wise's Jewish Institute of Re-

ligion, particularly those ordained through 1949, were consistently far
less likely to turn to Freehof than those ordained in Cincinnati. Only in
the 1950s—after Wise's death and the incorporation of the school with
HUC—did the New York percentage begin to approach the Cincinnati
percentage. The presence of a small number of more traditional students
at the independent New York school cannot account for the enormous
difference, so the answer must lie elsewhere. Perhaps Freehof's long association with the Cincinnati campus made its alumni more willing to
turn to him. Nevertheless, aside from these statistics, it should be noted
that the two rabbis who sent the most inquiries to Freehof—almost thirty
each—were Harold Waintrup (C '47), and Philip S. Bernstein (NY '26).
While the latter was a colleague and close friend from CANRA, the former had no personal relationship with Freehof at all, aside from possibly meeting at a CCAR convention.

The second-largest number of questions overall came from Reform
laypeople. Additionally, he received the occasional inquiry from Progressive rabbis in Europe, South Africa, South America, and Israel,
whom he often knew personally from his years as President of the World
Union for Progressive Judaism. He also received questions from Conservative rabbis, especially those in the Pittsburgh area; from a handful
of Orthodox rabbis, "reverends," and laymen; and the occasional Christian clergyman. As his reputation grew, so did his audience. Physicians,
hospital administrators, attorneys, and people who simply had random
questions about Jewish matters turned to him for answers. Even David
Ben-Gurion asked him for advice on what the state should do about Is-

Table VI: Distribution of Freehof's CCAR Questioners

DECADE ORDAINED	PERCENT OF RABBIS WHO SUBMITTED A QUESTION TO FREEHOF	
	HUC (CINCINNATI)	JIR (NEW YORK)
1920–1929	32%	8%
1930–1939	33%	13%
1940–1949	48%	13%
1950–1959	31%	22%
1960–1969	20%	10%
1970–1975	8%	7%

raelis who self-identified as Jews but whom the rabbinate regarded as gentiles ("Who Is a Jew?" *RRR* #14).

In addition to the subjects we have addressed, questions ran the gamut from the sublime to the ridiculous. Many correspondents asked about obscure folk customs, e.g., "Groom Not Seeing Bride" (*RR* #43); "Funeral Folklore" (*RR* #42 and *RRR* #32); "Kaddish and the Three Steps Backward" (*RRR* #47); "Spices and Passover," about a folk custom of not eating garlic on Passover (*CoRR* Inquiry #6); and "Sons at Father's Burial," about a tradition of sons not accompanying a father's coffin (*RROT* Inquiry #6). Freehof had long been fascinated with customs since his early interest in liturgy had led him to explore Ashkenazic *minhagbukher*; the enjoyment he derived from tracing the origin of strange customs is evident in his writing.

Others asked not about a specific problem they were having, but for the view of "Jewish tradition" on controversial contemporary problems such as end-of life issues, e.g., "Dying Patient Kept Alive" (*RR* #27) and "Determination and Postponement of Death" (*MRR* #34); new reproductive technologies, e.g., "The Fertility Pill" (*RROT* #44) and "The Test-Tube Baby" (*NRR* #47); and a host of other timely questions, e.g., "Psychodelic [*sic*] Drugs" (*CuRR* #60); "Occasional Gambling and State Lotteries" (*RROT* #49); "Malpractice Suits and the Physician" (*NRR* #50); "Deprogramming Young People" (*NRR* #51); and "The Hostages," about airplane hijackings (*TRR* #44).

Others were apparently motivated by sheer curiosity, without reference to specific problems. How should an astronaut keep to the Jewish calendar (*NRR* Inquiry #1)? What are a woman's rights regarding custody of children in Jewish law (*RR* #49)? What does the tradition say about menopause (*RRR* #48)? What does Jewish tradition say about the Soviet medical practice of taking the blood from dead bodies and storing it for use in transfusions (*CuRR* 59)? What does Jewish tradition say about earthquakes (*CoRR* Inquiry #7)? Would evidence obtained by wiretapping be admissible in a rabbinic court (*RROT* #56)? No question was too ridiculous for Freehof to answer with all seriousness after consultation with whatever sources he could muster. He invariably provided a carefully researched answer grounded as much as possible in normative halakhic texts.

Although he always cited both classical and modern halakhic authorities, he made particularly extensive use of contemporary Orthodox literature in the area of medical ethics, especially the responsa of Eliezer Waldenberg and Moshe Feinstein. In general he took a liberal stance on the use of medical procedures and new technologies, holding that "[t]he traditional law is completely liberal with regard to medical necessities,"[52] and dismissing the restrictive opinions of contemporary halakhists as sadly reflective of the general rightward trend in modern Orthodoxy. In permitting organ donations, for example, he first penned a lengthy digression on autopsy to demonstrate that that the law took a permissive attitude when autopsy would help someone else, and that recent Orthodox stringencies on the issue were an historical anomaly due to "political" conditions. Concerning an Orthodox rabbi who refused to support a community-wide Tay-Sachs screening program lest it lead to abortions, he commented that "he is stricter than the law requires," and explained why.[53]

The intersection of Freehof's personal stature within the CCAR with the postwar trend toward reintroducing ritual observance to Reform congregations[54] resulted in the efflorescence of responsa as a genre of Reform expression. In 1956 he reported that he had received approximately thirty inquiries; eight years later he was receiving about 200 inquiries annually. These, he noted, included difficult questions on which there were very few sources, such as the rights of veterans or the Jewish attitude toward athletics.[55] Freehof wrote all the committee's responsa himself and then sent the drafts to committee members for their approval, including a return postcard for them to vote yes or no. Occasionally a member sent a dissenting letter, and HUC-JIR Professor of Talmud Julius Kravetz once submitted a dissenting opinion,[56] but the committee generally enthusiastically endorsed whatever he wrote.[57]

Did Reform rabbis and congregants follow his guidance? On the one hand, most of his colleagues never asked him any questions, and there is no way to know to what extent they paid attention to his work. His responsa volumes were each issued once and then went out of print, although *RJP* was reissued twice. He did not succeed in influencing the movement's course in some of the areas about which he expressed himself most vehemently: mixed marriage, marriage on the Sabbath, synagogue membership for non-Jewish spouses, patrilineal descent, and acceptance of homosexuals.

On the other hand, there was definitely a demand for his direction.

Most of the questions he received were genuine requests for practical guidance. Occasionally the questioner would say that he had already looked in *RJP* and could not find an answer,[58] but usually a letter to Freehof seems to have been the first line of recourse. Questioners who wrote him heeded his responses. For example, asked whether women could be called to the Torah, he replied in the affirmative, explained why, and then offered guidance on how to proceed with the change. The questioner followed up with a reply saying that the synagogue Board of Trustees had all read Freehof's letter and unanimously endorsed it.[59] Likewise, the rabbi who had written about the Shabbat rummage sale wrote to tell him that the Sisterhood had voted not to do it again. Apparently quite chastened, they had also asked the rabbi to write Dr. Freehof and assure him that "the Sisterhood [was] in no way trying to subvert the Sabbath, but was only acting in the light of local custom and practice."[60] Another rabbi, unsure about the Jewish status of a young woman wishing to be married, sent an inquiry to Freehof and received an answer, but then had to let Freehof know that the couple had not waited for the answer but found another rabbi who married them with no questions asked. "I suppose," he wrote, "that some of our men feel that their instincts and opinions are good enough to decide even these fairly intricate problems and, I suppose, there is little that can be done about it. At any rate, I want to thank you for your kindness and the effort to which you went. It is marvelously reassuring to know that one can turn to you to resolve one's doubts in matters like these."[61] Many rabbis shared Freehof's responsa with their boards and used them as adult education material, thereby furthering Freehof's aim of raising awareness of the halakhah among Reform Jews.[62] In that respect, he succeeded.

The End of Freehof's Involvement with the Question of Reform Jewish Practice

From the 1970s on, the history of American Reform Judaism's relationship to Jewish law and the history of Solomon Freehof's role in determining that relationship began to diverge. There were three main reasons for this. The first was simply generational. Freehof, who retired from his pulpit in 1966, was getting old—not only aging physically, but in relation to the membership of the CCAR, for whom he became a figure increasingly revered from a distance. His unique stature in the Conference, which contributed so greatly to the members' interest in submitting questions to him and launching his Reform responsa work, had been the result of his exceptional leadership in the 1940s combined with the prestige of his military responsa activity. By 1975 these were ancient history. The second was the acceleration of the theological shift among Reform rabbis, toward the religious existentialism of Buber, Rosenzweig, and Heschel, or the religious-naturalism-plus-Jewish-folkways of Mordecai Kaplan, or the emerging covenant theology of Eugene B. Borowitz. All of these led to a renewed emphasis on Jewish ritual as something considerably more important than mere "ceremonies." Freehof's Kohlerian theology appeared hopelessly outmoded to a new generation of rabbis. Finally, as anxiety levels rose about assimilation, Jewish survival, and mixed marriage, Jewish community leaders wanted a more activist agenda for strengthening Jewish observance. In this context, Freehof's *laissez-faire* notion of minhag was not a helpful approach.

In 1976 Freehof relinquished the chairmanship of the Responsa Committee to Walter Jacob. He played no role in the writing or publication of any of the CCAR guides to Reform practice which appeared during his lifetime. The 1979 publication of *Gates of Mitzvah*, with its four essays on mitzvah representing four distinctly different theological perspectives, was an indication of the extent to which Reform had moved away from the Kohlerian paradigm of binding ethical law and non-binding ceremonial. "Deed" was, indeed, receiving far more emphasis than "creed," though how and why remained—and remains— problematic. Freehof, however, stayed aloof from the theological fray, and right up until his death continued to do what he had done since the 1940s—answer *she'elot*, one at a time.

10

REFORM RESPONSA SINCE FREEHOF

At first in the postwar years it was Freehof's unique personal stature that gave the responsa process its prominence in Reform Judaism. The ongoing challenges of boundary issues, however, coupled with the return to more traditional observance and the growing desire of a significant number of Reform Jews for ritual guidance, served to reinforce that prominence. By the time he stepped down as chairman in 1976, just as the movement was entering a quarter-century of turmoil over boundary issues, the committee was poised to play a significant but controversial role. For some rabbis, its decisions would acquire quasi-official status, while others would dismiss the committee as the voice of reaction, especially as its chairmen became involved in the effort to define and create a Reform halakhah.

The Responsa Committee after Freehof

In 1976 Freehof, age eighty-five and growing tired, turned over chairmanship of the committee to its hitherto vice chair Walter Jacob, his assistant and successor at Rodef Shalom. The minutes of the committee's January 1977 meeting at the CCAR's New York offices show that Jacob was eager to reorganize the committee by making it more participatory and broadening its scope. The committee at that time consisted of Freehof, Jacob, three HUC-JIR professors of rabbinics (Julius Kravetz from New York and Eugene Mihaly from Cincinnati, both long-time committee members, though the latter was about to end his association with it, and Stephen Passamaneck from Los Angeles), and two recently appointed congregational rabbis, Harry Roth and Herman Schaalman. Those present at the January meeting included CCAR President Arthur Lelyveld, CCAR Executive Director Joseph Glaser, and W. Gunther

Plaut, newly an *ex officio* Responsa Committee member by virtue of his chairmanship of the Committee on Reform Jewish Practice, which now included Walter Jacob *ex officio*. The reciprocity between these two committees was indicative of the new thinking: As the CCAR moved toward developing guides to Reform practice the leadership wanted the two committees involved with ritual observance to communicate with each other lest they issue conflicting materials.

The gathering (which Kravetz could not, and Mihaly did not, attend) reaffirmed that the committee's fundamental mission was still "the writing of responsa utilizing the traditional literature and providing modern Reform answers from it." They wanted, however, to regularize the committee's membership and procedures. First, they agreed that all committee members should take responsibility for writing responsa. In order to prepare for this responsibility, committee members expressed a desire to meet with Freehof so he could explain his methodology to them and also guide them in using the traditional literature. Responsa Committee members would no longer serve for open-ended periods of time but should have regular rotations, though these would be longer than the normal period of CCAR committee service, since it took time to develop expertise in writing responsa. Laypeople would not be represented on the committee as they lacked the necessary expertise, but the gathering expressed a desire to encourage younger colleagues to develop the expertise to serve as associate members and eventually as full members.[1]

How were rabbis chosen to serve on the Responsa Committee? Records do not exist and institutional memory is faint, but presumably it was by the same combination used for appointment to other committees: CCAR leaders would search out individuals with the necessary expertise and interest, and CCAR members would indicate their interest.[2] While CCAR members regularly rotate on and off most committees in order to share the opportunity to serve, some exceptions have always been made to take advantage of individual skills as needed. This is especially true of the Responsa Committee. Eleven men—five HUC-JIR professors and six other rabbis with textual expertise—served continually on the committee from before Freehof's appointment through the first nine years of his chairmanship.

Under Walter Jacob the committee makeup changed significantly, as the professors were replaced with active rabbis who generally served five-year terms. In 1983 the committee added a young rabbi studying for a doctorate in Talmud at HUC in Cincinnati, Mark Washofsky. In 1985 Moshe Zemer, the head of the Israeli Progressive Movement's *bet din*, was invited to serve on the committee *ex officio*, a nominal appointment until the early 1990s, when the committee became a genuinely deliberative body thanks to commercial access to email. Zemer was an active participant in the committee's decisions in the 1990s and remained on its mailing list until his death in November 2011. In 1994 or 1995 the CCAR leadership invited David Lilienthal of Amsterdam, founding head of the *bet din* of the European region of the World Union for Progressive Judaism, to join the Responsa Committee. Whether this was an *ex officio* appointment or a full appointment is unclear, and for all practical purposes irrelevant, since the committee's decisions are usually reached by consensus. Additionally, as with other CCAR committees, rabbis who are not committee members may become "corresponding members," meaning they may attend committee meetings and participate in all committee deliberations, but may not vote if a vote is necessary. Prior to the advent of email, this meant in practice that interested parties would attend the committee's annual open meeting at the CCAR convention, at which the chairman would present an issue or issues for discussion. In the cyberspace era, it has meant that corresponding members—many of whom are regular members whose terms have expired—may contribute equally to the committee's work as do the regular members. In practice, therefore, the Responsa Committee has come to comprise whichever CCAR members want to participate in its process.[3]

In the new, more collaborative procedure initiated by Jacob, "[m]atters of major concern to the Conference or to the future of the Reform movement [would] reflect the thought of the entire committee, not only of an individual." Each responsum would be written by an individual but circulated to the entire committee for discussion, and possibly dissenting opinions; this would be accomplished within one month of receiving the inquiry.[4] However, as HUC-JIR faculty were rotated off the committee and replaced with congregational rabbis, members of the committee generally lacked the chairman's expertise, and definitely lacked his access to Freehof's personal library, one of the finest rabbinic libraries in the world. Writing responsa, therefore, remained the responsibility of the chairman. Additionally, discussing responsa drafts by mail proved impractical. By 1979, when twenty-six responsa drafts were circulated among them, the committee decided that "[o]nly responsa which involves [*sic*] some major matter of principle or many members of the Conference should be circulated to the committee," and that fewer should be circulated altogether.[5]

To increase awareness of the responsa, Walter Jacob initiated two new projects. First, he entered into an agreement by which the editor of *Reform Judaism*, the glossy quarterly magazine sent to every member household affiliated with a Reform synagogue, would invite readers to submit questions about Reform practice. The editor could choose a question to answer by summarizing an existing responsum, with Jacob vetting the draft prior to publication. New questions would be referred to the Responsa Committee.[6]

Second, he brought to publication an anthology of responsa, which eventually appeared as *American Reform Responsa* (*ARR*). This volume included all responsa submitted to the *CCAR Yearbook* by the committee, significant decisions made by the CCAR prior to the creation of the Responsa Committee (e.g., *milat gerim*), and, setting a new precedent, all responsa that Jacob wrote and circulated to the committee because they involved significant Reform issues, whether or not they had been submitted to the CCAR in the committee's annual report. Combining all these responsa and having the volume published by the CCAR—rather than by the HUC Alumni Association and the HUC Press, like Freehof's collections—lent the collection a quasi-official status. It became in turn the model for five subsequent volumes: *Contemporary American Reform Responsa* (1987) and *New American Reform Responsa* (1992), from Walter Jacob's tenure as chair; *Teshuvot for the Nineties* (1997), from W. Gunther Plaut's six years as chair and current chair Mark Washofsky's early years; and the two volumes of *Reform Responsa for the Twenty-First Century* (2010). Each volume contains all responsa that the committee chair deemed of significant interest as Reform precedent. Meanwhile, 1990 was the last year in which responsa appeared in the *Yearbook*, as financial considerations led the CCAR to reduce the size of the annual volume (and to discontinue it completely after 2002, to the detriment of future historians of Reform Judaism). However, each issue of the quarterly *CCAR Journal* now usually included one or two responsa from the committee, so the quantity of responsa material being disseminated to the Conference actually increased.

Reform responsa became even more accessible in the first decade of the new millennium when they became available on the World Wide Web. For almost ten years the CCAR's old website included a searchable index of Reform responsa, including Freehof's books, which were long out of print. The index included free public links to full text versions of the more recent responsa, including those not yet in print. Today the demand for Reform responsa is great enough that the budget-conscious CCAR offers all these publications and all of Freehof's works for sale either as online subscriptions or as downloadable electronic books. The index alone to the complete Reform responsa runs seventy-six pages.[7]

In the 1970s other Reform bodies started turning to the Responsa Committee for guidance on questions that arose as they tried to fulfill their mandates. This was not a new phenomenon; the HUC Board of Governors had famously asked Jacob Lauterbach for a responsum on the ordination of women as rabbis in 1922, and the CCAR Committee on Justice and Peace had asked him for a responsum on birth control in 1927. In 1950 the same committee asked Israel Bettan for a responsum on the Jewish attitude toward euthanasia.[8] Now, however, there came a spate of inquiries, beginning in 1973 when UAHC President-Elect Alexander Schindler asked Freehof whether the Union should support the formation of congregations for homosexuals, a new phenomenon that had the support of at least one UAHC regional director.[9] Predictably, Freehof responded with a strong negative, but as events unfolded the responsum was ignored.

However, as Chapter 6 explained, in 1976 Freehof most unusually refused to answer a question from the CCAR concerning marriage on the Sabbath, lest its reference to the two exceptional precedents have the unintended consequence of providing justification for those rabbis who wanted to continue the practice. CCAR President Arthur Lelyveld wanted an answer, however, and so this was one of the first responsa Walter Jacob wrote when he acceded to the committee chairmanship. His argument proceeded exactly along the lines suggested by Freehof. After explaining the halakhic basis for not performing weddings on Shabbat as well as the two exceptional instances when they were performed, he shifted the grounds of the argument to arriving at a decision in a Reform context:

> We, however, are not concerned with an emergency, but with the usual social context for a modern wedding planned well in advance in the largest number of cases. From the sources cited above, we can see that the traditional prohibition against marriage on Shabbat as given in the Shulchan Aruch rests on foundations in the Talmudic tradition which we, as Reform Jews, no longer observe. One might, therefore, be led to argue that inasmuch as marriage is a *mitzvah*, it should override any objections to its performance on Shabbat. We disagree with that point of view for the following reasons. . . .

The reasons were: 1) not performing weddings on Shabbat has become a "widely observed *minhag* which supports the spirit of Shabbat"; 2) Reform has been trying to encourage the observance of Shabbat, and this runs counter to that aim; 3) we value *klal Yisra'el* and do not want to diverge from common practice simply for convenience; 4) even though couples may not be focusing on these, establishing a marriage does have economic and financial ramifications, and we should not be engaged in transactions with financial overtones on Shabbat; and 5) we should not raise an emergency permission to a normative standard. "We are opposed to the performance of marriages on Shabbat, as we prefer to give allegiance to a hallowed tradition rather than to honor mere convenience."[10]

It is doubtful whether publishing this responsum has had any effect one way or the other. As with mixed marriage, Reform rabbis make their own decisions on this matter. Today officiating before dark on Saturday nights in summer is commonplace, though officiating earlier than 6:00 pm remains rare and is usually limited to mixed marriages where non-Jewish clergy are also involved. Chelsea Clinton's well-publicized wedding in August 2010, at which a rabbi and a minister co-officiated on a Saturday evening before dark, led one Reform rabbi to write a public protest calling on Reform rabbis not to officiate before dark, citing Jacob's responsum at length;[11] when one rabbi posted the article approvingly on Ravkav, the CCAR listserv, it prompted both positive and negative replies including, not surprisingly, one raising the perpetual objection articulated by Samuel Schulman back in 1906 over Kaufmann Kohler's plan to include "Halakot" in the new Ministers' Handbook: By what right does Reform Judaism insist on adhering to halakhah on this matter when it does not on so many other matters?[12]

In 1977 the CCAR Family Life Committee submitted a laundry list of questions as it prepared to wrestle with crafting a Jewish response to changing sexual mores and family structures. Walter Jacob ultimately wrote seven responsa to answer their need.[13] In 1979 the Joint Commission on Education wanted to know the extent to which non-Jews could participate in a Jewish service, a question asked again fifteen years later by the Committee on Reform Jewish Practice.[14] The movement's *Berit Milah* Board wanted to know if Reform *mohalim* should be performing the ritual for children of dual-religion households who were also baptized, or for the children of "messianic Jews."[15] UAHC President Alexander Schindler sought guidance a second time when a Humanistic congregation applied for membership in the Union (see below). In the 1990s the CCAR Committee on Justice and Peace asked about nuclear war and the rights of disabled persons; the UAHC Commission on Social Action asked about the Jewish status of the Falas Mura; and the UAHC Commission on Outreach asked about conversion of a person whose spouse remains gentile.[16]

Freehof had received inquiries from a huge range of people, from within and outside the Reform movement, but he also received large numbers of inquiries from a small number of individuals who had some personal connection to him. Inquirers in the post-Freehof era had a different profile. Very few were from outside the Reform movement, a reflection not only of Freehof's unique stature but also of the growing polarization of the Jewish world. The questions came more or less equally from rabbis and laypeople. While a few rabbis submitted as many as five or six questions, the vast majority submitted only one or two. Clearly the era of sending a question to the master for the sheer delight of seeing how he answered it, or to afford him the pleasure of researching some obscure minhag, was past.

The categories of questions also changed somewhat. Although he did not indicate it explicitly in his tables of contents, Freehof organized the responsa in each of his volumes like traditional volumes, following the subject order of the Shulḥan Arukh. All five CCAR volumes have explicitly followed the same four-part division (although for some reason *CARR* switches their order). As Table VII shows, over the last twenty years there has been a significant rise in the percentage of questions on matters other than synagogue ritual, life cycle, and personal status.

Several factors help account for this trend. Most importantly, the responsa are functioning exactly as Freehof envisioned in 1941 (and as Max Heller envisioned in 1914). Detailed guidance on Reform precedent is available to rabbis and their congregants in quantities that were unimaginable thirty years ago. For example, published responsa provide answers to most questions that will arise with regard to conversion and personal status. Consequently there are far fewer responsa on these topics in the three latest volumes than in any previous volume, including Freehof's eight collections. Guides to Reform practice, including Mark Washofsky's comprehensive *Jewish Living: A Guide to Contemporary Reform Practice*,[17] obviate the need to ask a great many other questions. Second, controversial issues that divided Reform Jews in the second half of the twentieth century and generated numerous responsa, such as Shabbat observance, conversion, personal status, and gentile participation, have largely been resolved, or have at least receded from view as individuals have made up their minds where they stand. Third, since the advent of the internet individuals often just post questions on the CCAR listserv or the HUC-JIR alumni listserv and wait for responses, halakhically based or not, as they choose.

However, it appears that something else is going on. While the categorization is admittedly subjective, the Ḥoshen Mishpat sections in the last three volumes include a higher percentage of inquiries from people struggling with difficult ethical dilemmas in their daily lives, e.g., a synagogue board member accused of cheating a congregant out of money (*TFN* #5754.17); the obligation of physicians to treat indigent patients (*TFN* #5754.18); a severely handicapped individual's desire for sexual gratification (*TFN* #5751.9); privacy and the disclosure of medical information (*RR21/1* #5756.2); a rabbi's responsibility when the congregation knowingly violates tax laws (*RR21/1* #5758.4); working for a company that produces weapons technology for countries at war with Israel (*RR21/1* #5757.1); whether a synagogue may set minimum dues

Table VII: Questions Published per Section of Shulḥan Arukh

		ARR (Kohler)	ARR (Lauterbach)	ARR (Bettan)	ARR (Freehof)	Freehof responsa volumes	ARR (Jacob)	CARR	NARR	TFN	RR21/1	RR21/2
Oraḥ Ḥayim	number of questions	7	9	9	8	121	14	58	81	21	7	5
	% of questions in volume	23%	39%	36%	24%	28%	25%	29%	34%	30%	19%	11%
Yoreh De'ah	number of questions	17	10	9	21	211	22	107	128	16	10	14
	% of questions in volume	57%	44%	36%	61%	49%	39%	53%	52%	22.5%	27%	32%
Even HaEzer	number of questions	5	3	6	2	46	18	16	23	18	13	11
	% of questions in volume	17%	13%	24%	6%	11%	32%	8%	9%	25%	35%	25%
Ḥoshen Mishpat	number of questions	1	1	1	3	50	2	21	12	16	7	14
	% of questions in volume	3%	4%	4%	9%	12%	4%	10%	5%	22.5%	19%	32%

(*RR21/2* #5764.5); allowing a sex offender in the synagogue (*RR21/2* #5765.4); whether a synagogue must hire union labor for a major construction project (*RR21/2* #5761.4); and many more. For that matter, many responsa in the other sections also ask about difficult ethical dilemmas.[18] Freehof received about the same number of questions of this type, but his were spread out over forty years, while these are from a span of no more than fifteen years. Doubtless the Responsa Committee's higher profile makes it more likely that people will turn to it; but what appears to be an increase in non-ritual questions may reflect a need for guidance in the face of rapid and destabilizing social and technological change that generates challenging questions not only about medicine, but about interpersonal relationships and the marketplace.

The Post-Freehof Responsa Committee and the Halakhah

In 1949 Solomon Freehof delivered a remarkable sermon titled "What Would Grandfather Think of Us as Jews?" Likening Reform Judaism to a mature man whose elderly father is visiting his home, he portrayed the old man wandering about disoriented and disconsolate, because he can recognize nothing to mark it as a Jewish home.

> He would say, "Our house, as anybody knew, was a Jewish house, any hour of the day. The food was prepared in a certain special way. No child put a bit of food into his mouth, not even a morsel of bread, without thanking God. Every holiday was observed in some characteristic way. Our life was lived under the will of God." What he would object to in *our* life is that there is no visible evidence in our house that we worship the God of Israel, no religious ceremony. . . .
> We would have to explain to the old man . . . that we differ with him on principle. . . . The fact is that it is a principle of our Reform Jewish life that God does not command us, it is no mandate of God that [our home] has to be treated in a certain way. It may be desirable, but we will never believe that it is a religious mandate. It may be psychologically good to have lights on Friday night and on Chanuko, but we will never believe that this is ordained by God and a religious duty. We have a different religious point of view. We believe

that the essential of the worship of God is the ethical mandate and that the ceremonial is incidental, if anything. That is our principle. . . . We shall never make a religion for us out of all these observances. . . .

But, having silenced him, our conscience will still trouble us, because there is something in his argument that he did not realize. He is right, in a way, in a way which he did not see. We are right because ceremonial will never be a religious duty to us. No rabbi will ever try to persuade you that God commanded you to light lights on Friday night. I do not say that He did. Or that God commanded you to have a prayer before eating. These ceremonials are not duty. They are drama. It is the beauty which we lack. We have not only taken the learning away from adult Judaism, we have taken away its splendor. We should have more of this splendor of Judaism, not in the Orthodox sense that it is our duty to observe rituals, but in the Reform sense that they are beautiful, that they aid in creating a spiritual mood in the home. Whether God commanded or not that the mother of the house should light candles on Friday night and the father should make a blessing over wine or bread, whether or not all this is God's command, it does make the family think of God. It brings God into the home. We must work out our education in such a way not only that the habit of study becomes adult and permanent, but the desire to beautify our homes Jewishly shall no longer meet with silly and snobbish objection.[19]

Rejecting the notion that ritual was in any way obligatory, Freehof wanted Reform Jews to be moved to educate themselves to practice Judaism voluntarily, because of the ways in which daily observance in turn created a spiritual atmosphere. Paradoxically, Reform Judaism's premier halakhic decisor steadfastly resisted the idea that there could be a Reform halakhah, because halakhah was necessarily coercive, deriving its coercive force from the belief that it constituted a divine mandate. Others, however, adopted a different approach.

Virtually since its emergence as an organized movement, American Reform Judaism has struggled with three questions. The first is theological: Are Reform Jews obligated as Jews to do anything in addition to acting ethically, and if so, on what basis? The second is procedural:

How do Reform Jews decide how to carry out those acts? The third is pragmatic and pedagogical: How do rabbis and leaders move the people to act the way they are supposed to act as Reform Jews? The recent history of the Responsa Committee shows a committee actively involved with these questions as it tries to offer a coherent vision of a halakhic Reform Judaism.

The earliest attempts at reform in Europe were undertaken within the framework of the halakhah and were a deliberate effort to generate permissive rulings that would allow contemporary Jews to live simultaneously as observant Jews and as members of the larger society. The effort was eventually abandoned because of a combination of factors: the refusal of traditionalists to accept that questioning the halakhic status quo was even legitimate; the emergence of more radical new formulations of Judaism in which halakhah did not play a significant role, or even a positive role; and the disintegration of the Jewish "sacred canopy," so that more and more Jews no longer cared about observance, much less whether it was halakhically justified. Nevertheless, most Reformers continued to look to the past as expressed in texts for guidance in shaping the present, though this guidance quickly shifted from the search for normative precedent to historical-critical study. The study of the past, however, could also be used to justify radical reform, as it was in the US (e.g., the *milat gerim* decision). Thus the resort to halakhic texts and the desire for a Reform Judaism that was traditional in form and content are separate issues.

American Reform leaders expressed concern from the 1890s onward that their Jews did not practice enough. Reformers had been confident that the abandonment of Jewish observance in the nineteenth century was a rejection of a rigidified and meaningless traditionalism, and that a renewed form of Judaism would bring Jews back to the synagogue. Certainly this was true for many people. But the rabbis could not understand why it was that most of the people who were formally connected to their synagogues continued to have such a low level of religiosity. Whether they were classical Reformers who believed that correctly constituted observance inculcated piety, or the Columbus Platform generation who valued the non-rational sense of religiosity derived from observance, they viewed "ceremonials" as adjuncts—important adjuncts, but nonetheless adjuncts—to Judaism's essential ethical monotheism.

When Kaufmann Kohler used the term "Halakot" in 1906, he set off a firestorm of protest. Halakhah signified compulsion, and there could be no compulsion in matters of praxis. Freehof agreed. His use of the halakhic literature rested on the dual premises that it had lost its binding force with the demise of the legally autonomous Jewish community, and therefore even Orthodox Jews only adhered to it voluntarily and incompletely, and that it had no binding force for Reform Jews because they denied its divine origin. Therefore, it could only have the force of minhag in a Reform context. Freehof rejected the historical-critical approach in favor of an ahistorical appeal to the text for precedent, though the precedent was the "spirit of the law" rather than *nomos*. He loved the halakhah and valued it as the most important element, after the Bible, of the literary and spiritual heritage of Judaism. He wanted Reform Jews to turn to it for "guidance, not governance," in shaping Reform "practice." What he did not want, however, at least not in his own day or for some unspecified time to come, was for it to be used to tell Reform Jews that there were observances they were *obligated* to perform.

Freehof's attempt to identify minhag with the halakhic process itself ultimately was intellectually unsustainable, and Reform thinkers have generally ignored it. However, what he accomplished for Reform Judaism was to reintroduce and model a halakhic *process*, i.e., reading the text as precedent and interpreting it to apply it to a contemporary situation. All three Responsa Committee chairmen since Freehof—Walter Jacob, W. Gunther Plaut, and Mark Washofsky—assert that there is, indeed, Reform halakhah and that that is what the Responsa Committee does, and all three credit Freehof for that. As Walter Jacob wrote, "[H]e moved us in the direction of Reform Halakhah."[20] All three, however, also recognize that Freehof himself would not admit the possibility of Reform halakhah. All three also part company with Freehof on the pragmatic and pedagogical question of bringing Reform Jews to a richer and more observant Jewish life.

1. Walter Jacob, like Freehof, has left theology to others and focused on process. He stresses the similarity between the traditional halakhic process and the Reform halakhic process. Both, he points out, rely on "divine [authority as] transmitted through human interpretation, legis-

lation, precedent, and custom," though Reform also stresses diversity, individual freedom, and the right to interpret and change "if necessary." Like Freehof, he minimizes the significance of radical Reform and asserts that Reform has generally operated "within a broad framework of traditional authority." This traditional authority, the precedents of all the Reform conferences and synods, and the Responsa Committee are the three sources that provide "some degree of authority" in Reform.[21]

Jacob has been outspoken in calling for standards in Reform Judaism. The years of his CCAR presidency (1991–93) coincided with the peak years of controversy over the movement's blurring of boundaries with respect to mixed marriage, the status of children of mixed marriage, the role of non-Jewish spouses in the synagogue, and the inclusion of gays and lesbians. In his first presidential address he declared:

> A system of *mitzvot* and *halakhah* must be our way.
>
> We have moved along this new path rather gradually and that, perhaps, is an understatement. Our tempo has been glacial. We have taken as our motto the statement of my honored predecessor, Solomon B. Freehof, "guidance, not governance." That was fine for the forties, the vague beginnings of our halakhic efforts, but now we must set standards for ourselves and for the lifestyle of our people which will make it distinctly Jewish.
>
> When individuals turn to us for direction, to the Responsa Committee, as hundreds have done in the last few years, they are not looking for a menu of choices but for specific standards on which they could construct Judaism. . . .
>
> We, as Reform Jews, have not taught our people that Judaism must make demands; they must make conscious choices about their religious obligations, choices in every major area of concern.[22]

He wanted a "standard guide for all aspects of Reform Jewish life": not merely ritual, but also communal behavior—personal, communal, and business ethics, all the elements of social justice which Reform claimed to value. It did not matter that the theological underpinnings were as yet uncertain. The rabbis should not wait to define "the nature of the giver of those *mitzvot*" before declaring that some things are mitzvot. "Let 'standards now' be our motto."[23] In a polarized CCAR, however, the speech only added fuel to the fire.

Jacob did not wait for the CCAR to agree that there could be a Reform halakhah and that it should be applied to all aspects of life. Not content to address issues haphazardly as they came to the committee, in the late 1980s he founded the Freehof Institute of Progressive Halakhah to provide "a more thought out halakhic response to current issues than what responsa allowed," and also to do this from a less specifically American context.[24] His collaborator in this endeavor was Moshe Zemer, whose book *Halakhah Shefuyah* offered Progressive halakhic perspectives on vexing problems in Israeli society.[25] The Freehof Institute holds an annual symposium in conjunction with the CCAR convention and usually at least one other symposium each year, in the US, London, or Israel, and publishes an annual collection of papers on topics ranging from conversion to war and terrorism. (Jacob's vision of a Liberal halakhah to counter an ever-narrowing Orthodoxy also led him to open discussions with members of the Conservative movement's Committee on Jewish Law and Standards about the possibility of issuing joint responsa, but these efforts did not bear fruit.[26])

2. W. Gunther Plaut, who succeeded Walter Jacob in 1989, rooted his responsa writing in the covenantal approach of Doppelt and Polish's *Guide for Reform Jews*, of which the fullest theological exposition is that of Eugene B. Borowitz.[27] They rejected the paradigm of ethical monotheism, asserting that its categories of "ethical" and "ritual" commandments were alien to Judaism, inaccurate, and inappropriate. Judaism's foundation was the covenant, and covenant necessarily meant mitzvah. In their view, the mitzvot—e.g., *brit milah*—were all of those acts that arose from the historical encounter between God and Israel and which re-enacted the encounter each time they were performed. The *halakhot*, by contrast, were the specific details evolved by the rabbis to apply the mitzvot: Who may circumcise? What liturgy is to be said? The *minhagim* were the folkways with which the Jewish people embellished the mitzvot and *halakhot*: the *sandek*, the chair of Elijah. *Minhagim* varied enormously, according to popular creativity; and changing social circumstances could and should lead to change in the *halakhot*. But the mitzvot were "mandatory and certainly not elective."[28]

In 1968 Plaut bemoaned North American Reform's disconnection

from halakhah and called for a guide to Reform practice. While he credited Freehof for reconnecting Reform with the halakhic tradition, he also
criticized him for not going far enough. Freehof's insistence that Reform responsa could only be "advisory . . . gives even the most careful
student a shaky foundation for decision and ultimately leaves it to the individual Reform Jew to do 'that which is right in his own eyes.'"[29] He
also criticized Walter Jacob for not taking on the theological grounding
of his responsa. "His decisions are cast in the Freehofian model, and no
attempt is made to give his conclusions a comprehensive historical or
theological basis."[30]

Plaut held up instead the approach of Doppelt and Polish, praising
them for returning Reform to its early roots as a halakhically grounded
movement. He admitted, however, that no Reform theology could provide as powerful a basis for observing the mitsvot as the belief that they
were divine mandates. Traditional Judaism had halakhah, "practice-be-
come-law"; Reform could only offer "practice-by-consent," for which
Plaut coined the Hebrew neologism *halikhah*.[31] (He later abandoned the
term and reverted to using halakhah.[32]) *Halikhah* required individual
commitment. Reform Jews still retained a "sense of mitzvah," and
[m]ost . . . would give assent to the proposition that they *must do something to remain Jews*." Displaying a positively Freehofian sleight of
hand, Plaut neatly reconciled Freehof with Doppelt and Polish by explaining that Reform Jews had to be educated that the Jewish behaviors
they currently practiced were not simply what they *wanted* to do, i.e.,
minhagim, but were, in fact, what they *ought* to do, i.e., that they were
mitzvot. "As we invest various *minhagim* (not all, to be sure) with the
sense of *mitzvah* we will begin to reestablish a viable body of *halakhot*."[33]

In explaining how he interpreted the traditional texts to arrive at a
suitable Reform answer, Freehof had always emphasized the need to
search for the "spirit" of the law and to find the most liberal possible
answer, because popular minhag was to be validated as much as possible. And, of course, his answer was not halakhah. Plaut took a different
view. The committee's responsa most assuredly constituted Reform halakhah. They relied on two sets of precedents, halakhic texts and the
"legal corpus of our Liberal movement."

> We begin with Tradition and ask: how does it treat this
> *she'elah*? We then proceed to ask: What is there in our Lib-
> eral tradition that would have us disagree? Is there a previous
> ruling or other legal document that would have us decide oth-
> erwise? If not, our Tradition stands; if there is, we must ex-
> amine how our Liberal halakhah, as developed so far, can be
> applied in the case before us.
>
> In this way we are in fact creating a new body of refer-
> ence, a distinctly Liberal halakhah and we must have no hes-
> itation to call it just that.[34]

In other words, *the halakhah remains valid unless there is a Reform principle or a compelling consideration that overrides it.* This is exactly the
opposite of Freehof's approach, which was that the people's current
practice is valid unless there is a compelling reason to insist on the traditional way. The responsa issued during Plaut's chairmanship (written
jointly by him and vice-chair Mark Washofsky) reflect this process
through the regular use of subheadings such as "Halachic Precedents,"
"Reform Perspectives," and "Other Considerations."[35]

3. Mark Washofsky's responsa also assert that the halakhah is valid
unless there is a Reform principle or some other compelling reason to decide otherwise. His work is a model of scholarship demonstrating masterful use of classical and contemporary halakhic texts. In addition, he
has read widely in comparative legal studies and philosophy of law, especially Ronald Dworkin. He does not address the theological basis of
Reform halakhah, though his language is the language of covenant theology; but he repeatedly takes on the pragmatic and pedagogical task of
explaining to the Reform reading public what halakhic discourse is in a
Reform context and why it matters. His central message is that "if we
Reform Jews regard ourselves as students of Torah and our religious
practices as part of that tradition, then we, too, must continue to take
part in the conversation of halakhah, learning and speaking the language
in which the tradition creates our practices, gives them shape, and be-
queaths them to us."[36] He assures his readers that Reform responsa are
not binding but only advisory, but then reminds them that "[u]nlimited
religious autonomy is an oxymoron, since 'religion' is at its core an exercise in the setting of limits and the drawing of boundaries."[37] Reform

responsa advise where to draw those boundaries based on what the writer believes is the best reading of the texts within a Reform community of readers; the writer must then persuade the readers to accept that reading. "Each responsum is therefore an exercise in argumentation, an essay which seeks to elicit the agreement of a particular Jewish audience that shares the religious values of its author."[38]

For Washofsky, as for his predecessors, responsa are only one element in the process of developing a Reform halakhah. In addition to writing responsa, he also produced the long-desired guide to Jewish practice. *Jewish Living: A Guide to Contemporary Reform Practice* differs significantly from Freehof's *RJP.* Its very title, which relegates "Reform" to the subtitle, indicates the intent to minimize the separation between "Judaism" and "Reform Judaism." Unlike *RJP* it is comprehensive, covering all aspects of life as Walter Jacob envisioned, and not shying away from Shabbat, kashrut, and other unresolved questions.

Washofsky and his committee are writing responsa at least thirty years after the peak of Freehof's activity; Reform Judaism has changed a great deal in the interim. On occasion they explicitly disagree with Freehof's conclusions. Not infrequently they use a responsum to survey an issue on which there has been some reappraisal of an earlier Reform position that deviated from the codified law. A lengthy responsum about cremation illustrates this. A rabbi inquired on behalf of the children of a dying man who instructed them to have his body cremated. The children have strong religious objections to this. Are they obligated, as Freehof ruled, to carry out his wishes?

The responsum proceeds in careful steps. First, it explains Freehof's reasoning. He wrote that while the Talmud says it is a mitzvah to fulfill the wishes of the deceased, one is forbidden to do so if it involves a violation of Jewish law. But he insisted that only in the modern era did Orthodox authorities ban cremation, as part of their campaign against modernity, and that since the prohibition rests on weak halakhic grounds, Reform Jews are justified in ignoring it. The responsum rejects this reasoning.

> We would argue . . . that the times demand a different response. For one thing, the situation is no longer "so clear-

cut"; the Reform position on cremation is more complex today than it was when R. Freehof wrote his *t'shuvah* [responsum]. We also think that our attitude toward the maintenance and encouragement of traditional forms of Jewish observance has changed quite a bit over the last several decades. For these reasons, we hold that the children in this case may well be entitled to act upon their own religious beliefs and *not* to fulfill their father's request.[39]

There follows a survey of the halakhic sources on cremation, which finds them more persuasive than Freehof did. Next, a survey of Reform sources on cremation reveals "a perceptible shift of attitude" toward the practice, from complete acceptance to reservations stemming from two sources: acknowledgement that burial is the "normative traditional Jewish practice" and that cremation now inevitably carries overtones of the Holocaust.

This affords Washofsky the opportunity to do what he regularly does brilliantly and persuasively in his responsa—to make the case that "when there are no compelling moral or aesthetic arguments against that practice," Reform Jews should value and decide for traditional practice *because* it is traditional. "A Reform Jew today who finds special and satisfying meaning in the values and affirmations of Jewish tradition is thus entitled—though again, not obligated—to adopt this definition precisely because it flows from the religious and cultural heritage of our people."[40] While he carefully qualifies his language to avoid any hint of compulsion, the intent is clearly to persuade the reader to opt into the traditional practice, just as Reform halakhah uses the discourse of the halakhah and does not deviate in its conclusions except to the extent that Reform principles mandate.

The Responsa Committee and the Reform Kulturkampf

The upheavals in American society that began in the 1960s opened the way to a generation of controversies within American Reform Judaism. In the 1970s and 1980s the movement wrestled with mixed marriage; in the 1980s it produced a controversial new definition of who is a Jew; in the 1990s it struggled to retain its very Jewishness given the presence of so many non-Jews in its ranks, and moved through intense controversy toward extending formal recognition to same-sex couples. All of these controversies were conflicts over boundaries: Where were the limits of authentic Jewish religious expression? At what point did accommodation to the larger society become surrender of essential Jewish values and practice? On all of these issues except patrilineality the Responsa Committee argued vehemently against deviating from traditional norms. On mixed marriage the committee's halakhic and historical arguments counted for naught with those who were persuaded otherwise by sociological or pastoral concerns. On the question of non-Jewish participation in the synagogue, only a detailed survey of individual synagogue practices could show definitively whether the committee's 1995 responsum had an impact, but without a doubt in this area a majority of the rabbis were at least sympathetic to the committee's views. The committee ended up most definitively on the losing side on the same-sex marriage question.

1. Mixed marriage: In 1947 Freehof had joined a slim majority to defeat a strengthening of the CCAR's 1909 resolution against mixed marriage, convinced that it was only a problem because of the loose standards of a few elderly classical Reformers who would soon pass from the scene. Rates of Jewish marriage in the US were low, after all—below 7% through the 1950s.[41] As the rate rose through the 1960s and he received more and more questions about officiation, he remained convinced that some mixed marriage was part of the price of living in an open society, and that if rabbis would just refuse to normalize it, it would remain a marginal phenomenon.

By the early 1970s, however, it was obvious to everyone that the rate was going up significantly, though reliable figures were hard to come by.[42] The CCAR leadership was concerned not only about mixed marriage but about the growing pressure on rabbis to officiate, and therefore determined to strengthen the 1909 resolution. This it accomplished in 1973, with 62% of those present voting for the resolution;[43] but passions remained inflamed on both sides as the number of mixed marriages continued to rise.[44]

There had been no CCAR responsa on mixed marriage since 1919, when Kaufmann Kohler had pronounced that " . . . no rabbi who wants to be true to the tradition of Judaism can perform [a mixed] marriage ceremony . . . "[45] Freehof published only one responsum on the subject in his eight volumes of responsa; significantly, it appeared in 1969, as concern began to boil over. He used it to summarize all his arguments against rabbinic officiation.[46] Walter Jacob and the committee took an activist stance. A 1979 responsum ruled against pronouncing a public blessing for a mixed couple prior to their marriage, since to do so would be to give public approval to it. In 1980 the committee was asked whether a Reform rabbi could officiate at a mixed marriage and what the Reform attitude toward such officiation was. The question was obviously intended to provide an opportunity to restate the anti-mixed marriage case, which Jacob did in a lengthy and thorough historical survey reminiscent of a Lauterbach responsum. Two years later in response to a layperson who asked for "halachic and non-halachic" reasons against officiation, he added a responsum with fifteen reasons, thirteen of them strictly sociological.[47] The battle over mixed marriage raged with even greater heat in the 1980s. One group of rabbis defended the CCAR's official position in response to lay pressure on rabbis to officiate, while another funded the publication of a collection of responsa attacking that position and any attempt to claim binding authority for CCAR resolutions;[48] but the Responsa Committee itself was no longer involved.

There was especial outrage in the CCAR at the small number of rabbis who embarrassed them and scandalized the rest of the Jewish world by co-officiating with non-Jewish clergy. In 1982 the Conference accepted the report of its special Committee on Ecumenical Wedding Practices, which referenced the 1909, 1947, and 1973 resolutions and declared, "Mindful of these prior resolutions, we now call special attention to the most flagrant form of mixed marriage—co-officiating with non-Jewish clergy—and publicly repudiate that practice." A responsum applied that resolution equally to holding two separate marriage ceremonies, one Jewish and one Christian, declaring, "We vigorously reject this attempt at religious syncretism suggested by the question . . . "[49]

The Responsa Committee's efforts to reinforce the CCAR's official stance against officiation at mixed marriages may or may not have convinced some rabbis. A 1972 study found that 41% of Reform rabbis would officiate at a mixed marriage, under a variety of circumstances; in 1996 the figure was 48%.[50] In recent years the CCAR has stopped trying to assert that non-officiation is the norm from which some members deviate, and instead has focused on bringing its members together around the shared goal of creating households with an exclusive and unambiguous Jewish identity.[51]

2. Patrilineality: The rising rate of mixed marriage meant that there were more and more children with Jewish fathers and non-Jewish mothers. In 1978 UAHC President Alexander Schindler set off a furious debate by calling for a special committee, including representatives of the Responsa Committee, to find a way to make it possible to declare these children Jews.[52] Five years later the result was a CCAR resolution stating, in part, that "the child of one Jewish parent is under the presumption of Jewish descent. This presumption of the Jewish status of the offspring of any mixed marriage is to be established through appropriate and timely public and formal acts of identification with the Jewish faith and people."[53] Those who wanted to minimize the resolution's radical nature argued that this was essentially just an updated restatement of the guidelines for conversion of children of Jewish fathers proposed by Freehof and adopted by the CCAR in 1947. Since Reform in that era generally did not require any rituals for conversion, Freehof had argued that in effect, raising a child as a Jew was the same as converting it. Thus the 1983 resolution merely gave *de jure* recognition to what was already happening *de facto*. However, in the name of gender equality the 1983 resolution departed radically from both the 1947 guidelines and from rabbinic law by declaring that the child of a Jewish *mother* was not a Jew without being raised as such. Now birth was not sufficient to make the child of a Jewish mother a Jew, and no conversion, however effected, was necessary for the child of a Jewish father raised as a Jew. (Freehof opposed the decision on patrilineal descent, but he was beyond playing an active role in the movement's deliberations. While he applauded the goal, he felt there was no need to stir up intense Orthodox opposition by making "this drastic change in Jewish law [when o]ur system of conversion is so easy in the Reform movement that we can bring in these children in this way without difficulty."[54])

As with mixed marriage, the Responsa Committee again received a softball question to elicit a responsum explaining and justifying the CCAR's decision. Whatever his personal views may have been on this divisive issue, Walter Jacob produced another masterful historical responsum providing what was required. Key points were that biblical lineage was patrilineal and that the rabbinic shift was a function of historical circumstances and did not apply to all matters of Jewish status; that the Torah basis on which the rabbis ground matrilineal descent is weak; that the Reform decision was no different from the early rabbinic process, i.e., to change as circumstances demanded; that this decision's definition of Jewish status fell within the parameters of Israeli courts' definition of Jewish nationality; that the decision was a fulfillment of the Reform commitment to equality of the sexes; and that the new definition was the best way to resolve the ambiguity of many individuals' Jewish status given modern conditions.[55]

Subsequent responsa clarifying the Jewish status of children according to the 1983 resolution, with its dual requirements of biological and social elements of Jewishness for determining status, produced decisions no different than what Freehof's had been when the children had Jewish fathers. Biological descent through one parent was necessary, but not sufficient.[56] The adult son of a Jewish father who had no proof of *brit milah* and no Jewish education or upbringing was definitely not a Jew under the resolution. The young children of a Jewish man by two different non-Jewish wives, in order to be considered Jews, needed to attend religious school and go through bar/bat mitzvah and Confirmation. A young man descended from three generations of Jewish men married to non-Jewish women, with no Jewish education, was incorrect in assuming the 1983 resolution would enable him to claim Jewish status; he required formal conversion.[57] The committee never published any parallel responsa clarifying the status of children of Jewish mothers. While arguments from silence are less than definitive, it is likely that this reflects the reluctance of even rabbis who supported the 1983 resolution to decide flat out that the child of a Jewish woman is not a Jew, and therefore even one with the sketchiest of Jewish upbringings can be treated as leniently as necessary to avoid any problems.

As the 1990s brought an explosion in the number of intermarried Reform-affiliated households, including an increase in dual-religion households, the committee's focus in interpreting the 1983 resolution switched to stressing the need for exclusivity of Jewish identification. The following situation led to a momentous decision: A Jewish man applied to join a synagogue and send his young son to religious school. The man's wife was a practicing Catholic and they had agreed to raise their daughter as a Catholic and their son as a Jew. Mark Washofsky's responsum argued that it was wrong to assume that the 1983 resolution *automatically* conferred Jewish status on the child of one Jewish parent as long as the child had "appropriate and timely public and formal acts of identification with the Jewish faith and people." Neither the descent nor the acts were sufficient to establish Jewish status, he wrote, "in a situation in which the performance of these acts does not offer proof of exclusive Jewish identification—as in a case where the child's religious identity is torn, conflicted, or confused." He further declared that "[w]hether the child of a mixed marriage is in fact Jewish is a matter of judgment. It depends upon an evaluation of his or her conduct and commitment, a finding that the child's acts of identification with Judaism are sufficiently 'meaningful' to remove any doubt as to the genuineness of his or her Jewish identity."[58] The boy was presumed a gentile and was to be admitted to the religious school in order to study and become a Jew through conversion, which would have to be some sort of formal process *prior* to his becoming bar mitzvah.

This astonishing decision, which flew in the face of fifty years of attempts to clarify the status of children of non-Jewish parents, was a reaction to two problems. One was the issue that consumed Reform Judaism in the 1990s: In a Jewish community living with such open and porous boundaries, where were the limits of acceptable *Jewish* living? As Washofsky went on to write in this responsum:

> Our position flows from Reform Judaism's categorical rejection of the concept of religious syncretism, the notion that a child can be raised simultaneously in more than one religious tradition. We hold that Judaism is an exclusive religious identification, that one is either a Jew or one is not, that one cannot successfully be a Jew and something else. For this reason, in the case of a mixed marriage, until there exists in the family a firm and discernible intent and ability to raise the child as a Jew, that child is not regarded by us as Jewish. . . .
> It is up to the parents, through a sincere and credible commitment, to decide . . . And if there is any doubt as to the choice they have made, the child does not qualify as a Jew under the doctrine of patrilineal descent.[59]

The other problem was the lasting discontent with the 1983 resolution among many who had opposed it at the time as an unnecessary and destructive break with an historic Jewish norm, and as impossibly ambiguous. Members of the Responsa Committee, self-selected for their interest in halakhah, tended to fall into this category. In a postscript Washofsky asserted that the stringency of the decision was a necessary response not only because Reform was in a period "when mixed marriage is on the rise, where assimilation poses a constant challenge, and where the danger of religious syncretism is rife," but also because the case exposed the weaknesses of the 1983 resolution, i.e., its ambiguities, which were "unlikely [to be] . . . firmly and finally resolved without a concerted effort on the part of the Conference as a whole to re-examine the question of Jewish status in a thorough and thoughtful way."[60] In other words, the onus for this decision was on the people who had adopted "patrilineality." The CCAR has not modified the 1983 resolution, however, nor has the Responsa Committee dealt with a similarly difficult question about it.

3. Humanistic congregations: In the early 1990s furious controversy erupted over a theological boundary issue when Congregation Beth Adam, formerly affiliated with the small Society for Humanistic Judaism, applied for membership in the UAHC. The congregation's liturgy excluded all references to God, including the *Shema*.[61] After extended discussion both private and very public, the UAHC Board of Trustees overwhelmingly rejected the congregation's application. When the application was made, Alexander Schindler asked the Responsa Committee for its opinion. Its majority answer, from which three members dissented, made not a single reference to any halakhic text, but considered only what the congregation's own literature said about its theology in comparison to the theological pronouncements of the three Reform platforms. It concluded that the congregation's theological stance not only denied the reality of the deity but also of the covenant, and was therefore incompatible with Reform Judaism. Meanwhile, Beth Adam sought an opinion from Eugene Mihaly, the Cincinnati faculty member who had written a counter-responsum to the committee's responsum on weddings on Shabbat and festivals in 1976, and then written the counter-responsa on mixed marriage officiation in 1985. Mihaly obliged with a predictably contrarian responsum, the wide distribution of which Beth Adam funded.[62] This generated in turn a response from his Cincinnati

colleague, historian Michael A. Meyer. The final version of the committee's responsum in *TFN* includes a summary of their arguments.[63]

4. Non-Jewish participation: We have seen that Solomon Freehof received numerous questions over the years about the extent to which non-Jews could participate in regular Jewish worship and in the organizational life of the synagogue. While he advocated clear limits, he also made an important exception, suggesting that the Christian step-father of a bar mitzvah could be called to the Torah, since it was also sacred text for him, but recite an alternate blessing.[64] Such a permissive stance was not a problem when only 5% of Reform congregants had non-Jewish spouses and full membership for non-Jewish spouses was far from normative.[65] By 1992, after a decade of activity by the Commission on Outreach, however, *Reform Judaism* opened a story on "Non-Jews in the Synagogue" with the announcement that "Gentiles married to Jews are joining synagogues in record numbers," and that they were "emerging as congregational leaders, as committee members, as teachers, even as temple trustees."[66] Though this story gave the impression that most congregations were setting limits on ritual and organizational participation, there was enough evidence to the contrary that it appeared to many people that in its eagerness to reach out to non-Jewish spouses, the movement was in danger of losing its identity as a form of Judaism. Michael A. Meyer, who had recently published his magisterial history of Reform Judaism, warned that American Reform was well on the road to becoming a syncretistic sect, no longer part of historical Judaism.[67] "Syncretism" had become the buzzword among those who deplored the absence of limits on non-Jewish participation in many synagogues.

The UAHC's Commission on Outreach had published *Defining the Role of the Non-Jew in the Synagogue: A Resource for Congregations* in 1990, but offered congregations a range of options and no essential foundational principles on which to decide. The CCAR leadership felt, in any case, that this question was rightfully in its purview, and so the Reform Practices Committee asked the Responsa Committee for a comprehensive responsum on the role of the non-Jew in the synagogue. The result was *TFN* #5754.5, "Gentile Participation in Synagogue Ritual." It analyzed the halakhah on reciting liturgical blessings; counting in the *minyan*; serving as *sheliah tsibur*; and reading from, being called to, or handling the Torah scroll, and concluded that all of these were acts that non-Jews should not perform in a contemporary Reform context. To encourage rabbis to think through this issue, however, the CCAR also devoted a session to it at the 1994 convention. Recognizing that many CCAR members would not be persuaded by the halakhic reasoning of a responsum, the issue was intentionally not framed as a question of halakhah.[68] The plenary address on the topic was favorably received and anecdotal responses since then indicate that at least some rabbis found it useful, but no one can really say to what extent the responsum and the convention address were responsible for what appears to be the dissipation of the "syncretism" issue through the next few years.

5. Same-sex marriage: As a body with generally liberal social views, the Reform movement has a history of advocating for civil rights for gays and lesbians. Despite Freehof's negative responsa, the UAHC welcomed the first of several gay and lesbian synagogues as a member congregation in 1974.[69] Accepting gays and lesbians as religious leaders and formalizing same-sex relationships in a Jewish context were far more controversial issues, however. The CCAR struggled to adjust to the presence of gay and lesbian rabbis in its ranks as these began to come out in the late 1970s and through the 1980s, and HUC-JIR eventually abandoned its policy of trying to screen out gay and lesbian applicants. By the early 1990s the one unresolved issue was whether Reform Judaism would accord any formal recognition to same-sex relationships. Civil recognition for same-sex couples was one of the hot-button issues in the US culture wars; the CCAR readily staked out a liberal position by endorsing the idea in 1995, over a year before President Clinton signed the so-called Defense of Marriage Act. Growing numbers of rabbis were individually deciding to officiate at "commitment ceremonies" for same-sex couples. It was widely expected within the CCAR that its Ad Hoc Committee on Human Sexuality would favor rabbinic officiation, so it was not a surprise when its 1998 report did, in fact, declare that "*kedushah* [holiness] may be present in committed, same-gender relationships between two Jews, and . . . we believe that the relationship of a Jewish, same-gender couple is worthy of affirmation through appropriate Jewish ritual," with rabbis, of course, free to follow their consciences in choosing whether or not to officiate.[70] In 1996, however, before the Ad Hoc Committee presented its conclusion, an individual rabbi turned to the Responsa Committee. He had never officiated at a same-sex

ceremony, but the Ad Hoc Committee's interim presentation at that year's CCAR convention was leading him to change his thinking, and he now wanted clarification of "Judaism's opposition to such a union (beyond the Biblical injunctions)."[71]

The committee deliberations were drawn out over eight months of intense, emotionally wrenching, occasionally hostile controversy around two questions: Could a relationship between two Jews of the same sex constitute *kiddushin*, and could a Reform rabbi officiate at any ceremony, *kiddushin* or not, to formalize the relationship of a Jewish same-sex couple? Opinions fell into three categories. Two individuals at one end of the spectrum expressed vehement opposition to any Jewish recognition of same-sex couples, arguing that it ran counter to all Jewish family values, and that the synagogue should be resisting the decadence of contemporary culture, not joining it. On the other end, two members advocated a strong positive response largely rooted in arguments already made by Conservative rabbi Bradley Artson, who asserted that since sexual *orientation* was not a concept known to the classical Jewish tradition, which only considered sexual *acts*, its strictures could not be applied today to individuals whose orientation led them to find their deepest intimacy with members of their own sex.[72]

The majority of the committee strongly felt that extending *kiddushin* to same-sex couples, with all its halakhic implications, was simply too radical a departure from tradition for them to justify. Indeed, they looked on any formalization of same-sex relationships as an unjustifiable innovation, but if the CCAR wanted to invent a ritual, that was not the concern of the Responsa Committee. What the majority did *not* feel was that this was an ethical matter of fundamental justice (comparable to, e.g., equality of the sexes) that justified or even mandated a Reform departure from tradition. As Mark Washofsky recalls, "We were under no illusion . . . that our responsum would somehow 'stop the drive' toward CCAR approval of rabbinic officiation at same-sex weddings. I think we all knew that the majority of the Conference would soon vote to endorse officiation. The goal of the Committee's majority, at least as I saw it, was to provide a sufficiently liberal-halakhic rationale and rhetoric for those colleagues who did not want to officiate."[73] Contributing to this resistance, though not decisive, was the active involvement of the European and Israeli representatives, whose constituencies are more traditionally oriented than the American movement, and who also suffer more from Orthodox hostility. They had already experienced considerable abuse for the CCAR's 1983 "patrilineal" resolution, though they opposed it and never adopted it.

Not only was the committee unable to arrive at any agreement, but as Washofsky wrote, "In trying to talk to each other about this question, we discovered that we as a Committee had ceased to share the most elemental kinds of assumptions necessary for a common religious conversation. . . . [W]e were conducting a series of parallel monologues in place of the dialogue of text and tradition that has served us so well in the past."[74] Rather than issuing a majority decision with a minority dissent, he conceived the idea of writing a single responsum that would include both views, hoping that insight into the committee's difficulties would be of use to an intensely polarized CCAR. In retrospect Washofsky writes that he was under no illusion that the responsum would change anyone's mind. Rather, as he explains,

> It was more important, I thought, for our *teshuvah* to model a respectful debate between two irreconcilable positions, giving each side a chance to air its viewpoint in thorough manner. . . . What disappointed me the most is that few of our colleagues seemed to take the time to study and consider the arguments on both sides. All they remember, it seems, is that "the Responsa Committee came out against same-sex officiation."[75]

Indeed, they did. It cannot be denied that the majority of the committee wanted their colleagues to read and consider both sides—and be persuaded that the majority was correct. Wanting to appear "balanced," the CCAR leadership chose to publish the responsum two years after its issue, in the same yearbook volume that included the final report of the Ad Hoc Committee that endorsed same-sex officiation.[76] It was the only responsum published in a *Yearbook* after 1990. In 1999 the Women's Rabbinic Network, comprising women members of the CCAR, passed a resolution endorsing same-sex ceremonies that became the basis for a similar proposal brought to the CCAR the following year, when its adoption made national headlines. Many CCAR members concluded from the episode that the very attempt to root Reform practice in a process of interpreting the halakhah was misguided.

Conclusion

The Responsa Committee in the post-Freehof era has moved decisively to embrace the concept of Reform halakhah. In a period when controversy over boundaries and limits threatened to tear the Reform movement apart, the committee increasingly came to see its mission as setting limits and preventing *hefkerut*. Intentionally or not, it has become identified with an ideological stream within Reform Judaism, a significant change from the Freehof era. That, however, was as much a function of his unique personal status as it was of his carefully cultivated moderation. Large numbers of Reform Jews continue to value the committee's guidance, as they did in Freehof's day, but not necessarily because they are committed to Reform halakhah. Most of the questions are simply the most recent wrinkles on the same matters for which people turned to Freehof: synagogue life, conversion, Jewish status, life cycle, and medical ethics, though the noticeable uptick in questions of social and communal ethics does indicate an awareness that Jewish law can be a source of moral guidance in a chaotic world.

At the present moment, American Reform Judaism finds itself more consumed with economic and demographic challenges than with controversies over halakhah. The Great Recession exposed the fragility of an American Jewish communal establishment with too many organizations and not enough Jews to support them all; Reform institutions were not spared. Reform triumphalism at overtaking Conservative Judaism as the largest synagogue movement in North America has given way to fears of losing the next generation. "Post-denominational" Jews question whether the institutional label matters at all. The CCAR Responsa Committee as it is currently constituted can continue for many years to come to produce profoundly learned, thoughtful, and persuasive answers to difficult dilemmas, but its real influence will depend on what becomes of the community for which it interprets and creates the halakhah. The more successful the committee is in persuading Reform Jews to choose its vision of religious Jewish living, the more likely it is to assure itself a future community of readers.

GLOSSARY OF HEBREW, YIDDISH, AND ARAMAIC TERMS

Hebrew words are italicized and transliterated according to guidelines formulated by the Israel Academy of the Hebrew Language[1] with the following exceptions:

- The final silent *heh* is indicated because this is commonly done in an English language context.
- A few Hebrew terms in common use in English are not italicized and appear as they are most commonly spelled: bar mitzvah, bat mitzvah, mitzvah, halakhah. kashrut,etc.
- Names of holidays, prayers, and classic rabbinic texts are capitalized but not italicized, and appear as they are most commonly spelled.
- All quotations retain the original transliteration, with the result that the reader will encounter multiple transliterations of the same Hebrew word. In particular, the reader will note that Freehof's transliterations reflect his lifelong retention of the Ashkenazic pronunciation of Hebrew.

Yiddish words are transliterated according to the YIVO Institute guidelines.[2] All terms listed here are Hebrew unless otherwise noted.

agunah. Literally, "anchored [woman]." A woman who cannot remarry either because her husband will not issue her a *get*, or because he has disappeared and his death cannot be proven.

aliyah (pl. *aliyot*). Literally, "ascent." Being called to the Torah to recite the blessings before and after a passage is read in synagogue, traditionally restricted to adult male Jews.

arayot. The categories of forbidden sexual relations or the laws pertaining to them.

Arukh HaShulḥan. A halakhic compilation based on the Shulḥan Arukh, by R. Yeḥiel Mikhl Epstein (1829–1908).

Ashkenazic. Referring to the Jews of northern and eastern Europe or their cultural and legal traditions.

bet din. Rabbinical court.

Bet Yosef. A comprehensive commentary on the Tur, by R. Joseph Karo.

bimah. Raised platform from which the Torah is read and, in liberal synagogues, from which the service is led.

bittul Torah. Desisting from [the study of] Torah. A term applied by the tradition to any activity considered too frivolous for a Jewish man to spend time on.

brit milah. Literally, "covenant of circumcision." Ritual circumcision.

dina (Aram.). Law.

divre ḥaverut or ***ḥaverut.*** Formal act confirming an apostate's return to Judaism.

ger toshav. In biblical use, a foreigner who chose to reside among the Israelites.

get (pl. ***gittin***). Jewish divorce, issued by a *bet din.*

halakhah (pl. ***halakhot***). Jewish law as a whole or a specific law or laws, from the root *h-l-kh,* "walk, go."

hatafat dam. Literally, "drawing a drop of blood." If a male has already been medically circumcised, the ritual circumcision requires only the appropriate liturgy and a drop of blood from a symbolic cut where the foreskin was removed.

havdalah. Literally, "differentiation." The name of the ritual marking the end of the Sabbath and the beginning of the new week, originally fixed at the time when three stars are visible in the night sky.

hefkerut. Chaos, anarchy. A situation in which no authority prevails.

ḥalitsah. The ceremony of releasing a childless widow to remarry. When the brother of a deceased childless man does not follow the biblically mandated practice of marrying the widow in order to provide an heir for the deceased, he must formally release her. When monogamy became the law among Ashkenazic Jews, *ḥalitsah* became mandatory.

ḥamets. Leaven. Any food or utensils that cannot be eaten or used during Pesaḥ.

ḥol ha-mo'ed. The intermediate days of Pesaḥ and Sukkot, partial holidays on which ordinary activities are allowed but certain holiday practices are also in effect.

ḥuppah. Marriage canopy.

issur (Heb.), ***issura*** (Aram.). Prohibition; technical term for ritually permitted and forbidden matters and for the *halakhot* pertaining to them.

Kaddish. Prayer recited by mourners, requiring the presence of a *minyan* according to halakhah.

R. Joseph Karo (1488–1575). Sephardic rabbi who wrote the Shulḥan Arukh.

kedushah. Holiness, sanctity.

kehillah. In the pre-modern era, a legally constituted Jewish community.

ketubah. Marriage contract.

kiddushin. Technical term for a marriage according to halakhah, from the Hebrew root *k-d-sh*, meaning "set apart"; related to the word *kadosh,* "holy."

kinyan. Acquisition. The contractual transaction that establishes *kiddushin.*

kippah. Head covering (called in Yiddish a *yarmulke*).

klal Yisra'el. The totality of Israel, meaning the unity of the Jewish people.

kohen (pl. *kohanim*). Priest. A Jewish man who claims descent from the ancient Temple priesthood, and as such is subject to certain distinctions according to halakhah.

ma'ariv. The evening service.

mamzer (pl. *mamzerim*). The child of two Jews who cannot legally be married to one another, i.e., the offspring of an adulterous or incestuous union.

melakhot. The activities that according to halakhah are not to be performed on the Sabbath.

mikveh. Ritual bath.

milah. Circumcision.

milat gerim. Ritual circumcision of male proselytes.

minḥah. The afternoon service.

minhag (pl. *minhagim*). Custom.

minhagbukher (Yid.). Books by medieval Ashkenazic authorities detailing local customs.

minyan. The quorum of ten adult (male, according to Orthodox halakhah) Jews required for public worship.

Mishnah. The earliest (c. 200 CE) authoritative collection of rabbinic law.

mishnah. An individual pericope of the Mishnah.

Mishneh Torah. Comprehensive code of law by Maimonides (1138–1204).

mohel (pl. *mohalim*). Ritual circumciser.

R. Moses Isserles (1520–1572). Polish rabbi whose glosses on the Shulḥan Arukh reflected Ashkenazic practice, which differed in many details from the Sephardic practice codified in it by R. Joseph Karo.

motsi. Shorthand expression for the blessing over bread.

moytzi. Yiddish pronunciation of *motsi.*

pidyon haben. Redemption of the first-born son, the ceremony whereby a first-born son is "redeemed" for his parents from belonging to God. Since the destruction of the Temple in 70 CE it remains one of the few ritual roles for a *kohen.*

posek. Halakhic decisor.

R. Solomon Luria (1510–1573). Polish contemporary of R. Joseph Karo and R. Moses Isserles; he also wrote an important code, but it did not attain the widespread popularity of the Shulḥan Arukh.

Rabbenu Gershom (c. 960–1028?). Early Ashkenazic authority whose rulings were widely accepted.

Rabbenu Tam (1100–1171). Early Ashkenazic authority whose rulings were widely accepted.

Rishonim. Rabbinic authorities of the period from the close of the Talmud until the publication of the Shulḥan Arukh.

rosh ḥodesh. The beginning of the new month, a minor holiday on the Jewish calendar.

sandek. The person (usually an older male relative) who has the honor of holding the baby during a *brit milah*.

Sefer Mitsvot Hagadol. Halakhic work by R. Moses ben Jacob of Coucy (13th century).

Sephardic. Referring to the Jews of the Iberian Peninsula and, after 1492, their descendants elsewhere.

se'udat mitsvah. A meal that is an integral part of fulfilling a mitzvah, e.g., the Shabbat evening meal.

she'elah. Question.

sheliaḥ tsibur. Literally, "representative of the congregation," i.e., the individual who leads the service.

shofar. Ram's horn sounded as part of the liturgy on Rosh Hashanah.

Shulḥan Arukh. Comprehensive code of law by R. Joseph Karo, published in 1563. With the glosses of R. Moses Isserles added, it summarized both Sephardic and Ashkenazic practice and consequently became the most widely-accepted and definitive codification of halakhah. The Shulḥan Arukh employs the same four-part division as the Tur, and is also ordered similarly within each section, so that the same reference locator directs the user to the relevant passage in both texts.

sofer. Torah scribe.

tallit (pl. *tallitot*). Prayer shawl.

Talmud. The premier compendium of rabbinic law and legal reasoning, comprising the Mishnah and material generated from the third through the ninth centuries CE. The Talmud became the central text in rabbinic studies.

tefillin. Phylacteries.

teshuvah. Literally, "return:" (1) repentance; (2) responsum.

tevilah. Immersion in the *mikveh*.

Torah miSinay. Torah from Sinai, divinely revealed; also a figurative expression meaning "absolutely true."

treyf (Yid.). Something not kosher.

Tur, or **Arba'ah Turim.** "The Four Columns." Code of law by R. Jacob ben Asher (1270?– 1340). So called because R. Jacob divided his material into four sections: Oraḥ Ḥayim, dealing with liturgy, holidays, and the rituals of daily life; Yoreh De'ah, dealing with the permitted and prohibited; Even HaEzer, dealing with marriage, sexual relations, and other women's and family matters; and Ḥoshen Mishpat, dealing with contracts and civil law.

tsedakah. Charity.

ufruf (Yid.). The custom of calling a bridegroom to the Torah for an *aliyah* on the Shabbat before his wedding.

Yad, or **Yad HaHazakah** (The Mighty Hand). Another name for Maimonides' Mishneh Torah, so called because the work is divided into fourteen sections, and the number fourteen is represented by the letters *yod-dalet*, which spell *yad*, "hand."

yibbum. Levirate marriage.

Yiddishkayt (Yid.). Jewishness, cultural Jewish identity.

Yizkor. The memorial service traditionally included in the morning service on Yom Kippur and the three festivals.

yom tov sheni. The second day of the festivals, added in the Diaspora to the observance of the three festivals before the calendar was fixed by calculation. The extra day was retained afterward, but eliminated in Reform Judaism as an unnecessary holdover of the past.

yortsayt (Yid.). The anniversary of a death.

zeyde (Yid.). Grandfather.

NOTES

Abbreviations Appearing in the Notes
Archival Sources

AJA   American Jewish Archives

AJHS   American Jewish Historical Society

NJWB   National Jewish Welfare Board

RS   Rodef Shalom Congregation Archive, Pittsburgh

UAHC   Union of American Hebrew Congregations (now the URJ, Union for Reform Judaism)

Printed Sources

ARR   *American Reform Responsa*, Walter Jacob, ed. New York: CCAR, 1983.

CARR   *Contemporary American Reform Responsa.* Walter Jacob, ed. New York: CCAR, 1987.

CCARY   *Central Conference of American Rabbis Yearbook.*

CoRR   *Contemporary Reform Responsa*, Solomon B. Freehof. Cincinnati: Hebrew Union College Press, 1974.

CuRR   *Current Reform Responsa*, Solomon B. Freehof. Cincinnati: Hebrew Union College Press, 1969.

MRR   *Modern Reform Responsa*, Solomon B. Freehof. Cincinnati: Hebrew Union College Press, 1971.

NARR   *Questions and Reform Jewish Answers: New American Reform Responsa.* Walter Jacob, ed. New York: CCAR, 1992.

NRR   *New Reform Responsa*, Solomon B. Freehof. Cincinnati: Hebrew Union College Press, 1980.

RJP   *Reform Jewish Practice and its Rabbinic Background*, Solomon B. Freehof. Cincinnati: Hebrew Union College Press, 1944. Volume II, New York: Union of American Hebrew Congregations, 1952.

RR   *Reform Responsa*, Solomon B. Freehof. Cincinnati: Hebrew Union College Press, 1960.

RR21/1   *Reform Responsa for the Twenty-First Century*, Mark Washofsky, ed. New York: CCAR, 2010. E-book.

RR21/2   *Reform Responsa for the Twenty-First Century*, vol. II, Mark Washof-sky, ed. New York: CCAR, 2010. E-book.

RROT   *Reform Responsa for Our Time*, Solomon B. Freehof. Cincinnati: He-brew Union College Press, 1977.

RRR   *Recent Reform Responsa*, Solomon B. Freehof. Cincinnati: Hebrew Union College Press, 1963.

RWT   *Responsa in War-Time*, Solomon B. Freehof. New York: National Jewish Welfare Board, 1947.

TFN   *Teshuvot for the Nineties*, W. Gunther Plaut and Mark Washofsky, eds. New York: CCAR, 1997.

TRR   *Today's Reform Responsa*, Solomon B. Freehof. Pittsburgh: Rodef Shalom Congregation, 1990.

All unpublished correspondence identified only as "to [correspondent]" or "from [correspondent]" is to or from Solomon B. Freehof.

All unpublished material with archival designation BA- is from the Rodef Shalom Congregation Archive, Pittsburgh. Several references designated RS and the name of a file were among Freehof's papers, but cannot currently be lo-cated in the congregational archive.

All unpublished Freehof correspondence sourced as 2/6 or 2/7 is from AJA MS-435, Solomon B. Freehof Papers.

Introduction

1. Freehof, interview by Michael A. Meyer, 9 Mar 1973, AJA Tape 1203.

2. Jonathan D. Sarna, *American Judaism* (New Haven: Yale University Press, 2004), 222.

3. To R. Kenneth J. Weiss, 12 Dec 1978, BA-123 FF 9.

4. *Ibid.*

5. Diary of Jacob Rader Marcus, 25 Sep 1921, AJA MS-210 13/3.

6. *Reform Judaism in the Large Cities* (Cincinnati: UAHC, 1931), 10. Even so, the survey noted, they remained more open to traditional rituals than long-term Reform Jews.

7. Samuel Silver, "The Translation of That Impact," *CCARY* 56 (1946): 336–337; Deborah Dash Moore, *GI Jews* (Cambridge: Belknap Press, 2004), 126–132.

8. W. Gunther Plaut, "The Halacha of Reform," in *Contemporary Reform Jewish Thought*. Edited by Bernard Martin. (Chicago: Quadrangle Books, 1968), 89. For example, see Freehof's description of Judaism in his *Stormers of Heaven* (New York: Harper & Brothers, 1931), 34ff. and passim.

Chapter 1: Responsa in Reform Judaism

1. http://ccarnet.org/documentsandpositions/ (accessed 27 Jun 2008).

2. On responsa in Reform Judaism see Peter J. Haas, "Reform Responsa: Developing a Theory of Liberal Halakhah," in *Liberal Judaism and Halakhah: A Symposium in Honor of Solomon B. Freehof.* Edited by Walter Jacob. (Pittsburgh: Rodef Shalom Press, 1988), 35–71, and Walter Jacob, "Solomon B. Freehof and the Halachah: An Appreciation," in *RROT*, ix-xxvii.

3. Moshe Halbertal, *People of the Book: Canon, Meaning, and Authority* (Cambridge: Harvard University Press, 1997).

4. Menaḥem Mendel Steinhardt, *Divre Iggeret* (Rödelheim: 1812); *Nogah HaTsedek* (Dessau: 1818); *Eleh Divre HaBrit* (Altona: 1819). For a fuller description of these events see Michael A. Meyer, *Response to Modernity* (New York: Oxford University Press, 1988), 36–60.

5. Halbertal, 8.

6. Israel Bettan, "Early Reform in Contemporaneous Responsa," *HUCA* Special Issue, 1925: 425–26; Judith Bleich, "Menahem Mendel Steinhardt's *Divrei Iggeret:* Harbinger of Reform," *Proceedings of the 10th World Congress of Jewish Studies,* B/II: 207; David H. Ellenson, "A Disputed Precedent: The Prague Organ in Nineteenth-Century Legal Literature and Polemics," *Leo Baeck Institute Year Book* 40 (1995): 263; Meyer, *Response*, 158; Haas, "Liberal Halakhah," 38.

7. Judith Bleich, "Rabbinic Responses to Nonobservance in the Modern Era," in *Jewish Tradition and the Non-Traditional Jew.* Edited by J.J. Schachter. (Northvale, NJ: Jason Aronson, 1992), 41, n.5.

8. *Rabbinische Gutachten über die Verträglichkeit der freien Forschung mit dem Rabbineramte* (Breslau: 1842–43); S. A. Tictin, *Darstellung des Sachverhältnisses in seiner hiesigen Rabbinats-Angelegenheit* (Breslau: 1842); *Theologische Gutachten über das Gebetbuch nach dem Gebrauche des Neuen Israelitischen Tempelvereins in Hamburg* (Hamburg: 1842).

9. Solomon B. Freehof, *The Responsa Literature* (New York: Ktav, 1973), 172.

10. Haas, "Liberal Halakhah," 45.

11. Walter Jacob, "*Pesikah* and American Reform Responsa," in *Dynamic Jewish Law: Progressive Halakhah—Essence and Application*, Studies in Progressive Halakhah, vol. I. Edited by Walter Jacob and Moshe Zemer. (New York: Berghahn Books, 1991), 88–89.

12. Abraham Geiger, "A General Introduction to the Science of Judaism," in Max Wiener, *Abraham Geiger and Liberal Judaism: The Challenge of the Nineteenth Century* (Philadelphia: Jewish Publication Society, 1962), 149, 167; Michael A. Meyer, "Abraham Geiger's Historical Judaism," in *New Perspectives on Abraham Geiger.* Edited by Jakob J. Petuchowski. (Cincinnati: He-

brew Union College Press, 1975), 5; Nahum M. Sarna, "Abraham Geiger and Biblical Scholarship," in *ibid.*, 21.

13. Halbertal, 8–9.

14. See, e.g., the words of French rabbi Gerson-Lévy in W. Gunther Plaut, ed., *The Rise of Reform Judaism: A Sourcebook of Its European Origins* (New York: World Union for Progressive Judaism, 1963), 106.

15. Ellenson, "Prague Organ," 263.

16. See, e.g., R. Bernhard Felsenthal's comments on rabbis in his response to the question of *milat gerim, CCARY* 2 (1891): 87–94.

17. See Moshe Davis, *The Emergence of Conservative Judaism* (Philadelphia: Jewish Publication Society, 1963), 159–167, 231–234; Meyer, *Response*, 240–270; W. Gunther Plaut, ed., *The Growth of Reform Judaism* (New York: World Union for Progressive Judaism, 1965), 31–38.

18. Meyer, *Response*, 276–277.

19. Isaac Mayer Wise, "Address," *CCARY* 1 (1890): 19.

20. *CCARY* 1(1890): 23.

21. "The Milath Gerim Question," *CCARY* 2 (1891): 66–128.

22. *Ibid.,* 101.

23. Yad H. Milah 1:7; SM"G Neg. 116; Tur ShA YD 265:1.

24. *CCARY* 2 (1891): 85.

25. *CCARY* 3 (1892): 36.

26. *Ibid.*, 41.

27. *CCARY* 16 (1906): 58.

28. *Ibid.*, 59–60.

29. *Ibid.*, 61.

30. *Ibid.*, 67.

31. Discussion of President's Message, *CCARY* 17 (1907): 121–122.

32. *Ibid.,* 123.

33. "Report of the Responsa Committee," *CCARY* 23 (1913): 170–182.

34. Kaufmann Kohler, "The History and Functions of Ceremonies in Judaism," *CCARY* 17 (1907): 205–230.

35. Jacob, "*Pesikah*," 93–94; "Supplementary Remark by Prof. David Neumark," *CCARY* 23 (1913): 183–185.

36. *CCARY* 23 (1913): 181.

37. "Report of Committee on Responsa," *CCARY* 23 (1913): 167–170.

38. Meyer had succeeded the late Jacob Voorsanger at Congregation Emanu-El in 1909. In August 1912, with the support of some members of the Board of Trustees, he replaced the Hebrew Torah reading with English, reporting with satisfaction two months later at the annual congregational meeting that there was no more whispering from the congregation during the reading. After extensive discussion of this change, the membership voted to reinstitute the Hebrew reading and to prohibit any changes in ritual without congregational approval. Martin A. Meyer, "Rabbi's Report," *Annual Report of the Congregation*

Emanu-El, San Francisco, California, for the Fiscal Year 1911–1912 (San Francisco, n.d.), 21; handwritten minutes of the Annual Meeting, Sunday, 27 Oct 1912, in *Board Minutes, Congregation Emanu-El, San Francisco*, vol. "1906-1913," 317. I am grateful to Paula Freedman, Archivist of Congregation Emanu-El, for providing these references.

39. *CCARY* 23 (1913): 185–191.

40. *CCARY* 26 (1916): 133; *CCARY* 27 (1917): 87.

41. *CCARY* 25 (1915): 81.

42. This information is based on Walter Jacob, ed., *American Reform Responsa: Collected Responsa of the Central Conference of American Rabbis* (New York: CCAR, 1983), an anthology of all responsa that appeared in the *CCARY*. In some instances the titles differ from those that appear in the original *Yearbook* version. Some of these originally appeared as multiple issues combined into one responsum, but for the sake of clarity I have followed Dr. Jacob in treating them as separate. Dissenting opinions are also listed as separate responsa.

43. Peter Haas, "American Reform Responsa: An Oxymoron?" *Proceedings of the 11th World Congress of Jewish Studies*, D/I: 75 (Jerusalem: World Union of Jewish Studies, 1994). Haas also argues that Lauterbach's responsa were more textually-based than Kohler's, but this is more a difference of degree than quality.

44. Jacob Z. Lauterbach, "The Ethics of the Halakah," *CCARY* 23 (1913): 249–287.

45. Jacob, "Pesikah," 102–105.

46. Joan S. Friedman, "The Making of a Reform Rabbi: Solomon B. Freehof from Childhood to HUC," *American Jewish Archives Journal* vol. 58, nos. 1–2 (2006): 34.

47. *CCARY* 32 (1922): 51; *ARR* #7. For a complete discussion of the affair, see Pamela S. Nadell, *Women Who Would Be Rabbis: A History of Women's Ordination 1889–1985* (Boston: Beacon Press, 1998).

48. Jacob, *ARR*.

49. In 1926 the National Catholic Welfare Conference asked the CCAR Committee on Social Justice to join in lobbying against decriminalizing sending contraceptive information through the mail. The committee refused, saying that the Reform Jewish attitude was to embrace scientific change that improved the quality of human life; that limiting unwanted births was a good idea; that the use of contraceptives was virtually universal among the "well-to-do" classes; and that there should be more public knowledge and discussion of the issue, rather than less. To support their position they asked the Responsa Committee for an overview of the Jewish attitude. *CCARY* 36 (1926): 102–105.

50. Jacob Z. Lauterbach, "The Ceremony of Breaking a Glass at Weddings," *Hebrew Union College Annual* 2 (1925): 351–380.

51. *Jacob*, "Pesikah," 105.

52. Jacob, *ARR*.

53. AJA C-72.

54. AJA C-72; *CCARY* 32 (1922): 41–43.

55. Haas, "American Reform Responsa," 58.

56. "Report of the Committee on Responsa," *CCARY* 24 (1914): 154.

Chapter 2: How Freehof Became the Reform *Posek*

1. Haas, "Liberal Halakhah," 60.

2. See, e.g., Kaufmann Kohler, "The Spiritual Forces of Judaism," *CCARY* 5 (1894): 134–143; William Rosenau, *The Sabbath Question* (Baltimore: Kohn & Pollock, 1897); Henry Berkowitz, *Kiddush, or Sabbath Sentiment in the Home* (Philadelphia, 1898); Bobbie Malone, *Rabbi Max Heller: Reformer, Zionist, Southerner, 1860–1929* (Tuscaloosa: University of Alabama Press, 1997), 130. On these Reformers as part of a larger American Jewish religious revival see Jonathan Sarna, "A Great Awakening: The Transformation that Shaped Twentieth Century American Judaism and its Implications for Today," *CIJE Essay Series* (New York: Council for Initiatives in Jewish Education, 1995).

3. Kohler, "Ceremonies," *CCARY* 17 (1907): 222.

4. Morton White, *Social Thought in America: The Revolt Against Formalism* (Boston: Beacon Press, 1957).

5. Lynn Dumenil, *The Modern Temper: American Culture and Society in the 1920s* (New York: Hill & Wang, 1997); Morris Feuerlicht, "What Will the Gentiles Say?" and Harry Ettelson, "Possessing Our Possessions: Conference Sermon," *CCARY* 30 (1920): 194 and 201–202; Louis Witt, "The Spirit of the Synagogue," *CCARY* 31 (1921): 125–129; Julian Morgenstern, "The Achievements of Reform Judaism," *CCARY* 34 (1924): 267–269; Marvin Nathan, "The Trend Today of the Reform Movement," *CCARY* 36 (1926): 313.

6. See, e.g., David Philipson, *My Life as an American Jew* (Cincinnati: John G. Kidd & Son, Inc., 1941), 203. On the complexities of "race" with regard to American Jews see Eric L. Goldstein, *The Price of Whiteness: Jews, Race, and American Identity* (Princeton, NJ: Princeton University Press, 2006).

7. Classical Reformer Louis Wolsey fiercely attacked the notion of a Jewish culture in his President's Message, *CCARY* 36 (1926): 145ff.; see also Philipson, *My Life*, 379.

8. See Seth Korelitz, "The Menorah Idea: From Religion to Culture, from Race to Ethnicity," *American Jewish History* vol. 85, no. 1 (1997): 57–74.

9. *Reform Judaism in the Large Cities* (Cincinnati: UAHC, 1931), 10.

10. *Ibid.*, 31–33 and 47–50.

11. William Rosenblum, *CCARY* 39 (1929): 496–497, and Samuel Gup, "Currents in Jewish Religious Thought and Life in America in the Twentieth Century," *CCARY* 41 (1931): 306–311.

12. Jacob D. Schwarz, *Ceremonies in Modern Jewish Life* (Cincinnati: UAHC, 1937).

268 *Notes*

13. "Report of Committee on Ceremonies," *CCARY* 49 (1939): 187.
14. Irving Reichert, "Shall We Teach Ceremonies in the Religious School?" *CCARY* 33 (1923): 293–294.
15. Marvin Nathan, "Survey of Jewish Religious Conditions," *CCARY* 36 (1926): 312–318.
16. Philipson, *My Life*, 392.
17. "Report of the Recording Secretary," *CCARY* 45 (1935): 23.
18. "Proceedings of the Thirty-Fifth Council," *Proceedings of the Union of American Hebrew Congregations* 13 (1936–40): 312.
19. *Ibid.*, 191–193.
20. "Guiding Principles of Reform Judaism," *CCARY* 47 (1937): 100.
21. Jakob J. Petuchowski, *Prayerbook Reform in Europe: The Liturgy of European Liberal and Reform Judaism* (New York: World Union for Progressive Judaism, 1968), 146.
22. Samuel S. Cohon, *Judaism: A Way of Life* (Cincinnati: UAHC, 1948), 261–262. See also his comments regarding the proposed revision of the *Union Haggadah*, "Report of Committee on Revision of Union Haggadah," *CCARY* 31 (1921): 38.
23. Max Heller, "Casuistry in Reform Judaism," *HUC Monthly* vol. 1, no. 2 (Nov 1914): 21.
24. Louis Binstock, "Dogma and Judaism," *CCARY* 35 (1925): 261–267.
25. Sefton Temkin, ed., "Biographical Sketch," *His Own Torah: Felix A. Levy Memorial Volume* (New York: Jonathan David Publishers, 1969), 3–33.
26. "President's Message," *CCARY* 47 (1937): 182–183.
27. Of the fourteen committee members, four had been ordained in the 1880s, six between 1890–1900, three in 1904, and one in 1918. They could scarcely be considered representative of the Conference's makeup in 1937.
28. "Report of Committee on President's Message," *CCARY* 47 (1937): 164–165.
29. "Report of the Committee on Synagog and Community," *CCARY* 48 (1938): 62.
30. Friedman, "Reform Rabbi," 21–22. The fraternity identified itself by three Hebrew letters, יכה, which in the kabbalistic system of letter substitution called *at-bash* were actually the initials of the Hebrew phrase "Whoever is for the LORD, to me! (Ex. 32:26)."
31. "Report," *CCARY* 48 (1938): 64–65.
32. "Report of Recording Secretary," *CCARY* 50 (1940): 31.
33. Solomon B. Freehof, "A Code of Ceremonial and Ritual Practice," *CCARY* 51 (1941): 289–297.
34. To R. J. Marshall Taxay, Terre Haute, IN, 20 Oct 1930 and to R. Irving Reichert, San Francisco, CA, 22 Jan 1932, BA-89 FF 12.
35. From Prof. Jacob Z. Lauterbach, 17 Nov [no year]. BA-89 FF 17.
36. *RRR*, "Introduction," 7.

37. Freehof, "Code," 1941, 290. Subsequent citations are from this paper.

38. *CCARY* 1 (1890): 31.

39. Joan S. Friedman, "The Writing of *Reform Jewish Practice and its Rabbinic Background,*" *CCAR Journal*, 51, no. 3 (Summer 2004): 50–51.

40. "Report of Recording Secretary," *CCARY* 52 (1942): 36.

41. "Report of the Committee on Code of Practice," *CCARY* 52 (1942): 123–124.

42. Solomon B. Freehof, *Reform Jewish Practice and its Rabbinic Background* (Cincinnati: Hebrew Union College Press, 1944) and *Reform Jewish Practice and its Rabbinic Background*, vol. 2 (New York: UAHC, 1952).

43. Freehof, "Code," 1941, 295.

44. *Ibid.*, 15.

45. Moses Mielziner, *The Jewish Law of Marriage and Divorce in Ancient and Modern Times and its Relation to the Law of the State* (Cincinnati: Bloch, 1884; repr. Littleton, CO: Fred B. Rothman, 1987).

46. Ibid., 117–118.

47. Solomon B. Freehof, "Reform Judaism and the Halacha," *CCARY* 56 (1946): 276–292.

48. *Ibid.,* 304.

49. *Ibid.*, 307.

50. *Ibid.,* 316.

51. E.g., Solomon B. Freehof, "Each Generation and Its Truth," *CCARY* 60 (1950): 256–265; to Morton Berman, Chicago, 26 Feb 1953, BA-74 FF 3.

52. Frederic A. Doppelt and David Polish, *A Guide for Reform Jews* (New York: Bloch Publishing Co., 1957); Morrison David Bial, *Liberal Judaism at Home* (New York: UAHC, 1971).

53. Friedman, "Reform Rabbi," 29.

54. Solomon B. Freehof, *The Small Sanctuary—Judaism in the Prayerbook* (Cincinnati: UAHC, 1942) and *In the House of the Lord—Our Worship and Our Prayerbook* (Cincinnati: UAHC, 1942), mimeographed.

55. *The Union Prayerbook for Jewish Worship*, 2 vols. (Cincinnati, Central Conference of American Rabbis, 1940 and 1945).

56. *CCARY* 52 (1942): 169–182; Meyer, *Response*, 330–32; Howard Greenstein, *Turning Point: Zionism and Reform Judaism*, Brown Judaic Studies 12 (Chico, CA: Scholars' Press, 1981), 35ff.

57. Joan S. Friedman, "Solomon B. Freehof and the Shaping of American Reform Judaism" (PhD diss., Columbia University, 2003), 283–287.

58. Meyer, *Response*, 333–334; Greenstein, *Turning Point*, 51ff. For a very different perspective on the controversy, see Thomas A. Kolsky, *Jews Against Zionism: The American Council for Judaism, 1943–1948* (Philadelphia: Temple University Press, 1990), 80–99.

59. To Leopold L. Meyer, President, Congregation Beth Israel, Houston, TX, n.d., AJA MS-435 1/5.

60. On Freehof's military service see Friedman, "Reform Rabbi," 26ff.

61. "Report of the Committee on Chaplains," *CCARY* 53 (1943): 117–119.

62. Philip S. Bernstein, *Rabbis at War: The CANRA Story* (Waltham, MA: AJHS, 1971), 1–2; CANRA Minutes, 9 Feb 1942, AJHS I-249, NJWB Military Chaplaincy Records, Box 1.

63. On Jung, see Leo Jung, *The Path of a Pioneer: The Autobiography of Leo Jung* (London: Soncino Press, 1980) and Jacob J. Schachter, ed., *Reverence, Righteousness, and Rahmanut: Essays in Memory of Rabbi Dr. Leo Jung* (Northvale, NJ: Jason Aronson, 1992). On Steinberg, see Simon Noveck, *Milton Steinberg: Portrait of a Rabbi* (New York: Ktav, 1978).

64. To R. S. Andhil Fineberg, New York, NY, 13 Nov 1979, BA-123 FF 10.

65. Friedman, "Shaping," 219–250.

66. To Isaiah Berger, Brooklyn, NY, 15 Aug 1947, RS "Books 1947–48"; to R. Philip Graubart, 10 Oct and 23 Oct 1945, BA-92 FF 16.

67. To R. Jacob Honig, 24 Nov 1944; to Chaplain Marvin Reznikoff and to R. Lee Levinger, 27 Jul 1945, BA-92 FF 16; from Chaplain Henry Tavel, 17 May 1950 and 7 Apr 1950, BA-70 FF 74; from R. Leo Jung, 23 Dec 1948 and to Jung, 29 Dec 1948, BA-70 FF 41.

68. To Louis J. Freehof, 15 Apr 1968, BA-120 FF 40. He mastered bookbinding as a hobby and gave away hundreds of rescued rebound *seforim* (sacred texts) to colleagues over the years.

69. *Ibid.*; Laurel Wolfson, Administrative Librarian, Klau Library, HUC-JIR, email communication to author, 7 Jun 2011.

70. To R. S. Andhil Fineberg, New York, NY, 13 Nov 1979, BA-123 FF 10.

71. Haas, "American Reform Responsa," 79.

72. Philip S. Bernstein, "The Faith of the Jew in the Armed Forces," *CCARY* 53 (1943): 253; Samuel Silver, "The Translation of That Impact," *CCARY* 56 (1946): 336–337. Not all Reform chaplains were so accommodating of tradition; see Deborah Dash Moore, *G.I. Jews* (Cambridge: Belknap Press, 2004), 125–131.

73. This figure was reached by comparing chaplaincy rolls with CCAR membership lists.

74. *Responsa in War Time.* New York: National Jewish Welfare Board, 1947.

75. *CCARY* 57 (1947): 158–172; discussion of the Report, 172–184.

Chapter 3: Freehof on Reform Observance, Halakhah, and Responsa

1. Dr. A. Stanley Dreyfus, oral communication to the author, 2 Oct 2000.

2. Solomon B. Freehof, *What Is Reform Judaism?* Popular Studies in Judaism, no. 27 (Cincinnati: UAHC, 1937).

3. Kaufmann Kohler, *Jewish Theology Systematically and Historically*

Considered (Cincinnati, Bloch Publishing Co., 1918; reprint, New York: Ktav, 1968), 263ff.

4. Freehof, *What Is Reform Judaism?,* 6.

5. *Ibid.,* 6–7.

6. *Ibid.,* 7–8.

7. Kohler, "Ceremonies," 315, quoted in Freehof, *Reform Judaism,* 18.

8. Freehof, *Reform Judaism,* 19.

9. Kaufmann Kohler, Gotthard Deutsch, Henry Englander, and Julian Morgenstern to Student Committee, n.d., inserted at page 233 in Faculty Minutes 1898–1921, AJA MS-5 Box B-3.

10. Schwarz, *Ceremonies,* 2.

11. "Report of the Committee on Synagogue Music," Discussion, *CCARY* 40 (1930): 102.

12. Kohler, "Ceremonies," 222.

13. Solomon B. Freehof, interview by Kenneth J. Weiss, 1 Sep 1978, AJA C-229.

14. See, e.g., Barnett Brickner's comments, *CCARY* 39 (1929): 514.

15. Classical Reformer Hyman Enelow attacked Buber in his spirited defense of Reform in "The Theoretical Foundation of Reform Judaism," *CCARY* 34 (1924): 230–246.

16. See, e.g., William G. Braude, "Liberal Judaism in a Reactionary World," *CCARY* 52 (1942): 290–292.

17. Michael A. Meyer, "Samuel S. Cohon: Reformer of Reform Judaism," *Judaism* 15 (1966): 321.

18. Michael A. Meyer, "A Centennial History," in *Hebrew Union College-Jewish Institute of Religion at One Hundred Years.* Edited by Samuel E. Karff. (Cincinnati: HUC Press, 1976), 60.

19. Introduction, *RRR,* 12; *CCARY* 52 (1942): 263–264; "The Reform Revaluation of Jewish Law," Louis Caplan Lectureship on Jewish Law, 1972 (Cincinnati: HUC Press, n.d.), 14–15.

20. Lauterbach, "Ethics," 256, 261.

21. From Prof. Jacob Z. Lauterbach 29 Apr 1941, BA-89 FF 17.

22. To Prof. Jacob Z. Lauterbach, 2 May 1941, BA-89 FF 17.

23. Freehof, "Halacha," *CCARY* 56 (1946): 290.

24. *RJP,* 7.

25. *Ibid.,* 13.

26. *Ibid.,* 14–15.

27. For a detailed discussion of this issue see Joan S. Friedman, "A Critique of Solomon B. Freehof's Concept of Minhag," in *Re-examining Progressive Halakhah.* Studies in Progressive Halakhah. Edited by Walter Jacob and Moshe Zemer (New York: Berghahn Books, 2002), 111–133.

28. *RJP,* 9.

29. Menahem Elon, *Jewish Law: History, Sources, Principles,* vol. I.

Translated by Bernard Auerbach and Melvin Sykes. (Philadelphia: Jewish Publication Society, 1994), 122ff.

30. *Ibid.*, 131.

31. *Ibid.*, vol. II, 910, citing Resp. Rashbash #419.

32. *Ibid.*, vol. II, 885, 882.

33. *RJP*, 11.

34. *RJP*, 8, citing Y. Sofrim 14:18.

35. *RJP*, 15.

36. Freehof, "Halacha," 276–292.

37. *Ibid.*, 278.

38. *Ibid.*, 279–280.

39. Friedman, "Reform Rabbi," 6ff.

40. Freehof, "Halacha," 279.

41. *Ibid.*, 285–286.

42. *Ibid.*, 287. He used very similar language in response to a 1959 inquiry about standards of ritual observance in Reform Judaism. To Dr. Samuel Newman, Danville, VA, 19 May 1959, BA-118 FF 86.

43. *Ibid.*, 288–289.

44. *Ibid.*, 289–290.

45. *Ibid.*, 290.

46. To R. Steven S. Schwarzschild, Fargo, ND, 1 Feb 1954, BA-74 FF 14.

47. See, e.g., "Introduction," *RR*, 19; Solomon B. Freehof, "Reform Judaism and the Law," Louis Caplan Lectureship on Jewish Law, Cincinnati, 4 Apr 1967 (Cincinnati: HUC, n.d.), 20; "Introduction," *CuRR*, 5–6.

48. Meyer, *Response*, 324–325.

49. Solomon B. Freehof, "What Would Grandfather Think Of Us As Jews?" sermon delivered at Rodef Shalom Congregation, Pittsburgh, PA, 13 Feb 1949, BA-176 FF 23.

50. Solomon B. Freehof, interview by Kenneth J. Weiss, 1 Sep 1978, AJA C-229.

51. "Report on Changes in Reform Jewish Practice," *CCARY* 64 (1954): 127.

52. "A Responsum on the Sabbath Question," *CCAR Journal* no. 1 (Apr 1953): 28–30 (=*ARR* #43, 1952); "Funeral Rites of Fraternal Orders," *CCAR Journal* no. 3 (Oct 1953): 29–30, 43 (= *ARR* #92, 1954); "The Marriage of a Negro Boy to a Jewish Girl" and "Permissibility of Circumcision on a Day Other than the Eighth Day," *CCAR Journal* no. 4 (Jan 1954): 38–39 (=*ARR* #144 and *ARR* #55, 1954); "National Flags Displayed at Religious Services" and "Physician Keeping the Truth from His Patient," *CCAR Journal* no. 5 (Apr 1954): 30–31, 36 (=*ARR* #21 and *ARR* #74, 1954); "Bas Mitzvah Has No Place in Reform Practice," *CCAR Journal* no. 6 (Jun 1954): 26–27, 46 (=*ARR* #32, 1954); "Propriety of Using Discarded Practices in Reform Services," *CCAR Journal* no. 7 (Oct 1954): 40–41 (=*ARR* #1, 1955).

53. "Report of the Recording Secretary," *CCARY* 65 (1955): 25; "Report of the Committee on the Purpose, Scope, and Role of the Responsa Committee, *CCARY* 66 (1956): 110–115. Subsequent quotations are from this Report.

Chapter 4: Marriage and Divorce

1. Freehof, "Code," 294–297.

2. Milton Barron, "The Incidence of Jewish Intermarriage in Europe and America," *American Sociological Review* 11, no. 1 (Feb 46): 8–13. http://www.jstor.org/stable/2085270 (accessed 6 Jul 2011).

3. These are reflected in *RWT* #16, "Conversion"; #17, "Performance of Marriage of Protestant Girl to Jewish Lieutenant—Conversion"; and #22, "Emergency Mixed Marriage." Also to Chaplain Myron Silverman, Ft. Sill, OK, 28 Dec 42; from Chaplain William B. Schwartz, Fort Jackson, SC, 14 Dec 44; to Schwartz, telegram text, n.d.; to Chaplain Alvin Fine, US Forces, China Theatre; and to R. Philip S. Bernstein, New York, 8 Jun 45, RS BA-89 FF 48. See also Lance J. Sussman, "A 'Delicate Balance:' Interfaith Marriage, Rabbinic Officiation, and Reform Judaism in America, 1870-2005," *CCAR Journal* 53, no. 2 (Spring 2006): 49.

4. "Report on Mixed Marriage and Intermarriage," *CCARY* 57 (1947): 158–172.

5. *RJP*, 56.

6. Mielziner, *Law of Marriage*, 33–41, 59–60; "Minister's Handbook Committee Report," *CCARY* 37 (1927): 163–164.

7. Martin Ottenheimer, "Lewis Henry Morgan and the Prohibition of Cousin Marriage in the United States," *Journal of Family History* 15, no. 3 (Jun 1990): 325–334, http://gateway. proquest.com/openurl?url_ver=Z39.88-2004&res_dat =xri:pao-us:&rft_dat=xri:pao:article:h179-1990-015-03-000005:1 (accessed 25 Jun 2011); Diane B. Paul and Hamish G. Spencer, "It's OK, We're Not Cousins by Blood: The Cousin Marriage Controversy in Historical Perspective," *PLoS Biology* 6, no. 12 (Dec 2008): e320. doi:10.1371/journal.pbio.0060320 (accessed 25 Jun 2011).

8. *CCARY* 1 (1890): 112–113, 119–120; Mielziner, *Law of Marriage*, 54–58.

9. Samuel S. Cohon, "Marrying a Deceased Brother's Wife," *CCARY* 35 (1925): 369–371.

10. Kaufmann Kohler, "The Harmonization of the Jewish and Civil Laws of Marriage and Divorce," *CCARY* 25 (1915): 335–378.

11. "Report of the Responsa Committee," *CCARY* 27 (1917): 87; "Report of the Responsa Committee," *CCARY* 33 (1923): 59–60, 64.

12. Cohon, *CCARY* 35 (1925), 371.

13. *Ibid.*, 371–379.

14. *RJP*, 60.

15. To Eugene Strassburger, Pittsburgh, 8 Jun 1948, BA-70 FF 19.

16. To R. Joseph Rudavsky, River Edge, NJ, 24 Oct 1963, 2/6; to R. Milton Rosenbaum, Oak Park, MI, 6 Jan 1965, 2/7.

17. To R. J. Marshall Taxay, Clearwater, FL, 12 Aug 1964, 2/6.

18. To R. Bernard Kligfeld, 25 May 1956; also to R. Leonard Helman, Hartford, CT, 2 Jan 1958; BA-118 FF 86.

19. Solomon B. Freehof, "Questions Asked by the Editor," *CCAR Journal* 11, no. 1 (Apr 63): 16.

20. *CuRR* #53, "Answers to *C.C.A.R. Journal*," 223.

21. From R. Milton Rosenbaum, Oak Park, MI, 22 Apr 1965, 2/7.

22. Deut. 24:4.

23. *RRR* #35, "Woman Returning to Her First Husband," 164.

24. ShA EH 10:1; Yad H. Gerushin 11:13.

25. Alfasi to Yevamot 11b; Nimuke Yosef *ad loc.*; Paḥad Yitsḥak, s.v. "*Gerushah im niset*," 72c.

26. *RRR* #35, 166–167.

27. *CuRR* #56, "Homosexuality," 238; to R. David Polish, Evanston, IL, 30 Oct 1972; to Dr. Murray Kohn, 15 Nov 1972; to R. Joseph Narot, 8 Oct 1973, 2/7; Dana Evan Kaplan, *American Reform Judaism: An Introduction* (New Brunswick, NJ: Rutgers University Press, 2005), 212-215; http://www.bcc-la.org/content/history/ (accessed 21 Jun 2011).

28. *CoRR* #4, 24.

29. To R. Harold Waintrup, Abington, PA, 5 Jan 1970, 2/7.

30. *RJP*, 60.

31. Plaut, *Rise,* 222; Meyer, *Response*, 135; Alan Todd Levenson, "Reform Attitudes, in the Past, Toward Intermarriage," *Judaism* 38, no. 3 (Summer 1989): 322.

32. Levenson, "Reform Attitudes," 326–329.

33. *CCARY* 19 (1909): 170, 177, 181.

34. To R. Norman Diamond, Daytona Beach, FL, 16 May 1972, 2/7. On Einhorn's comment see Meyer, *Response*, 247, 451 n. 73.

35. To R. Joseph Taxay, Terre Haute, IN, 20 Oct 1930. BA-89 FF 12.

36. Friedman, "Shaping," 246.

37. "Most of us interpret 'discourage' to mean that the rabbi should refuse to officiate, and a significant minority interpret the term to be more flexible." "Report of the Special Committee on Mixed Marriage," *CCARY* 72 (1962): 89.

38. *RJP*, 65.

39. Yehuda Leib Zirelsohn, *Ma'arkhe Lev* #87 (Kishinev, 1932; reprinted 1971); A.H. Freimann, *Seder Kiddushin VeNissuin Aḥare Ḥatimat haTalmud* (Jerusalem: Mossad HaRav Kook, 1947; reprinted 1964), 355–361.

40. M. Ketubot 1:4; B. Yevamot 60b, B. Kiddushin 78a; Yad H. Ishut 11:1-2; Tur ShA EH 67:3; *CCARY* 1 (1890): 111.

41. Jacob Z. Lauterbach, "The Attitude of the Jew Towards the Non-Jew," *CCARY* 31 (1921): 200, 217.

42. To R. Philip S. Bernstein, Rochester, NY, 25 Jan 1962, 2/6.

43. To R. Abraham I. Shinedling, Albuquerque, NM, 25 Oct 1971, 2/7.

44. A sampling of the data on this issue over a period of decades yields contradictory results. See, e.g., Bernard Lazerwitz, "Jewish-Christian Marriages and Conversions*," Jewish Social Studies* 43, no. 1 (Winter 1981): 40–41, http://www.jstor.org/stable/4467110 (accessed 24 Jun 2011); Yisrael Ellman, "Intermarriage in the US: A Comparative Study of Jews and Other Ethnic Groups," *Jewish Social Studies* 49, no. 1 (Winter 1987): 12, http://www.jstor.org/stable/4467356 (accessed 24 Nov 2009); Sylvia Barack Fishman, *Double or Nothing?* (Hanover, NH: University Press of New England, 2004), 44–45. Nevertheless, it has been a widely accepted truism among both Jews and Christians. See, e.g., Robert Gordis, *Judaism in a Christian World* (New York: McGraw-Hill, 1966), 204, and "Religion: Interfaith Marriages," *Time,* 31 Jan 1949, n.p., http://www.time.com/time/magazine/article/0,9171,794557-2,00.html (accessed 5 Jul 2011).

45. "Report on Mixed Marriage and Intermarriage," 164.

46. *Ibid.*, 161.

47. *Ibid.*, 172–184.

48. To R. Philip S. Bernstein, Rochester, NY, 11 Jun 1962, 2/6.

49. For a brief survey of trends see Dana Evan Kaplan, *Contemporary American Judaism* (New York: Columbia University Press, 2009), 166–170. More detailed statistics for the postwar decades are in Larry D. Barnett, "Research in Interreligious Dating and Marriage," *Marriage & Family Living* 24, no. 2 (May 1962): 191–194, http://www.jstor.org/stable/347013 (accessed 19 Jul 2011); Norval D. Glenn, "Interreligious Marriage in the United States: Patterns and Recent Trends," *Journal of Marriage and Family* 44, no. 3 (1982): 555–566, http://www.jstor.org/stable/351579 (accessed 19 Jul 2011); Ellman, "Intermarriage in the United States."

50. To R. Philip S. Bernstein, 25 Jan 1962, 2/6; to R. M.M. Landau, Cleveland, MS, 29 Nov 1965; to R. Norman Goldburg, Augusta, GA, 29 Nov 1965; to R. Samuel Silver, Stamford, CT, 10 Feb 1969; to R. Harold L. Gelfman, Macon, GA, 13 Mar 1969; to R. Jerome Grollman, St. Louis, MO, 18 Apr 1969; to R. Kurt Metzger, Altoona, PA, 6 Apr 1970, 2/7.

51. To R. Norman Goldburg, Augusta, GA, 12 Nov 1968, 2/7.

52. *CuRR* #43, "Rabbi Participating in a Christian Funeral." From R. Kurt Metzger, 2 Apr 1970, RS Responsa Corr Mar-Jun 1970.

53. To R. Kurt Metzger, 6 Apr 1970, 2/7. Also to J. Leonard Ostow, Erie, PA, 28 Nov 1962, BA-71 FF 4.

54. To R. Harold L. Gelfman, Macon, GA, 13 Mar 1969, 2/7.

55. To R. Benjamin Schultz, Clarksdale, MS, 20 Dec 1972, and to R. Gerald Kaplan, Midland, MI, 15 Mar 1974, 2/7.

56. To R. Abraham I. Shinedling, Albuquerque, NM, 25 Aug 1978, and to R. Howard Bogot, Philadelphia, PA, 16 Mar 1979, 2/7.

57. To R. Philip S. Bernstein, Rochester, NY, 11 Jun 1962, 2/6.

58. To R. Meyer Marx, Sarasota, FL, 17 Dec 1964, BA-71 FF 7.

59. "Report of the Special Committee on Mixed Marriage," *CCARY* 73 (1963): 86–94.

60. To R. Robert A. Raab, Wantagh, NY, 20 Dec 1966, 2/7.

61. To Dr. Eugene Mihaly, Cincinnati, 5 May 1972, RS Responsa Corr May Jun 72.

62. *MRR* #19, "Mixed Marriage on Temple Premises," 115.

63. Solomon B. Freehof, "The New Marriage Problems," unpublished paper, n.d., 3. RS Responsa Feb Mar Apr 1972.

64. "Report on Mixed Marriage," 163.

65. He relied on Freimann, *Seder Kiddushin veNissuin*.

66. "Report on Mixed Marriage," 164, 172.

67. To R. William Kramer, Hollywood, CA, 4 Sep 1957, BA-118 FF 88.

68. "The Assembly of Jewish Notables, 'Answers to Napoleon,'" in *The Jew in the Modern World: A Documentary History*, 2nd ed. Edited by Jehuda Reinharz and Paul Mendes-Flohr. (New York: Oxford University Press, 1995), 128–129, 131.

69. Mielziner, *Law of Marriage*, 89.

70. David Ellenson, "Samuel Holdheim on the Legal Character of Jewish Marriage," in *Marriage and its Obstacles in Jewish Law*, Studies in Progressive Halakhah, vol. 8. Edited by Walter Jacob and Moshe Zemer. (Freehof Institute of Progressive Halacha: Pittsburgh, 1999): 1–26.

71. Mielziner, *Law of Marriage*, 25–26; Kohler, "Harmonization," 350; *Rabbi's Manual* (Cincinnati: CCAR, 1928), 159.

72. All halakhic authorities understand M. Kiddushin 1:1 to mean that the groom must acquire the bride, based on Scripture. Most Orthodox authorities refuse to allow a double-ring ceremony since it may give the incorrect impression that the ring the bride gives to the groom is part of the kinyan. See, e.g., Aaron Rakeffet-Rothkoff, *The Rav: The World of Rabbi Joseph B. Soloveitchik*, vol. 2 (New York: Ktav, 1999), 32–33. Moshe Feinstein ruled that a reciprocal statement and giving of a ring to the groom was meaningless and did not invalidate the *kiddushin*, but that it was a meaningless and foolish act. *ShU"T Igrot Moshe EH* III (New York, 1961), #18.

73. Plaut, *Rise*, 217–219.

74. Meyer, *Response*, 255–258.

75. Plaut, *Rise*, 219; Mielziner, *Law of Marriage*, 92–93.

76. Moses Mielziner, "The Marriage Agenda," *CCARY* 1 (1890): 39–41; "Report of Committee on Marriage-Agenda," *CCARY* 13 (1903): 45.

77. *Minister's Hand Book* (New York: Bloch Publishing Co., 1917), 37.

78. *Rabbi's Manual*, 42. The 1961 revised *Rabbi's Manual* introduced the bride's statement in Hebrew, but still kept the double-ring ceremony optional. The current manual lays out the text in such a way as to obscure any distinction

between normative and optional in two wedding services and offers a fully egalitarian text in two others. *Rabbi's Manual*, revised edition (New York: CCAR, 1961): 27, 31, 39, 129–130; *Ma'aglei Tzedek: Rabbi's Manual* (New York: CCAR, 1988): 54, 65, 75, 80.

79. "Witnesses to the Marriage," unpublished responsum, n.d., to R. Nathan Kaber, Altoona, PA, BA-72 FF 27.

80. *Ibid.*

81. *NRR* #43, "Apostate Wedding Attendants," 190–192.

82. Bava Kama 68a; Yad H. Edut 9:1; Tur ShA HM 35:14.

83. "Wedding Formula Recited by the Bride," undated draft of unpublished responsum, and letter to R. Leonard Winograd, Johnstown, PA, 3 Aug 1966, BA-72 FF 21.

84. *RROT* #41, "Reform Marriage Formula," 194–195.

85. To R. Robert I. Kahn, Houston, TX, 11 Feb 1963, 2/6.

86. Friedman, "Reform Rabbi," 34.

87. "Responsa Committee Report," *CCARY* 80 (1970): 56.

88. *RJP*, 99.

89. Ibid., 106.

90. To R. Nathan Kaber, Altoona, PA, 8 Apr 1963, 2/6.

91. To R. Robert I. Kahn, Houston, TX, 11 Feb 1963, 2/6.

Chapter 5: Conversion and Jewish Status

1. Freehof, "Code," 295–296.

2. Levenson, "Reform Attitudes," 321; "Resolutions of the Augsburg Synod," *CCARY* 1 (1890): 114; *CCARY* 3 (1892): 33–36; Meyer, *Response*, 190.

3. See comments of Adolph Moses in Plaut, *Growth*, 284–285; and Isaac Schwab, "Response," *CCARY* 2 (1891): 84.

4. See Robin Judd, *Contested Rituals: Circumcision, Kosher Butchering, and Jewish Political Life in Germany, 1843–1933* (Ithaca: Cornell University Press, 2007).

5. Plaut, *Rise*, 209.

6. See n. 10 and Michael A. Meyer, "*Berit Milah* Within the History of the Reform Movement," in *Berit Milah in the Reform Context*, edited by Lewis M. Barth. (Berit Milah Board of Reform Judaism, 1990), 146–147.

7. Plaut, *Rise*, 206–209; Plaut, *Growth*, 284–285; Meyer, *Response*, 257; *CCARY* 1 (1890): 122.

8. *CCARY* 3 (1892): 36–37.

9. *CCARY* 24 (1914): 58, 65.

10. David L. Gollaher, "From Ritual to Science: The Medical Transformation of Circumcision in America," *Journal of Social History* 28, no. 1 (1994): 22–23 http://www.jstor.org/stable/3788341 (accessed 24 Jun 2011).

11. *Minister's Hand Book*, 33–34.

12. Kaufmann Kohler, "Children of Mixed Marriages," *CCARY* 29 (1919): 76–77.

13. *RJP*, 70.

14. *Ibid.*, 70.

15. On the CANRA policy on conversion see Friedman, "Shaping," 238ff., and "Conversions" in *Responsa in War Time*, 22–23.

16. David Ellenson, "The Development of Orthodox Attitudes to Conversion in the Modern Period," *Conservative Judaism* 36, no. 4 (Summer 1983): 57–73; Marcus Horovitz, *Mateh Levi*, II (Frankfurt: Y. Kaufmann, 1933), #54 and #55; David Tsvi Hoffman, *Melamed LeHo'il* (Frankfurt: Hermon, 1925/26 – 1931/32, repr. New York: 1954), Part II, #83.

17. From R. Leo Jung, 17 Feb 1943, BA-89 FF 48. On at least one occasion the committee relied on this precedent to allow a chaplain to perform a conversion. Chaplain Alvin Fine, China Theatre, to R. Philip S. Bernstein, 8 Jun 1945, and draft responsum, n.d., RS BA-89 FF 48.

18. See also *RRR* #14, "Who Is a Jew?" 74. The 1907 *Jewish Encyclopedia* skirted this sensitive issue, though by 1972 the *Encyclopedia Judaica* agreed with Freehof's characterization of the change in rabbinic attitudes toward conversion. http://www. jewishencyclopedia.com/view_page.jsp?pid=0&artid= 556&letter=P (accessed 7 Jul 2011) and *Encyclopedia Judaica*, 1972, *s.v.* "Proselytes."

19. "Report," *CCARY* 57 (1947), 162; "*Hakol lefi re'ot ene bet din*," e.g., Bet Yosef to Tur YD 268.

20. "Report," *CCARY* 57 (1947), 162.

21. M. Ketubot, 4:3; B. Ketubot 11a.; B. Kiddushin, 3:12; Yad H. Issure Bi'ah 15:3–4.

22. The Cradle Roll was a program of the National Federation of Temple Sisterhoods to bring young children into the synagogue from the earliest possible age. Participating congregations celebrated the child's registration in the program with some formal announcement such as a bulletin announcement or a certificate. Eleanor Schwartz, former Executive Director, National Federation of Temple Sisterhoods, telephone communication to author, 14 Oct 2009.

23. Resolution on Patrilineal Descent, *CCARY* 93 (1983): 160.

24. *RR* #21, "Circumcision Before Eighth Day."

25. To R. Joseph Utschen, Gastonia, SC, 8 Apr 1960, BA-71 FF 19.

26. *Rabbi's Manual*, 12.

27. "Report," *CCARY* 57 (1947), 172. Yad H. Issure Bi'ah 14:2.

28. *CoRR*, Inquiries #1, "Questions from Israel on Proselytism."

29. From R. Floyd Fierman, El Paso, TX, 14 Mar 1955, BA-118 FF 39.

30. To R. Floyd Fierman, El Paso, TX, 17 Mar 1955, 2/6.

31. To Chaplain Aryeh Lev, 24 Aug 1953, BA-118 FF 39.

32. *RR* #19, "Converting a Married Woman," 85–87; to R. Harold

Waintrup, Abington, PA, 16 Apr 1962, 2/6; to R. André Zaoui, Paris, 7 Aug 1973, 2/7.

33. *RR* #18, "Conversion and Church Membership"; *RR* #20, "Conversion Without Marriage"; *RRR* #15, "A Questionable Conversion"; *CuRR* #29, "Converting a Gentile Mother Whose Children Remain Christian."

34. To R. Phillip Segal, Pittsburgh, 15 Nov 1974, 2/7.

35. To R. Herman Schaalman, Chicago, 5 Mar 1965, 2/6. See also *CoRR*, Inquiry #1: "Questions from Israel on Proselytism," 274.

36. To R. Abraham Shinedling, Albuquerque, NM, 6 Aug 1974. See also *RRR* #16, "Miscegenation and Conversion of Negroes"; to Anna Oxenhandler, Ferndale, MI, 4 Aug 1970, 2/7; and to Rev. Donald W. Smith, 11 Dec 1969, RS Responsa Corr Dec 69, Jan, Feb 70.

37. *RRR* #16, "Miscegenation and Conversion of Negroes"; to R. Perry Nussbaum, Jackson, MS, 25 Sep 1968, BA-71 FF 15.

38. *RR* #18, "Conversion and Church Membership."

39. To R. Sidney Akselrad, Los Altos Hills, CA, 8 Aug 1977, 2/7; *NRR* #17, "Questions Concerning Proselytes," 73–74.

40. From R. Joseph Herzog, Sharon, PA, 18 Feb 1964, BA-71 FF 6; to Herzog, 21 Feb 1964, 2/6.

41. To R. Alvin Fine, Seattle, 26 Sep 1972, 2/7; *RROT* #14, "Converts and the Rabbi's Responsibility."

42. To R. Philip S. Bernstein, Rochester, NY, 7 May 1973, 2/7, and 25 Jan 1962, 2/6. See also to R. Arthur J. Kolatch, Bakersfield, CA, 20 Dec 1966, 2/6.

43. To R. Sidney Akselrad, Los Altos Hills, CA, 12 Sep 1980, 2/7.

44. *RRR* #14, "Who Is a Jew?" 76.

45. *NRR* #18, "An Incomplete Conversion."

46. *RRR* #21, "Circumcising Son of Gentile Wife"; *RR* #47, "Adoption"; *CuRR* #20, "Conversion of Infants"; *MRR* #29, "Circumcision for Children of Mixed Marriages"; *CoRR* Inquiry #1, "Questions from Israel Concerning Proselytism"; *NRR* #18, "An Incomplete Conversion"; *ARR* #61, "The Status of a Gentile-Born Child Adopted into a Jewish Family"; to R. Abraham J. Brachman, Fort Worth, TX, 20 Apr 1956, BA-72 FF 13; R. Joseph Utschen, Gastonia, SC, 8 Apr 1960, BA-71 FF 19; R. Norman Diamond, Daytona Beach, FL, 1 Feb 1966, BA-71 FF 10; Judge Joseph J. Shapiro, Bridgeport, CT, 9 May 1963; R. David Polish, Evanston, IL, 20 Aug 1963; R. P. Irving Bloom, Mobile, AL, 23 Sep 1963; R. Daniel Kaplan, Needham Heights, MA, 16 Jan 1964, 2/6; R. Jay Goldburg, Des Moines, IA, 9 Dec 1968; R. Philip S. Bernstein, Rochester, NY, 3 Aug 1971; R. Jack D. Spiro, Richmond, VA, 4 Mar 1974; R. Daniel Syme, NY, 18 Mar 1980; Madeleine Solomon, Pittsburgh, 12 Apr 1982; and R. Kenneth J. Weiss, El Paso, TX, 20 Sep 1982, 2/7.

47. To R. Harry A. Roth, Lawrence, MA, 28 Nov 1972, 2/7.

48. To R. Norman D. Hirsh, Seattle, 30 Sep 1975, 2/7.

49. To R. Philip S. Bernstein, Rochester, NY, 5 May 1969, 2/7. See also *CuRR* #53, "Inquiries to the *CCAR Journal*," (5), 221.

50. To Chaplain Michael B. Eisenstat, Keesler AFB, MS, 4 Oct 1967, 2/7.

51. *RR* #21, "Circumcising Son of Gentile Wife," 104.

52. "Circumcising a Child of a Mixed Marriage," BA-70 FF 82; *Responsa to Chaplains 1948–1953* (Commission on Jewish Chaplaincy, Division of Religious Activities, NJWB: New York, 1953), 20–21. He based his decision on Isserles to ShA YD 263:5, ShA YD 268:9, and R. Shabtai Cohen *ad loc.* to both.

53. To R. Arthur J. Kolatch, Lakewood, NJ, n.d., BA-118 FF 86.

54. To Mr. Howard Smigel, Westport, CT, 24 Aug 1959, BA-71 FF 19.

55. To R. Alan Fuchs, Somerville, NJ, 8 Feb 1968, 2/7.

56. "Naming Child of Gentile Father," unpublished responsum, RS Responsa 1961. Also to R. Daniel L. Kaplan, Needham Heights, MA, 29 Nov 1967, 2/7.

57. To Mr. [Chester G.] Bandman, [Pittsburgh,] 19 Jan 1960, BA-71 FF 19.

58. To R. Mordecai I. Soloff, Los Angeles, 31 Dec 1968, BA-71 FF 15.

59. To Chaplain Hirshel Jaffe, Travis AFB, CA, 1 Nov 1963, 2/6.

60. *RRR* #21, "Circumcising Son of Gentile Wife," 100.

61. *Ibid.*, 104.

62. *MRR* #29, "Circumcision for Children of Mixed Marriages," 167, 169.

63. *CCARY* 93 (1983): 160.

64. See, e.g., *RR* #46, "Marrying Apostate Daughter of Jewish Mother," 192–195.

65. To R. Harold Waintrup, Abington, PA, 4 Mar 1980, 2/7.

66. *RJP*, 139–140.

67. John J. Appel, "Christian Science and the Jews," *Jewish Social Studies* 31, no.2 (Apr 1969): 102ff., http://www.jstor.org/stable/4466485 (accessed 23 Jul 2011); Ellen M. Umansky, *From Christian Science to Jewish Science* (New York: Oxford University Press, 2004), 12ff.; Meyer, *Response*, 314–315.

68. *RJP*, 140. In 1918 a rabbi asked the Responsa Committee if he should officiate at the funeral of one member of a Jewish couple who had both become Christian Scientists, and who wanted him to co-officiate with one of their practitioners, with the burial in a Christian cemetery. Kohler's response was a firm negative, but Julius Rapoport dissented, advocating officiation as outreach to the family on the grounds that an apostate may be buried in a Jewish cemetery. Kohler followed up in 1919 by drawing a distinction between the type of person in question and "the Christian Scientist in general who has not left the fold altogether." The latter was to be encouraged to rejoin the community; the former was to be excluded. "Report of the Committee on Responsa," *CCARY* 29 (1919): 75.

69. *Ibid.*, 144.

70. *RR* #46, "Marrying Apostate Daughter of Jewish Mother." The original inquiry is from Sep 1957 (RS Responsa CCAR 1957–58).

71. B. Yevamot 47b and Rashi *s.v. de'i hadar be*; B. Sanhedrin 44a; Yad, H. Issure Bi'ah 13:17; ShA YD 268:2; Maggid Mishneh to Yad H. Yibum Veḥalitsah 1:6, *s.v. mi sheyesh*; Yad H. Ishut 4:16. For one recent example see *Mishpete Uzziel,* vol. II (Jerusalem, 1998), YD #54.

72. *RRR* #10, "Jew Joining the Unitarian Church"; #26, "Status of Apostates (Children and Adults)"; #27, "Burial of an Apostate"; #28, "Kaddish for Apostates and Gentiles"; *MRR* #28, "The Reverting Proselyte"; #30, "Our Attitude to Apostates"; *NRR* #43, "Apostate Wedding Attendants"; *TRR* #24, "Circumcising Child of an Apostate Mother."

73. *RR* #46, 195.

74. *Ibid.*, 197.

75. See the opinion of the Ritba, cited in the Nimuke Yosef to Alfasi Yevamot 47b, s.v. *kiddushav kiddushin.* This opinion is cited by the Bet Yosef, YD 268 s.v. *katav ba'al haTur*, though he also notes that the Tur apparently does not require a returning apostate to immerse (YD 267: *hare hu keyisra'el mumar she'eno tsarikh tevilah*). He also cites the responsum of R. Solomon Duran concerning the Marranos (see below).

76. ShA YD 268:10.

77. For example, Eliezer Waldenberg expected a young woman who had become an Anglican prior to marriage to undergo immersion and make a formal declaration of *divre ḥaverut* (*ShU"T Tsits Eliezer* XIII, [Jerusalem, 19??], #93), while in the case of a woman whose parents had had her baptized as a child and who wished to live as a Jew, Jacob Jehiel Weinberg ruled that her monthly immersion was sufficient (*ShU"T Seride Esh* I [Jerusalem, 1998], #64).

78. *ShU"t Rabbenu Gershom Me'or HaGolah* (New York, 1956), #4.

79. Solomon B. Freehof, *A Treasury of Responsa* (Philadelphia: Jewish Publication Society, 1962), 88–89.

80. Solomon b. Simon Duran, *Responsa* (Leghorn: 1742), #89. Translated by Freehof, *Treasury*, 91.

81. *Ibid.*, 92.

82. Chaplain Irving Ganz to R. Aryeh Lev, 21 May 1947; from R. Aryeh Lev, 3 Jun 1947; to Lev, 7 Jun 1947; from Lev, 18 Jun 1947; to Lev, 19 Aug 1947, BA-92 FF 36.

83. To R. Judah Cahn, Lawrence, NY, 6 Jan 1948, BA-70 FF 9; to Azriel Grishman, New York, NY, 7 Jan 1949, BA-70 FF 38; from R. Alvin Fine, San Francisco, 6 Oct 1949; to Fine, 10 Oct 1949, BA-70 FF 49; to R. Herman E. Snyder, Springfield, MA, 1 Dec 1955, BA-118 FF 88; "Status of Children of Doubtful Religious Background," *ARR* #61 (also published as *RRR* #26, "Status of Apostates (Children and Adults)."

84. From R. Benno Wallach, 11 Feb 1965, 2/6.

85. *RRR* #10, "Jew Joining the Unitarian Church;" to R. Norman Diamond, Daytona Beach, FL, 5 Aug 1969, 2/7.

86. To R. Merle Singer, Boca Raton, 11 Mar 1980, 2/7.

87. "Religious Rights of Christian Scientists and Spiritualists," unpublished responsum sent to R. W. Blumenthal, Johannesburg, 1961, BA-72 FF 2; to R. Frederick Eisenberg, Cleveland, 30 Mar 1976, 2/7.

88. *RRR* #20, "Baptism of Child Before Adoption By Jewish Couple."

89. To R. David Polish, Evanston, IL, 20 Aug 1963, 2/6. Also to R. Philip S. Bernstein, Rochester, NY, 31 Dec 1964; to R. Leo Trepp, Napa, CA, 12 Feb 1965; to R. Benno Wallach, Orlando, FL, 15 Feb 1965, 2/6; to R. Robert A. Kaufman, Warren, OH, 24 Oct 1966; to R. Harold Waintrup, Abington, PA, 9 Feb 1967; to R. Nathan Kaber, Altoona, PA, 28 Jul 1967; to R. Alan Fuchs, Philadelphia, 8 Mar 1972; to R. Stanley M. Davids, Springfield, MA, 15 Mar 1972; to R. Allan S. Maller, Culver City, CA, 19 Apr 1972; to R. Philip J. Bentley, Curaçao, 6 Oct 1975, 2/7.

90. *ARR* #61.

91. To R. Philip S. Bernstein, 31 Dec 1964, 2/6.

92. To R. Benno Wallach, 15 Feb 1965, 2/6.

93. From Bernstein, 29 Jun 1965, and to Bernstein, 30 Jul 1965, 2/6.

94. To R. Robert A. Kaufman, Warren, OH, 24 Oct 1966, 2/7.

95. To R. Norman D. Hirsh, Seattle, WA, 3 May 1967, 2/7.

96. "Answers to *CCAR Journal*," *CoRR* #53, 218.

97. To R. Alan D. Fuchs, Philadelphia, 8 Mar 1972. Also to R. Stanley M. Davids, Springfield, MA, 15 Mar 1972; to R. Allan S. Maller, Culver City, CA, 19 Apr 1972, 2/7.

98. "Reconverting an Ex-Nun," *CoRR* #31, 142.

99. *Ibid.*, 144–145.

100. *RRR* #28, "Kaddish for Apostates and Gentiles"; unpublished responsum "Burial of a Jewess Converted to Catholicism in a Jewish Cemetery," n.d., sent to R. Bernard D. Rosenberg, Stockton, CA, BA-72 FF 20; to R. Amiel Wohl, Baltimore, 27 May 1965, 2/6; *TRR* #24, "Circumcising Child of an Apostate Mother" to R. Martin Ryback, Evansville, IN, 22 Oct 1956, BA-72 FF 5.

101. *MRR* #30, "Our Attitude to Apostates," 174–175.

102. To R. Paul Tuchman, Dothan, AL, 1 Dec 1981, 2/7.

103. To R. Samuel A. Friedman, Wilmington, NC, 3 Dec 1957, BA-118 FF 86.

104. *MRR* #30, "Our Attitude to Apostates," 171–174.

105. To Rev. Neil Ferris, 16 Mar 1961, BA-72 FF 14. On the discomfort of earlier generations of Reform rabbis with Unitarianism, see Benny Kraut, "The Ambivalent Relations of American Reform Judaism with Unitarianism in the Last Third of the Nineteenth Century," *Journal of Ecumenical Studies* 23 no.1 (Winter 1986): 58–68, and Benny Kraut, "Judaism Triumphant: Isaac Mayer

Wise on Unitarianism and Liberal Christianity," *AJS Review* 7 (1983): 179–230, http://www.jstor.org/stable/1486410 (accessed 1 Aug 2011). See also the website of the Unitarian Universalists for Jewish Awareness, http://www.uuja.org (accessed 1 Jul 2011).

Chapter 6: Shabbat and Kashrut

1. Resolutions of the Breslau Conference, *CCARY* 1 (1890): 95–96.

2. *Ibid.,* 108–109; Plaut, ed., *Rise*, 192–195.

3. Samuel S. Cohon, "Kaufmann Kohler the Reformer," in *Mordecai M. Kaplan Jubilee Volume.* Edited by Moshe Davis. (New York: Jewish Theological Seminary of America, 1953), 143.

4. Kaufmann Kohler, "Is Reform Judaism Destructive or Constructive?" *CCARY* 3 (1893): 111–112.

5. E.g. Henry Berkowitz's *Kiddush, or Sabbath Sentiment in the Home*; Joseph Krauskopf, *Kiddush* (Philadelphia: Reform Congregation Keneseth Israel, 1907).

6. Jacob K. Voorsanger, "The Sabbath Question," *CCARY* 12 (1902): 105–121.

7. "Report of the Sabbath Commission," *CCARY* 13 (1903): 155–171.

8. Discussion of the "Report of the Sabbath Commission," *CCARY* 15 (1905): 62.

9. Jacob Voorsanger, "Report of the Sabbath Commission," *CCARY* 13 (1903): 149–154; "The Sabbath Question," *CCARY* 12 (1902), 121.

10. Heller, "Casuistry," 20.

11. "Proceedings of the Thirty-Fifth Council," *Proceedings of the Union of American Hebrew Congregations* 13 (1936–40): 312.

12. See Lance J. Sussman, "The Myth of the Trefa Banquet: American Culinary Culture and the Radicalization of Food Policy in American Reform Judaism," *American Jewish Archives Journal* 57, no.1-2 (2005): 29–52; Bernard C. Rosen, "Minority Group in Transition: A Study of Adolescent Conviction and Conduct," in *The Jews: Social Patterns of an American Group.* Edited by Marshall Sklare. (Glencoe, IL: The Free Press, 1958), 342; Marshall Sklare and Joseph Greenbaum, *Jewish Identity on the Suburban Frontier* (New York: Basic Books, Inc., 1967), 50–56; Jenna Weissman Joselit, "Jewish in Dishes: Kashrut in the New World," in *The Americanization of the Jews.* Edited by Robert M. Seltzer and Norman J. Cohen. (New York: New York University Press, 1995), 247–264.

13. "Code," 292.

14. "Authentic Report of the Proceedings of the Rabbinical Conference Held at Pittsburg, Nov. 16, 17, 18, 1885," in *The Pittsburgh Platform in Retrospect*, edited by Walter Jacob. (Pittsburgh: Rodef Shalom Congregation, 1985), 94.

15. *RJP*, 14–15.

16. "Sabbath Observance," *ARR* #43. Subsequent quotes are from this responsum.

17. W. Gunther Plaut, *Tadrikh le-Shabbat: A Shabbat Manual* (New York: CCAR, 1972).

18. To R. Sidney L. Regner, New York, 10 Apr 1957, BA-72 FF 5.

19. "Gift Corner Open on the Sabbath," *RR* #9, 51. Subsequent quotes are from this responsum.

20. To R. Martin I. Silverman, Monroe, LA, 12 Oct 1962, 2/6. The author can attest that the synagogue in Terre Haute, IN, was holding its annual rummage sale on Saturdays in the early 1990s.

21. To R. Hillel Gamoran, Hoffman Estates, IL, 16 Nov 1964, BA-71 FF 7; also to R. Joseph Rudavsky, 20 Apr 1971, 2/7.

22. From R. Morton Hoffman, San Rafael, CA, 5 Mar 1964, BA-71 FF 6.

23. To Hoffman, 12 Mar 1964, 2/6.

24. *RJP*, 72.

25. To R. Joseph Baron, Congregation Emanu-El B'nei Jeshurun, Milwaukee, WI, 14 Apr 1950, BA-70 FF 49.

26. *RRR* #36, "Wedding on Saturday Before Dark," 167–170.

27. To R. Samuel Silver, Stamford, CT, 27 Jan 1969, 2/7.

28. R.Theodore L. Steinberg, Malvern, NY, to R. Joseph B. Glaser, 11 Aug 1971, BA-100 FF 35.

29. To R. Joseph B. Glaser, 16 Aug 1971, 2/7.

30. B. Shabbat 12b: *Halakhah ve'en morin ken.*

31. To R. Arthur Lelyveld, Cleveland, 24 Sep 1976, 2/7.

32. Isaac Klein, *A Guide to Jewish Religious Practice*, Moreshet Series: Studies in Jewish History, Literature and Thought, vol. 6 (New York: Jewish Theological Seminary of America, 1979), 89–90. For an Orthodox parallel see Norman Lamm, *The Sabbath: Model for a Theory of Leisure* (New York: Jewish Education Committee of New York, 1969), 14–16.

33. From Mr. Fred Levinthal, Chicago, 12 Jan 1965, BA-71 FF 8, and reply, 14 Jan 1965, 2/6. Also to R. Victor Weissberg, Chicago, 15 Jan 1965, BA-71 FF 8; to R. Robert Schreibman, Arnold, MD, 19 Aug 1965, 2/6, and to R. Seymour Prystowsky, Lafayette Hill, PA, 3 Aug 1971, 2/7.

34. To R. Joel Zion, Lawrence, NY, 3 Sep 1976; also to R. Joseph Glaser, New York, 10 Sep 1976, 2/7.

35. To R. Leonard Mervis, Oak Park, IL, 28 Mar 1966, 2/7.

36. Although Freehof was on solid ground in citing halakhic distaste for card playing, the reason for that was that card playing, in addition to being a *bittul Torah*, was a form of gambling. A quick search through the Bar-Ilan Responsa Project CD-ROM, for example, turns up eight references to card playing in twentieth-century responsa, six of which are in the context of gambling. The seventh is a responsum of Moshe Feinstein ruling that children's card games are not *muktseh* (objects not to be handled on the Sabbath, lest one accidentally vi-

olate the Sabbath by using them) for an adult (*Igrot Moshe* OḤ 5, #35). The eighth, also by Moshe Feinstein, forbids card playing, bingo, and mixed dancing in the social hall of a synagogue, even if the community's reason for holding dances for young single Jews is to prevent them from going out to places where they would dance with gentiles (*Igrot Moshe* OḤ 4, #35).

37. Dr. Jay Azneer, Brooklyn, NY, email communication to the author, 24 Nov 1999; Dr. Walter Jacob, Pittsburgh, PA, email communication to the author, 8 Aug 2011.

38. Sachar had received a scathing letter from R. Simon G. Kramer, President of the New York Board of Rabbis (and a CANRA colleague of Freehof's), to which he replied that "[a] very diversified athletic program is part of the tradition of every great American university. Brandeis will stand or fall ultimately on its academic program, but it will fit into the American tradition only if it includes the ancillary athletic activities which are expected of a university." Abram L. Sachar to R. Simon G. Kramer, 30 Jun 1950, BA-74 FF 11.

39. To Abram L. Sachar, 2 Oct 1953, BA-74 FF 11.

40. To R. Harold Waintrup, Abington, PA, 11 Sep 1958, BA-71 FF 1. He thought the source was R. Ḥayim Benveniste's *Kenesset Hagedolah*, but was not sure if he remembered correctly.

41. Published as *RRR* #5, "School Dance on the Sabbath."

42. *Treasury*, 206. The responsum is *ShU"T Zikhron Yosef* (Jerusalem, 1995), OḤ #17.

43. From Mr. Arthur Sherr, Tarrytown, NY, 27 Feb 1962, and reply, 3 Apr 1962, BA-71 FF 4.

44. To R. Sanford Jarashow, Framingham, MA, 3 Aug 1963, 2/6.

45. To R. H. Philip Berkowitz, Pontiac, MI, 14 Mar 1974; also to R. Nathan Kaber, Altoona, PA, 1 Mar 1974, 2/7.

46. From Dr. Samuel Newman, Danville, VA, 3 May 1959, and reply, 19 May 1959, BA-118 FF 86.

47. From R. Philip S. Bernstein, Rochester, NY, 16 Mar 1965, BA-71 FF 8; reply, 19 Mar 1965, 2/7.

48. To R. Chaim Asa, Buenos Aires, 4 May 1965, 2/7.

49. *RR* #8, "Congregational Meeting on the Sabbath," 46–50.

50. To R. Alexander Schindler, New York, 20 Mar 1967, and to R. Joseph Rudavsky, River Edge, NJ, 20 Apr 1971, 2/7.

51. *CuRR* #53, "Answers to *CCAR Journal*," 226.

52. To R. Israel J. Gerber, Charlotte, NC, 13 Feb 1967, 2/7.

53. To Mr. Leonard Simons, 13 and 18 Jan 1960, BA-71 FF 19.

54. From R. Morton M. Applebaum, Akron, OH, 13 May 1965, BA-71 FF 8, and to Applebaum, 27 May 1965, 2/6.

55. To R. Paul Levenson, Brookline, MA, 18 Dec 1961, BA-71 FF 3.

56. From R. Paul Levenson, 26 Mar 1962, BA-71 FF 4.

57. To R. Sydney Hoffman, Lima, OH, 7 Jan 1963, 2/6.

58. The editorial contrasted the Men's Club's action with the behavior of a previous rabbi of the same Reform temple, who had often asked the *Jewish News* not to advertise events scheduled for Friday nights if they were sponsored by Jews, as a way of encouraging Jews to honor the Sabbath. It asked provocatively, "[I]s such a service sacred when those serving as substitutes for Christians desecrate their own Sabbath?" *Southfield [MI] Eccentric*, 30 Dec 1971, n.p.; "Ecumenism . . . Good Will . . . Sanctity and Self-Abnegation," *Jewish News*, n.d., n.p.; and from Philip Slomovitz, Southfield, MI, 2 Jan 1972, RS Responsa Feb Mar Apr 72.

59. From R. Richard Hertz, Detroit, 3 Jan 1972, RS Responsa Feb Mar Apr 72.

60. *CoRR* #29, "Substituting for Christians on Christmas."

61. To Hertz, 9 Mar 1972, and to Slomovitz, 9 Mar 1972, RS Responsa Feb Mar Apr 72.

62. From R. Bertram Korn, Philadelphia, 1 May 1972, RS Responsa Corr Feb, Mar, Apr 72.

63. To R. William Sajowitz, 19 May 1955, BA-118 FF 39. Another rabbi asked whether he should march in the Memorial Day parade when it fell on the Sabbath; unfortunately the response is not in the files. From R. Albert Belton, 1 May 1959, BA-71 FF 2.

64. W. Gunther Plaut, "The Sabbath in the Reform Movement," *CCARY* 75 (1965): 168–193.

65. "Report of the Committee on the Sabbath," *CCARY* 78 (1968): 122.

66. To R. W. Gunther Plaut, Toronto, 28 May 1965, BA-71 FF 8.

67. To R. W. Gunther Plaut, Toronto, 9 Sep 1968, BA-71 FF 15.

68. *Shabbat Manual*, 9–13.

69. Dr. Walter Jacob, email communication to the author, 8 Aug 2011.

70. To R. Sanford Jarashow, Framingham Center, MA, 29 Dec 1962, 2/6.

71. To R. Abraham Shusterman, Baltimore, MD, 14 Jan 1963, 2/6.

72. *CuRR* #53, "Answers to *CCAR Journal*," 227.

73. To R. Sheldon Harr, West Palm Beach, FL, 2 Oct 1975, 2/7.

74. To R. Paul Feinberg, Chicago, 17 Apr 1978, 2/7.

75. From and to R. Maurice Eisendrath, New York, 2 Nov and 6 Nov 1964, BA-71 FF 7.

Chapter 7: Looking Outward: The Boundaries of Judaism

1. Plaut, *Growth*, 30.

2. *CCARY* 1 (1890): 121.

3. Arnold M. Eisen, *Rethinking Modern Judaism: Ritual, Commandment, Community* (Chicago: University of Chicago Press, 1998), 107.

4. To R. Kenneth J. Weiss, 12 Dec 1978, BA-123 FF 9.

5. Karla Goldman, *Beyond the Synagogue Gallery: Finding a Place for*

Women in American Judaism (Cambridge: Harvard University Press, 2000), 211.

6. To Judge Joseph G. Shapiro, Bridgeport, CT, 16 Mar 1959, BA-72 FF 2; also to R. Melvin Weinman, Waterbury, CT, 10 Apr 1957, BA-71 FF 18; to R. S. Andhil Fineberg, 26 Aug 1954, BA-118 FF 39; to R. E.M. Rosenzweig, Chapel Hill, NC, 14 Dec 1959, BA-71 FF 19.

7. *RRR* #12, "Temple Membership of Mixed Couple," 65–66.

8. To Mr. Max I. Ossinsky, 1 May 1964, 2/6; also to R. Laszlo Berkowitz, 12 Nov 1968 and to R. Simon Friedman, Cape Coral, FL, 18 Aug 1970, 2/7; to R. Sanford Jarashow, Chevy Chase, MD, 24 May 1968, BA-71 FF 14; to R. Joseph Rudavsky, 19 Apr 1974, BA-30 FF 11.

9. *RROT* #47, "Gentile Membership in Synagogue," 221-224; *NRR* #7, "Gentiles' Part in Sabbath Service," 33.

10. From R. Simon Friedman, Cape Coral, FL, 21 May 1970, RS Responsa Corr Mar–June 1970. Freehof's reply is missing.

11. The handwritten missive, obviously not from a native English speaker, explained that the rabbi's original affiliation had been Conservative, but then the congregation decided to become "Reform, leaned toward Conservatism." Since attending a CCAR convention the rabbi had begun allowing non-Jews to participate in the service, explaining that this was acceptable in Reform congregations. The rabbi had also said, according to this congregant, that any gentile woman who becomes sisterhood president "'accepts Jewdaism and automaticly becomes Jewish.' Is this true? I have never been as confused in my entire life, and I suffer very much on account of it. Please, give me some of Your valuable time and answer me." Mrs. David (Sylvia) Gottlieb to Jacob R. Marcus, Cincinnati, 18 Jul 1970, and Marcus to Freehof, 26 Jul 1970, RS Responsa Corr Aug, Sep, Oct 70.

12. *CuRR* #22, "Pre-converts Participating in Sabbath Services."

13. To Prof. Jacob R. Marcus, 1 Sep 1970, RS Responsa Corr Aug, Sep, Oct 70. The distressed congregant was thrilled to receive it and wrote back, "May G-d bless you for the great Mitzvah in giving me the restoration in G-d's eternal truth. I sincerely feel that you have enlightened my life, as I am fully convinced that Reform Judaism is not a religion of convenience, as I was told, it does have a שולחן ערוך," concluding with a flowery Hebrew salutation. From Mrs. David (Sylvia) Gottlieb, 30 Aug 1970, RS Responsa Corr Aug, Sep, Oct 70.

14. *RROT* #53, "Gentile President for Sisterhood," 249–251.

15. "Gentiles' Regular Synagogue Attendance," unpublished responsum, n.d., RS Responsa Apr May Jun 71; to R. Gerald Raiskin, Burlingame, CA, 8 Apr 1983, 2/7.

16. To R. Eric Hoffman, Cleveland, OH, 12 Apr 1976, 2/7.

17. To R. Gerald Zielonka, Easton, PA, 20 May 1974, 2/7.

18. To R. Jerome Grollman, St. Louis, MO, 10 Mar 1958, BA-118 FF 86; R. Walter Jacob (for Freehof) to R. Leo Turitz, Decatur, IL, 26 Jun 1963, BA-

71 FF 5. Also to R. Leon Jick, Mt. Vernon, NY, 16 Apr 1962 and to R. Daniel Kaplan, Needham Heights, MA, 16 Jan 1964, 2/6; to R. Minard Klein, Park Forest, IL, 25 Nov 1968 and to R. Michael M. Szenes, Schenectady, NY, 13 Apr 1971, 2/7; *NRR* #7, "Gentiles' Part in the Sabbath Service."

19. To R. Bernard Frank, Philadelphia, 2 Feb 1965, 2/6.

20. Joan S. Friedman, "The Role of the Non-Jew in the Synagogue: Challenges and Choices, *CCARY* 104 (1994): 25–32.

21. To R. Norman H. Diamond, Daytona Beach, FL, 18 Aug 1978, 2/7.

22. To R. Bernard Frank, Philadelphia, 2 Feb 1965; to R. Minard Klein, Park Forest, IL 25 Nov 1968; to R. Michael M. Szenes, Schenectady, NY, 13 Apr 1971; to R. Norman Patz, Cedar Grove, NJ, 6 Aug 1973; to R. Gerald Zielonka, Easton, PA, 20 May 1974; to R. Norman H. Diamond, Daytona Beach, FL, 18 Aug 1978; to R. Deborah Prinz, New York City, 2 Mar 1979; to R. Harold Waintrup, Abington, PA, 19 Mar 1979; to R. Alfred J. Kolatch, Middle Village, NY, 9 Nov 1982, 2/7.

23. To R. Charles Kroloff, Westfield, NJ, 28 Dec 1966, 2/7; *CuRR* #23, "Gentile Stepfather at Bar Mitzvah," 91.

24. "Blessed be God who has freed me from the burden of [responsibility for any transgressions committed by] this one." As a minor the boy's conduct was the father's responsibility; having now attained his religious majority, he is responsible for his own conduct.

25. To R. Norman Patz, Cedar Grove, NJ, 6 Aug 1973, 2/7.

26. *TRR* #3, "A Gentile Bridegroom Called to the Torah," 7–9.

27. To R. Daniel L. Kaplan, Worcester, MA, 28 May 1962, and to R. J. Marshall Taxay, Clearwater, FL, 2 Jan 1964, 2/6.

28. To R. Bernard Kligfeld, 2 Apr 1954, BA-118 FF 39.

29. *ARR* #100, "Cremation from the Jewish Standpoint"; *ARR* #98, "Burial of Non-Jewish Wives in Jewish Cemeteries"; *RJP*, 123, 137–139.

30. Gen. 23:9, 25:9, 49:31, 50:13; I Sam. 31:12-13; Is. 22:16; Jer. 34:4-5; Amos 6:10.

31. *RJP*, 123.

32. To R. Joseph Narot, Miami, FL, 2 Jan 1958, BA-118 FF 86; to Mr. Isadore Moshein, 21 Jan 1959, and to Mr. Robert Weiner, 31 May 1959, Clarksburg, WV, BA-71 FF 1-2; to R. Emmett Frank, Alexandria, VA, 4 Jan 1960, BA-71 FF 19; to R. Albert S. Goldstein, Brookline, MA, 5 Feb 1963, BA-72 FF 15-16; *ARR* #99 / *CuRR* #39, "Non-Jewish Burial in a Jewish Cemetery."

33. To Dr. H.S. Kopsofsky, Braddock, PA, 10 Nov 1964, BA-71 FF 7; to R. Jack Segal, Houston, 5 Aug 1969, BA-71 FF 17.

34. To R. Norman Diamond, Daytona Beach, FL, 2 Nov 1964, BA-71 FF 7; to R. Leonard Winograd, McKeesport, PA, 7 Mar 1975, 2/7.

35. To R. Jerome S. Gurland, Cranston, RI, 30 Nov 1965, 2/6.

36. To R. William G. Braude, Providence, RI, 22 Jan 1962, 6/2.

37. *RJP* II, 101–103; to R. Leon Fram, Detroit, 16 May 1972, 2/7.

38. While his sentiments were admirable and reflected reality, on this occasion his resistance to popular minhag may have stemmed from concern for the damage such arrangements would make to the bottom lines of Jewish funeral homes, such as the one his brother directed in San Francisco. " . . . [T]he consultation with the funeral director is a useful element in the pious and considerate attention to the dead. . . . [The] modern Jewish funeral director has taken the place of the European Chevra Kadisha [burial society]. He serves the *entire* community . . . I am sure that American Jewry will be harmed if congregations take steps to diminish and eventually to abolish the Jewish funeral director." To Mr. Burton Hirsch, Pittsburgh, 14 Dec 1976, 2/7.

39. To R. Emmett Frank, Alexandria, VA, 4 Jan 1960, BA-71 FF 19. On this topic he also published *RR* #33, "Burial in a Christian Cemetery."

40. To R. Martin Ryback, Evansville, IN, 9 Jan 1961, BA-71 FF 20.

41. To R. Robert I. Kahn, 23 Jan 1950, BA-70 FF 49.

42. To R. Leo Turitz, Meridian, MS, 7 Apr 1975, 2/7.

43. To R. Philip S. Bernstein, Rochester, NY, 23 Sep 1974, 2/7. He cited Tosefta Gittin 3:14, B. Gittin 61a and Rashi *ad loc.*, B. Ta'anit 16a, and ShA OH 579:3.

44. *Entsiklopedya Talmudit, s.v. "Ḥukkot Hagoyim."*

45. To R. Nathan Kaber, Altoona, PA, 4 Apr 1950, BA-70 FF 49.

46. To Mr. Eugene Ebbert, Pittsburgh, 16 Apr 1962, 2/6.

47. RH 3:3. To R. Harold Waintrup, Abington, PA, 30 Nov 1965, 2/6.

48. To R. Morris Kipper, Coral Gables, FL, 30 Mar 1964, 2/6.

49. *CuRR* #24, "Halloween Masks"; to R. William Sajowitz, Flint, MI, n.d., BA-72 FF 3-4; to R. Joshua O. Haberman, Trenton, NJ, 24 Oct 1957, BA-118 FF 86.

50. From R. Paul Liner, Davenport, IA, n.d., and to Liner, 22 Nov 1963, BA-71 FF 5; "Sisterhood Selling Christmas Cards," unpublished responsum to Liner, n.d., BA-72 FF 17.

51. "Custodian's Christmas Tree on Temple Premises," unpublished responsum, n.d., BA-13 FF 18.

52. *CuRR* #9, "Church Use of Synagogue Building," and #3, "Joint Building for Synagogue and Unitarian Church," 21–22.

53. To Dr. James I. McGuire, Western Pennsylvania Hospital, Pittsburgh, 7 Jan 1963, 2/6; to R. John Rosenblatt, Lake Charles, LA, 28 Mar 1966, and to R. Z. David Levy, Morristown, NJ, 9 Aug 1974, 2/7.

54. http://www.knightsofcyprus.org/index.php?topic_id=3 (accessed 17 Dec 2009).

55. To R. Morris Kipper, Coral Gables, FL, 26 Mar 1971, 2/7.

56. To R. Morris Kipper, 20 Apr 1971, RS Responsa Corr Apr May Jun 71.

57. *ARR* #25, "Carillon Music," 71.

58. To R. Byron T. Rubinstein, Westport, CT, 29 Dec 1964, 2/6; R. Philip

S. Bernstein, Rochester, NY, 15 Jan 1965, 2/7; R. Samuel Jaffe, Hollywood, FL, 5 May 1959, BA-71 FF1-2.

59. *RROT* #34, "Ashes of Cremation in a Temple Cornerstone," 169.

60. To R. Louis J. Sigel, 23 May 1961, BA-72 FF 2.

61. To R. Wolli Kaelter, 2 Feb 1964, and R. Morris Kipper, Coral Gables, FL, 30 Mar 1964, 2/6.

62. "Sisterhood Selling Christmas Cards," unpublished responsum, n.d., to R. Paul Liner, Davenport, IA, Jan 1964, BA-72 FF 17.

63. To R. Morris A. Kipper, Coral Gables, FL, 26 Mar 1971, 2/7; to R. Jack Segal, Houston, 7 Aug 1969, BA-71 FF 17.

64. "Masonic Service at a Funeral," *ARR* #91, 308.

65. To R. Joshua O. Haberman, 16 Aug 1971, 2/7; "Honoring a Pet Dog," unpublished responsum, n.d., to R. Albert Michels, Hot Springs, AR, RS Responsa Aug Sep Oct 1971.

66. *MoRR* #30, "Our Attitude to Apostates," 173.

Chapter 8: Looking Inward: The Boundaries of Reform Judaism

1. Schwarz, *Ceremonies*, 14.

2. Meyer, *Response*, 358, 469, n. 12.

3. *ARR* #1, "Propriety of Using Discarded Practices in Reform Services," 1.

4. *ARR* #35, 91, "Time of a Bar Mitzvah."

5. *ARR* #1, 1–3.

6. To Prof. Israel Bettan, 14 Sep 1954, BA-118 FF 39.

7. *RRR* #40, "Breaking a Glass at Weddings," 187–188.

8. To R. James Wax, Memphis, TN, 2 Dec 1957, BA-118 FF 86; also to R. Robert Blinder, Galveston, TX, 20 Mar 1967, 2/7.

9. To R. Philip S. Bernstein, Rochester, NY, 16 Oct 1963, 2/6.

10. To R. Sydney Hoffman, Lima, OH, 7 Jan 1963, 2/6.

11. To R. Malcolm Cohen, Pueblo, CO, 2 Jan 1957, BA-72 FF 5; R. Chaim Asa, Buenos Aires, 15 Feb 1965, and Mr. Samuel Stahl, Cincinnati, 11 Feb 1965, 2/6.

12. Solomon B. Freehof, "30th Anniversary Commission on Jewish Education" (UAHC, 1953).

13. *What Is Reform Judaism?*, 18; to Mr. Leopold L. Meyer, Congregation Beth Israel, Houston, n.d., AJA MS-435 1/5.

14. Freehof, interview, AJA C-229.

15. To R. Albert H. Michels, 13 Sep 1972, 2/7.

16. To R. Philip S. Bernstein, Rochester, NY, 19 Sep 1972, 2/7.

17. To Mr. Arthur Alintuck, Wellesley Hills, MA, n.d., BA-72 FF 22.

18. To R. Edward Ellenbogen, New Shrewsbury, NJ, 27 Oct 1969, 2/7.

19. Friedman, "Reform Rabbi," 17.

20. To R. Morris A. Kipper, Coral Gables, FL, 9 Feb 1967, 2/7.

21. To R. Randall Falk, Erie, PA, 11 Dec 1957, BA-118 FF 86.

22. *ARR* #3, "Less than a Minyan of Ten at Services."

23. The author recollects that at the New York campus of the Hebrew Union College-Jewish Institute of Religion in the 1970s, where the daily service frequently lacked a *minyan* on days other than Mondays and Thursdays, inclusion of the *devarim shebikedushah* (elements of the service requiring a *minyan* according to halakhah) was at the discretion of the student leading the service.

24. From Mr. Allen Sinsheimer, Chetek, WI, 6 Aug 1963, BA-71 FF 5; from R. Norman D. Hirsch, 19 Sep 1973, RS Responsa Corr Aug Sep 1973.

25. To R. Sanford Jarashow, Framingham Center, MA, 24 Oct 1963, 2/6; unpublished responsum, "Minyan for Pidyon Ha-Ben, Etc.," to R. Norman D. Hirsch, Seattle, WA, n.d., RS Responsa Aug Sep 1973; *TRR* #16, "The Minyan."

26. To R. Sanford Jarashow, Chevy Chase, MD, 7 Mar 1966, 2/7.

27. To R. Maurice Bloom, Bronx, NY, 30 Apr 1962, 2/6.

28. To R. Michael Szenes, Schenectady, NY, 7 May 1962, 2/6, and to R. Joel S. Goor, San Diego, 22 Feb 1966, 2/7.

29. *RJP*, 113.

30. Gollaher, "From Ritual to Science," 23–24; Ann Reid Slaby and Terrence Drizd, "Circumcision in the United States," *American Journal of Public Health* 75/8 (Aug 1985): 878–880, http://search.ebscohost.com/login.aspx?direct=true&db=ehh&AN=4949509&site=ehost-live (accessed Aug 26, 2010); Meyer, "*Berit Milah*," 147.

31. Standard medical procedure in at least one hospital in 1961 was to keep the baby in the hospital for 36 hours when parents came back for a *brit milah* on the eighth day. From Chaplain Paul Levenson, 18 Apr 1961, BA-72 FF 2.

32. To R. Leo Jung and R. Milton Steinberg, 25 Mar 1946, BA-92 FF 16; from R. Robert I. Kahn, Houston, 19 Feb 1952, BA-70 FF 81; from Chaplain Edwin Schoffman, Langley Air Force Base, VA, 12 Mar 1952, BA-118 FF 45.

33. *ARR* #55, "Circumcision on a Day other than the Eighth Day of Birth," 144. When the same question was posed to the CCAR Responsa Committee in 1977, newly under the chairmanship of Walter Jacob, the answer was also a firm negative, for the same reason. See *ARR* #56, "Circumcision Prior to the Eighth Day."

34. "Circumcision Before the Eighth Day," *RR* #21; to Chaplain Paul Levenson, Ft. Hood, TX, 20 Apr 1961, BA-72 FF 2; to R. Martin Ryback, Evansville, IN, 29 Jan 1962, 2/6.

35. To R. Samuel Silver, Stamford, CT, 12 Mar 1964, and to Dr. Robert Shestack, Hagerstown, MD, 12 Aug 1964, 2/6.

36. The first bar mitzvah at Rodef Shalom took place only three months after he retired, in Nov 1966. Board Meeting Minutes, 8 Nov 1966, BA-120 FF 30.

37. To R. Ariel Goldburg, Richmond, VA, 11 Sep 1959, BA-120 FF 14.

38. To Mr. Glenn Olbum, 30 Jul 1965, BA-120 FF 14.

39. To R. Edgar Magnin, Los Angeles, 1 Apr 1964, BA-120 FF 7.

40. From R. Bernard Bamberger, 26 May 1959, RS Responsa and Correspondence 1958–59; from Mr. M.J. Rothschild, Birmingham, AL, 8 Oct 1957, BA-118 FF 88; Rachel Kranson, "More Bar than Mitzvah: Anxieties over Bar Mitzvah Receptions in Postwar America," in *Rites of Passage: How Today's Jews Celebrate, Commemorate, and Commiserate*, Studies in Jewish Civilization 21. Edited by Leonard Greenspoon. (West Lafayette, IN: Purdue University Press, 2010), 9–24; Stuart Schoenfeld, "Folk Judaism, Elite Judaism, and the Role of Bar Mitzvah in the Development of the Synagogue and Jewish School in America," *Contemporary Jewry* 9, no. 1 (Fall 1987): 69–72, http://search.ebscohost.com/login.aspx?direct=true&db=sih&AN=11592699& site=ehost-live (accessed 5 Jul 2011).

41. Oral communication from Dr. A. Stanley Dreyfus, Brooklyn, NY, Mar 2001.

42. Kranson, "More Bar Than Mitzvah," 12.

43. To R. Saul Applebaum, Rockford, IL, 16 Mar 1953, RS Responsa and Correspondence 1958–59.

44. *ARR* #35, "Time of a Bar Mitzvah," 91.

45. *RR* #4, "Bar Mitzvah on a Sunday," 35–37.

46. To R. Ariel Goldburg, Richmond, VA, 11 Sep 1959, RS Bar Mitzvah 1965–66. See also his comments on the way contemporary American Jews have "perverted" bar mitzvah in Solomon B. Freehof, "American Jewish Education in the Future," *CCARY* 65 (1955): 176.

47. *RRR* #2, "Bar Mitzvah on a Saturday Afternoon."

48. From R. Samuel Silver, 12 Mar, and to Silver, 16 Mar 1964, BA-71 FF 6.

49. OḤ 293:2.

50. To R. Harold Silver, Pittsburgh, 18 Oct 1961, BA-71 FF 3; to R. Harold Hahn, Norfolk, VA, 19 Oct 1964, BA-120 FF 14.

51. To Mr. Allen Sinsheimer, Chetek, WI, 6 Aug 1963, BA-71 FF 5.

52. Friedman, "Reform Rabbi," 34.

53. To R. Emanuel Bennett, Duluth, MN, 24 Oct 1957, BA-118 FF 86.

54. To Mr. Arthur Sherr, New York City, 31 Dec 1962, 2/6.

55. To R. Norman D. Hirsch, Seattle, 5 Sep 1973, 2/7.

56. To R. Harold Waintrup, Abington, PA, 30 Nov 1965, 2/6.

57. To Mrs. Miriam Greenberg, Newark, DE, 8 Mar 1972, 2/7.

58. AJA MS-5 Box B-2/7.

59. The author recalls this anecdote circulating among rabbinic students at HUC-JIR in the 1970s.

60. Friedman, "Reform Rabbi," 4.

61. *Large Cities*, 10.

62. To R. David Polish, Evanston, IL, 26 Jan 1955, BA-118 FF 11.

63. R. Mark Staitman, oral communication to the author, Apr 1999.

64. To R. Jerome W. Grollman, St. Louis, MO, n.d., BA-72 FF 3-4. Also to R. David Polish, 24 Jan 1955, BA-118 FF 11; R. Paul Liner, 4 Mar 1975, 2/7; R. Wolli Kaelter, Long Beach, CA, 7 Apr 1978, 2/7; R. Sanford Jarashow, Massapequa, NY, 13 Aug 1983, 2/7; and *CuRR* #15, "Gambling for the Benefit of the Synagogue."

65. To R. Paul Levenson, Temple Emanu-El, Fords, NJ, 12 Sep 1963, 2/6.

66. Jeffrey S. Gurock, "American Judaism Between the Two World Wars," in *The Columbia History of Jews and Judaism in America*. Edited by Marc Lee Raphael. (New York: Columbia University Press, 2008), 93–113.

67. Frank Rosenthal Memorial Tribute, *CCARY* 90 (1980): 238–239.

68. From Dr. Frank Rosenthal, Huntington Woods, MI, 3 Nov 1953, BA-118 FF 39.

69. *RR* #16, "Social Hall of Synagogue."

70. To Rosenthal, 4 Nov 1953, BA-118 FF 39.

71. To Rosenthal, 5 Nov 1953, BA-118 FF 39.

72. To Dr. Solomon Strouse, Chicago, 30 Jan 1934, BA-89 FF 13.

73. The author recalls that when her parents moved to a suburb on Boston's North Shore in 1959, becoming the only Jewish family on the street, her mother warned her brother and her to behave themselves when they went out to play, lest the neighbors think badly of Jews.

74. David Kaufman, *Shul with a Pool: The "Synagogue-Center" in American Jewish History* (Hanover, NH: University Press of New England, 1999), 279–280.

75. *Ibid.*, 10ff. See also Alan Silverstein, *Alternatives to Assimilation: The Response of Reform Judaism to American Culture, 1840–1930* (Hanover, NH: University Press of New England, 1994).

76. To R. David Polish, Evanston, IL, 26 Jan 1955, BA-118 FF 39.

77. To R. Samuel Silver, New York, NY, 16 Aug 1952, BA-74 FF 3.

78. Kaufman, *Shul*, 277.

79. To R. Samuel Uman, Manchester, NH, 29 Jan 1964, 2/6.

80. To Dr. Frank Rosenthal, 4 Nov 1953, BA-118 FF 39.

81. To Dr. Frank Rosenthal, 5 Nov 1953, BA-118 FF 39. Subsequent citations are from these two letters.

82. B. Berakhot 34b, *ve'amar Rabi Ḥiya bar Abba . . . ;* Rashi *ad loc. s.v. dematzle bevikta;* ShA OḤ 55:22; OḤ 90:5 and Magen Avraham *ad loc.* #6; ShA OḤ 150:1; ShA YD 245:1, 4, 7; Isaac Weiss, *Siaḥ Yitshak*, vol. 2 (Jerusalem: Mif'al Moreshet Yahadut Hungaria, 1950): 34–35.

83. *RR* #16, "Social Hall of Synagogue," 77. Even Moshe Feinstein, writing twelve years later, raised no objection to a multipurpose space when funds were insufficient to build separate facilities. *Igrot Moshe* OḤ I, #27.

84. R. Joseph Klein, Temple Emanu-El, Oak Park, MI, telephone interview by author, 17 May 2010.

85. From R. Harry Essrig, Grand Rapids, MI, 4 Feb 1960, BA-71 FF 19.

86. To Mr. David Firestone, Silver Spring, MD, 7 Jan 1964, BA-71 FF 6. In *TRR* #11, "New Year Party in the Sanctuary," he again reacted negatively to screening off the Ark for a New Year's party after the Friday evening service. On that occasion, however, he made no comment about the fact that it was a Friday night, despite his consistent objections to such events. The inconsistency is best explained by Freehof's advanced age when he answered this question. All the responsa in *TRR*—which was published posthumously—are of significantly poorer quality than those in his earlier volumes.

87. *NRR* #2, "An Operetta in the Sanctuary," 14–15; "A Play with a Pig in the Social Hall," unpublished responsum, n.d., BA-13 FF 23.

88. "Gentiles' Regular Synagogue Attendance," unpublished responsum, BA-13 FF 19.

89. *RRR* #14, "Who Is a Jew?"

90. Solomon B. Freehof, interview by Kenneth J. Weiss, 1 Sep 1978, AJA C-231.

91. "Introduction," *RR*, 12; Solomon B. Freehof, "Reform Judaism and the Legal Tradition," Tintner Memorial Lecture, 7 Feb 1961 (Association of Reform Rabbis of New York City and Vicinity, 1961), 4; "Introduction," *MRR*, 8ff.; "Introduction," CoRR, 2ff.; to R. Moshe Zemer, 14 Dec 1973, BA-30 FF 10.

92. Freehof, "Reform and Halacha," 1946, 281–282.

93. *Ibid.*, 284–285; "Reform Judaism and the Law," 1967, 8.

94. To R. Aryeh Lev, New York City, 19 Nov 1973, 2/7.

95. Friedman, "Shaping," 257ff.

96. *HaMa'or* was a monthly journal of halakhah and commentary on Jewish affairs, published by R. Meir Amsel of Brooklyn from 1950 through 1959. *HaPardes* was a similar bi-monthly publication founded in Poland in 1912 by R. Samuel Pardes, who continued to publish from Chicago. His co-editor and successor, R. Simḥa Elberg of Brooklyn, kept the journal going into the 1990s. Both periodicals served the ultra-Orthodox community.

97. To R. Wolf Leiter, Pittsburgh, 5 Jun 1956, BA-72 FF 3-4; 31 Oct 1963, BA-71 FF 5; 19 Feb 1968, BA-71 FF 14.

98. To R. Aryeh Lev, New York City, 19 Jan 1955, BA-118 FF 39.

99. To Mr. Morton Berman, Chicago, 26 Feb 1953, BA-74 FF 3.

100. To Mr. Gabriel Cohen, *The Jewish Post*, 31 Aug 1954, BA-118 FF 41.

101. The ad copy read: "'There can be no doubt that the burial in ancient Israel was more like mausoleum burial than earth burial.'—Rabbi Solomon B. Freehof, Past President of the Central Conference of American Rabbis." Clipping included in letter of Mr. Bertram Schlein, Philadelphia, to Freehof, n.d., BA-71 FF 7.

102. From Schlein and to Schlein, 8 Apr 1964 BA-71 FF 7.

103. To R. Rav A. Soloff, Newark, NJ, 13 Feb 1959, BA-71 FF1-2; *RRR* #37, "Weddings and Other Ceremonies on Hoshana Rabba," and #38, "Wedding on the 9th of Av."

104. To R. Norman M. Goldburg, Augusta, GA, 17 Feb 1959, BA-72 FF 2.

105. From R. James Wax, Memphis, TN, 29 Nov 1957, and to Wax, 2 Dec 1957, BA-118 FF 86.

106. *Ibid.*

107. To Mr. Leonard Simons, Detroit, MI, 13 Jan 1960; to Mr. Louis Caplan, Pittsburgh, 3 Mar 1960, BA-71 FF 19; to R. Maurice Eisendrath, New York City, 6 Nov 1964, 2/6.

108. "Jewish Center Activities on the Sabbath," unpublished responsum, to Judge Moss, n.d., BA-72 FF 14.

109. To R. David Sherman, Cape Town, South Africa, 14 Feb 1966, 2/7.

110. E.g., to R. Herman Heilperin, Tree of Life Synagogue, Pittsburgh, BA-71 FF 18 and 2/6; R. Pincus Miller, Pittsburgh, BA-246 FF 3 and 2/7; Dr. Eric Hirsch, Geneva, NY, BA-71 FF 8; Mr. Isadore Moshein, Clarksburg, WV, BA-71 FF1; R. Philip Sigal, Pittsburgh Hillel Center, RS Responsa Corr Sep 1974-. R. Jack Segal was a young rabbi in a Pittsburgh suburb researching his D.H.L. thesis when he first contacted Freehof with questions about finding sources, but throughout his career he continued to send his halakhic questions to Freehof. From Segal, Homestead, PA, 11 May 1956, BA-72 FF 3.

111. To R. Eli Bohnen, Providence, RI, 10 Feb 1966, 2/7; Freehof, "Reform and Halacha," 1946, 283–284; and *RR*, "Introduction," 13.

112. To R. Herman Heilperin, Pittsburgh, 11 Mar 1957, BA-71 FF 18; to R. Joel Zion, Lawrence, Long Island, NY, 27 Jan 1964, 2/6.

113. To R. Levi Olan, 14 Apr 1969; from Olan, 10 May 1969, BA-71 FF 16.

114. From R. Theodore H. Gordon, 19 Nov 1961, BA-71 FF 3.

115. Unpublished responsum, n.d., to R. Theodore H. Gordon, BA-72 FF 14.

116. To R. Eli A. Bohnen, Providence, RI, 10 Feb 1966, 2/7; also to R. Abraham Shinedling, Albuquerque, NM, 10 Oct 1968, 2/7; to R. Bennett Herman, East Meadow, NY, 23 Aug 1977, 2/7.

117. To R. Hirshel Jaffe, Dallas, TX, 11 Mar 1968, 2/7; also to R. Robert Blinder, Galveston, TX, 20 Mar 1967; to R. Alexander Schindler, New York City, 22 May 1981; and to R. Larry Kaplan, Danville, VA, 8 Aug 1983, 2/7.

118. Freehof was undoubtedly commenting indirectly on some well-known but unsavory practices. The author personally recalls the 1981 case of a man who went through a rigorous conversion program under Reform auspices, including *milah* and *tevilah*; his fiancée's grandmother, however, refused to attend the wedding unless he had an Orthodox conversion, which she obtained for him from an Orthodox rabbi in Montreal for $500.

119. ShA YD 268:11 and B. Kiddushin 76b.

120. To R. Sidney Akselrad, Los Altos Hills, CA, 12 Sep 1980, 2/7.

121. To R. Paul H. Levenson, Brookline, MA, 16 Apr 1962; to R. David Polish, Evanston, IL, 16 Apr 1962, 2/6; to R. W. Gunther Plaut, Toronto, 1 Nov

1977; to R. Bennett Herman, East Meadow, NY, 10 Mar 1978; to R. Isaac Richards, Durban, South Africa, 28 Aug 1978; and to Mr. Jacob Davis, Pittsburgh, 21 Dec 1979, 2/7. Freehof elaborated on these views in an unpublished position paper for the CCAR Mixed Marriage Committee titled "The New Marriage Problems," RS: Responsa Feb Mar Apr 72.

122. B. Gittin 81b: *En adam oseh be'ilato be'ilat zenut*, "A man does not intend his act of intercourse to be lewdness," meaning that when a Jewish man has intercourse with a Jewish woman, we presume it was with the intention of contracting a marriage with her.

123. *Igrot Moshe* EH Part I, #76.

124. From Dr. W. Van der Zyl, 23 Jul 1959, BA-71 FF 19.

125. *RRR* #42, "Orthodox Aspersions Against Reform Marriages."

126. *Ibid.*, 198.

127. *Ibid.*, 198, 202–203.

128. "The Challenge to Jewish Brotherhood," unpublished manuscript by R. Hayim Halevy Donin, includes citation from Immanuel Jacobovits, *Journal of a Rabbi* (New York: Living Books, 1966), 46. From R. Hayim Halevy Donin, Southfield, MI, 31 Oct 1969, 2/7.

129. To R. Hayim Halevy Donin, 25 Nov 1969, 2/7.

130. To R. Paul Levenson, Brookline, MA, 16 Apr 1962, 2/6; to M. Greihammer, Paris, 13 May 1963, 2/6; to R. David Sherman, Cape Town, South Africa, 14 Feb 1966, 2/7; to R. André Zaoui, Jerusalem, 10 Mar 1970, 2/7; to R. Herman Schaalman, Chicago, 12 Sep 1972, 2/7; to R. W. Gunther Plaut, Toronto, 1 Nov 1977, 2/7; to R. Bennett Herman, East Meadow, NY, 10 Mar 1978, 2/7.

Chapter 9: The Significance of Freehof's Responsa

1. From R. Steven S. Schwarzschild, 11 Mar 1955, BA-118 FF 38.

2. Dan Cohn-Sherbok, "Law in Reform Judaism," in *A Traditional Quest: Essays in Honour of Louis Jacob*, Journal for the Study of the Old Testament Supplement Series 114. Edited by Dan Cohn-Sherbok. (Sheffield, England: Sheffield Academic Press, 1991): 179. See also his extraordinary attack on Freehof, "Law and Freedom in Reform Judaism," *CCAR Journal* 30, no. 1: 88–97, and the responses in the same issue by Walter Jacob and Mark Staitman and by Peter Haas.

3. W. Gunther Plaut, "Reform Responsa as Liberal Halakhah," in *Dynamic Jewish Law: Progressive Halakhah Essence and Application,* Studies in Progressive Halakhah, vol. I. Edited by Walter Jacob and Moshe Zemer. (Pittsburgh: Rodef Shalom Press, 1991), 113.

4. R. Arnold Jacob Wolf, oral communication to the author, Jun 1999.

5. See the brief discussion of Freehof in Eugene B. Borowitz, "'Halakhah' in Reform Jewish Usage," *CCAR Journal* 49, no. 4 (Fall 2002): 10–11.

6. To R. Steven S. Schwarzschild, 15 Mar 1955, BA-118 FF 38.

7. Elsewhere he emphasized that this would be an extended, multi-generational process. "Reform Judaism and the Law," 1967, 20; Introduction, *CuRR*, 5–6.

8. Introduction, *RR*, 19–22.

9. Introduction, *RR*, 17.

10. "Reform Judaism and the Legal Tradition," 1961, 9; "The Reform Revaluation of Jewish Law," 11; Introduction, *NRR*, 4.

11. To R. J. Marshall Taxay, 20 Feb 1959, BA-71 FF 1-2.

12. Introduction, RR, 21; Introduction, *RRR*, 12-13; Introduction, *CuRR*, 7; "The Reform Revaluation of Jewish Law," 1972, 13–15.

13. Introduction, *RRR*, 12; Introduction, *CuRR*, 4–5.

14. Introduction, *RR*, 15–17; Introduction, *RRR*, 8; Introduction, *CuRR*, 3.

15. "Reform Judaism and the Jewish Life," sermon delivered at Rodef Shalom Temple on Sunday, January 13, 1952, in "Reform Judaism and the Changing World: A Series of Three Addresses," 7–8.

16. Introduction, *RR*, 21.

17. To R. John D. Rayner, London, 3 Oct 1961, 2/6. He expressed the same commitment to fluidity in 1978. "My sole criterion of what makes us Reform Jews is not how many ceremonies we observe or we don't, but our judgment of our ceremonies. In other words, if I believe, if I've gotten to believe that *minhag Yisroel Torah hu*, and I take Torah to be *Torah miSinay*, then every *minhag* is sacrosanct. Don't believe it. If it's useful, it'll continue. If it ceases to be useful, it'll drop out. In other words, what's essential in Judaism are its great doctrines and its tremendous intellectual tradition." Solomon B. Freehof, interview by Kenneth J. Weiss, 1 Sep 1978, AJA C-229.

18. Frederic A. Doppelt, "Criteria for a Guide of Practices in Reform Judaism," Judaism 4, no. 3 (Summer 1955): 254–262 http://gateway.proquest. com/openurl?url_ver=Z39.88-2004&res_dat=xri:pao-us:&rft_dat=xri: pao:article:6137-1955-004-03-000006 (accessed 21 Dec 2011); idem and David Polish, "A Guide for Reform Ritual Practice," *CCAR Journal* 18 (Jun 1956): 10–18.

19. Doppelt and Polish, Guide, 5–9. In 1971 the UAHC, which always had its finger on the pulse of the Reform laity, published R. Morrison David Bial's *Liberal Judaism at Home: The Practices of Modern Reform Judaism*. Bial had originally published the volume privately in 1967 for his congregation's use.

20. "Report of the Committee on the Sabbath," *CCARY* 78 (1968): 122.

21. Meyer, *Response*, 377.

22. Introduction, *CuRR*, 5–6.

23. Simeon J. Maslin, "Foreword," in *Gates of the Seasons: A Guide to the Jewish Year*. Edited by Peter S. Knobel. (New York: CCAR, 1983), vii.

24. *Shabbat Manual*, 7, 9.

25. *Ibid.*, 7–11.

26. Simeon J. Maslin, ed., *Gates of Mitzvah: A Guide to the Jewish Life Cycle* (New York: CCAR, 1979).

27. *Ibid.*, 2.

28. *Ibid.*, 3.

29. Mark Dov Shapiro, *Gates of Shabbat: A Guide for Observing Shabbat* (New York: CCAR, 1991).

30. *Gates of Mitzvah*, 82, n.65.

31. See Klein, *Guide to Jewish Religious Practice*, 434ff., and Washofsky, *Jewish Living*, 141–142.

32. See, e.g., *TFN* 5751.5, "Annual Meeting on Shabbat"; 5755.12, "Delayed *Berit Milah* on Shabbat," n. 7; 5753.22, "Communal Work on Shabbat," n. 2.

33. *Gates of Mitzvah*, v.

34. Introduction, *RR*, 11–12; Introduction, *MRR*, 3–6; Introduction, *RROT*, 3; Introduction, *NRR* 1–3.

35. See, e.g., Nathan Glazer, *American Judaism*, second revised edition (Chicago: University of Chicago Press, 1989), 141 and 144ff.; and Kimmy Caplan, "The Ever-Dying Denomination: American Jewish Orthodoxy 1824–1965," in *The Columbia History of Jews and Judaism in America*. Edited by Marc Lee Raphael. (New York: Columbia University Press, 2008), 182–183.

36. "Reform Judaism and the Legal Tradition," 1961, 2–3; "Reform Judaism and the Law," 1967, 6–8.

37. "Reform Judaism and the Legal Tradition," 1961, 8.

38. "Report of the Committee on the Purpose, Scope, and Role of the Responsa Committee," *CCARY* 66 (1956): 111.

39. Solomon B. Freehof, interview by Kenneth J. Weiss, 1 Sep 1978, AJA C-229.

40. Saul Berman, "Methodology of Response to New Questions in Jewish Law," lecture, conference on The Contemporary Study of Halakhah: Methods and Meaning, Hebrew Union College-Jewish Institute of Religion, New York, NY, 18–20 Mar 2001.

41. E.g., to R. Norman A. Goldburg, Augusta, GA, 26 Dec 1962, 2/6; to Mrs. Albert L. Martin, Bridgeport, CT, 28 Dec 1962, 2/6; to R. Sanford Jarashow, Framingham Center, MA, 3 Aug 1963, 2/6; to R. Paul H. Levenson, Fords, NJ, 12 Sep 1963, 2/6.

42. Freehof, interview, 1 Sep 1978.

43. Introduction, *RR*, 22–23.

44. *RROT* #15, "Circumcision of Proselytes," 76–77.

45. Edward A. Purcell, Jr., "American Jurisprudence Between the Wars: Legal Realism and the Crisis of Democratic Theory," *American Historical Review* 75, no. 2 (Dec 1969): 426, http://www.jstor.org/stable/1849692 (accessed 8 Aug 2012).

46. Heller, "Casuistry."

47. To R. Steven S. Schwarzschild, Fargo, ND, 1 Feb 1954, BA-74 FF 14, and to R. Meyer Heller, San Francisco, 12 Oct 1953, BA-74 FF 11.

48. To Prof. Israel Bettan, 28 Sep 1956, BA-118 FF 86.

49. Responsa Committee Report, 1 May 1956, BA-118 FF 86.

50. From *ARR*.

51. While Freehof's files are now carefully archived, the contents of individual files are somewhat disorganized, making an exact count virtually impossible.

52. *MRR* #22, "Surgery for Trans-sexuals," 129.

53. *CoRR* #49, "Bequeathing Parts of the Body," 217–219; *TRR* #19, "The Tay-Sachs Program," 19.

54. "Report of the Committee on Ceremonies, *CCARY* 63 (1953): 138–146; Jacob J. Weinstein, "Trends in Reform Judaism," *CCAR Journal* 19 (Oct 1957): 1–12.

55. "Report of the Committee on Responsa," *CCARY* 66 (1956): 104; Report to the "Omnibus Committee Reporter," BA-72 FF 8.

56. Addendum to *ARR* #75, "Choosing Which Patient to Save."

57. From R. Abraham Brachman, Ft. Worth, TX, 8 May 1958, BA-118 FF 86; from Prof. Julius Kravetz, New York, NY, 28 Apr 1966, BA-71 FF 10. This same file includes fulsome return postcards from Prof. John Tepper ("I thoroughly enjoyed reading your responsum and most heartily agree with you"), R. Joshua Bloch ("The תשובה is superb"), and R. William Braude ("Dear Sol—I agree with your decision concerning Kaddish. A few years ago I decided on my own as you did with regard to Kaddish for a non-Jew. Affectionately, Bill.")

58. E.g., from R. Martin Ryback, 11 Feb 1953, and from R. Sidney Jacobs, 22 May 1953, BA-74 FF 11.

59. To Mr. Arthur Sherr, New York City, 31 Dec 1962, 2/6; from Sherr, n.d., BA-71 FF 4.

60. From R. Martin Silverman, Monroe, LA, 15 Mar 1963, BA-72 FF 16.

61. From R. Herman Schaalman, Chicago, 2 Oct 1957, BA-118 FF 88.

62. From R. Joshua O. Haberman, Trenton, NJ, 28 Oct 1958, BA-71 FF 2; from R. Leon Jick, 4 May 1962, BA-72 FF 14; from R. Harry Essrig, Grand Rapids, MI, 4 Feb 1960, BA-71 FF 19.

Chapter 10: The Responsa Committee Since Freehof

1. "Report of the Committee on Responsa" and "Supplement to the Report of the Committee on Responsa," *CCARY* 87 (1977): 96, 103–104.

2. http://www.ccarnet.org/media/filer_public/2011/11/18/ccarnewsletter-2005-01.pdf (accessed 21 Dec 2011).

3. R. David Lilienthal, email communication to the author, 27 Dec 2011. In an email communication to the author, Committee chair Mark Washofsky could not tell the author who among the thirty names on the email list were the committee's current official members, 26 Dec 2011.

4. "Report of the Committee on Responsa," 96.

5. "Report of the Committee on Responsa," *CCARY* 89 (1979): 80; Dr. Walter Jacob, email communication to the author, 3 Nov 2011.

6. "Report of the Committee on Responsa," *CCARY* 89 (1979): 109.

7. http://ccar-ebook.com/Index_of_Responsa/1 and http://ccar-ebook.com/Reform_Responsa_Collection (accessed 25 Dec 2011).

8. *ARR* #8, #156, #78.

9. *ARR* #13, "Judaism and Homosexuality," 1973.

10. *ARR* #136, "Marriage on Shabbat or Yom Tov," 414–415.

11. http://www.thejewishweek.com/editorial_opinion/opinion/call_moratorium_shabbat_weddings (accessed 21 Dec 2011).

12. R. Ariel Edery, email to Ravkav mailing list, 28 Aug 2010, http://list-serv.shamash.org/cgi-bin/wa?A3=ind1008&L=RAVKAV&E=quoted-printable&P=472351&B=—&T=text%2Fplain;%20charset=iso-8859-1&header=1 (accessed 28 Dec 2011).

13. *ARR* #137, "Marriage of Transsexuals," 1978; *ARR* #63, "Adoption and Adopted Children," 1979; *ARR* #133, "Concubinage as an Alternative to Marriage,"1979; *ARR* #152, "An Inquiry about Virginity," 1979; *ARR* #153, "Masturbation," 1979; *ARR* #154, "Jewish Attitude Toward Sexual Relations Between Consenting Adults," 1979; and *ARR* #155, "Sexuality of a Maturing Child,"1979.

14. *ARR* #6, "Participation of Non-Jews in a Jewish Public Service"; *TFN* #5754.5, "Gentile Participation in Synagogue Ritual."

15. *NARR* #109, "Berit and Baptism," and *NARR* #110, "Berit for 'Messianic' Jews."

16. *TFN* #5750.2, "Nuclear War"; #5752.5, "Disabled Persons"; *RR21/1* #5757.3, "The 'Falas Mura'"; *RR* 21/2 #5760.5, "Conversion When the Spouse Remains a Gentile."

17. Mark Washofsky, *Jewish Living: A Guide to Contemporary Reform Practice* (New York: UAHC, 2001).

18. E.g., *CARR* #25, "Gifts to Organizations Inimical to Reform Judaism"; *CARR* #26, "Children's Support of Parents"; *CARR* #202, "Parental Obligation to a Severely Retarded Child"; *NARR* #32, "A Bat Mitzvah and Her Estranged Mother"; *TFN* #5752.12, "Congregation Choosing to Remain Small"; "Divorce of an Incapacitated Spouse (*RR21/1* #5756.15).

19. "Grandfather," sermon, 13 Feb 1949. He expressed the same view in an interview in 1978. Freehof, interview, 1 Sep 1978.

20. Dr. Walter Jacob, email communication to the author, 3 Nov 2011.

21. Walter Jacob, "The Source of Reform Halachic Authority," *CCARY* 90 (1980), part 2: 31–36.

22. Walter Jacob, "Presidential Address," *CCARY* 101 (1991): 121–122.

23. *Ibid.*, 125.

24. Jacob, 3 Nov 2011.

25. Moshe Zemer, *Halakhah Shefuyah* (Tel Aviv: Dvir, 1993). Published in English as *Evolving Halakhah: A Progressive Approach to Traditional Jewish Law* (Woodstock, VT: Jewish Lights Publishing, 1999).

26. "Report of the Committee on Responsa," *CCARY* 89 (1979): 108.

27. Eugene B. Borowitz, *Renewing the Covenant: A Theology for the Postmodern Jew* (Philadelphia: Jewish Publication Society, 1991).

28. Doppelt, "Criteria for a Guide," 262. See also Jakob J. Petuchowski, "Problems of Reform Halacha," in *Contemporary Reform Jewish Thought*. Edited by Bernard Martin. (Chicago: Quadrangle Books, 1968), 105–122.

29. W. Gunther Plaut, "The Halacha of Reform," in Martin, *Thought*, 94.

30. W. Gunther Plaut, "Reform Responsa as Liberal Halakhah," in *Dynamic Jewish Law: Progressive Halakhah—Essence and Application*. Studies in Progressive Halakhah, vol. I. Edited by Walter Jacob and Moshe Zemer. (Pittsburgh: Rodef Shalom Press, 1991), 114.

31. Plaut, "The Halacha of Reform," 97.

32. Plaut, "Liberal Halakhah," 114.

33. Plaut, "The Halacha of Reform," 98–99.

34. Plaut, "Liberal Halakhah," 115.

35. *TFN, passim.*

36. Mark Washofsky, *Jewish Living: A Guide to Contemporary Reform Practice* (New York: UAHC, 2001), xxi.

37. Mark Washofsky, "Introduction: Reform Responsa and the Reform Rabbinate," *TFN*, xvii.

38. *Ibid.*, xx.

39. *RR* 21/2 #5766.2, "When a Parent Requests Cremation," 194. The Freehof responsum in question is *CoRR* #51, "Family Disagreement Over Cremation."

40. *Ibid.*, 199–200.

41. Sarna, *American Judaism*, 361.

42. Leonard J. Fein, "Some Consequences of Jewish Intermarriage," *Jewish Social Studies* 33, no. 1 (Jan 1971): 44. http://gateway.proquest.com/openurl?url_ver=Z39.88-2004&res_dat=xri:pao-us:&rft_dat=xri:pao:article:1106-1971-033-01-000004:1 (accessed 19 Jul 2011). The study of Reform congregations commissioned by the CCAR in 1969 found that 25% of married couples ages 20–24 in its study involved a Jew married to an unconverted non-Jew. Theodore I. Lenn et al, *Rabbi and Synagogue in Reform Judaism* (New York: CCAR, 1972), 217–218.

43. "Report of Committee on Mixed Marriage," *CCARY* 83 (1973): 89.

44. A survey of delegates to the 1985 UAHC biennial convention— i.e., congregational lay leaders—found that of their married children, 31% were married to non-Jews. Another study has found that from 1971–1990 "only 44% of the marriages among Reform adherents were between two Jewish individuals

or involved a convert to Judaism." Mark L. Winer, Sanford Seltzer, and Steven J. Schwager, *Leaders of Reform Judaism* (New York: UAHC, 1987), 66; Bernard Lazerwitz and Ephraim Tabory, "A Religious and Social Profile of Reform Judaism in the United States," in *Contemporary Debates in American Reform Judaism*. Edited by Dana Evan Kaplan. (New York: Routledge, 2001), 28.

45. *ARR* #148, "Rabbi Officiating at Mixed Marriage," 466.

46. *MRR* #19, "Mixed Marriage on Temple Premises."

47. *ARR* #147, "Prayer for Couple Contemplating Intermarriage"; *ARR* #146, "Reform Judaism and Mixed Marriage"; *ARR* #149, "Rabbi Officiating at a Mixed Marriage."

48. Committee of 100, "Reform Rabbis and Mixed Marriage," (Elkins Park, PA: Congregation Keneseth Israel,1984); Eugene Mihaly, *Responsa on Jewish Marriage* (Cincinnati, 1985).

49. "Report of the Committee on Ecumenical Wedding Ceremonies," *CCARY* 92 (1982): 132; *CARR* #190, "Dual Wedding Ceremonies," 284.

50. Lenn, *Rabbi and Synagogue,* 128; Kaplan, *American Reform Judaism*, 177. Though in both cases there is some question about the exact results, as ball park figures they are reliable.

51. http://admin.ccar.webfactional.com/media/filer_public/2011/11/18/ ccarnewsletter-2007-02.pdf; http://admin.ccar.webfactional.com/media/filer _public/2011/11/18/ccarnewsletter-2007-04.pdf (accessed 21 Dec 2011).

52. Alexander M. Schindler, "Outreach: The Case for a Missionary Judaism" (address to UAHC Board of Trustees, Houston, Dec 1978), reprinted in *The Reform Judaism Reader: North American Documents*. Edited by Michael A. Meyer and W. Gunther Plaut. (New York: UAHC, 2001), 166–167.

53. "Report of the Committee on Patrilineal Descent," *CCARY* 93 (1983): 160.

54. To R. Philip Hiat, New York City, 10 Mar 1980, 2/7.

55. *CARR* #38, "Patrilineal and Matrilineal Descent."

56. *NARR* #125, "Conversion of a Child."

57. *CARR* #39, "Patrilineal Descent and a Questionable Background"; *CARR* #58, "Intermarried Russian Jewish Family"; *CARR* #59, "Three Generations of Mixed Marriage."

58. *TFN* #5755.17, "The Dual Religion Family and Patrilineal Descent," 254–255.

59. *Ibid.,* 255–256.

60. *Ibid.,* 257.

61. For a detailed narrative of the affair, see Kaplan, *American Reform Judaism*, 54ff.

62. Eugene Mihaly, "Qualifications for Membership in the Union of American Hebrew Congregations" (Cincinnati: Beth Adam, 1990). The pamphlet includes the inquiry from Beth Adam's rabbi, Robert Barr, a graduate

of the Cincinnati school, and was distributed to all CCAR members, UAHC Board members, and other people within the movement with a cover letter from him advising them that they could obtain a copy of the responsum by Responsa Committee chairman W. Gunther Plaut from the CCAR office.

63. *TFN* #5751.4, "Humanistic Congregation."

64. *CuRR* #23, "Gentile Stepfather at Bar Mitzvah."

65. Lenn *et al.*, *Rabbi and Synagogue*, 217. The same study reported that only 1% of Reform congregants were non-Jews.

66. Nina Mizrahi, "Non-Jews in the Synagogue," *Reform Judaism* 20, no. 4 (Summer 1992): 5.

67. Michael A. Meyer, "On the Slope Toward Syncretism and Sectarianism," *CCAR Journal* 40, no. 3 (Summer 1993): 41–44.

68. This author was then a member of the Responsa Committee and had written the first draft of the responsum (*TFN* #5754.5, "Gentile Participation in Synagogue Ritual"). She was invited to address the plenum by CCAR Executive Vice-President Joseph Glaser but expressly charged with framing the responsum's conclusions in a way that would persuade rabbis for whom halakhah was not a concern. Joan S. Friedman, "The Role of the Non-Jew in the Synagogue: Challenges and Choices," *CCARY* 104 (1994): 25–32.

69. http://www.bcc-la.org/history/ (accessed 28 Dec 2011). For a more detailed narrative on the acceptance of gays and lesbians by Reform Judaism see the chapter on "The Acceptance of Gays and Lesbians" in Kaplan, *American Reform Judaism*, 209–232, to which this summary is indebted.

70. "Report of the Ad Hoc Committee on Jewish Sexual Values," *CCARY* 108 (1998): 34.

71. Name withheld to Mark Washofsky, Cincinnati, OH, 5 Apr 1996. This author was a member of the Responsa Committee at the time. The account of this matter is based on her records of the committee's debate, including extensive email printouts, which are necessarily still confidential. Committee members' final votes, however, are included in the published responsum, *RR21/1* #5756.8, "On Homosexual Marriage."

72. Bradley Shavit Artson, "Judaism and Homosexuality," *Tikkun* 3, no.2 (Mar-Apr 1988): 52–54, 92–93; idem, "Enfranchising the Monogamous Homosexual" and "Response to Rabbi Joel Roth," *S'vara: A Journal of Philosophy, Law, and Judaism* 3, no.1 (1993): 15–26, 35–38.

73. Mark Washofsky, email communication to the author, 4 Nov 2011.

74. *RR21/1* #5756.8, 213–214.

75. Washofsky, 4 Nov 2011.

76. "CCAR Responsum on Homosexual Marriage," *CCARY* 108 (1998): 43–76.

Notes

1. http://hebrew-academy.huji.ac.il/hahlatot/TheTranscription/Documents/ATAR1.pdf (accessed 8 Aug 2012).

2. http://www.yivoinstitute.org/archive/yiddish/alefbeys_fr.htm (accessed 8 Aug 2012).

INDEX

179, 181, 184; and churches, 158; cornerstones of, 160; and dancing, 181, 184, 185, 185; design of, 159–60; and food, 141–42, 144; and fund raising, 179–80, 185; and gambling, 179–80, 183; and gentile custodians, 136; and gentile funerals, 154; and gentile leadership, 149; and gentile membership, 114, 146–48; and gentile musicians, 133; and gentile participation, 146–55, 161, 218, 233, 234, 240, 246, 252–53; and gentile service participation, 148–49, 149–50, 151–52; gift shops, 125–26, 135, 158, 161, 219; and holidays, 157; and Jewish Community Centers, 186; and leisure activities, 130–31; life, 256; membership, 146, 218, 224; multipurpose spaces in, 181–86; and New Year's celebrations, 131, 157; and non-kosher caterers, 136; observances, 34; and the organ, 29; recreational programs, 123; Reform, 178–87; sale of, 15t; services, 38; and Shabbat observance, 125–30, 133–36; and smoking, 133–35, 164; and social activities, 21; and sports, 131–32; suburban, xxv; and tradition, 12; use of, 181–86

tallit, 87, 148, 164, 166, 168, 170, 219
Talmud, 52; and *brit milah*, 102; and circumcision, 216; and conversions, 92, 94, 96, 98, 100, 104; and Freehof responsa, 214; and instruction at Hebrew Union College, 51; and Jewish life, 206; and Judaism development, 5; and Lauterbach, 16; and ritual, 52; and Shulhan Arukh, 32; and social services, 138; and synagogues, 183
tefillin, 170

Temple Emanu-El (San Francisco), 11–12
Teshuvot for the Nineties, 230
tevilah, 57, 99, 104, 168, 196
Tiktin, Solomon, 3
tombstones, 18t, 19t, 19t, 154
Torah, 29–30, 57, 177, 184–85; and apostates, 108; and circumcision, 173; and forbidden marriage, 70–74; and gentile practices, 155–56; and halakhah, 30; and Jewish community, 1; laws of, 52; loyalty to, 165; and marriage, 73, 74; and matrilineal descent, 249; and *milat gerim*, 7; and minhag, 56; ornaments, 156; processionals, 150; Reform version of, 62; and ritual, 61; and Rosh Hashanah, 194; and Shabbat, 194–95; study of, 105, 131; and women, 178. See also *aliyah*; ul Torah; Sefer Torah
Torah miSinay, 168
Torah processionals, 150
Torah reading, 14t, 18t, 104, 152, 168, 170, 171, 175, 252; and bar mitzvah, 174; language of, 11–16, 14t; on Friday night, 171
transplant surgery, 20t
Treasury of Responsa, 108, 132
trumpets, 157, 178
tsedakah, 212
Tzena Urena, 178

ufruf, 152
Union of American Hebrew Congregations, 5, 105, 147, 164, 231, 233, 251, 253; Commission on Outreach, 233, 252; Commission on Social Action, 233; Commission on Synagogue Activities, 26, 163–64; Council, 27; Joint Commission on Jewish Education, xxii, 31, 41, 233; Joint Committee on Ceremonies,

ABOUT THE AUTHOR

Joan Friedman is Associate Professor of History and Religious Studies at the College of Wooster in Wooster, Ohio. She received her doctorate in Jewish history from Columbia University and her rabbinic ordination from Hebrew Union College-Jewish Institute of Religion in New York.

MONOGRAPHS OF
THE HEBREW UNION COLLEGE

1. Lewis M. Barth, *An Analysis of Vatican 30*
2. Samson H. Levey, *The Messiah: An Aramaic Interpretation*
3. Ben Zion Wacholder, *Eupolemus: A Study of Judaeo-Greek Literature*
4. Richard Victor Bergren, *The Prophets and the Law*
5. Benny Kraut, *From Reform Judaism to Ethical Culture: The Religious Evolution of Felix Adler*
6. David B. Ruderman, *The World of a Renaissance Jew: The Life and Thought of Abraham ben Mordecai Farrisol*
7. Alan Mendelson, *Secular Education in Philo of Alexandria*
8. Ben Zion Wacholder, *The Dawn of Qumran: The Sectarian Torah and the Teacher of Righteousness*
9. Stephen M. Passamaneck, *The Traditional Jewish Law of Sale: Shulḥan Arukh, Ḥoshen Mishpat, Chapters 189–240*
10. Yael S. Feldman, *Modernism and Cultural Transfer: Gabriel Preil and the Tradition of Jewish Literary Bilingualism*
11. Raphael Jospe, *Torah and Sophia: The Life and Thought of Shem Tov ibn Falaquera*
12. Richard Kalmin, *The Redaction of the Babylonian Talmud: Amoraic or Saboraic?*
13. Shuly Rubin Schwartz, *The Emergence of Jewish Scholarship in America: The Publication of the Jewish Encyclopedia*
14. John C. Reeves, *Jewish Lore in Manichaean Cosmogony: Studies in the Book of Giants Traditions*
15. Robert Kirschner, *Baraita De Melekhet Ha-Mishkan: A Critical Edition with Introduction and Translation*
16. Philip E. Miller, *Karaite Separatism in Nineteenth-Century Russia: Joseph Solomon Lutski's Epistle of Israel's Deliverance*
17. Warran Bargad, *"To Write the Lips of Sleepers": The Poetry of Amir Gilboa*
18. Marc Saperstein, *"Your Voice Like a Ram's Horn": Themes and Texts in Traditional Jewish Preaching*
19. Emanuel Melzer, *No Way Out: The Politics of Polish Jewry, 1935–1939*